"William Christian makes all this come alive, evoking time, place, and character so well, not forgetting the private life too in probing the anatomy of a Victorian marriage between the teacher and his star student, and the remarkable family they produced."

TERRY COOK, *Department of History, University of Manitoba*

"Seldom in my life have I been so excited about a book. I did not want to lay the book down. William Christian has a winner not only in the person of Parkin but in the style of writing."

HAROLD NUTTER, *Archbishop of Fredericton*

"As founding secretary of the Rhodes Scholarships, Sir George Parkin had a powerful and lasting impact on American education, politics, and culture. William Christian admirably shows us why, and how."

PROF. MARTYN THOMPSON, *Tulane University, New Orleans, and Fellow of The Huntington Library, San Marino, California*

"William Christian tells the story of a Canadian who deserves far more attention if one is to understand the evolution of Canadian foreign policy."

HON. MICHAEL CHONG, P.C., M.P.

Front Cover

Sir George Parkin with grandson George Parkin Grant on the beach at Cap à l'Aigle, Quebec, 1921. The photograph has been attributed to Vincent Massey, one of Parkin's sons-in-law and later Canada's first native-born governor-general.

Courtesy of Sheila Grant

Opening Page

George Parkin passionately believed that the English-speaking peoples of the world should be united and that Canada be a part of this great imperial federation.

Courtesy of Sheila Grant

PARKIN

*Canada's Most Famous
Forgotten Man*

William Christian

THINK FREE, BE FREE

© William Christian

All rights reserved. No part of this publication may be copied, stored, transmitted or reproduced by any method or in any format without the written permission of the publisher or a valid licence from Access Copyright.

Blue Butterfly Book Publishing Inc.
2583 Lakeshore Boulevard West, Toronto, Ontario, Canada M8V 1G3
Tel 416-255-3930   Fax 416-252-8291   www.bluebutterflybooks.ca

Complete ordering information for Blue Butterfly titles is available at:
www.bluebutterflybooks.ca

First edition, paperback: 2008

LIBRARY AND ARCHIVES CANADA CATALOGUING IN PUBLICATION

Christian, William, 1945–
Parkin : Canada's most famous forgotten man / William Christian.
Includes bibliographical references and index.
ISBN 978-0-9781600-3-6

1. Parkin, George R. (George Robert), 1846–1922.
2. Educators—Canada—Biography. 3. Authors, Canadian (English)—
19th century—Biography. 4. Imperial federation. I. Title.
FC541.P37C47 2008   370.92   C2008-903507-0

Design and typesetting by Fox Meadow Creations
Text set in Adobe Caslon, a digital typeface based on the work of the
18th-century English typefounder William Caslon

No government grants were sought nor any public subsidies received for publication of this book. Blue Butterfly Books thanks book buyers for their support in the marketplace.

To Terry Cook and the memory of Raleigh Parkin

Contents

Preface xiii

1 A Farmer's Son 1

2 The Passionate Young Teacher 14

3 The Magic of Oxford 26

4 Reka Dom and Annie 43

5 Imperial Federation 56

6 Foreign Travels and Domestic Tragedies 68

7 The Knight-Errant 88

8	Colouring the Empire Red	101
9	Money Troubles and the Death of the IFL	125
10	Home Again	142
11	Principal Parkin	152
12	Canada's Imperial Mission	171
13	The Most Delightful Man in Canada	186
14	I, Cecil Rhodes	204
15	Home and Away	222
16	Settling Down?	236
17	This Great Struggle for Humanity	254
18	A Radiant and Triumphant Personality	275
19	Epilogue and Legacy	287
	Timeline	295
	Notes	301
	Sources	320
	Index	329
	Credits	340
	Author Interview	343

Preface

When Sir George Parkin died in 1922 he was quite possibly the best-known Canadian in the world. At least, it would be safe to place him among the top ten. He was one of the most-admired orators of his age; he published prolifically in newspapers, magazines, and scholarly journals virtually everywhere that English was spoken. He saved Toronto's leading private boys' school from bankruptcy and he created the institutional foundations for the most prestigious academic awards in the world, the Rhodes Scholarships. He was extremely charismatic. Vincent Massey, later Canada's governor-general, described him as "charged with magnetism." His portrait, by the distinguished Canadian painter F.H. Varley, which now hangs in the National Gallery of Canada, reveals a man of unmistakable greatness.

He was driven by a political vision which formed when he was relatively young and was shared with a fairly small but influential group of intellectuals and politicians clustered mainly in Ontario, England, and several Australian states. Together, these men worked tirelessly for something they called imperial federation, a movement to bring closer political, economic, and cultural ties between the United Kingdom and what were called the settler colonies: Canada, New Zealand, and what became Australia and South Africa.

In Canada their numbers included Principal Grant of Queen's University, Charles Tupper (Canada's first high commissioner to the United Kingdom and very briefly prime minister of Canada), and the excitable and eccentric but nonetheless formidable Colonel George Denison. In the United Kingdom, the two leaders of the movement were lords Rosebery and Milner. Although Rosebery had been foreign secretary and briefly prime minister, he seemed to enjoy the role for which he was more suited: political gadfly. He lent his prestige and parts of his immense fortune to promoting the imperial federation movement. The other figure, Alfred Milner, married a powerful intellect with an immense capacity for hard work and was an administrator of genius. But it was Parkin who held the movement together. He gave it vitality. His apparently limitless energy connected Scotland to Toronto to Melbourne. By boat and train he visited every one of the self-governing colonies and dominions, promoting closer ties between the British peoples.

In the latter years of the nineteenth century, the young country of Canada was feeling its way in the world, trying to find an identity. In many ways it faced choices very similar to those Canada faces now. Goldwin Smith, Canada's greatest journalist of the period, called for free trade with the United States and hoped for eventual political union. The 1891 federal election in Canada was fought over this issue. The imperial federation movement said that Canada should move in the other direction, forging closer military, economic, or political ties with the United Kingdom and the settler colonies.

Parkin wanted nothing so limited for Canada. He was Canada's first prophet of globalization. For him, the British Empire was not a series of states subservient to the United Kingdom. It was an interconnected network of telegraph lines, interoceanic cables, cheap postage, and coaling stations that fuelled the new steamships that sustained commerce and warfare. He called for a closer union of the British peoples—he called it the British nation—whom he believed were the supreme cultural force for good in the world. He created a great map, a giant map that he used for lectures to show these connections. The British Empire, "on which the sun never sets," was marked in glori-

Preface

ous red. Take away one link, Parkin argued, and you weaken, perhaps destroy, the whole.

Why did Parkin want Canada to achieve a global reach? Today we call it internationalism and as Canadians we are very proud of it. Because Parkin called his ideal "the British nation," for many people, the word "British" will stand as a barrier between them and Parkin. It shouldn't. It may be an old-fashioned word, but the basic ideals for which it stood are not. Parkin despised the corruption of American politics and democratic excesses such as the election of judges. He thought that the values of fairness, moderation, and balance were superior and that the British tradition represented them. He wanted them maintained, enhanced, and where possible, spread. He stood for the kind of values that Canadian troops now fight for in Afghanistan. It is only appropriate that former Conservative cabinet minister Michael Chong has described him as someone who should be studied if we want to understand the evolution of Canadian foreign policy.

Parkin's compassion also extended to the poor who lived in squalor in the great cities of the United Kingdom. For Parkin, a united empire was a means of salvation for the malnourished in Britain, ridden with lung diseases from coal heating, and infected with disease caused by inadequate sanitation. Emigration, Parkin thought, could provide for the poor of Britain what they could never enjoy at home: fresh air, clean living conditions, proper nourishment, and the opportunity for vigorous exercise.

He was also a notable educational reformer and a political visionary. A disciple of Edward Thring, headmaster of Uppingham School in England and one of the foremost figures in Victorian education, Parkin attempted to adapt Thring's educational ideas to North American circumstances. This meant the creation of a non-denominational but profoundly Christian boarding school whose primary aim was to form the character of all the boys in its charge, rather than to foster the academic excellence of a few high-flyers. Parkin's attempts to implement this philosophy in New Brunswick in the 1870s and 1880s met with failure, but when he was called in 1895 to rescue Upper Canada College in Toronto from near collapse, he had the right circumstances in which to work. He transformed it from a languishing, near-bankrupt, government-dominated institution into a financially sound, educationally innovative private institution. "In challenging times," according to Dr. Jim Power, UCC's principal in 2007, "George Parkin launched initiatives that continued to benefit Upper Canada College students more than a century later, including establishing the first endowment to secure UCC's future." When he left in 1902, Parkin's influence on education extended across the province and throughout the country.

Parkin's greatest achievement arose from his eighteen years as founding secretary of the Rhodes Scholarships. Cecil Rhodes, an Englishman who had grown rich in the diamond-mining industry in a country he named, with a typical sense of his importance in the world, Rhodesia. When he died he left a famous will that was long on sentiment and short on operational details: most of his vast fortune was designated to the establishment of scholarships for study at Oxford University. The Rhodes Trustees called on Parkin to see if he could turn Rhodes's dream into a living reality. We take it for granted now that everyone would want a Rhodes Scholarship, but in 1902 it was by no means certain that Mormons in Utah or French-Canadians would want to send their brightest students to study in Oxford. Parkin faced a thousand other problems, great and small. With eighteen years of heroic labour, he overcame them, and when he finally retired at the age of seventy-four, in the words of Sir Colin Lucas, warden of Rhodes House, "It was Parkin more than anyone else who laid the ground for the vigorous survival of the Rhodes Scholarships right to the present day." Thanks to his work with the Rhodes Scholarships, Parkin became one of the most influential educational figures in the English-speaking world.

His role with the Rhodes Scholarships gave him one last—and great—opportunity to fulfil his vision. Unlike some of his fellow members in the imperial federation movement, Parkin did not hate or fear the United States. He believed that the fragmentation of the English-speaking world that occurred after American independence was recognized by the United Kingdom in 1783 after the American Revolution had been a great tragedy. Cecil Rhodes shared this view. Of course neither of them thought that they could bring the United States back into the British Empire, but they wanted to promote closer ties and greater understanding. It was in this spirit that Rhodes gave the greatest number of his scholarships to the United States, and Par-

Preface

kin worked tirelessly to achieve his goal that the scholarships would not turn Americans into little Englishmen, but would give Americans an opportunity to understand British traditions, politics, and culture. Although many American Rhodes scholars achieved high office, both elected and in the bureaucracy, nothing would have pleased Rhodes or Parkin more than to see Bill Clinton, who won a Rhodes Scholarship in 1968, inaugurated as president of the United States.

There was a price for his success, but it was mostly borne by his wife, Annie. Twelve years younger than her husband—in fact one of his former students—she was regularly left alone with the children and with insufficient finances. She also experienced the death of three children. The relationship between an ambitious man who rose in the world and outgrew his wife, and the wife who was forced to stay behind and bear all the domestic responsibilities largely single-handedly, may not have been unusual for late-Victorians, or perhaps even for couples in the twenty-first century. In recognizing Parkin's achievements, I try to keep Annie, who suffered increasingly from depression, in view. It was not easy, she once remarked, to be married to the tail-end of a comet. She would figure more prominently if there were more documentation.

Most of the story told here is based on the Parkin's diaries and the letters written from, to, and about him that can be found in various archives, most particularly Library and Archives Canada. Any uncited quotation in the text comes from an archival source.

1

A Farmer's Son

———◆———

> *He was commonly alluded to by surname only;*
> *and besides Laurier, I can think of no other Canadian*
> *of whom this is the case. Parkin was Parkin.*
>
> —W.A. Deacon, *Ottawa Citizen*, 1929

In 1873 George Parkin, a twenty-seven-year-old high school principal, boarded a train in Fredericton and set off for Halifax. There he caught a steamer bound for Liverpool. He planned a year of study at Oxford. He had a slight reputation within his own province of New Brunswick as an educational reformer and a public speaker. He was intelligent, ambitious, and capable of extraordinary commitment to his work. His mentor, John Medley, Anglican Bishop of Fredericton and an Oxford man himself, had put the idea to him that he take a year's leave from his school and gain the learning and culture that only Oxford and England could provide. Parkin jumped at the opportunity once he learned that it was a real possibility. The bishop offered Parkin the money to make the project feasible. He was the first of many who would freely and generously contribute to advance Parkin's careers and the causes that were indistinguishable from them: educational reform and closer ties between the English-speaking peoples.

Who were the Parkins? Parkin himself was curious. During the Christmas vacation of 1873 he set out for Yorkshire to visit his relatives. Taking the train, he arrived at Barnard Castle in Yorkshire on 24 December. The moon shone romantically on the river and the castle as the train pulled into the station. It was a pleasant welcome to his ancestral ground. Barnard Castle had belonged to the thirteenth-century Northern baron John de Baliol who had given scholarships to Oxford in 1263 and in whose memory his widow had founded Balliol College in 1269, an institution to which Parkin had a life-long attachment.

By ten that evening he was in Middleton-in-Teesdale, where he stayed at an inn. After breakfast on Christmas morning he set off on foot. Once across the River Tees by bridge, he asked directions of a local lad who told him that the shortest route to his cousin's at Wythe Hill was to "gang over the fell, frae ane gate to the ither, past a wee bit o' plantin, and down the way to the dale." He started over the fell, the weather like a clear, beautiful spring day. At the top of the fell, he then paused to admire the view, the long-horned Scottish sheep dotted about the green dales, grazing peacefully, only their occasional baaing to disturb the silence.

He resumed his journey and descended into the dale, where he picked up the Lunedale Road. After a short while he ran into a man who introduced himself as Parkin Raine. He turned out to be a cousin, and Parkin recognized a close resemblance to his father. Together they walked to the home of another cousin, Barbara. She had made ready a large room for him. A day or so later they made their way through the light snow to Raine's, where he was given one of the chairs that John Parkin had made as a wedding gift some half century earlier. Raine fiddled for him and the children sang. On Friday Parkin went to Middleton for the yearly pay-day for the lead miners of the district. He found the village crowded and the streets crammed with the covered stalls of merchants hoping to relieve the miners of some part of their pay packet. Most of his time was spent studying and writing, fortified with large quantities of milk and cream supplied by his cousin. With his free time he studied the local farming practices and learned a little of the Yorkshire dialect.

He made some inquiries of a neighbour, a Mr. Ball, who helped him trace a probable lineage, though the task was made difficult because Parkin, Perkin, Parkyn, Perkyn (diminutives of Peter-Peterkin=Little Peter) was a common name in Yorkshire, Lancashire, Durham, and Derbyshire, stretching back to the late Middle Ages. Later in January he went to Ronaldkirk, two miles south of Mickleton, where with the help of the local vicar he searched the church register. He found a John Parkin who had been buried 9 August 1625, the bans for another John Parkin and Agnes Bell from 31 August 1678, the marriage of William Middleton and Isabel Parkin from 13 April 1702, the baptism of Anne Parkin on 18 June 1763, and the death of William Parkin on 29 March 1827 at age sixty-nine. Whether any of these Parkins were direct ancestors was impossible to determine. The best that can be said is that the Parkins, the Raines, and the Watsons from the North Riding of Yorkshire had been yeomen farmers from time immemorial and that the families had frequently intermarried. The houses of their descendants pointed to hardworking, substantial farmers, but not to men of great wealth.

A local woman, Mrs. Brecken, remembered John Parkin from many years earlier and told his son that he had always been "a very steady young man." It was the two sons of William Parkin and Elizabeth Watson, John and William Parkin, who set sail in 1817, possibly from Sunderland on the Durham coast, for Halifax. They spent several years in Nova Scotia before moving on to New Brunswick about 1820, where they settled in Albert County in the north of the province.

A younger brother, Robert, had not been so lucky. He had sailed for Quebec in the summer of 1823. As his ship approached its destination, Robert, almost alone on deck early in the morning, noticed an empty boat floating downstream. Thinking to "possess himself" of the boat, he tied a rope around his waist and jumped into the river. About fifteen minutes later, some of the other passengers noticed no sign of him, and when they pulled in the rope, they found his dead body at the end of it. He was buried in the "English burying-ground in as respectable a manner as appeared necessary."

In Hillsborough, John Parkin (1795? to 3 May 1877) met and married Elizabeth McLean (1802 to 20 May 1862) on 21 October 1820. They likely lived there until the birth of their first child, William, in 1822, then moved to 210 acres of Crown land wilderness on a branch of the Coverdale River. There they lived for the next twenty-two years in a backwoods settlement first known as Thriftyville, but which eventually became known as Parkindale. Elizabeth gave birth to ten children there, all of whom survived infancy: Ann, 1823; Jane, 1824; Mary, 1825; John, 1828; Alice, 1829; Watson, 1830; Elizabeth, 1832; Eliza, 1833; Olivia, 1835; and Charlotte, 1837. James may have been born there too, in 1845.

John Parkin prospered. He purchased an adjoining 210 acres of land from James MacLatchey, along with two mills in which MacLatchey may have retained an interest. In 1827, John acquired a further 89 acres, and on 17 September 1836 he bought 573 acres in the village of Salisbury. Salisbury, with a population of about three hundred, was situated on the Petitcodiac River twelve miles west of Moncton. The Parkins' move there in 1845 added noticeably to the local population, which was further increased by one on 8 February 1846 when Elizabeth Parkin gave birth at the age of forty-four to her thirteenth, and last, child, George Robert Parkin. The eldest son, William, stayed in Parkindale and married the year Parkin was born. He appears to have lived there his whole life, since he is buried in its cemetery.

The property for which John Parkin paid £500 included the Jacques Tavern, a coaching stop on the north side of the river. John Parkin converted the tavern into a home for his numerous family. As Parkin was growing up, there were six or seven of his brothers and sisters living with the family. The farm lay at the confluence of the Petitcodiac and Coverdale rivers. As a child, Parkin and his siblings often wandered the woods and fields, gathering strawberries, choke cherries, hazelnuts, and other wild fruits and berries. In the winter, there were rabbits to catch, and the two brooks flowing through the farm supplied enough trout in the spring and summer to ignite a life-long love of fishing. The tide from the Bay of Fundy brought smelt and even salmon in the early years, before the settlement became too dense.

Parkin remained close to his family throughout his life and Salisbury was special to him. He always made an effort to visit New Brunswick whenever his travels brought him to North America. He was particularly close to his brother Watson and his sister Olive. Although Watson married and had two children, he appears to have lived with his wife in the Parkin home, and was still there when it burned down in 1903. Olive, who taught in the Salisbury Baptist Sunday School for over seventy years, interrogated her brother whenever he visited to assure herself that he had not succumbed to the corrupting influences of the world beyond Salisbury.

John Parkin came from an Anglican background, but there were no Anglican churches in the vicinity. The Parkins readily accepted the comfort of the Baptist minister in Salisbury. An evangelical movement spread through rural New Brunswick in the 1840s and 1850s, and although Parkin never formally joined the church, his family accepted many of its basic values. These included strict and regular church attendance on the Sabbath, with strong social and even legal pressure brought to bear on those who profaned the Lord's Day.[1]

In later life, Parkin recalled his mother as "a woman of high ideals and marked mental force," and remembered her beautiful voice as she sang to him. She died in 1862, when Parkin was sixteen. His father, a man of immense energy, retained clarity of mind until his death at eighty-seven. John Parkin's interest in education led him to donate land for the erection of a new school building, and Parkin recalled with pleasure the "good poetry" that his father made him learn by heart. It was up to Watson, though, to find where his little brother was hiding in the morning, saddle a horse, put George in front of him, and ride him to school. When he was not at school, Parkin helped with the chores and, when he could, "tickled for trout," a recreation that lasted a lifetime. He also had the knack of whittling a whistle out of a willow stick, a talent that stood him in good stead with his own children and grandchildren.

Since Parkin's older brothers and sister do not appear to have gone far in school, it is possible that he showed an innate gift, and as the benjamin of the family, was indulged. We know that a Baptist minister named George Seeley lent him books when he was about fourteen. Since no records survive about teachers in New Brunswick before 1877, it is impossible to know the identity of the local schoolmaster who might have inspired Parkin's love of learning.

In 1862 Parkin turned sixteen. In the autumn of that year he boarded the train for what was likely his first significant trip beyond Salisbury. He was headed for Saint John on the Bay of Fundy in southern New Brunswick to attend the Saint John Provincial Training School, the Normal School, to qualify as a teacher. His excitement was intense. Compared with Salisbury, Saint John was a major metropolis. The city was then at the height of its economic growth, with a population of some 50,000 and many new buildings, due to the rebuilding of the city after the fire of 1837. "No entrance to the great capitals of the world," he later wrote, "has moved me so deeply since—save perhaps one's first approach to Rome."

Little is known about his year in the brown-and-grey fog-drenched city, but he did formulate two principles that guided him through the rest of his life. The first was that education was the basis of civilized life. The second was the importance of the teacher, who had the power to form the manners and morals of his students in a decisive way. Once Parkin received his certificate that allowed him to teach in any primary school in the province, he set out for Buctouche, a largely Acadian lumbering town twenty-five miles north of Moncton, to put these principles in action.

His time there was short; by the autumn of 1863, Parkin was teaching on the Island of Campobello in the Bay of Fundy, later famous as the summer home of American president Franklin Roosevelt. The first settlement occurred in 1770, and although its ownership was disputed between New Brunswick and the United States, it was awarded to New Brunswick in 1817. The small island (about twelve miles long and three or four wide) was a curiosity, since it was managed much like a feudal tenancy. The British government had originally granted it to a naval veteran, Admiral Owen, who bequeathed it to his daughter. The fisher folk, who were the island's chief source of income, settled on the coast and paid rents for their plots of land and shore rights.

Parkin had a reasonable number of students at his school, though they were mostly younger ones. He seemed to enjoy his year. As he wrote to his brother Watson, in somewhat curious idiom: "I am still sound on the goose; and flourishing considerable, if not more. I had a few pretty sick days about a fortnight ago, but I am well again like a thousand of brick. I have engaged with the people to remain three months longer, and I expect to put in a pretty good summer, as Campobello suits my taste very well." He was also prepared to combine a little professional development with flirtation: "The inspector has sent for all us teachers to go up to St. Andrews, and myself and one or two other fellows are going to get a boat and take all the schoolmistresses we can get, both here and on Deer Island up the river. It is for the purpose of forming a teachers Institute.... You may calculate that we will have a spree seeing that some of the ladies are young, funny and pretty." Still, he missed his family. "It would tickle me to a great size to see some of you," he wrote.

A different type of romantic thought also attracted the eighteen-year-old Parkin. He toyed with the idea of fighting on the Confederate side in the American Civil War. However, he received a sharp rebuke from his cousin Maria, who reminded him that a young man, even one who wants to make his mark, should think before he acts. In supporting the Confederacy, she lectured, "I have no fears of you 'helping Jeff Davis in his glorious struggle for liberty.' You made a very great mistake; instead of liberty he is fighting for slavery! He helped drive a part of the south to secede, the other part were as bad as he was. The struggle for liberty is on the other side, and they will come off as conquerors in the end. Of course they will." Besides, she teased, there was a Yankee girl boarding at her mother's, a school teacher, a nice girl who enjoyed a good time and was waiting for a letter from him; but, she warned, Parkin should be mum about politics: "I should advise you not to say a word about politics—if you do you will drop a peg or so in her estimation very suddenly."

It's not clear why the young Parkin's sympathies were with the South. Opinion in the United Kingdom on balance was pro-Confederacy because cotton from the South fed the mills in the English Midlands. There was a body of pro-Southern opinion in Ontario, which was really more anti-American opinion, and welcomed anything that brought misery to the Great Republic. Parkin seems to have been inspired by idealism, in this case incredibly naïve. This idealism never left. It was the core of his being, but as it matured, it drove Parkin to heroic levels of service to his ideals.

Once his contract was finished, Parkin decided to enrol as a student at the University of New Brunswick in Fredericton, the provincial capital. As he prepared to leave Campobello Island for the mainland, he was given some fatherly advice by one of the local fisher folk, a certain Captain Nehemiah Mitchell, who addressed him in a tone that reminded him of the traditional nasal utterance of the Cromwellian soldier. Mitchell was to take him to Eastport where he would join the steamboat. A large party of pupils and parents gathered to bid him farewell. While waiting for high tide, "Uncle" Nehemiah took off his hat, turned his eyes heavenwards, and taking as his text "With all your getting, get understanding," exhorted him on the dangers, and the opportunities, of an intellectual life, while the assembled community was silently attentive. "The deep sincerity of his remarks and their wisdom redeemed the ludicrousness of the situation and have remained impressed on my recollection. When the exhortation was completed he instantly became his sailor self again and with a natural quarter deck voice ordered his young men to launch the boat and take oars."

There were two ways to get to Fredericton from Saint John, where he landed: one was to take the train, a journey of less than sixty miles; the other was the more leisurely and picturesque route up the Saint John River, following its twists and turns, some eighty-four miles by boat.[2] In a hurry, Parkin took the train.

When Parkin arrived on 1 September 1864, he found a wealthy city with about 6000 inhabitants. The city had been founded by United Empire Loyalists, American colonists who, by choice or necessity, had to flee the United States in 1783 after the United Kingdom recognized American independence. Because of them, New Brunswick later came to call itself the "Loyalist Province." Many spent the first winter living in tents, close to death from either cold or starvation. They petitioned London to create a colony for them so that they would be separately governed from the largely francophone residents of what is now Nova Scotia, and London granted this in 1784. The governor, Sir Thomas Carleton, removed the capital inland to a spacious, sweeping curve of ground watered by small brooks and wooded with stately elms. Fredericton was a planned city, intended to give a place of refuge to the king's friends, easily defended (as Saint John was not) and free from the bustling commercial spirit of the port city.

There was little industry. Fredericton's economic base rested on two sources: it was a centre of the lumber trade and it was also the political, ecclesiastical, and intellectual centre of the young province. It boasted

A Farmer's Son

a fine Gothic cathedral, constructed between 1846 and 1853 under the guidance of the Anglican bishop, John Medley; the Normal School (teachers college) building; and a city hall with, in the words of one contemporary observer, "a supremely ridiculous little tower stuck upon its rear" matching the big clock-tower on the front, and looking like "the back of some prehistoric mammal with a rudimentary tail, in an attitude of alert expectancy." The parliament buildings, though, were an attractive structure of free stone and grey granite, with fluted square pillars up the front, surrounded by some of the city's most beautiful elms and butternuts.

The university consisted of a single rectangular stone building of four storeys and mansard roof, built in 1828, the year it received a royal charter. There was a splendid view from its cupola. "It is a bright afternoon in September," a former student wrote, "and an early frost has startled out the leaves into their full splendour. Behind rises the remnant of the hill, dark-green with spruce and hemlock; directly beneath is the level sward of the terraces, walled off from the keener winds by a dense thicket of cedars at the north end." For miles in every direction one could see the pale green valley of the Saint John River, spotted with the occasional square of rich saffron, the yet unharvested grain.

Fredericton was the centre of Parkin's life for the next twenty years. Although Parkin arrived on the wrong day, there was no problem with his admission and he was awarded a county scholarship of $60, which he held each year until he graduated. Parkin had saved some money from his year of teaching, but he still needed to borrow some money from his father, starting with "3 or 4 dollars to do me until October." He spent $8 on books, a larger sum than some others "because I had not a very good supply before." Instead of living in residence, Parkin tried to save money by living in a boarding house, though even that cost him $2 a week. The university's annual fee of $150 included board, tuition, some books, fuel, and laundry.

The university fell on hard times in the 1840s and 1850s, but a blue ribbon committee had restructured it as the first provincial and non-denominational institution in British North America. By any standards, the university was tiny. Its teaching staff consisted of four professors. William Brydon Jack, who doubled as president, taught mathematics and natural philosophy. Loring Woart Bailey, who joined the faculty in 1861 from Harvard (where he studied with Asa Gray and Louis Agassiz, two of the most important scientists involved in the evolution controversy), was professor of chemistry, though his responsibilities also included natural history; that is, botany, zoology, and, of particular interest to Bailey, geology and mineralogy.[3] George Montgomery-Campbell, a Cambridge graduate, taught classics. Joseph Marshall de Brett, second Baron d'Avray, maréchal de France, chevalier de St. Louis, was professor of French and English literature, as well as serving as the head of the Normal School, editor of a newspaper, and chief superintendent of education.[4] The faculty, then, was small, but no one could doubt their intellectual ability. If you wanted to get an education you could—and Parkin did.

He found the university, if anything, better than he expected. "Coming here just shows a fellow how ignorant he is," he informed his father. He rose at four or five in the morning. From nine until one he spent an hour with each of the professors, studying Latin, Greek, French, Mathematics, and Rhetoric. After lunch, he spent the time until ten in private study. On Sundays, he attended the Anglican Cathedral. "We all have to attend Church in our college gowns, which make a person look quite reverend," he observed with awe.

Not long after his arrival at UNB some of the city mice decided they would play a prank on the new country mouse. Since he attended services at the cathedral, they concluded that he was an Anglican, and thought they might get a laugh at the tall, awkward nineteen-year-old's expense. They told him that there was a college rule requiring all communicants to make a courtesy call on the bishop. The thought of the country mouse in his ill-fitting homespun suit arriving unannounced at the bishop's door was a vision they found irresistibly funny. Parkin, not for the last time, was prepared to do his duty, and he knocked on the door and was shown into the Lord Bishop's study. He halted spellbound at the door, not from embarrassment, but because he was amazed at the bishop's library, a famous one in its day, with shelves of books on every wall, floor to ceiling. "Books!" he exclaimed. "How wonderful to live with all these beautiful books." Medley failed to notice the ill-fitting suit, and saw only the upturned face lost in admiration of his treasured library. He placed his hand on Parkin's shoulder. "My boy," he said, "as long as you stay in Fredericton, this library's at your disposal. You may come here whenever you wish and stay as long as you like and read all the books you want." Even many years later, after the bishop's death, his widow liked to tell the story of the tall country boy who used to sprawl on the hearth rug beside the fire in the study where he spent hours reading the bishop's books.[5]

John Medley was a central figure not just in Parkin's academic life, but in the religious life of New Brunswick. Born in 1804, he graduated from Oxford in 1826 and became a priest in 1829. The early years of his ministry were spent in the English county of Devon, where he became a prebendary of Exeter Cathedral in 1842. The diocese of Nova Scotia had become too large for one bishop and the Church of England decided to create a new one, to which Medley was appointed in 1845.[6] Saint John, as the leading city, naturally expected him to establish his seat there rather than Fredericton, then an unincorporated town of 4000. Their expectations were not unfounded because, under English ecclesiastical law, the bishop's seat had to be a city.[7]

A spirited controversy erupted in the newspapers. Saint John wits suggested that it was contrary to scripture for a cathedral to be built on sand, and that Fredericton was therefore out of the question. Fredericton replied that the best masonry in the world would crumble and become unfit after a few years of Saint John's relentless fogs.[8] Medley prevailed, Fredericton became a city, church music was refined, the great new cathedral was undertaken, and the new bishop set about to rebuild the Anglican Church in New Brunswick with vigour and a greater sense of the importance of the intellect. William Gladstone, a British prime minister, called him "the wisest head that ever wore a mitre."[9]

Although Medley represented advanced English theological opinion, the conflict between religion and science did not erupt in Parkin's UNB. Loring Bailey, the professor of natural science, himself only six years older than Parkin, had come to Fredericton from Harvard and Brown. At Harvard, he had studied with Asa Gray, a botanist and one of the leading proponents of Darwin in North America, whose *Origin of the Species* (1859) had created vigorous divisions and a conflict of faith in England. However, Bailey had also studied with Louis Agassiz, famous for his theories of glaciation, who was opposed to Darwin, and Bailey's courses from the 1860s and 1870s make no mention of evolution, although he did teach about historical geology, palaeontology, plant and animal distributions, and classification.[10] Even had Bailey been interested in teaching Darwin's theories, it is unlikely that he would have done so in such a way that would have challenged the faith of his students. More than twenty years later Bailey published an elementary text for schools in which he praised the Divine plan and the manifestations of divine wisdom in nature.[11] Parkin was much moved by Bailey's lectures, and later declared that they had opened a new world to him. He was also much influenced by another work to which Bailey would have introduced him, Guyot's *The Earth and Man: Lectures on Comparative Physical Geography* (1849) in which he discovered that "civilization has been influenced by the configuration of the continents, the position and character of the mountains, plains, and rivers, and the relations of sea and land. That was to me a profound awakening...."[12]

Every summer Parkin returned home to Salisbury to help his father on the farm. So deep was his love of his new-found learning that it consumed his every spare moment. As the horses slowed down to turn at the end of each row of ploughing, he took a copy of the Virgil's Latin poetry from his pocket and read a few lines.

In his second and third years, Parkin lived in residence. Athletics was not a central factor in university life, though there was a modest gymnasium and an opportunity to play cricket. What grabbed Parkin's attention was the debating society, where he could test himself against people like his friend George Foster (later dominion finance minister). There were other less structured recreations like boating on the Saint John River.[13] At the end of each year, towards the end of June, the university erupted with tar barrels and tin horns. "Then the ground shakes with the thunderous report of a huge rusty cannon, which was presented to the students ... by the spirit of an old French General, whom, tradition says, they had rudely awakened out of his centuries' sleep. The student glee club was wont to meet for practice, on moonlit nights, in a secret part of the grove where the General had been buried. He arose and bribed them with the cannon; and thenceforth the club met no more in that place."[14]

A few days before New Brunswick and Nova Scotia joined with Canada to form a new political unit, Parkin graduated magna cum laude. The printed degree certificate, dated 27 June 1867, left blanks for Brydon Jack to complete. The president found Parkin's attendance regular, his conduct highly becoming, commendable in diligence, and his academic achievements entirely satisfactory. He won the prize for natural science and, with the money, began to pay off his debts. He took with him the words of L.A. Wilmot: "My young friend," said the New Brunswick Supreme Court Justice, as if trying to condense all his ideas on the subject into one short maxim—"My young friend, get principles of action—get principles, get principles—they are everything."

2

The Passionate Young Teacher

———◆———

Parkin was now twenty-one. Six feet tall, with striking blue eyes and a prominent forehead, he was filled with energy and driven by an ambition that he sought to subject to God's purposes, whatever they might turn out to be. As a university graduate, he had several professional careers open to him. He considered law, he considered the church, but he was attracted to the idea of forming minds and characters, so he accepted the position of headmaster of the Gloucester County School in northern New Brunswick at Bathurst, a respectable though not particularly lucrative first job in 1867. He boarded with a Presbyterian couple.

Bathurst was a town situated at the head of a spacious landlocked harbour on the Bay of Chaleur. Built on both sides of a shallow estuary, it was joined by a wide road built on piles. A declining lobster fishery, the Elm Tree and Nigadoo silver mines, and New Brunswick's major staple products, lumbering, shipbuilding, and sawmills, formed its economic base. The population was mixed, mostly English and Scottish, with some French-Canadians and workers of various European nationalities. Parkin found it agreeable, with "wealth and leisure, scholarly men and attractive women, a free hospitality and a devotion to intellectual pursuits."

The school itself was considered one of the better ones in the province, but its quality was only comparative, since the New Brunswick school system was "crude, voluntary, and often starved for adequate means."[1] In geography, for example, Parkin was supposed to use a globe for teaching purposes, but none was provided. Attendance was sporadic; about half the pupils attended regularly. Only about one in five took courses in classics and mathematics, both of which were necessary to enter university. In the face of these difficulties, Parkin also had to deal with students as young as ten, and some even younger. Under the circumstances it was somewhat surprising that Parkin survived Bathurst with his love of teaching and his enthusiasm for moulding the minds and characters of the young intact.

The head of Bathurst's small upper class was John Ferguson, a lumber merchant and politician, who became a senator in the first dominion parliament, and a member of the legislative council (cabinet) of New Brunswick three years later. In the nineteenth century, and well into the twentieth, New Brunswick politics was rough, and money played a bigger role than principles, so it is not surprising that business found politics profitable. Sanford Fleming, with whom Parkin formed a lifelong friendship, was the chief engineer of the Intercolonial Railway, an instrument designed to link the new country together.

Parkin's life was a paradox. He naturally gravitated toward the rich and powerful. He enjoyed their company and the comforts of life in which he could indulge through their friendship, comforts which would otherwise have been outside his financial reach. But he was driven by a social conscience. Moral improvement is not fashionable today, but for Parkin the central mission of public figures, whether they were politicians, businessmen, or humble school teachers, was to make the poor happy by making them better people. For this to happen, attitudes had to change and Parkin, at the age of twenty-three, was the man to change them. He delivered two public lectures at the Bathurst Courthouse: "Life from the Stand-point of Youth" and "Education." "Life" survives as a neatly handwritten text, serious and earnest. Pedestrian as much of it is, it contains flashes of the passion that drove Parkin's life. "We owe a duty to our fellow men," he told his audience, "a duty to do good to all, to help the poor and the oppressed, to educate the ignorant, to redeem the wicked, to shake off superstition. The advancement of civilization, that is the Christianization of the human race, is the one great object to strive for."

The success of his first talk gave him confidence and when he spoke again, he already showed greater fluency and he spoke more personally. Teachers were, he believed, without the world knowing it, true dreamers, inspired artists labouring with greater inspiration than the sculptors of ancient Greece or modern Italy. They took boys and girls and tried to transform them into good, true, and noble men and women who scorned everything mean, false, or deceitful. The artist-teacher gave his pupils the unflinching eye of innocence, the window of a soul conscious of itself of right.

In both his lectures he denounced the abuse of alcohol. "The social, friendly glass that they took now could, like the cloud on the horizon, spread and darken the whole bright firmament of [their] existence." As a teacher, he saw the effect it had on their children. There was no doubt that much heavy drinking took place in the lumber camps of New Brunswick, then as now. In fact, when the dominion government passed general legislation regulating the sale of liquor, its authority to do so was upheld by the Judicial Committee of the Privy Council, the highest court of appeal for the empire, on the grounds that drunkenness must have been on such a scale as to constitute a national emergency.

A powerful temperance movement started around 1847. In 1852 the Sons of Temperance presented a petition to the legislative assembly demanding prohibition of the import of alcoholic beverages. Although the Baptists and the Methodists were the spearhead of the movement, it was interdenominational in scope, as well as intergenerational. There were Daughters of Temperance and Cadets of Temperance, though the moderation implied by the word temperance usually meant abstinence. The temperance movement had the kind of influence wielded today by important single-interest groups such as right-to-life, and, led by S.L. Tilley of Saint John, a future premier, it wielded social and political power. That Parkin sympathized with these views can be inferred from a letter his nephew wrote him. "I neither smoke, 'chew,' drink," he boasted, "and above all I have preserved my virtue which I am afraid not one of my fellow clerks can say."

In the context of a rough working-class town like Bathurst, Parkin's campaign for total prohibition made perfect sense. It's very easy to cross over the line from being helpful to being a busybody. John Stuart Mill published his classic work *On Liberty* in 1869 because he was afraid that the amount of state interference in the private lives of citizens was increasing. But Parkin understood that the uneducated workers in New Brunswick had few opportunities for entertainment or relaxation after their hard week of labour other than one of the eighteen taverns in the town; and the tavern consumed their income and led to ragged and hungry children and poorly supported schools and churches. With prohibition all this was expected to change. Dissolute workers would, under prohibition, have the time, energy, and money to pursue self-improvement. Anyone, Parkin claimed, could rise from obscurity to affect the lives of millions "and make their mark in history," as Parkin himself was to prove. Self-improvement was open to everyone, and Parkin liked to quote Longfellow's verse from "The Ladder of Saint Augustine":

> The heights by great men won and kept,
> Were not attained by sudden flight,
> But they—while their companions slept,
> Were toiling upward in the night.

Parkin's earnest desire for improvement included himself. He had never been outside New Brunswick in his life and he wanted to see a little of the world. In the summer of 1869 he boarded the Intercolonial Railway, stopped in Quebec to see the Plains of Abraham, where the British general Wolfe had defeated the French general Montcalm in a battle that led to Canada becoming a British possession. Then Parkin set out for Montreal and Chicago, cities larger and more complex than any he had known in New Brunswick. In Chicago, he marvelled at the bursting American energy that had created such a place. As Parkin travelled through the newly created dominion and the United States, he was struck by the differences between the political systems of the two countries. At this time, though, Parkin's concerns were not so much political as spiritual. Parkin attended the cathedral regularly when he was a student at UNB and he continued to maintain his connection with Anglican Church. During the Christmas break of 1870, he took the train to Fredericton. On New Year's Day 1871, Bishop Medley confirmed Parkin in the Anglican tradition at the cathedral, where Parkin took Holy Communion for the first time. His old teacher from UNB, Professor d'Avray, invited Parkin to dinner. Parkin attended two services at the cathedral the next day.

In terms of doctrine, Medley believed in the key importance of the institutional apostolic church, the church that can trace its roots directly back to St. Peter. For Medley, the Anglican Church was a divine, not a human creation. It may be a reformed and protestant church, but it was apostolic all the same and the ritual of the church was necessary for human spiritual well-being. Medley also affirmed the central importance of the Book of Common Prayer in Anglican worship. It was, for Medley, the absolute standard by which the Scriptures were to be interpreted. It and the Bible were the only two books to which he was willing to assent without reservation to every phrase.

Parkin agreed with part of this. In its beginning, Parkin wrote, Protestantism was a refusal to assent to the corrupt doctrines of the Roman Catholic church. However, the early Protestants were not driven to revolt by a set of doctrines. "The courage which carried men triumphantly through the pains of a terrible death at the stake was not inspired by an intellectual belief in a creed, but by a heartfelt faith in the truth and power and mercy of Almighty God, which made all the pains which man could inflict of small moment compared with his first indignation at hypocrisy and lying beliefs. It almost seems as if men's faith grew weak in proportion as they succeeded in bringing down to defined limits in creeds and formulas of belief the ideas which aroused that faith." Throughout his life, Parkin read the Bible and attended divine service on Sunday regularly. Even when he was travelling he went to church on Sundays, an Anglican one if handy, but another denomination if necessary and without much sign of complaint that the service was not the traditional one to which he was accustomed. His Christianity was an intensely personal matter; all great spirits, he observed, "are nourished best in self-communion and silence. We see that forty years of it were required for Moses—perhaps it would be better for all of us if we had more of it than we do...."

Parkin's Baptist childhood influenced him more, perhaps, than he knew, and prevented him from fully accepting his mentor's theological beliefs. The conflict between what he believed in his heart and what he wanted to believe surely caused him a deep sense of spiritual unease.

This spiritual loneliness was accompanied by a deep, personal unhappiness. "A happy state of mind," he reminded himself in his diary, "is most easily maintained by one who has the power of forgetting the things of the present and fixing his mind on the past or the future. Memory seems to soften the outlines of the sorrows and brings out in stronger relief those of the joys of the past, while Hope always touches the canvas of the future with glowing colours. But when our pleasures and trials are present with us we are almost invariably dissatisfied with the one and overwhelmed by the other." He worried that he annoyed other people through certain "angles" in his character or habits. He was also worried that he suffered from "vanity & self-conceit and foolish pride." There are few indications that the sacraments or the mediation of the institutional church between him and God were a consolation. This agony, this self-doubt, this concern with pride was real and pointed.

About 1869 or 1870, Parkin faced one of the great moral challenges of his life, one which pushed him spiritually and emotionally to his breaking point. He recalled it later to his son, who, at eighteen, was just about to enlist for the Great War. "I was the youngest of thirteen, he said, but at twenty-four, I had to consider myself the head of the family." It is difficult to say for certain what caused this great change in Parkin's life. It appears there were pressures on Parkin to abandon his teaching career and return home.

Parkin's eldest brother, William, never moved to Salisbury with the family; he remained in Parkindale. John, the second son, married Maria Small, and by the mid-1860s was a grocer in the St. Stephen-Milltown region of the province, a considerable distance from the family farm. He died at the age of forty-three in September 1871. Charlotte was unmarried and may have been living with her father. Jane was in Saint

John, where she died in April 1873. Watson, who married in the early 1860s, had returned with his wife to live on the family farm after his mother's death. James was living there too, but he was a carpenter and a contractor who emigrated to Fairfield, Maine, where he operated his own firm, Parkin & Son. It is likely, but not certain, that James's desire to leave might very well have precipitated a family crisis, and Parkin might have been under some pressure to leave his teaching career and return to the confines of Salisbury to look after the family. In any case, if James were going, someone had to resolve the problem, and there was no one else but Parkin.

In spiritual turmoil, Parkin felt wracked by guilt; he was, he said, "subject to Satan's assaults and tempting wiles." He had just been offered the most important educational position in the province, the headmastership of the Collegiate School in Fredericton. His diary over this period is of very little direct help. It is more a record of Parkin's mood swings. One day he thinks that it is fine to have ambition because through the power of prayer, one can rise above its temptations. Another day he wonders where he will get the strength to perform his duty.

By the autumn of 1871, matters were resolved. Parkin was back at work, teaching school in Fredericton and throwing himself into various activities. On 7 October he spoke at a public peace meeting at the city hall on the question of a grand international council of arbitration. "I did better than I expected in speaking," he confessed in his diary. It was on Sundays that Parkin seemed to be most reflective of his own life. After church, he often meditated on the readings and the sermon by the bishop. He was "trying hard all day to crush down the aching of the heart that will come on one sometimes in spite of oneself. I suppose it will last as long as life lasts, in one form or another. In God alone can we look for fixed and certain happiness. Teach me Lord, to say 'Thy will be done.'"

Parkin was to be appointed principal of the Collegiate School at Fredericton, a position recently vacated by Dr. Roberts, at a salary of $600 to be paid in quarterly instalments. Parkin had concluded that it was his Christian duty to strive for self-improvement: "I think that nothing can be more profitable for us, as young men, than to place often before our minds the image of glorious and noble lives, that imbued with the principle that actuated them we may be developed toward a higher and perfect manhood...when we study the lives of men, we are in reality getting a glimpse of the plans and purposes of God in the government of the world...." Parkin had a calling and he felt that he had a Christian duty to use his abilities to God's purpose, but he also felt that he had a duty to his family, and more important, he loved them. He had figured out a way, with his new income, to sort matters out at home that would make everyone happy.

On New Year's Day 1872, he set out for Salisbury. He and Jim agreed to take financial responsibility for their brothers and sisters. Parkin provided $45 immediately and gave another $25 worth of Christmas presents, in total more than ten per cent of his annual salary. A week later he set out for Saint John to meet with E.B. Chandler to make the final arrangements. Chandler was seventy-one and a distinguished New Brunswick politician who later became lieutenant-governor. Chandler agreed to transfer the deed and the mortgage for the farm to his brother Jim and him.

On 13 January 1872 he noted in his diary that he was "bothered by the row at College and know now all the horrors of doubt." It looked as if there might be some problem with his appointment. A week later, he was in the throes of worry and self-doubt, steeling himself against the worst. "Why cannot the heart be patient and bide God's time? Would we be happy if we got all we wanted? I suppose not, for we would go on creating new desires. How wrong it is to feel as if we were hardly used, when only one thing is withheld of all that we have asked, something that may, after all, for aught we know, prove rather a curse than a blessing. And that, I suppose, is the thought that should give strength to our faith. The very fact that it is kept from us is proof that God finds it best for us to rule it so."

It appears that there was some delay in the paperwork, but he received the official copy of his appointment to the head mastership, and by his twenty-sixth birthday, he was installed in Fredericton, presiding over his new school. His mood, as he wrote in his diary, had improved wonderfully: "I have been blessed with good health—with hosts of kind friends and acquaintances—have never felt great want—

have been able to acquire some education and have met with greater success and advancement in life than I have often hoped for. I believe all these things have come from God's hand, and I wish to be thankful for this—I hope to live in the future a truer and more faithful life in His service." The newly formed Fredericton School Board had taken over responsibility for schooling, since free schools now operated in the city. Parkin was now in charge of the Fredericton High School, under an agreement with the university by which the university financed the classical section of the school for the next twenty years.[2]

As a town, Fredericton was hot in the summer, cold in the winter, miles from anywhere, provincial, and smug. With the legislature, the cathedral, the garrison, the lieutenant-governor, and the university, Fredericton was a Lilliputian London. Its social elite had rigid expectations about what was done and not done. One historian suggests that self-respect and personal honour were so highly valued that duels were a common occurrence.[3] As headmaster of the high school, Parkin was eligible for admission to the upper reaches of good society. He was educated, personable, eloquent, and hard-working, and he threw himself into a wide range of activities associated with church and school. He joined the British and Foreign Bible Society, the YMCA, the Christian Union, taught Sunday school, and sat in on debates at the legislature, as well as giving the occasional public lecture. In reward he received an invitation to the Speaker's Ball in the city hall, part of "a great crowd."

Parkin read classical writers such as Juvenal, and history. Like many of his contemporaries he was fascinated with the historian Thomas Carlyle, particularly *Oliver Cromwell's Letters and Speeches*, *The French Revolution: A History*, and his novel *Sartor Restartus*. He also read a history of the Reformation by Carlyle's disciple, J.A. Froude, and made notes on it in his diary. Shakespeare's plays, Gibbon and Arnold on Rome, Horace, Corneille, Hazlett, Longfellow, Greek, Latin, and French also formed part of his efforts at self-improvement. Such names as crop up in his diary for this period are those of educational figures such as Dr. Jack, the president of UNB, and T.H. Rand, superintendent of education in New Brunswick. He also mentions a visit to a Mr. Hildebrand, with the comment: "How hard it must be, to be so poor as he is with such a cultivated mind." There is little indication that he spent any significant part of his time in the company of Fredericton's social and economic elite.

Towards the end of April 1872 Parkin succumbed to an illness that kept him in bed for almost six weeks. This illness may well have been a nervous breakdown. On 3 March he had written in his diary: "I've been thinking today how little my life is governed by steady principles—or more particularly—my work. I wait too much for impulses from without. I should know more definitely what I work for—and strive with more fixedness of purpose. Only once in a while I catch a clear glimpse of the beauty and nobility of a life of faith and patient work. I feel too, that I am not wielding a sufficiently strong moral influence over the boys in school." And two days later: "How I long tonight to live a life good and true and brave." And on 14 April Parkin spoke of suffering "something like religious dissipation, with perhaps a lower state of feeling within than usual." On the fifth of June, when he managed to make it downstairs for the first time, he commented, "it seems as if I were really going to pick up the threads of life again after all these weary weeks."

Ambitious, Parkin certainly was, but at the age of twenty-seven, he had every reason to feel happy in his accomplishments. He was a farm-boy who had worked hard, studied hard, and accomplished more already than he could ever have hoped for himself. He had the best teaching position in the province, a reasonable income for a bachelor, and, perhaps most important, there were none of his contemporaries or siblings with whom he was likely to compare himself and find himself wanting. "I cannot be too thankful for the kindness almost without limit which every one has shown me and above all for God's merciful goodness."

The explanation that seems most plausible for Parkin's collapse: stress induced by overwork. Parkin was a man of enormous energy, a quality he believed he inherited from his father and their Yorkshire yeoman ancestors. He also had a high, though reasonable, belief in the nobility of the vocation of teacher and in his responsibility to form young minds and characters, and as a result, he pursued those goals with a passion. Above all, though, was his religious vocation. In his deepest religious instincts, Parkin was not the Anglican of his adult communion, but the Calvinist Baptist of his childhood upbringing. "How deep and intense," he wrote in his diary, "must be his joy who receives the prizes of life in the consciousness that they are deserved, having been won by his own right hand, compared with his feelings who receives them merely as gifts from the hands of Fortune, who bestows her favours alike on the fool and the wise." Parkin believed that if his hard work and faith resulted in success, then he would be one of the elect. Reading Carlyle's work also helped convince him that there was a mission, even in an age a mediocrity and materiality, for spiritual men of vision.

On 27 June 1872, exactly five years after he received his Bachelor of Arts, he walked to the university and applied for his Master of Arts. This was not an earned degree, but was available to any university graduate prepared to pay the appointed fee. Its only real use was that it allowed the holder to play an active role in certain aspects of university governance. Clergymen and teachers were more likely than businessmen or lawyers to bother with this step, since it conferred an enhanced status in the genteel professions.

The next day Parkin set out for Saint John to visit his sister Betsy, and then spent the next ten days on the farm before taking off on a holiday to Prince Edward Island, Halifax (the naval dockyard and fortifications were of particular interest), down the Annapolis Valley to Annapolis, then by boat across the Bay of Fundy to Saint John, and thence on 27 July back to Fredericton.

On 7 February 1873, he lectured in the city hall. He had spoken there the previous October on the topic of the formation of an international peace council, and had done better than he had expected. This time the topic was more controversial. Parkin had already established a reputation as a speaker and the hall was full. His topic was modern science. "They say the lecture was a good one—but I know its faults better than they do. Once I got so weak from the exertion that I thought I would have to give up. The lecture took an hour and twenty minutes." According to the editor of the *New Brunswick Reporter and Fredericton Advertiser*, the address was florid and ornate, but still chained the attention of the audience and elicited their rapturous applause. Although he was critical of the content, the editor wanted to publish it, but Parkin declined and spent almost an entire day writing a letter in reply to the editorial. He was quite pleased with himself when it appeared four days later on 26 February and the editor retracted many of his criticisms. He was gaining confidence as a public speaker. He had also just learned an important lesson about how to handle the press: journalists might back down if you made a vigorous counterattack.

The most amazing thing about 1873 came quite unexpectedly. Bishop Medley suggested to Parkin that he spend a year at Medley's alma mater, Oxford. Parkin could save what he could out of his salary; the bishop would make a substantial contribution personally.[4] On 5 August 1873 Parkin formally wrote to Dr. Jack to ask permission to spend the next year in Oxford. Two days later he received a favourable reply, and by the middle of September he was packing for his trip. On 19 September he said goodbye to the boys at the school, who gave him a dressing case as a gift. It was "hard work," he said, to part from them.

He took the train to Halifax. The steamship, *The Austrian*, arrived late from Montreal. He wasn't able to board until 11:30 and slept poorly because of the racket as the ship took on coal. On 23 September 1873, at six in the morning, he set sail for England. All the passengers were on deck for a chance to see what Halifax looked like from the Atlantic Ocean. "Soon we got seasick," he lamented in his diary.

3

The Magic of Oxford

On Saturday, 4 October 1873, Parkin caught his first sight of England. When he reached Oxford, there was no way for him to know that this was going to be more than an exciting and fulfilling year of study and travel. It was the beginning of a life-long relationship that left him an honorary doctor of the university and a knight of the realm.

On 11 October he enrolled in the university and paid his fees of £1.2.6. His first contact was with G.W. Kitchin, a handsome and charming man, who supervised non-collegiate students. Most students at Oxford enrolled in individual colleges, where they lived and ate. Although they attended lectures occasionally, they received most of their education from weekly meetings with their college tutor. The university itself existed largely as an administrative convenience (or inconvenience). Parkin could not afford the luxury of college membership. Kitchin had been appointed to his office in 1868 to make the necessary arrangements for such students to benefit from their association with Oxford. He led his charges to the Convocation Hall at Christ Church College where Parkin signed his name in Latin as Georgius Robertus Parkin. The great classical scholar Dean Liddell, father of a little girl who was immortalized by Lewis Caroll as *Alice in Wonderland*, delivered a short speech of welcome in Latin, and then dismissed them to go where they pleased with the new dignity of members of the university.

Oxford suited Parkin. He was, he wrote to his father, in the very best of health, never unwell, even for an hour, while in Fredericton he couldn't depend on being well for a week at a time. There were about two thousand men studying at the university, and Parkin was impressed by the fact that they wore their college caps and gowns around the streets; "it gives the place a very learned look," he noted. He boarded with the Misses Buckingham, "two old maids," as he described them, who were kind to him. They gave him apples and grapes from their garden. He shared the house with two other boarders, with whom he rarely socialized. To economize, he used wax candles for light. They cost him a shilling a week out of the pound he had budgeted for his expenses.

Although formally an unattached student, Parkin formed a close informal association with Balliol College. Architecturally, Balliol is not spectacular. It is built in the form of a quadrangle, but little of the original mediaeval building survives.[1] The architect Alfred Waterstone transformed the facade in the Scottish-baronial style of Balmoral Castle in 1867–8. In 1870, three years prior to Parkin's arrival at Oxford, the legendary Plato scholar and philosopher Benjamin Jowett succeeded to the mastership of Balliol. "A heroically industrious Tutor, he kept an ever-open door. His students worshipped him, despite the disconcerting long silences for which he was notorious, and his impatience with small talk and ill-considered remarks, which often led to a devastating snub."[2] Jowett was a liberal in his interpretation of Christianity, but he was the model of a political talent scout: he recruited students of every social rank with a view to grooming them for power. Balliol was already becoming *the* place to be for the politically ambitious, and Parkin developed an informal relationship with it. One of the dons at Balliol gave Parkin tutorials in Greek, and Parkin dined there from time to time; indeed, he even managed to secure invitations to the Senior Common Room and to dine at High Table. Parkin also hired another unattached student, James Deen Keriman Mahomed, to tutor him in Latin. Lectures, then as now, were free.

On 20 October, Parkin first attended John Ruskin's legendary lecture series on art. They moved him deeply. Ruskin, at fifty-four, was one of the most controversial figures of his age. A poet, a social revolutionary, and an early conservationist, Ruskin fascinated Parkin. He was, Parkin noted, "a rather spare, thin-faced man but tall. His brows somewhat overhang his eyes, at times hiding them almost altogether, giving them—especially when he speaks in an angry tone—a kind of piercing, scornful look. The upper part of his face has delicate outlines, the mouth is large and ugly, the nose aquiline. His hair is rather light and not all tinged with grey and so he looks much younger than I fancied he would be. His hair is a good deal longer than it is usually worn and gives him a somewhat shaggy look. He wore a frock coat buttoned up over a light waistcoat and he had on a large blue tie, wound around the neck after the old fashion. On the whole he was a rough-looking person, [with] a careless, negligent manner of walking." But when he spoke, Parkin encountered a man "full of energy and action, vehemently accentuating words and sentences with gestures of hand and body."

Ruskin lectured in art history, but more and more the focus of his interests turned to social and political questions. His causes included a national education policy, old age pensions, and council housing for the poor. He was much distressed by the urban squalor of the industrial revolution, and he affirmed the dignity of labour in the face of the *laissez faire* economics of the Manchester school. In 1874, he attacked the Oxford preoccupation with rowing, a sport he described as eight fools on a toothpick.[3] Instead, he invited undergraduates to join in building a road from North to South Hinksey, villages outside Oxford. Although the project seemed quixotic, for Ruskin it had both a practical and a spiritual element. It was a project intended to keep the countryside beautiful and it also reminded undergraduates of the pleasures of useful muscular work. If digging were properly done, Ruskin thought, it could be raised to the level of an art at least the equivalent to rowing.[4] Ruskin's project offered physical exercise, moral uplift, and breakfast with the master; it attracted a number of talented undergraduates, among them Alfred Milner, Arnold Toynbee, Oscar Wilde, and Parkin.

As well as lectures, Parkin enjoyed attending the university chapel, where "the very cleverest men there are in England preach." On 16 November, Arthur Stanley, a brilliant scholar who had taught under the most famous headmaster of the nineteenth century, Thomas Arnold of Rugby School, delivered the sermon. Stanley was dean of Westminster Cathedral and a celebrated preacher. Long before the service was scheduled to begin, there were great crowds outside St. Mary's Church, and Parkin had to use all his strength to avoid injury in the pushing, writhing crowd. Once in the church, he noticed that Ruskin was there as well. Stanley's sermon was "broad to the last degree. He [Arnold] quoted from Watts, Hall, Dr. Cudlish, and others of all creeds—and said good could be found in all," a view with which Parkin was in substantial sympathy. The immense congregation listened to it in breathless admiration.

Parkin also made friends with some of the dons. Kitchin, a modern historian, was in the process of publishing his most ambitious literary undertaking, a three-volume history of France. Richard Nettleship, the same age as Parkin but a Fellow of Balliol and a brilliant student of Plato, had him for tea. Bonamy Price, the Drummond professor of political economy, invited him for dinner, where they discussed colonial politics. Parkin described his host as a "small, well-built man with a fine-looking pleasant face and very bright eyes. He is a great talker, scarcely anybody much can get in while in conversation with him. He is a great laugher and when talking full of action and gesture, a man I should say of irrepressible spirits."[5] Price came to Oxford from Rugby School and this connection to one of the great reforming schools of the nineteenth century, in itself, was enough to commend him to Parkin. Price was not an original thinker. He rejected the attempts to turn political economy into a science, eschewed the use of mathematics, and, taking Adam Smith as his model, taught that the role of economics was to express everyday practices intelligibly.[6] Politically, he was an old liberal who believed in free trade, democracy, and progress. Just as important for Parkin, he thought that Smith's invisible hand created a natural harmony between the interests of capital and labour, and therefore advocated free trade and a free labour market.[7] All in all, the charming, enthusiastic Canadian schoolmaster was getting his money's worth. People liked Parkin and he liked them. His enthusiasm for ideas and for the people who propounded them was genuine and infectious.

In November, Bishop Medley sent Parkin a very pleasant and welcome surprise: "I do rejoice with all my heart at your good fortune; and now my dear Mr. Parkin you must do me a favour. I want you to see a great deal besides Oxford—especially I would like you to see York. Durham—Ely and Canterbury....At Canterbury you would see St. Augustin's as well....And if you go to Canterbury you must go through London and of course visit the British Museum. I therefore enclose a cheque for £15 and I request you to devote to so much of this purpose as you can effect." This generous gift financed Parkin's travels over the Christmas vacation.

Before he visited his relatives for Christmas, Parkin wanted to learn what he could about education from the great English public schools (fee-paying private schools). He first went to Windsor, not far from Oxford, to visit Eton, founded by King Henry VI in 1440, to meet with Edmond Warre. Warre had come to Eton in 1860 and opened a boarding house, to which he attracted distinguished pupils. Later, in 1884, he became headmaster, where he sought to raise the moral tone and intellectual standards of the school, which had become notoriously lax. Warre affirmed mainstream British educational theory. He believed in the central importance of an education in Greek and Latin grammar and literature, which helps, he told Parkin, even the most stupid boy, for the drill in construction of a Latin sentence enables the student to think clearly about the construction of an English one. By the time a boy left Eton, he had read six books of Virgil, twelve of Homer, most of Horace, eight or ten Greek plays, about half of Thucydides, Xenophon, and a good deal of Livy.

After Eton and a short visit with his friends the Ketchums in London, where he was enveloped by one of London's famous pea-soup fogs, Parkin headed for Winchester, where he arrived in time to see the enthronement of the new bishop. He then went for an interview with the Rev. Dr. George Ridding, like Warre a former Balliol man, who was in his seventh year as headmaster, and was considered the second founder of the school in recognition of his building program and his educational reforms. Ridding disagreed with the heavy emphasis on classics at schools like Eton. He even favoured the co-education of the sexes, a radical idea at the time, provided that it could be achieved under the most careful and delicate restrictions.

Following Medley's wishes, Parkin returned to London where he spent the next ten days immersing himself in the cultural life of the capital. He visited St. Paul's Cathedral, Westminster Abbey, Whitehall, the parliament buildings, Kensington Museum, the Crystal Palace, and the National Gallery, where he was especially impressed with the collection of Turners.

The British Museum raised a challenge for Parkin. He was committed to the moral and intellectual improvement of the poor, and institutions like it offered the means of public education, provided by public expense. He regretted, though, that it was not fulfilling its mission: there seemed to be an unbreachable gap between the virtually limitless educational opportunities it provided and the ability of the people who needed that education to take advantage of its riches. This moment was not an epiphany, but the significance of the insight stayed with him. It's not enough to have good ideas, it seemed to Parkin: one must be able to communicate them. For him, there was no point in building a great museum and filling it with treasures from around the world, if one couldn't get the working people of London to walk up its marble steps and through its classical columns.

On 23 December, Parkin set out again for Winchester, this time to attend the Headmasters' Conference. Ridding had invited Parkin for a visit, and Parkin found himself in Ridding's study enthusiastically expounding his views on education. Listening with the amused scepticism of experience to the dreams of youth, Ridding heard the door open at the end of the long room and saw a man enter. "Here is the man who can tell you more about education than anyone else in England," said Ridding to Parkin, and introduced him to the newcomer, Edward Thring, headmaster of Uppingham.[8] Parkin spent much of the next day in conversation with Ridding and Thring. They discussed three questions at length: the importance of teaching science; how to prevent "the injurious influence of excessive amusement and luxurious habits"; and how the boys should spend Sunday at school.

In his conversations with Thring and the other headmasters at the conference, Parkin's combination of enthusiasm, earnestness, intelligence, and charm seems to have made a favourable impression, and several of the headmasters invited him to visit their schools. The one he accepted, Thring's to Uppingham in late March 1874, proved a decisive experience in his life.

> Edward Thring
> This was a leader of the sons of light,
> of winsome cheer and strenuous command.
> Upon the veteran hordes of Bigot-land
> All day His vanguard spirit, flaming bright,
> Bore up the brunt of unavailing fight.
> Then, with the iron in His soul, one hand
> Still on the hilt, he passed from that slim band
> Out through the ranks to rearward and the night.[9]
> —*Bliss Carman*

The Rev. Edward Thring was one of the great reforming headmasters of English public schools in the nineteenth century, ranking with such well-known names as Thomas Arnold. He was fifty-two when Parkin made his acquaintance. Thring was the fifth son of a comfortably well-to-do vicar. He had done well as a student at Eton and had gone on to King's College, Cambridge, where he scored brilliant successes in classics and earned a fellowship. Ordained in 1846, he became a curate in the city of Gloucester, where he displayed a strong interest in the local parochial schools. In 1853, he accepted the position of headmaster at Uppingham, a country grammar school. Although it was founded in 1584, the school was small and had only two masters and twenty-five pupils, and its buildings were distinctly shabby. Thring came to Uppingham with a well-formed blueprint for the construction of a new type of public school.[10]

His trustees were strangely indifferent to his plans to re-found the school, but Thring had a dominating personality that combined a capacity for affection with the temper for combat. His central principles were that a public school should train the characters as much as form the minds of the boys in its charge, and that its main concern should not be preparing a select few for university scholarships, but to improve all of its students, including the average and less-than-average pupil. As a British politician later told Parkin: "Thring was the most Christian man of his generation because he was the first man in England to assert openly that in the economy of God's world a dull boy had as much right to have his power, such as it is, fully trained as a boy of talent, and that no school did honest work which did not recognise this truth as the basis of its working arrangements."

Thring explained his theory of how to organize a school to achieve these ends to Parkin. According to Thring, the overall size of a school should not be more than 300, since in a larger school the headmaster would not be able to know each of the boys individually. When he himself had been a student at Eton, the boys spent much of their time in large dormitories, and Thring expressed his concern that where too great numbers are massed together the opportunity for individual development is lost in the overmastering influence of the mob. Thring wanted to decentralize the organization of the school. To this end, he encouraged his teachers to establish their own houses within the school, and contrary to the prevailing practice, allowed each master to keep the profits from his boarding pupils. This decision represented a very substantial sacrifice for Thring, and Thring was also constantly advancing his own money for school improvement or borrowing on his own credit for improvements to the school. Decentralization kept the number of boys per house to thirty, and this, Thring told Parkin, ensured that each boy had a direct connection with the master and the master's family. He also insisted that the rowdiness and bullying of Eton could be reduced if each pupil had a small study area of his own, furnished by himself. "Most of them are quite tasteful, and hung round with pictures. During certain hours of the afternoon a boy may have a friend in the study with him and on Sundays from 7 till 8 in the evening, at other times this is not allowed."

There would be a core curriculum of languages, especially classics, and mathematics and theoretical sciences. Lessons in these subjects began at seven and were over by noon. In the afternoon, there were classes in French, German, and chemistry. As well—and this was one of Thring's most significant innovations—there were also classes in carpentry, drawing, and music, which students might take as electives. Thring also built workshops, an aviary, laboratories, and a gymnasium, the latter in addition to the traditional playing fields.

Concerned as he was with character development, Thring placed a very strong emphasis on truth-telling. He told Parkin that the best way to punish lying was to make the punishment the natural consequence of the offence. If a boy told untruths, then, in the future, when he offered any sort of excuse for an action, he would be presumed to be lying, and nothing he could say would be an extenuation of his conduct. "This course would soon induce the boys to invariably speak the truth, even on the low ground of its being the best policy."

Parkin also noted Thring's opinion about state regulation of schools. Thring was opposed to government regulation, except to the extent that the government should provide inspection to ensure that the school provided a certain minimum standard. Beyond that, Thring felt that it should be left to the schools to compete for students by providing excellent education. A set curriculum would encourage teachers to prepare students to pass examinations, rather than to learn, and would stifle originality in teaching methods.

Uppingham also tried to provide students with an aesthetically pleasing and morally uplifting environment. There were regular concerts, and the classrooms were decorated with pictures that symbolically or historically pertained to the subjects of instruction. Although Thring encouraged athletics, he did not give it the central place that it held in other public schools as training for leadership. It was, after all, the ordinary, rather than the extraordinary boy, at whom Uppingham aimed. When Parkin left, Thring gave him letters of introduction to other headmasters and told Parkin how much he and his family had enjoyed the visit.

Over the Easter break, Parkin set out on a holiday, his ultimate destination Rome, the city he had dreamed about ever since he had been a young boy reading Latin verse in his father's house. He caught the train at London Bridge Station, but he had to wait several hours for his boat to catch the tides, and then had an unpleasant voyage during which he became seasick. After a day in Paris, he took the train to Burgundy, and then proceeded on to Turin. The thirty-nine-minute trip through the tunnel was oppressively hot, but when the train emerged on the Italian side, he came at once into cooler and more pleasant weather.

He pressed on toward Rome—past the fig trees, cypresses, almond, and pear trees then in bloom to Florence, where he changed trains again. On 5 April, he arrived and found a room on the top floor of a *pensione*, the Alliergo Pace, in the via Felice. He quickly ate breakfast and went to St. Peter's Square in the Vatican for Easter Sunday. His journey had taken him "about two or three hours from London to New Haven. Seven from New Haven to Dieppe. Five from Dieppe to Paris. Twenty six from Paris to Turin. Twenty five from Turin to Rome." No one would ever doubt his stamina in a good cause.

The next day, Parkin started by visiting the Church S. Giovanni, and there he met Caroline Erskine, in the term of the day a spinster, perhaps twenty years older than him. They quickly became close friends, and she became a mentor to him. Erskine came from a distinguished English family. Her grandfather, Thomas Erskine, first Baron Erskine (1750–1823) was one of the most distinguished lawyers of his age, a liberal who sympathized with the French Revolution. He was also an advocate for the abolition of the slave trade and for Greek independence, and reached the pinnacle of the British legal system as lord chancellor. Her father was the dean of Rippon Cathedral.

When Parkin and Miss Erskine entered the cloister, the guide told them that the pillars supporting the marble were the exact height of Jesus. Parkin, to his amazement, found that "it was precisely my height when standing upright under it." Parkin spent Tuesday morning studying the arrangement of the Forum, and the afternoon at the Vatican, where he found the Sistine Chapel initially disappointing, but soon was overwhelmed by its grandeur. On Wednesday, he and Miss Erskine went to the catacombs and on Thursday they went with some other acquaintances to the Palace of the Caesars. On Monday, they went to the Lateran Museum, and on Tuesday to the Etruscan Museum and the baths. On Thursday, he boarded the train to return to England.

Parkin decided to spend a few days in London, and on 24 April spent the evening in the House of Commons. Both Gladstone and Disraeli were in the House and Parkin observed them closely. Disraeli was the more impressive, Parkin felt, sitting on the front bench, affecting an attitude of total self-absorption. He sat the whole evening, his arms folded, and though the House was from time to time convulsed with laughter, he never smiled, except in private conversation. Gladstone's manner was as different as his politics. Fidgety, restless, taking notes, and eager to get at his opponent, when he rose to his feet he was, nevertheless, completely calm and the words and sentences poured out in a steam of perfect eloquence. His speech was lean, directly addressed to the substance of the current debate. "They both have fine voices," Parkin observed.

Once Parkin was back at Oxford, nothing could have been more congenial to the aspiring young orator than to take an opportunity to display his rhetorical talents before his fellow Oxonians. At UNB, Parkin had engaged in formal debates. At Bathurst, he gave public lectures at the courthouse. In Fredericton, he was called on from time to time to give public addresses. Not surprisingly, when he came to Oxford, he sought out one of its most famous clubs, the Oxford Union. "We have great fun down in the Union Debates," he wrote to his old UNB professor, Bailey. "The society is a rather famous one, as most of the great English statesmen got their first training in it as speakers." He began to attend the debates regularly and first spoke on 13 November in a debate on depriving denominational schools of their government grants.

The Oxford Union was already one of the most famous clubs in Oxford, and it is strange that the New Brunswick schoolmaster was not intimidated to speak in it. The debating hall was constructed in the early 1850s, and in 1857 William Morris took his friend the painter and poet Dante Gabriel Rossetti to Oxford to see the new hall. Rossetti immediately noticed the bare walls and offered to decorate them. Morris agreed to help and together they covered the walls with scene from Mallory's *Morte D'Arthur*.[11] The rising star of the union in Parkin's time was H.H. Asquith, a future prime minister, the third who was a product of the union. In the Trinity term of 1874, Asquith became president of the union.

H.H. Asquith came to Balliol from the City of London School, and was treasurer of the union in 1872. He ran for the presidency the next year, but was too aggressively Liberal and too aggressively Balliol. He ran again in the Trinity term of 1874 and won. He asked Parkin to serve as secretary and Parkin became the only non-collegiate student to hold any office in the union between 1841 and 1928. H.A. Venables of New College as treasurer and Ashton Cross of Balliol as librarian completed the slate.

The Magic of Oxford

As president, Asquith's reforms were modest. He introduced afternoon tea, an undoubted improvement, and lifted the ban on smoking. He spoke rarely in debates and when he did he was formidable, since he combined meticulous preparation with an extraordinary intelligence and an eloquence that made him one of the best orators of his age. Since he was a Liberal and came from a non-conformist (non-Anglican) background, he was at odds with the typical Balliol student, who was both Anglican and Tory. Asquith's maiden speech argued for the removal of bishops from the House of Lords.[12]

Parkin spoke in that debate too; he moved an amendment for the substitution of life peerages for hereditary succession. He also spoke on 1 December 1873, and on 12 February and 26 February 1874.[13] Earlier in the term he had written a topic on a piece of paper and put it in the suggestion box. It had been chosen as the subject of the debate on the evening of 8 May. He had been feeling sick during the day but he went to dinner as arranged with his friend Arthur Sloman, a classics scholar. After they had eaten they strolled over to the union, where Sloman was to succeed Asquith as president. It was an important evening for the tall, sinewy, gaunt Canadian with the winning smile and easy manner. Parkin rose in the room surrounded by the muted frescoes of Camelot and the mythical King Arthur. He read his motion: "That in the opinion of this house a closer union than at present exists between England and her Colonies is essential to the highest future prosperity of both, and should, as soon as possible, be effected by such an Imperial Federation as will secure the representation of the more important Colonies in the Imperial Council." He spoke quickly; his words flowed smoothly. A confederation of England and its colonies, he maintained, was possible, and once achieved it would dominate the world. The audience was large; he noted the presence of Prince Leopold, Queen Victoria's eighth child. As he later noted: "Did pretty well considering how unwell I felt."

The debate was continued on 15 May, when Asquith himself left the chair to oppose the motion. When the votes were counted, Parkin carried the day twenty-eight to six. Asquith wasn't used to defeat. This was the only time he lost. The debate became an Oxford legend and was certainly "the chief feature of Mr. Asquith's term of office." The novelty of the subject and Parkin's own "powerful and effective speech" made for "one of the most memorable debates ever held in the Union...." The later imperial prominence of its chief participants also caused the tradition of the encounter to linger around Oxford for years.[14] Asquith later testified "that he owed his deep interest in imperial organization to the influence of a Canadian fellow-student at Oxford named George Parkin."[15]

After the first evening of debate a young undergraduate approached Parkin. As he recalled the incident about twenty years later: "I am not likely to forget my first meeting with [Alfred Milner, later Alfred, Viscount Milner] when we were at Oxford together. It was at the Union; I had been leading a Debate on Imperial Federation, and many young fellows, now prominent in the Empire, had taken part in it. When the evening's debate was over Milner came up to me, gave me his card, asked me to breakfast with him, adding that he would try to get ten or twelve of the best men to join us and try to see if something practical might not be evolved from what we had been discussing. We met and talked, and I cannot but think that our discussions have had their influence in the world."

Like Parkin and Asquith, Milner, too, was an outsider. Born to a middle-class British family in Germany, he took his early education in Tübingen, before his family moved to London. When he approached Parkin, he was twenty-three. On 9 May, Parkin had dinner with his friend Tom Raleigh, and then went to Raleigh's rooms at Balliol, where they spent the evening with Asquith, Milner, and a couple of other friends discussing the imperial federation idea. Parkin and Milner met several times over the next month or so to have dinner or to work on Ruskin's road. According to one of Milner's biographers, it was a happy circumstance for Milner that "just when he was becoming interested in the British Empire there should have arrived at Oxford a young Canadian, who was absorbed in the future development and co-operation of a group of nations of which his motherland, Canada, was an important member... few men in the Kingdom or in the Dominions have every worked more whole-heartedly for Imperial Federation than he did."[16]

Where did Parkin's views on imperial federation originate? He may first have come across the idea on his trip to Montreal and Chicago. While he was on the train, he read a newly published book by

The Magic of Oxford

Charles Dilke, a brilliant British politician and author, who had travelled through the English-speaking countries in 1866 and 1867, and in 1868. The newly elected twenty-five-year-old MP published *Greater Britain: A Record of Travel*. The book caused a sensation. Dilke was the first person to travel throughout the English-speaking world as Alexis de Tocqueville had through America, with the intention of analyzing it and writing about it. His conclusion was that it formed a great cultural unity. It had enormous powers to assimilate immigrants, and nowhere could that be seen better than in the United States, with the consequence that the United States still remained a British country. "If I remarked that climate, soil, manners of life, that mixture with other peoples had modified the blood, I saw, too, that in essentials the race was always one....In America, the peoples of the world are being fused together, but they are run into an English mould; Alfred's laws and Chaucer's tongue are theirs whether they would or no."[17] For him, the greatest tragedy that had ever befallen the English-speaking people was the rupture of 1776, and the highest priority was to heal the rift.

The idea of empire was in the air. In June 1868, the Royal Colonial Institute was founded for the study of colonial problems, and grew over the years to become a prominent institution.

In 1870, J.A. Froude, one of England's leading popular historians, contributed on important series of articles on imperial unity to London's *Fraser's Magazine*. Froude made three points. First: emigrants, especially those who left Ireland after the famine, settled predominantly in the United States, where they created a body of public opinion hostile to the United Kingdom in a country whose economic interests rivalled the United Kingdom's. Second: as England became an increasingly industrial and urban nation, it was declining in character. Crowded conditions produced drunkenness, which sapped the vigour of mind and body "industrious, energetic, ingenious, capable of great muscular exertion, and remarkable along with it for equally great personal courage."[18] Third: population needed to grow so that England could keep pace economically and militarily with its rivals. The solution to these problems was assisted emigration to the colonies with their "virgin soil sufficient to employ and feed five times as many people who are now crowded into Great Britain and Ireland."[19]

Previously, closer political union was impossible because of the vast distances that separated the United Kingdom from its colonies. "The problem now is but to reunite the scattered fragments of the same nation, and bridge over the distance which divides them from us. Distance frightens us; but steam and the telegraph have abolished distance."[20] For Froude, such questions as the terms of the federation, the nature of the imperial council, the functions of the local legislatures, the present debt of the colonies, and the apportionment of taxation were matters of detail, not insuperable difficulties. Froude's ideas were sufficiently appealing that Lord Carnarvon, the Conservative secretary of state for the colonies, sent him on a mission to South Africa in 1874-5 to promote confederation.[21]

In the January and April 1871 numbers of the *Contemporary Review*, Edward Jenkins went into more detail. Jenkins was encouraged by the success of the Canadian confederation, an idea that was described as "visionary" in 1856, but was brought to fruition a mere eleven years later. Following the Canadian example, Jenkins proposed the creation of an imperial parliament to deal with empire-wide matters, with representatives from all the constituent parts. He also favoured free trade within the empire. His slogan, "Federation or Disintegration," became the rallying-cry of the movement, as did his rationale: "[T]his vast stretch of empire represents not alone the energy of a race unrivalled in history, not only physical and moral forces which might perhaps beard the world in arms, but principles of freedom, of justice, and of Christianity, however, and however often marred by invidious accidents, yet shedding over the whole a surpassing and peculiar lustre."[22] Jenkins was one of the principal speakers at a conference in July devoted to imperial unity at the Westminster Palace, which also attracted the participation of public figures such as the Duke of Manchester and the Earl of Shaftesbury. F.P. de Labillière read a paper on "Imperial and Colonial Federalism," his first contribution on a subject of which he was destined to become one of the ablest and most prominent advocates. Both he and Jenkins spoke on the same subject again at the Social Science Congress held at Devonport in 1872; and Jehu Mathews published his detailed proposals, *A Colonist on the Colonial Question*.[23]

On 24 June 1872, the great Conservative leader Benjamin Disraeli announced at the Crystal Palace that one of the great aims of the

Conservative Party was to preserve the empire. "No minister in this country," he stated, "will do his duty who neglects an opportunity of reconstructing as much as possible our Colonial Empire, and of responding to those distant sympathies which may become the source of incalculable strength and happiness to this land."[24] Parliament held a debate in 1873 and the *Times*, which in 1872 suggested that it might be the moment for Canadian independence, by 1874 was celebrating the loyal union of the colonies to the vast, united empire.[25]

Then there were the more immediate influences. Parkin visited Thring, who supported the idea, shortly before the debate. And he was attending Ruskin's lectures.

Ruskin believed in the importance of the British Empire as an agent for spreading British civilization throughout the world. As Ruskin put it in his inaugural lecture in 1870: "There is a destiny now possible to us, the highest ever set before a nation to be accepted or refused. We are still undegenerate in race; a race mingled of the best northern blood. We are not dissolute in temper, but still have the firmness to govern and the grace to obey. We have a religion of pure mercy. This is what England must do or perish. She must found Colonies as fast and as far as she is able, formed of her most energetic and worthiest men, seizing every piece she can get her feet on and teaching these Colonists that their chief virtue is to be fidelity to their country, and that, though they live in a distant plot of land, they are no more to consider themselves therefore disfranchised from their native land than the sailors of her fleet do."[26] These words were particularly cherished by Cecil Rhodes, and Parkin made them the centre of his life's work.

According to Richard Symonds, "Ruskin's social and economic ideas made themselves felt in the Empire in diverse ways. Though by no means uncritically accepted by Milner, Parkin and Toynbee, Ruskin's ideas contributed to their belief in a more positive role for the state in the development of the Empire than was prevalent either in Conservative or Liberal contemporary circles."[27] Ruskin's views on the importance of harmony in the British Empire were reinforced by a speech delivered to the Society for the Propagation of the Gospel by an archdeacon from Manitoba. The reverend gentleman, Parkin noted, "made some good points in regard to the immense importance of Canada to the British people and the greatness of the country."[28]

The difference between Parkin and most other advocates of closer imperial ties was that Parkin made the idea the centre of his life's work. Unlike anyone else, Parkin's vision evolved from a British empire to a global union of the English-speaking peoples, where neither trade nor military might but a desire to do good in the world was the binding force. Parkin stood out from the rest, not just by his dedication and energy, but by the idealism that drove him. Given how far out of step he was with most of the generals, businessmen, and politicians of his age, it is remarkable how much he accomplished.

Once the third and last of Parkin's terms at Oxford finished, and he dug for the last time on Ruskin's road, he received an invitation from Thring to travel with the family in their railway carriage and spend a few days with them at Grasmere in the beautiful Lake District, an area the railway had opened up to tourism. Parkin spent a few days in London, visited Miss Erskine and escorted her to a Handel festival, then set out via Nottingham for Uppingham, where he spent his first evening with the Rev. John Skrine. Skrine, a couple of years younger than Parkin, had just joined the staff at Uppingham after a successful degree at Oxford. Both men idealized Thring, but it was Parkin who accompanied the family on vacation and spent a pleasant few days rowing on the lake, bathing, and touring the neighbourhood. On 30 June, Parkin boarded a boat in Liverpool. He landed in Halifax on 12 July and set out immediately to see his family in Salisbury.

4

Reka Dom and Annie

Parkin returned to Fredericton in September 1874 ready for work. The house in which he boarded was about one hundred yards from the school, and from his window he could see Medley's cathedral, his alma mater on the hill, surrounded by maple trees which turned to brilliant reds and oranges in October, and Government House, where he now dined occasionally. His boys, he assured Miss Erskine, shared his ambitions to be true, pure, and good, and wished to grow up into faithful men. His moods continued to fluctuate, but he found solace in his dreams, which "throw a halo around even disappointment and defeat."

Socially, there was a fair amount for the bachelor to do. Fredericton society was divided between the self-employed and the salaried on the one side, and those who worked for wages. The first group, which included Parkin, could take the opportunity to participate in the various special occasions, such as the visit of the governor-general and his wife, Princess Louise, fourth daughter of Queen Victoria. There was the annual lieutenant-governor's ball, which coincided with the opening of the legislature. This attracted politicians, soldiers and anyone else who could contrive to get an invitation. The university had an annual Conversazione, or "Con," an event where men and women came together and, instead of dancing, were given topics as the basis for short conversations. There were innumerable ceremonial occasions—laying foundation stones, sod turnings, opening of bridges, railways, and buildings, ship launchings, funerals, memorial services for the death of royalty, celebration of military victories, and the most important of all, the celebration of Queen Victoria's birthday on the 24th of May.[1]

The Exhibition Palace displayed flowers and local fruits. It also contained a small pottery and a collection of minerals organized by professors Hind and Bailey. Almost all the most famous circuses visited Fredericton in the summer, and there were travelling theatre companies and entertainers who usually included Fredericton on their North American tours. After 1876, Fredericton had a venue suitable for more important productions, the Opera House, as the upstairs of the new city hall was called. Bands also played an important role. Although the bands of the British regiments had left, the civilian bands of the Fredericton Juvenile Band or the Temperance Reform Club Band filled the gap. There was skating, and later curling, tobogganing, and snowshoeing in the winter, and swimming and canoeing in the summer. When the weather did not co-operate, there was always checkers, either at home or in the hotel lobby, the barber's, or the blacksmith's shop. Although the evangelicals considered playing cards as the "devil's instrument," whist was fashionable. On the Sabbath, walking was one of the few permitted recreations.[2]

Parkin engaged in some of these activities with his students. Charles G.D. Roberts and Bliss Carman became life-long friends. Outside school, he told them stories about his year in Oxford, and reminisced about the world of arts and letters. He filled their pockets with apples. He was addicted to apples, Roberts said. In their hikes across country, he told stories and, in his rich voice,[3] recited the poems of Swinburne and Rossetti, "ecstatically, over and over till we too were intoxicated with them, the great choruses from 'Atalanta in Calydon,' passages from 'The Triumph of Time,' and 'Rococo'—but above all, 'The Blessed Damozel,' which he loved so passionately that Carman suspected him of sometimes saying it instead of his prayers." But Parkin's love and understanding of poetry was not confined to the work of the pre-Raphaelites. He quoted Tennyson, Browning, and Arnold and taught them Homer and Horace as supreme poets and masters of verbal music. In conversation, Parkin quoted from Horace as easily as from the English poets. One occasion particularly delighted Roberts. Parkin, Carman, and he were trout-fishing on the upper waters of the Nashwaak—or rather, Parkin and Roberts were fishing, while Carman, paying no attention, let his flies trail over a sunlit shallow that no trout was likely to visit. Suddenly Roberts hooked such a small trout that he inadvertently flung it into the upper branches of a neighbouring elm tree. Pointing upward to the fish, Parkin declared solemnly: "*Piscium et summa genus haesit ulmo* [When fish were in the elm-tops caught]."[4] Horace and Latin had in that instant become a living reality for two New Brunswick schoolboys.

Bliss Carman remembered this tall and spare teacher with a quick, swinging step, dressed in a well-cut suit of rough grey or heather mixture tweeds, looking like a country gentleman. "Often you would see him swinging along with that free debonair carriage of loosened energy, with a book or two gathered up in his left hand, and swinging a heavy stick in his right.... His face too was striking, dark skinned and lean, with a tawny moustache, and rather deep-set dark grey-blue eyes, not large nor flashing, but very penetrating and observant, and at times glaring with intensity of feeling and conviction."[5] When he joined the boys for football, he played with energy and zest.[6] In the summer of 1875 he took four of his favourite boys with him on his month-long vacation to Prince Edward Island, fishing, bathing, and baking oysters.

However, it was as a teacher that he made his mark on his students. He had, according to Carman, a great power to arouse and inspire his pupils, "a power he possessed in such abundance and spent so lavishly."[7] He brought the dry study of classics to life, recalling how he too had seen a honey-coloured moon rising over the roofs of Rome or flooding the Forum with its radiance. When Carman entered UNB, Roberts welcomed him to the university where, he predicted, he would "win the highest honours," but reminded him that half of these "are due/To your own strength of brain, and half accrue/To that wise master from whose hands you came/Equipped to win, and win yourself a name."[8] As his protégés matured, Bliss Carman and Sir Charles G.D.

Roberts, two of Canada's most important poets, freely acknowledged the important influence that Parkin's love of nature, fishing, and his pre-Raphaelite romanticism had on their development as artists and as men.

Inspired by Thring's ideas and ideals, Parkin decided in the autumn of 1875 to try to make his school the dynamic centre of education for the province as a whole. At the time, the school had only day students from Fredericton. Parkin wanted to establish something closer to an English public school, and that meant residential accommodation. He proposed to raise $5000 to build a residence so that boys from all over the province could board, and follow a curriculum that led to university. Since he expected his plan to bolster enrolments, he hoped for strong UNB support.

Central to his vision of the school he intended to create was a religious spirit. Over the summer he was offered the headmastership of the Collegiate School in Windsor, Nova Scotia, connected with King's College. This was an Anglican establishment, and since the school buildings had recently burnt to the ground, the governors promised Parkin $12,000 with which he could build a new school building. Although he thought that he could make a success of the project, and attract boys from both New Brunswick and Nova Scotia, he declined the offer in favour of staying in Fredericton and trying to create a religious institution that was non-denominational. He also had family responsibilities. His youngest sister, Charlotte, died while he was in PEI, and he interrupted his vacation to attend her funeral in Saint John. As well, a flurry of letters and telegrams from Watson had informed him that their father was so seriously ill that Parkin returned to Salisbury and took Holy Communion with him.

In the meantime, he remained very active. He founded an old boys' society for the school, helped to form a branch of the Temperance Society, led a discussion about teaching classics at the Teachers Institute, and threw himself into church work. At a meeting of the church synod, he spoke on "Mission Work: a Special Duty on the part of the Anglo-Saxon Race," a matter about which he felt strongly, and also helped organise the contributions to the Melanesian mission. The latter effort arose from the recent visit of Medley's friend, George Selwyn, the first Bishop of New Zealand.

Reka Dom and Annie

In 1874 Bishop Tozer, who had served in Zanzibar, and Bishop Selwyn had visited Fredericton. Selwyn preached twice at the cathedral and gave a "beautiful address" to the Sunday school about missions. Parkin also met with him for dinner and then for breakfast at Bishop Medley's where they had interesting conversations about the aboriginal peoples of the Pacific. During his meeting with Selwyn, Parkin asked, "Will the Maoris of New Zealand rise? Have they the capacity to lift themselves up into civilization that we English people have?" "That is race impertinence," Selwyn replied. Although the Maori were now in a childlike state, he went on, they had the capacity, under the right influences, to rise as high as the British race.[9]

Late nineteenth-century science had not determined whether there was one human race or several, or if there were several, whether they had all arisen at the same time. Anthropologists, archaeologists, geneticists, and others are still debating questions such as the nature of the Neanderthals, whether there were one or several migrations from Asia to North America, and whether Homo Sapiens arose elsewhere than in Africa. For Victorian Christians, such as Parkin, the matter was not relevant. Christ's message was meant for all human beings, and it was the responsibility of Christians to ensure that the good news reached all people, wherever they lived and whatever their background, so that they could understand Christ's redeeming sacrifice. Missionary societies, such as the Society for the Propagation of the Gospel in Foreign Parts, always commended themselves to Parkin for precisely these reasons.

Parkin shared the opinions of his age. He was not certain whether or not race meant destiny. However, he was open to persuasion, when many people were not. As we shall see, he thought that there was such a thing as the British race, and that that entity had evolved through long historical struggle, interbreeding between Celtic and Germanic tribes, the Reformation, and the rise of England. In other words, the English race had evolved, but it had taken some fifteen hundred years for the rude tribes of the Anglo-Saxon heptarchy to produce the nineteenth-century British Empire. Parkin was not sure how long it would it take the Maori of New Zealand, but Bishop Selwyn had assured him that it was possible, so Parkin contributed to the mission to Melanesia. He was not dogmatic in his attitude to race.

Parkin continued to press for his educational reforms. He was the university orator for 1876 and he launched a plea to create a residential public school along Thring's model. Edward Wilmot responded with a pledge of $1000 if four others could be found to do the same, but that proved impossible. An important figure such as Dr. T.H. Rand, chief superintendent of education, deplored Parkin's efforts to graft the educational institutions of one country on another, whose social situation was completely different.[10] Parkin refused to accept this setback. Thring had not been deterred by the indifference or the hostility of his governors; neither was Parkin. In April 1877, he rented the largest available house, and set out to convert it into a residence for boarding students.

The house Parkin rented was called Reka Dom, Russian for "river home." One of its previous occupants was Juliana Horatia Ewing, a novelist, and also, coincidentally, a friend of Thring's. It was a wooden, four-storey house on the Saint John River, several hundred yards from Parkin's school.[11] Reka Dom was Parkin's first home of his own, after, in his words, fifteen years among strangers. He hired a housekeeper, Mrs. Leonard, to help inspire the boys with the ideal of Christian manliness, and with her assistance bought a stove, carpets, and other furnishings. On 21 April Mrs. Leonard's own furniture arrived, and a week later Parkin moved in himself. Mrs. Leonard, Parkin thought, was thorough, energetic, and practical, and perhaps more important, a friend of Bishop and Mrs. Medley. Miss Erskine marked the occasion by sending him some new books, and Parkin replied that he had "never been so comfortable, happy or contented."

To help feed him and five students, Parkin planted potatoes, lettuce, radishes, tomatoes, and other crops. He also acquired a cow, which arrived by boat, and two pigs. However, Parkin's plans for the house were temporarily interrupted in June by the news of a fire that devastated Saint John. Parkin went down to the city on 23 June and two days later was at a public meeting that raised $5000 in relief. The strain of these activities proved too great for him. School resumed on 22 August, but on the 24th Parkin recorded in his diary that he was experiencing heart troubles. His condition lasted for about a week.

Other problems also arose. Over time, Mrs. Leonard proved an unsatisfactory housekeeper, more concerned with providing for her

Reka Dom and Annie

own declining years than undertaking a bold educational experiment. More serious, the gentry of New Brunswick were unwilling to send their children away to school, except for those who were serious discipline problems. When Mrs. Leonard quit in 1880, the experiment came to an end.

Parkin had another reason to give up the project. He had proposed to a former student, twelve years his junior, whom he had courted for twenty months. Annie Connell Fisher was, as Parkin described her to Miss Erskine, a happy cheerful girl, in perfect sympathy with his work, an earnest student and practical woman who might help him in his teaching, since she also had proved herself a good classical scholar. Miss Erskine replied with words of blessing, but noted that Parkin had neglected to tell her the name of his intended, perhaps an omen of the future imbalance in their relationship. Annie was barely twenty when Bishop Medley married them on 9 July 1878 at the cathedral. They went to Saint John by boat and honeymooned until 14 August. Parkin was so happy that he did not write in his diary again until October.

Parkin described his bride as "poor like myself." However, she came from an interesting family.[12] The earliest Fishers of whom there are records, are not Fishers at all, but Fischers. Lewis Fischer was born about 1740, probably in New Jersey, the son of German or Dutch parents. He married Barbara Till in 1772, the daughter of German immigrants. At the outbreak of the American Revolution, Lewis Fischer enlisted in a loyalist regiment, the New Jersey Volunteers. He saw action during the war, first in the way of raids, and then as part of the attack on Fort Griswold, where the loyalists massacred the garrison and burnt the village of New London, Connecticut. Fischer's battalion was one of the last to evacuate New York.

Although his ship, the *Esther*, was nearly lost, it arrived safely at the mouth of the Saint John River in the early autumn of 1783. The family travelled up river by schooner, and then by foot and canoe to St. Ann's Point (Fredericton), where they found other United Empire Loyalists, as they came to be known, of his regiment. The first winter was particularly trying, due to the lack of food and the necessity to live in tents. As a loyalist, Fisher was entitled to free land, which he formally received in 1788; he acquired another land grant in 1803.

Peter Fisher was born 9 June 1782, and grew up in Fredericton. He married Susannah Williams in 1788. She bore eleven children before her death in 1836 at the age of forty-eight. Peter started life as a blacksmith, but by 1821 he had acquired a store that sold drapery, ribbons, hardware, carpeting, wines, tea, coffee, sugars, etc. He was also engaged in the lumber business, and it is this that may have been the source of his wealth. As well as his business activities, Peter Fisher published *Sketches of New Brunswick* in 1825 and a similar work, *Notitia of New Brunswick*, in 1838. These two works earned him the title of the first historian of New Brunswick. He cared deeply about education, published a school primer, and ensured that his children had an excellent education. He was active in the civic life of Fredericton, and attained a commission in the local militia in 1825, a mark of substantial social progress in one whose father had been a private. His commission was a mark of acceptance by the Fredericton establishment.

Peter and Susannah's fifth child, William, was born 21 December 1818, and was baptised in the Anglican Church. In 1852, he married a widow, Catherine Clawson of Saint John. She died in 1854 and on 10 April 1856, he married his second wife, Charity Ann French. Annie, their first child, was born 13 June 1858. She was eighteen when her mother died. William was a merchant or trader—and not a particularly successful one, if we credit Parkin's comment that the family was poor. In the late 1870s, William became Indian Agent for New Brunswick, but resigned his office after a few years in protest against the endemic corruption.

Two of Annie's uncles achieved a prominence in New Brunswick politics. Charles Connell, who married Peter's daughter Anne, was one of the leading lumber merchants in Woodstock. Elected to the legislative assembly in 1846, he was appointed to the legislative council in 1849, and in 1858 he became postmaster-general in Charles Fisher's government. In the office, he achieved notoriety by issuing a stamp containing his own portrait rather than the queen's, a blunder that led to his resignation. Peter's son, Charles Fisher, was more prominent. He had a major impact on New Brunswick politics. He introduced responsible government and was one of the Fathers of Confederation. However, he did not always scruple about the methods he used. According to Donald Creighton, Fisher's "career in New Brunswick politics had been prominent, tempestuous, and, at times, extremely unsavoury, even by provincial standards."[13] Far from being a member of the New Brunswick establishment, Fisher led a movement known as "The Smashers," and his government contained no members of the ruling elite who had previously dominated provincial politics. Fisher was driven from office in 1861 over allegations of improprieties concerning the purchase of crown lands and, although other cabinet ministers such as Samuel Tilley were also implicated, they sacrificed their leader and retained office. However, Fisher was far from finished. When his electors returned him to the legislature in a by-election in 1862, he joined with Tilley to lead the confederation movement, although the project was generally unpopular in the province. He took part in the Quebec conference, and in 1866 returned to office as attorney-general in Tilley's administration. He retired from politics in 1868 to serve as a judge on the New Brunswick Supreme Court.

Marriage to Annie, then, brought Parkin closer to the centre of Fredericton society. He continued his activities in the Anglican Church and related societies. He taught regularly at the Sunday school and in 1878 became superintendent. He regularly attended the mid-week scripture class that Medley offered, and continued to support interdenominational institutions such as the Bible Society and the Church Temperance Society, on whose behalf he spoke frequently. Parkin also sat on the Church Temperance Society's executive committee and helped to plan its concerts and picnics. Although under Medley's influence, he began to practise what he preached—temperance rather than abstinence—he never took beer or wine in more than modest amounts and still thought intemperance to be a major source of poverty, crime, and irreligion.

It was through the Anglican diocesan synod, the governing body for Bishop Medley's jurisdiction, and the Diocesan Church Society, that Parkin began to make real inroads into the Fredericton elite. He sat on many of its committees with prominent Frederictonians.[14] The thirty-two-year-old also thought that he might get the recently vacated position as superintendent of education, but the position went to someone else.

The collegiate school itself was flourishing. Parkin persuaded one of his assistant masters to rent a house and take boarders. He was also pleased that the school was achieving his interdenominational ideals:

most of the boys were Anglicans, but he had also recruited a Baptist, two Presbyterians, a Methodist and, best of all, he said proudly, a Jew. There was even interest from a Roman Catholic. "If I could only get a Turk and an infidel my happy family would be complete and a fit subject for Christian anxiety. As it is I believe there is a Christianity broad enough to embrace them all." His theory was that only the moral force of a nondenominational Christian school could check the inevitable decadence that comes to children who inherit wealth.

Late in 1878, the university approached Parkin with the offer of a teaching position. He was well qualified. He had had his year at Oxford and was administering the school well. He also showed a scholarly disposition. In 1876, for example, he recorded in his diary that he translated Plato's *Apology* from the original Greek. Bishop Medley urged him to take it, and his doctor advised him that the position would be better for his health than the dawn-to-bedtime regimen he was putting in as principal. However, Parkin felt that there was no one to continue his reforms with the same zeal and concluded that it was his duty to remain in his post.

During his hectic years running a school and trying to reform education in New Brunswick, Parkin's interest in imperial federation never disappeared. He continued to read English books and periodicals, and his involvement in support of Anglican missionary works ensured that the cause of the Christianization of the "heathen" parts of the empire continued to absorb his interests.

The British Empire that Parkin hoped for had Christianity and justice at its centre, what Parkin called "the purer air of ideal good." Even if disappointment and defeat meant that it was impossible to realize dreams, it was better to dream a utopia, even the wild utopia that filled the thoughts, teachings, and life of Christ. "For even if we cannot see it realized in fact in the world generally, it is no small thing that the picture of it should exist in our minds. Besides, I am convinced that mere faith, and bare assertion of that faith, are the very best things to lead others to believe as we do."

Parkin's conversations with Bishop Selwyn had had a deep impact on his view of both the role of the Christian churches and the spiritual mission of the British Empire. In 1875, according to the *New Brunswick Reporter*, Parkin told a Diocesan Church Society meeting in

June that mission work was a special duty of the Anglo-Saxon world. Although the United Kingdom had won great commercial successes and her armies had triumphed in distant fields of battle, its achievements to date were nothing if they did not serve to bring God's truth to the nations. Void of this moral mission, the country would sink into ruin or decay. The July 1876 the Saint John *Daily Telegraph* reported a speech by Parkin in which he reiterated his view that, although the destiny of the British Empire was pre-eminently as a moral force, its past had been less than noble. It had piled up vast hoards of wealth by robbing its colonies rather than civilizing them. The exploitation of India and the slave trade were only the most egregious examples. An empire of force was dehumanizing to the conquered and enervating for the conquerors. For Parkin, the empire was the United Kingdom's destiny, but that fate might be for either good or ill, depending upon the use it made of it. One thing was sure: it was not simply good because it was British. Religion, as Parkin's first biographer, John Willison, observed, was the deepest thing in him. In these beliefs, Parkin foreshadowed what became, a hundred years later, the main thrust of Canada's foreign policy. From its role in the founding of the United Nations, its creation of peacekeeping, and the sponsoring of the land mine treaty, Canada's foreign policy has been guided by moral concerns. Parkin needs to be acknowledged as one of the earliest and most eloquent voices for this approach.

Parkin's view that Canada's true role was global was sustained by his correspondence with Miss Erskine and with Thring. Miss Erskine sent him copies of some of the leading British periodicals. He was, she told him, making history by educating young Canadians. The United Kingdom itself was becoming more crowded and there were fewer opportunities; many, whose brains would lie fallow for lack of work, could expand their talent and their energies in Canada and it was important for more and more emigrants of all ranks to go to Canada. Thring was another bubbling font of encouragement. Public opinion, he assured Parkin in January 1879, was "very cordial towards Canada, very, present." He was especially encouraged by how sports, particularly rowing and cricket, were helping to weld the English-speaking world together.

A leader of the imperial federation movement, William Forster, formerly under-secretary for the colonies under Gladstone, had recently been in the United States where he urged a closer alliance between the USA and the United Kingdom with the aim of making a union of the English-speaking peoples that might "soon be able to practically control the world." In Ontario, a movement called Canada First stood for the maintenance of the British connection and the consolidation of the empire. In the interim, Canada First proposed a Canadian voice in the making of treaties, closer trade relations with the West Indies (with the eventual aim of absorbing them), and a tariff intended to foster the growth of Canadian industry.[15] The dominant sentiment of the Canadian people, claimed Colonel George Denison, its leading spokesman, was "Canada first within the empire."[16]

Parkin's involvement in the imperial federation movement and his various other activities necessarily affected his ability to meet his family obligations. Annie had just turned twenty-one and was still living in Reka Dom when she gave birth to their first child, Alice Stuart, on 1 July 1879. In the late summer of 1880 Annie was pregnant again, due early in September. Parkin had been elected a delegate to the Anglican Synod to be held Montreal roughly at the same time as her expected confinement. According to Parkin, he wanted to stay, but his wife "so far overcame her woman's anxiety as to be resolute in her determination that I should not follow my own inclination to remain with her," and Parkin attended the synod where he was a brilliant success.[17]

An experienced orator, Parkin had the knack of rousing large bodies. He rarely used platitudes, since his ideas, although not intellectual, were not commonplace either. He never overwhelmed or intimidated an audience; he certainly never spoke over their heads. He had the orator's art of creating a mood of complicity with his audience. They were decent, earnest, moral Victorians; so was he. They wanted to make the world a better place; so did he. In Montreal, his cause was a great missionary drive to the new territories of the Canadian Northwest, which the Rev. George M. Grant, principal of Queen's University in Kingston, Ontario, had visited and spoken so movingly about in Fredericton several years before. This great area stood, Parkin argued, in grave moral peril. Could it be allowed to face the social and spiritual demoralization which marked the settlement of the western states of America? Or would we do our duty and win this area for Christian righteousness? The latter was the missionary destiny of the English race. It was the destiny of the British Empire, evidently designed by Providence for just this purpose, to carry the Gospel to every land, he concluded.

The assembly rose to its feet in appreciation. Churchmen from all over the dominion offered their congratulations. When Parkin returned to Fredericton, he wrote to Miss Erskine, "as a boy writes to his mother of his school victories," not to boast, since it was, he said, not his personal success or pride in his powers of speech that moved him. Rather he was aware that the great mission was to save "this vast country" for the Church of England, and not let it fall into the hands of other denominations. In his absence, Parkin noted Annie had given birth to a daughter on 14 September 1880. He asked if he might be allowed to name her Maude Erskine Parkin.

5

Imperial Federation

Parkin's growing family did not keep him home for long. In December 1880, he travelled to Saint John to give an address that united his two themes: Canada's mission as a moral force, and its need to reach out on a global scale.

Parkin's adversary was formidable: Goldwin Smith. His book, *The Political Destiny of Canada*, had made a strong case for Canadian integration with the United States. Born in 1823, Smith, who was about twenty-three years older than Parkin, had received an elite education at Eton and Magdalen College, Oxford, where he was an outstanding student and won a fellowship. Although not a great scholar, he was a brilliant writer, and he became Regius Professor of History in 1858 at the unusually young age of thirty-five. Smith was a political and economic liberal. His journalism attracted the attention of the leading intellectual, literary, and political figures of the day. Resigning his chair at Oxford, he participated in the founding of Cornell University, then a small rural institution emerging out of donated farmland in upper New York State. In 1871, he moved to Toronto, where he remained for the rest of his life. In 1875, at the age of fifty-two, he married Harriette Boulton, a widow who lived in the Grange, a splendid house on John Street in Toronto.[1] Although Smith was stationed in one of the outposts of the empire, he still played a role at the centre of British political and intellectual life. He wrote extensively for British newspapers and periodicals and founded two of his own, *The Week* and *The Bystander*. If anything, his reputation was higher in the United Kingdom than it was in Canada, though he was arguably the best journalist in Canada and one of the finest in North America.

In opposition to John A. Macdonald and his National Policy of protectionist tariffs and state intervention to foster national development, Smith was a Manchesterian liberal and free trader. He saw Macdonald's protectionism as a misguided policy that arose from the selfishness of vested interests and that would inevitably lead to the impoverishment of the country. The victory of the Tories in the 1878 election, he believed, would lead to a weakening of liberal principles in general, which only an alliance with the Great Republic could redress.

Parkin fought back. Had we forgotten the ideals and the sacrifices of the Loyalists, he asked a receptive audience? They had not left the United States for an easy and prosperous life, but "for principles, and ties [to the Crown, the Mother Country, the concept of loyalty, and the organic British constitution] held far more dear than any prosperity." To abandon these spiritual values for the utilitarian principles and material advantages that Smith preached would lead to nothing else than "public shame and degradation...." Canada's choice was not between independence and annexation. There was another option, Parkin believed, one that would achieve three great goals: national honour, commercial prosperity, and the ideal of active participation in the civilizing mission of the Anglo-Saxon race.[2]

The issue of the Saint John *Daily Telegraph* in which Parkin's remarks were printed came to Smith's attention. Smith replied in a long letter to the editor. In it, he made several shrewd observations that showed that he and Parkin were, on some points, not all that far apart in their analysis of the national sentiment of the new country. Earlier in the decade Smith had briefly associated with the nationalists in Canada At that time they shared a common desire to promote Canada's interests in the face of the United Kingdom's persistently self-centred attitude to its overseas possessions. Little Englanders and free traders believed that prosperity was best attained by pursuing purely commercial ties. They often pointed to the example of British trade with the United States, the value of which was far larger than her trade with any settler dominion, and to the economic importance of the United States, which was growing, in spite of independence and diplomatic relations that generally varied in a range between fair and poor.

For the free traders, Canada was a particular case in point. Canada attained the semi-independence of dominion status precisely because it suited the British colonial office.[3] The existence of British North America was a continuing irritant to Anglo-American relations. Militarily, there was no possibility that the United Kingdom could counter an America determined on the conquest of Canada; the success of Northern forces in the Civil War demonstrated just how effective a fighting force the United States could mount. Canada insisted on the presence of British forces, but was unwilling to defray the costs of their maintenance. On the contrary, Canada insisted on the United Kingdom's duty to support garrisons and to provide the capital for the canals and railways that any hope of effective defence would need. In return, Canada offered the United Kingdom raw materials and an outlet for British manufactured goods. The free traders argued that many of these benefits could be attained elsewhere at lower cost.

The British Conservatives, committed to imperialism after Disraeli's Crystal Palace speech of 1872, disagreed, though only in part. They saw the empire as an economic benefit to the United Kingdom, but when they spoke of the empire, they subtly, though not explicitly, divided it into three parts. One part was Africa and the Far East. In particular, Africa was an uncharted wilderness whose wealth in gold and other resources had yet to be proved, but for which there was every hope of munificence. India, the jewel in the crown, appealed to Disraeli's and the British people's sense of oriental mystery and magic. With the queen as empress and with the great project of a Suez canal allowing for an easy connection between Britain and India, the wealth of the orient could be harnessed to the manufacturing and commercial genius of the British people, producing wealth beyond the dreams of avarice, for those prepared to dream and to dare. Finally, there were the settler colonies—Canada, New Zealand, Australia, and

South Africa—which served as new homelands for the United Kingdom's surplus population, as Miss Erskine had suggested to Parkin. The settler colonies were not supposed to be the rivals of the United Kingdom but adjuncts, loyal to the motherland, subordinate to her vision of the best interests of the British peoples. Loyal they began; loyal would they remain, in the spirit of the motto of the province of Ontario.

However, on one matter, both free traders and imperialists were in complete agreement. The touchstone by which the value of the colonies was to be judged was economic benefit to the United Kingdom. Where that benefit lay was a matter for dispute, and not just among mainstream British interests. Smith concluded that the interests of the settler colonies like Canada were irreconcilable with those of the United Kingdom. Canada wanted the United Kingdom to use its economic and military power to protect Canadian interests; the United Kingdom saw Canada as an instrument in advancing its own.[4] To some extent, Parkin agreed with Smith's analysis. He implicitly conceded Smith's analysis that Canada's material prosperity was best served by union with the United States, calling this "the strictest conclusions of logic." Where Parkin disagreed directly with Smith, and indirectly with prevailing British opinion, was his belief that the common national purpose in social and Christian progress would trump material benefit as a *raison d'être* for Canada and the empire. Common political institutions, a common history, and a common political culture, which Parkin called "a unity of blood," would serve as a basis to lift the British peoples above the desire for mere crass commercial advantage.

Goldwin Smith was not the only writer pushing Canada towards union with the United States. In the November 1880 issue of the *Contemporary Review*, William Clarke began his article on the future of Canada with the announcement that he intended to state "the case on behalf of the annexation of Canada to the United States."[5] Unlike Smith, Clarke's argument for union was primarily political. Canada had not established a strong separate political identity. To the contrary, it lacked the advantages of both Europe and the United States. Stranded among the snows and ice of the north, it was "separated alike from the historic culture of Europe and from the heroic aspirations of America; sharing none of the precious traditions of England, and untouched by the breath of democratic freedom which sweeps through the United States."[6]

Despite the opposition of men like Smith and Clarke, however, closer union within the empire began to enjoy something of a vogue in the 1870s and 1880s. Many of the schemes advanced were pipe-dreams, because they did not take into sufficient account the political or economic realities in the United Kingdom or in the colonies. One type of scheme, the representation of the colonies in the imperial parliament, was old in inspiration. It had been suggested during the middle of the eighteenth century as a way of providing representation for the American colonies, but it failed because of the time—between eight and ten weeks—that it took for a sailing ship to cross the North Atlantic. Its nineteenth century proponents argued that the invention of the steam ship, the telegraph, and the transatlantic deep-sea cable now made it a practical possibility. However, colonial representation in Westminster posed insuperable difficulties of another sort. If representation were proportionate to the population of the various jurisdictions, the United Kingdom would so dominate for the foreseeable future as to make a mockery of the whole idea.

A second idea, which seemed more practical, was to adopt a federal imperial system on American or Canadian lines. There were several objections to this sort of plan. First, would there still need to be a separate British legislature dealing exclusively with British domestic matters and would it be bicameral or unicameral? Second, what would be the basis for representation in the imperial parliament's upper chamber? The American model of equal representation of each constituent part would give New Zealand and the United Kingdom, say, equal representation, a result completely disproportionate to their relative populations and wealth. Third, would the new federal imperial parliament have powers of taxation? And if so, how would these be levied and how would they be collected? Even in New Zealand, opinion was roughly evenly divided on this question. Between 1883 and 1885, when its legislature debated imperial federation, seven speakers spoke in favour, five against, with three adopting more guarded positions.[7] The opposition in New Zealand and elsewhere often stemmed from a sus-

Imperial Federation

picion that any scheme that involved powers of taxation was a thinly disguised plan by Westminster to extract contributions for imperial defence from the reluctant colonies.

The final concern was perhaps the most serious from a theoretical point of view: who would decide which matters lay in the jurisdiction of the federal parliament and which in the British parliament, and who would resolve disputes? In the United States, the Supreme Court had assumed that role, though opposition to the Supreme Court's ultimate jurisdiction continued right up to, and was one of the causes of, the Civil War in that country. However, the Supreme Court's power could be grounded in the sovereignty of the people.

In Canada, the power of the courts to decide jurisdictional disputes between the dominion government and the provinces had a sound basis but was irrelevant to the matter at hand. The power of the Supreme Court of Canada and ultimately of the Judicial Committee of the Privy Council to rule whether legislation was or was not within the power of the enacting body arose from the powers granted to British courts under the Colonial Laws (Validity) Act of 1865, which gave British courts the power to review the enactments of colonial legislatures. Since the British North America Act of 1867, which created the Canadian confederation, was an act of the British legislature, the courts had jurisdiction over enactments by subordinate bodies such as the dominion parliament.

This theoretical problem was not a minor irritant. The conflicting ideas of a limited government and of an unrestricted parliamentary sovereignty had been a major cause of the American Revolution. By the late nineteenth century, the concept of parliamentary sovereignty had become unquestioned dogma for constitutional theorists, and many simply could not conceive of a British parliament being overseen and overridden by a court of its own creation. These various problems led some of the proponents of imperial federation to suggest some sort of council of advice, with advisory powers. Although this seemed a weak and vacuous suggestion to many, in some ways it was the father of the colonial and imperial conferences, and later the Imperial War Cabinet, and perhaps even the grandfather of the modern Commonwealth.[8]

The movement for closer imperial ties was given a powerful boost when J.R. Seeley, professor of Modern History at Cambridge from 1869 until his death in 1895, delivered a series of lectures that received wide attention when they were delivered, and more subsequently when they were published as a book, *The Expansion of England*. Seeley's lectures, if they are known at all now, are famous as the source of the phrase that England "conquered and peopled half the world in a fit of absence of mind."[9] In an address given at the time of Seeley's death, Parkin praised the historian as someone who had taken the ideals of mere enthusiasts and woven the themes of history together to "develop a powerful chain of reasoning which showed that the true life and history of this nation could well be worked out on a scale commensurate with its past, and that it was not unreal to hope for a great united Britain in the future...."[10]

At its best, Seeley's argument came close to an understanding that the United Kingdom, and by extension, Greater Britain, were not natural or organic growths. Instead, he shrewdly observed that Greater Britain was an expansion of the English state. As a consequence, English colonists were united with one another and with the motherland by a common understanding of the way they associated with one another, namely as free individuals. This insight allowed him to reject the idea that the colonies were somehow enterprises developed by England merely to exploit the natural resources of the colonies for the benefit of the metropolis, that the colony was an estate to be worked for the benefit of its owners.[11] In the past, especially with the Americans, British policy had collapsed incoherently because it claimed to rule the colonists as Englishmen, but it treated them as if they were a conquered and backward people. At the same time, it afforded them sufficient liberty that they could easily rebel.[12]

However, Seeley was too much taken with nineteenth-century ideas of nationality to follow his insight to its radical conclusion. Although he rejected a simple racialist explanation, he clearly affirmed the existence of an English race that had been created through the contingency of history and the religious changes introduced by the Protestant Reformation. The formative factors for a people were race, religion, and economics, Seeley argued, and the ten million English who lived outside the United Kingdom were a great homogenous people "one in blood, language, religion and laws."[13] It was only recently, Seeley

Imperial Federation

observed, that the idea had taken hold that the "people of one nation, speaking one language, ought in general to have one government."[14]

Given these general principles, three conclusions seemed to follow. First: the English peoples should have their own state. Second: some sort of federal structure could address the factors of distance and local particularities. Third: the United States, the other centre of the English peoples, would be a factor of some as yet undetermined sort in whatever happened.

On 29 July 1884, some of the more important names in British politics met at the Westminster Palace Hotel to discuss imperial federation. They were united by a determination that England's relationship with its colonies would be a moral one, not simply an economic one. One of those present, W.E. Foster, Liberal MP for Bradford, a former under-secretary for the colonies and a member of Gladstone's cabinets 1868–74 and 1880–2, was the force behind the conference. The empire, he said, was at a crossroads; it couldn't stand still. It had two options and only two options: disintegration, as the Little Englanders of the Manchester School desired, or a tighter political unity based on the principle of equality between Englishmen. Technological advances in transportation and communication, steam, and electricity had created possibilities for closer integration. Should they be seized and developed, or ignored? The British Empire could be a moral force for good in the world, Foster argued, while the disintegration of the British Empire would lead to the increased probability of war among Christian nations, and the throwing back of the progress of civilisation. (Cheers arose from the audience on this point.) A moral imperial policy and prosperity were not incompatible goals, he felt, but complementary: "[T]here is no fact more proved by practical experience than that the trade does follow the flag."[15]

When Foster had finished his remarks, W.H. Smith, Conservative Member of Parliament and First Lord of the Admiralty in Disraeli's cabinet 1877–80, rose to propose the following motion: "That the political relations between Great Britain and her Colonies must inevitably lead to ultimate Federation or disintegration. That in order to avert the latter, and to secure the permanent unity of the Empire, some form of Federation is indispensable."[16] Lord Rosebery, a future prime minister, spoke in support, as did Lord Bury. From the colonies, Charles

Tupper, Canada's high commissioner, assured the audience that Canadians supported the maintenance of the imperial connection, and W. Gisborn from New Zealand looked forward to practical conclusions resulting from the public discussion. The conference adopted the resolution and voted to create a steering committee to give a more permanent form to the new organization, which was achieved at a second meeting on 18 November.

There were favourable comments from the London press. The *Times* was sympathetic, though it feared that the conference had sought strong support for a weak and vague resolution. The *Standard* hoped that a Federated British Empire would prove "an immense material advantage to ourselves and a guarantee of peace and progress to the world." And the *Pall Mall Gazette* saw imperial federation as a happy middle ground between the bombastic rhetoric of Disraeli and the fallacies of the non-interventionist school.

During this period, Parkin and Thring were exchanging letters in support of imperial federation and railing against its opponents. The idea of federation, Thring observed in one, was a simple law of nature, resulting from railways, telegraphs, and steam, just as Great Britain itself had evolved from the Anglo-Saxon heptarchy as a consequence of the development of roads.[17]

Parkin in turn drew Thring's attention to Goldwin Smith's most recent polemic. Smith had written an article in the *Contemporary Review* in response to Seeley's lectures. In it, he had made a series of telling points against the idea of imperial federation. The movement had arisen in England in response to the increasing independence of the colonies, the progressive concession of self-government that extended to a separate tariff policy, and, in the Canadian case, virtually to the ability to negotiate separate commercial treaties. In response, Smith thought, Downing Street wanted to politically reincorporate the colonies into the mother country under the name of imperial federation.[18] The constitutional problems were great, he argued, but more serious was the fact that colonies like Canada had developed a social system that was out of sympathy with England, one that was "thoroughly and unalterably democratic."[19] That meant that Canada had much more in common with the United States, and Canada's future lay with the continental version of Greater Britain rather than with the transoceanic variety. This argument infuriated Parkin. He told Thring that he wanted to try to get a hearing for real Canadian views on the subject of Colonial annexation.[20] Imperial federation was certain, Thring replied; however, he advised, Parkin would do well not to concentrate on the ideals towards which the movement aimed, though "never despising the present, though it be Job's dunghill...."[21]

On 9 May 1885 at three o'clock in the afternoon, D'Alton McCarthy, MP, called the organizing committee of the Canadian branch of the Imperial Federation League to order in the Windsor Hotel in Montreal. It enjoyed the support of eleven senators, forty-six MPs, and G.R. Parkin, M.A., of Fredericton, N.B.

The committee agreed to put the following two resolutions to a public meeting that evening:

1. That this meeting has observed with satisfaction the increased interest in the outlying portions of the Empire, displayed by the people of the mother country, and the formation under the auspices of many distinguished practical statesmen of the IMPERIAL FEDERATION LEAGUE.

2. That to the end that the mother country and the colonies may remain perpetually under a common sovereignty, a United Empire in its foreign affairs, with constitutional liberty for every part as regards internal administration, a re-adjustment of the several constitutional authorities of the Empire should, as occasion arises, be made in such manner as to increase the practical efficiency of Imperial unity.[22]

The evening was dark and wet, but when McCarthy rose to speak at 8 p.m. the crowd of seven or eight hundred people, including a "fair sprinkling of ladies," who had assembled in the Queen's Hall, burst into loud and prolonged applause. MPs, senators, distinguished clergymen, Sir William Dawson, principal of McGill, and George Monro Grant, principal of Queen's University in Kingston, flanked him.

Canada's welfare, McCarthy proclaimed to cheers, was bound with the empire's. Its political, social, and intellectual interests were best served by entering into a close and perpetual partnership with the Mother Country and the other self-governing colonies.[23] More cheers from the crowd. Then Professor Schuman of Dalhousie spoke. Remember, he said, the United Empire Loyalists, the exiled martyrs, whose very name evoked the vision that had brought the crowd together that night. George Foster followed. He argued that the prosperity of the various parts of the empire depended on the wealth of the whole, and that Canadians could be equal partners, free citizens, with common rights, equal privileges, and mutual aspirations.[24] Loud applause erupted.

Then, as Principal Grant, the star of the evening, rose to his feet, he was met with loud and hearty cheers. The empire, he affirmed, was a powerful and efficient organization which nourished liberty, defended the principles of righteousness, developed manhood, and extended its benefits to all classes, creeds, and colours. A few fine young fellows, he conceded, were naturally impatient, as the young often are, with the condition of colonial inferiority, and independence indeed sounded like an attractive idea. But its true name was isolation, and in Canada's case, that meant intolerable dependence.

Others, Grant noted, openly advocated annexation, which its ablest proponents called continentalism and some of these honestly believed that the addition of loyal Canadians to the United States would tip the balance of opinion in that country sufficiently that the English-speaking peoples could again be united. Yet, Grant argued, they deceived themselves. Annexation meant nothing less than revolution. (Cheers.) "I believe in Evolution not Revolution. (Cheers.) Evolution is the divine plan, and it is much better than revolution. (Hear, hear.)"[25]

Hitherto, Grant continued, Canada had relied on the British fleet for its security, but had contributed not a cent to its cost. Was this consistent with honour or self-respect that such a state of affairs continue? "No," cried the crowd. Well, then, Grant concluded, we must create such a passion for unification in the Mother Country for a free and equal association of England and its self-governing colonies that they can become full partners in the richest, truest, grandest nation in the world.[26]

Grant's commanding presence and eloquence carried the audience through every step of his argument. When he closed, the crowd enthusiastically broke into an ovation of cheers, and soon the audience spontaneously broke out into "God Save the Queen." The resolutions were unanimously adopted, and the League was launched with 224 members, an entirely satisfactory beginning to the new enterprise.

There was great enthusiasm, but the weakness of the Canadian League was the same as that of its British cousin: what did its supporters really want? Closer economic ties? Federated institutions? Military integration? John A. Macdonald, who had long experience of the selfishness of Downing Street, dismissed imperial federation as an idle dream. Edward Blake, leader of the opposition, called it the dream of yesterday. The league faced an uphill battle in persuading Canadian public opinion that the drift towards independence had not already gone too far.

Yet, whatever they called themselves, the men and women who met that night in the Windsor Hotel were agreed that Canada should be an outward-looking country, open to the world, and ready to assume its responsibilities.

Soon after his return to Fredericton, Parkin suffered from what Thring described in a letter as a breakdown. He counselled his young friend to be very careful for a year, and to be careful not to overextend himself for two or three years after that. "For goodness sake," Thring pleaded, "take care of yourself...husband your strength. I shall be in a great rage if you don't take my advice...." Parkin did not take Thring's advice, and since they both possessed what Parkin described as a "passionate earnestness," Thring was not surprised. Blessed with incredible stamina and energy and driven by a passion to make the world better, Parkin never learned to pace himself. His regular pattern into his seventies was to push himself to the breaking point and stop only when his body told him that it could do no more. There then followed a period of complete rest, which allowed him to recover his energy, ready for the next heroic exertion.

6

Foreign Travels and Domestic Tragedies

Parkin had become one of the leaders of Fredericton society, and that involved further duties, such as presiding over seventy-five alumni at the university's annual dinner on 26 June 1884, attending the synod in Saint John on 1 July, and speaking at the Teachers' Institute on 10 July. He was driven to further journalism and public speaking because he needed recognition, but he now also needed to supplement his income. As a bachelor, Parkin had not been much concerned about his finances. Content to live in lodgings, he could afford to save enough money to take a year off in Oxford. The experiment with Reka Dom undoubtedly required subsidy from his income, but his hero, Thring, had taken even greater financial risks to build Uppingham.

By the early 1880s Parkin was in his mid-thirties, with a growing family to support. Fredericton High School had two streams, a classics-based stream, meant to prepare students for university entrance, and a more practically oriented stream, intended to get students ready to earn a living. For the first, he received part of his salary from the university senate. The city trustees, whose contribution varied according to the city's financial circumstances and their inclination to generosity, provided the rest. In 1883, Parkin threatened to resign if his salary were not increased. The university responded by fixing his remuneration at $800 and added a further $200 in 1885. However, the city fixed its share at $400, $50 less than previously, and, according to Parkin, less than a third what rival cities such as Saint John paid. Parkin was able to supplement this income with his freelance journalism, though this paid little then as now. Parkin also borrowed money from friends and family and was reduced at one point to advising Annie that she needed to take special care with the piano, since he had pledged it as security for a loan.

Parkin developed a plan that would allow him to pay his emotional debt to Thring at the same time as he raised the funds to satisfy his more mundane creditors. He proposed to write an article on Uppingham for *Century Magazine* to mark the school's tercentenary. *Century Magazine* was one of the American journals with the widest circulation and the most generous fees for contributors. An illustrated article that featured Thring's teaching ideas, the houses, gardens, and workshops of the school, would prove a vehicle for spreading Thring's ideas more widely in the United States, and, as Parkin wrote to Thring, might also provide enough additional cash to allow Parkin to make "a pilgrimage over the water to join with you." Thring replied immediately to both the text and the subtext of the letter. He offered to contribute £50 towards Parkin's expenses in undertaking the article and elegantly replied to Parkin's comment regarding his lack of a contribution to the tercentenary. "I am really glad you cannot give to our Tercentenary. It is quite enough to have our friendship and work in the same field." What made Parkin valuable in this and other areas was his empathy, his articulateness, his unbounded enthusiasm in a cause he deemed worthy, and perhaps most of all, his integrity and his sincerity. Thring told him as much: "I don't care if a mere magazine article is to be written....It would probably be full of false glory, and misleading views; but if you write it knowing as you do the inner meaning, and in close communion with me I should prize it very much indeed."

For both of them, education was as much a political matter as a social or moral one. In a review of Thring's *Theory and Practice of Teaching* of 1883, Parkin warned against the developing practice of national standards and uniform examination. Intellectual death, Parkin wrote, "is the only possible result that can come from making the teacher a mere machine, with his work and its worth tested and ticketed by another examining machine, which compels all that come under its control to pass through one and the same intellectual hole which it has drilled as the gauge of merit."

The state and its examiners must be kept at a distance. It was the role of the public school to form the national character, not reflect it. It was the boarding school that made the English such an adventurous race, Thring argued, and he likened it to the mediaeval custom of sending the children of the nobility to serve as pages in other noble houses. In subsequent letters, Thring continued to furnish Parkin with information regarding the character of Uppingham, and in May 1886 Parkin decided to take Annie's advice and visit Uppingham again. Annie thought that a sea voyage might consolidate her husband's health, and a trip would give Parkin the opportunity to take in an educational conference in London in July. Parkin contacted Richard Gilder at the *Century* and was reassured that the editor still wanted an article on Thring. The magazine was Parkin's first choice, since its circulation ran into the hundreds of thousands. Gilder was glad to have the piece, though he did ask Parkin to make it as light and readable as he could.

Parkin received $100 for his Uppingham article; he was disappointed that it was not more, since the research had cost him a fair amount. Perhaps, some day, his market value would rise, he mused. At least he had his foot in the door.

In the article, he emphasized the points about Uppingham that over time Parkin adapted and made his own: boarding schools provided a healthy environment for the sons of the wealthy; they should be egalitarian and the classes must be small; they must address the whole child, not just the intellect.[1]

Thring's ability to innovate depended on the fact that Uppingham was an independent school whose curriculum and standards were not dictated by the state. For almost a century, a growing movement had preached universal state education as a means of improving the social, economic, and political condition of the poor. Industrialization increasingly required a literate and numerate workforce, with a minimum and standardized level of achievement. The Reform Act of 1832 began a process of an expansion of the electorate and the beginnings of the democracy in British politics. Disraeli and Gladstone continued to expand the franchise so that, by the end of the nineteenth century, Major John Cartwright's wild, utopian dream of the 1770s of a universal manhood franchise was almost in place.

For Thring, state-regulated education, in the name of democracy, would impose a sterile uniformity on all education. As he pithily summed up his objections in a letter to Parkin, free education meant:

> Education judged by the mob, and directed by mob officers. Education with its course laid down by government, examined, inspected, and every original movement in teaching strangled. Education with religion damped off, or forbidden and the thrifty made to pay for his scoundrelly neighbour's lusts....

As far as Thring was concerned—and he had some grounds for this view—Uppingham was his school. Yet his trustees did not see things entirely this way. Thring was openly at war with them. Parkin's efforts at celebrating Thring's achievements in the United States gave Thring powerful weapons to deploy. "I want to show my power in every possible way," Thring wrote Parkin. He was willing to escalate the arms race, and spend £30 or £40 if Parkin was prepared to write more favourable pieces for American journals. "I shall not grudge expense, more if necessary, at a corresponding increase of artillery." Any weapon that came to hand would be useful "to show my power...to my insolent oppressors." By the end of August the reinforcements had arrived. Parkin's article was everything that could be desired and arrived in the nick of time. A telegram demanded 100 more copies to throw into the battle. Parkin, though, was feeling increasing pressure to provide for a growing family. Though they had lost a son, who was either stillborn or lived only a few hours or days in April 1884,[2] they had three daughters, and Annie was three months into her fifth pregnancy in seven years of marriage. The baby was born on 7 September 1885. They called her Muriel Thring Parkin. She became very ill the following spring and for two or three days Parkin and Annie feared for her life, but the doctor was pleased with her recovery and pronounced her completely out of danger.

Parkin wrote Thring to tell him that they might soon meet. There was a meeting of the Imperial Federation League in London in July, which Parkin wanted very much to attend; it was a chance to meet interested men from all over the world and the opportunity might not soon return. He could combine this meeting with the task of representing the diocese at the Church of England Temperance Society meeting in London later in the month, since Leonard Tilley was prepared to give up his place for him. Annie was once again in the early stages of pregnancy, but this time he would be back in plenty of time for the birth.

Parkin left for England on 16 June and arrived in Liverpool on the 26th. He found the port city oppressive. Great cities like this, he wrote home, "have in them to me something of the terrible." Nonetheless, he was able to buy a top hat and some other items of clothing that he thought were necessary for London and his other visits. It was just this sort of expenditure that strained the family budget. Were they necessary for a New Brunswick schoolmaster? Strictly speaking, no, but clothes do make the man. There is no evidence that Parkin cared at all for the clothes he wore, but just like comportment, a certain code of behaviour, knowledge of the rules of etiquette, they contributed to his respectability and, as such, were a necessary expenditure if he were to get a hearing for his ideas among the political elite, where important decisions were as likely to be made at a country house weekend or dinner at a private club as in a public forum. Whether they were an expenditure he could afford is another matter. However, Parkin did not forget about his wife's needs back in Fredericton. His hostess offered to help him pick out "dress stuff" for her. Then he could get a dress made up "which would do real well, that is the skirt—sending the stuff for the body."

On Thursday, 1 July 1886, Parkin spoke briefly at the imperial federation conference meeting. He had made a name for himself on the topic twelve years before in Oxford and again the impression he made was favourable, so much so that the next morning when he returned to the conference, the secretary asked him if he would speak again. The room he was in had a great map of the empire. As he gazed on it, his thoughts quickly came together. He had been allotted ten minutes, but when they expired, the audience wanted more, so he spoke for another ten, perhaps fifteen. He stood with a large pointer, jabbing at the map, the words flowing easily, his mind focused, filled with sensations of great intensity and energy. He felt the exultation that comes to an orator who has established an intimate bond with his audience and captivates them with his effortless mastery of his subject.

The speech changed Parkin's life. A Scottish MP rushed over to ask if he would come to Edinburgh to speak to the Chamber of Commerce. Captain Colomb devoted the closing remarks of his paper to the enormous power with which Parkin had treated the subject. Others asked if he would speak at halls in London where they would guarantee an audience of two or three thousand. Morton Frewen, Lord Randolph Churchill's brother-in-law, asked him to lunch and arranged for an interview with a London newspaper.

After the conference finished, Parkin headed off to the Albert Hall for a concert. When the celebrated Patti sang "Home, Sweet Home," it was, as Parkin put it, "a complete upsetter for a fellow so far away from his own." But he soon recovered his equilibrium and rushed back to dress for the evening's banquet at the Freemason's Tavern. He was tempted to send Annie the printed lists of all the great people who were there, the menu, the music, "but it will cost something in postage and can keep till I come." The highlight of the evening was a ten-minute audience with the great Catholic prelate, Cardinal Manning. "Many of us colonists have come from very far," he told the cardinal, "but none from any place so far that your name has not reached there." "I think this was fair without being flattering," Parkin prided himself.

He also tried to re-establish contacts with some of his friends from Oxford. Milner had worked as a writer for *Pall Mall Gazette* and then taken a position as private secretary to George Goschen, a chancellor of the exchequer. Milner offered to help Parkin find outlets for his journalism, and arranged a meeting for him with W.T. Stead, his former editor at the *Gazette*. The trio of Parkin's fellow Oxford Union debaters—Raleigh, Milner, and Asquith—had been marked for greatness by fellow undergraduates and by the talent-spotting dons at Balliol, and the debate centred on which of them would eventually become prime minister. It turned out to be Asquith. He first step was his election to Parliament in 1885; Milner and Raleigh ran unsuccessfully.

After the Imperial Federation Conference, Parkin had lunch with a Mr. Morgan at the Devonshire Club, "very gorgeous and epicurean," in Parkin's words, and then took the train to Oxford to stay with Raleigh, his old debating club friend from Oxford, who was now a Fellow of All Soul's, an Oxford college, and a barrister in London. Living at All Soul's was a different Oxford experience for Parkin than boarding with two sisters who supplemented his diet with their apples. Here he dressed for dinner with MPs and other swells, then strolled across the quad for port, before settling down in the common room to chat over coffee. "All very stately and fine," Parkin pronounced it. He then went to Hornblotton in the county of Somerset to visit Thring's brother Godfrey.

Parkin's attention then turned to the Temperance Congress, which had been called to collect comparative information about the voluntary and legislative efforts throughout the empire to restrain intemperance. Parkin spoke about the movement in New Brunswick and argued that the fight for temperance should be organized on an imperial rather than a local scale. The *Times* reacted to this suggestion with the observation that "federation by means of temperance legislation is surely an entirely novel idea...[and] strikes us as a singularly impractical one."[3] Parkin was not intimidated by the Thunderer's editorial, and fired off a letter in his defence.

His letter attracted the attention of a Mrs. Flower, a Rothschild by birth, who was so impressed that she invited him to lunch at what was generally thought as the most sumptuous house in London. Parkin was overwhelmed by the opulence. "I think it must have cost a million to furnish it," he observed with awe. In spite of the aristocrats and parliamentarians present, she spent the luncheon talking to him, and they were both so overcome with emotion when they found out that they had a friend in common that she urged him to stay with them until Sunday. When Parkin left, she saw him to the door and insisted that he let her know when he was returning to London. He left "scarce knowing whether I were my own self or not." Parkin also visited Lord (Henry) Thring, a distinguished parliamentary draftsman and Edward's elder brother, spoke in Kensington and Tower Hamlets, and then stayed with the IFL secretary and book publisher, Hugh Arnold-Foster. The last three days were planned for his relatives in Barnard Castle. "I feel sure, dearie, now, that if my life and health are spared, the trip may prove to be a good investment directly or indirectly," he wrote home. "I only pray that it may in some way turn out to make life pleasanter for you. Looking back from this distance I feel how hard a time you have had these years past and am resolved to make it lighter if love and help can do it."

He sailed for New York, making landfall on 12 August. When he docked, a letter was waiting for him. Muriel had fallen ill again. The doctor had thought there was no danger, but the next time that Annie went to her crib, she found her cold and lifeless. It had taken Annie several days before she could make sense of what happened. He took the train to Boston and then rushed to Fredericton. Parkin thought about recent parallel events: he had been in visiting Thring's brother, enjoying the conversation, when Muriel died, and was in Wiltshire walking in the garden when she was buried. Thring wrote, trying to console him with the thought that his daughter's death might "consecrate and hallow by a purifying source the work in which you were engaged. It seems, I mean, intended to blend with the great movement sent to ennoble you, and deepen your heart, and make your whole spirit move in a higher, holier sphere."

Her baby's death made Annie's pregnancy very difficult. She gave birth to a daughter early in the morning of 15 February 1887. "Our Valentine," Parkin wrote in his diary. She seemed in perfect health, but two weeks later she became very ill and Parkin summoned the minister to baptize her Annie Connell. She died on 1 March. "The Lord giveth and the Lord taketh away. Blessed be the name of the Lord," Parkin wrote in his diary. It was possible that her heart had been damaged during the pregnancy.

Parkin, however, always had the option of immersing himself in work. He threw himself back into his attempts to raise the standard of education, trying to persuade the New Brunswick government to enact free public education. By the end of September, there were even more family worries. Parkin's diary for 30 September notes that Maude was ill with "Scarlet Rash" (probably scarlet fever). On 2 October, Alice showed the first symptoms; on the next day, so did Grace. Fortunately, they all recovered.

Annie never did. She had been shattered emotionally and she never regained her strength. These events triggered a serious clinical depression in her, though the family referred to it as "the Fisher nerves." Over the years, though Parkin loved his wife, he regularly put his ambition and his idealism ahead of her needs. The combination of their age difference, the social expectations of the Victorian era, and Parkin's compelling personality meant that his wife really had little chance of forcing him to balance her needs with his. Often, as we will see, she found herself almost a penniless single mother relying on the charity of friends to keep a roof over her children and food in their mouths, since her husband had miscalculated her financial requirements.

This, perhaps, is an all-too-common story—a man rises to greatness only because his wife stays at home to raise the children and look after domestic matters. In the case of this story, the impact is multiplied. Parkin travelled the world and stayed in some of the great stately homes of Europe before Annie even left New Brunswick. Annie appears only occasionally in this story, not because she isn't important, but because the documents that relate to her are available mainly only when there is a crisis. Parkin's greatness was built on Annie's hardship and suffering, not because Parkin wanted Annie to suffer, but because he wanted to be great.

By the end of the year, Parkin was giving lectures on imperial federation again. He also approached Gilder at the *Century* magazine about the possibility of writing something for him on the subject. Gilder replied cautiously, and informed Parkin that he would not be able to use the articles on Rockingham Castle or the Earl of Stafford that Parkin had submitted. However, he did send Parkin a second $100 as a contribution towards the expense of his Uppingham article.

As well as providing Parkin with some money, his Uppingham article also had a major effect on Thring. Indeed, Thring made a resolute decision: When he died, Thring said in a letter to Parkin, he didn't want a half-gelded creature who couldn't see practical truth to write his biography and explain his ideas. He wanted a real man; he wanted Parkin. That was, he said, a kind of last will and testament.

When Thring made this request, he was sixty-five and in good health. However, in the middle of October, he caught a cold and felt very faint as he left the chapel. He went to bed, but the cold fastened on his lungs, and he steadily weakened. At half-past four in the morning, his three daughters, who were sleeping in the visitors' room, were called in. Thring was unconscious, his pulse getting weaker. Each of the girls kissed her father and then retired to the drawing-room. At a quarter to eight in the morning, the doctor summoned them again. They sat with their father until he passed quietly away. One of his daughters, Grace, wrote to Parkin the same day, 22 October 1887.

A month later, Parkin received a long letter from John Skrine, a teacher at Uppingham whom Parkin knew well. Skrine had expected to be appointed Thring's biographer and was shocked and rather angry that he was not the chosen one. Skrine felt that Parkin should stand aside since Skrine thought that his was the superior claim. He had been Thring's favourite pupil, seven years a boarder in his house, and five years in his class. For fourteen years, he had served as a master under Thring. Furthermore, Skrine stated that one day, while Thring and he had been reading a poem of Skrine's, Thring had turned to him and said with deep feeling in his voice, "Skrine, you shall write my epitaph." In spite of the pain Thring's decision caused him, Skrine was determined to write some sort of memorial even if he was denied the role of official biographer.

Parkin replied with a letter that Skrine described as a noble, unselfish, and sincere, almost brotherly response. Parkin said that he believed it was the feeling of the family that they had a responsibility to carry out their father's wishes. To this, Skrine replied that the family had treated him as if he were to have the task until they learned of their father's letter to Parkin.

How did the school's Old Boys and Thring's friends feel? According to Skrine, they were shocked that a virtually unknown stranger was to do the work. This latent hostility, Skrine feared, might hamper Parkin in his research. What of Thring's own expressed wishes? Skrine speculated that Thring had chosen Parkin exactly because of his distance from the school, which allowed him to speak of Thring's relations with the trustees and other teachers without prejudice. However, Skrine rejoined, the situation had changed completely; he had now broken his ties to Uppingham and resigned his position. He now had both the knowledge of the situation and the freedom to write about it without constraint. Parkin certainly agreed that Skrine had the advantage over him: it would be difficult to write the biography when all the documents were on the other side of the ocean. Skrine agreed that he had both the time and the resources.

After considerable thought, Parkin told Skrine that he considered the request from Thring the moral equivalent of a command, and also sent him a passage from Thring's diary supporting his decision. The Thring family was very happy with his decision. "We all feel very much the sacrifice you are thinking of making for him and for us, it is wonderful to us to think of it, I could not help a sob rising when Mother told me how near his last wish was to fulfilment." Nevertheless, both Skrine and H.D. Rawnsley, another of Thring's teachers, wrote short memorial sketches of their beloved friend, which appeared long before Parkin's much delayed biography in two volumes.

On 13 June 1888, Parkin left Fredericton for England to begin work on what he described as his sacred duty, writing Thring's biography, and to work on his imperial federation ideas. It was hard, he allowed, to be parted from all his dear ones, but it was a sacrifice he had to make. While in England, he stayed with Thring's immediate family in Uppingham and also with Thring's brothers, Godfrey, a hymnologist, and Lord Thring, whose country house was near Eton, where Thring had gone to school. These visits allowed Parkin to collect material for the biography, while the family hospitality reduced his expenses.[4] Parkin wrote letter after letter to Old Boys, teachers, and parents to seek copies of correspondence or reminiscences or anecdotes about life at Uppingham, and collected a trunk full of letters that he hoped would allow him to complete his biography in Canada.

His other reason for visiting England was to agitate on behalf of the Imperial Federation League, and in the service of the cause, he spoke in Oxford, Canterbury, Cambridge, Eton, Yorkshire, as well as Wales and Scotland. He dined at the House of Commons with sympathetic members of parliament such as Herbert Asquith and Bruce and George Trevelyan, and met John Morley, Gladstone's senior colleague.[5]

During this period Colonel George Denison took charge of the organization of the Imperial Federation League; Parkin was more its proselytizer. Denison formally organized the Toronto branch on 1 February 1888. It passed a resolution calling on "our friends in parliament" to support its aims, which were, in Denison's colourful words, to call on the patriotic sons of Canada "to rally round the old flag and frustrate the evil designs of traitors."[6] Denison called a public meeting for

Foreign Travels and Domestic Tragedies

24 March at the Association Hall in Toronto to promote imperial federation and to demolish the delusive theory of unrestricted reciprocity and commercial union between Canada and the USA. For him, imperial federation amounted to the implementation of a preferential tariff against the importation of foreign production. For the next three years, Toronto rather than Montreal was the dynamic centre of the movement and the league, in Denison's view, became a "strong and effective influence upon the public opinion of Canada."[7] The establishment of the branch in Toronto was soon followed by others in Brantford, St. Thomas, Port Arthur, Orillia, Ottawa, and Halifax.

Fortune and character play about equal roles in men's lives, Machiavelli said, and so it proved for Parkin. The Executive Committee of the Imperial Federation League met in London on 31 July 1888. The mayor of Melbourne, Downes Carter, who was president of the league in the colony of Victoria, was scheduled to address the group, as was D'Alton McCarthy, the founding president of the Canadian League. During Carter's speech, word came that McCarthy was delayed. Would Parkin say a few words from the Canadian perspective? His speeches around the United Kingdom has already established him as a force within the movement and this impromptu speech so impressed Carter that he invited Parkin to tour of Australia and New Zealand. He thought he could easily find £400 for the three-month engagement, a sum Parkin calculated was more than double his schoolteacher's salary, and one he hoped would both help eliminate the family's debt, as well as lift him "out of that rut of accepted mediocrity or inferiority in which I was placed in [Fredericton]...." He decided that he would quit his teaching post at Fredericton, and seek a new life based in England.

This was one more case—and not the last—of Parkin deciding that sacrifices needed to be made for the sake of the family's long-term prospects. Unfortunately for Annie, this invariably involved her husband setting off on his travels, while she had to be resourceful and cope somehow during his absence. In this case, she and the children stayed with his relatives on the family farm. This would be a good solution, he said, since Annie could study and read and do lots of things that might improve her spirits, and the children would get familiar with rural conditions and the rhythm of country life. "It is so healthy for them mentally I think." Once again, while she was left behind in rural

New Brunswick, he was learning to play lawn tennis, visiting Lord Thring, and travelling to Oxford, Cambridge, Edinburgh, and Yorkshire, to "say nothing of minor places, with a good bit more of time in London...." "If you can be brave, I can," Parkin concluded a letter to her, quite genuinely believing that their sacrifices were roughly equal.

By the beginning of September, Parkin, exhausted with travel and work, was suffering from one of his bouts of depression, when everything seemed so large and difficult that his courage oozed away. Thring himself, he noted, experienced the same dramatic variations in mood, on the mountaintops one day and in such a state of hopelessness soon after that life scarcely seemed worth living. In a letter to Annie at this time, Parkin wrote that he felt he would be happy living in a smaller house and not entertaining, but he felt strongly the fact that he was depriving Annie of a pleasant life. But, he reminded her, poor Thring suffered from debt, year after year, and Parkin's current sacrifice was an effort to avoid this fate for his family. He added that he had enjoyed a pleasant stay with Bishop Branch, coadjutor of Antigua in the West Indies, with whom he had a delightful talk about imperial federation, especially about the possibilities that the West Indies might join Canada.

A few weeks later, the plans for an Australian visit were moving along. It was agreed that he should have the £400 for the three months, though £150 of that was earmarked for expenses. It was hoped that he could earn extra money from journalism along the way, and perhaps the Canadian Pacific might allow him free passage across Canada, which would reduce the expenses. Carter telegraphed Australia to see if there was local interest.

Annie, however, was growing restless with her in-laws in Salisbury and wanted to move back to Fredericton. She wrote her husband for advice and also for money. Parkin himself was comfortable, since he was staying with the Thrings and other friends of means in England, but Annie had to pay her own way in New Brunswick. A possible general election in one of the Australian colonies was making the timing of Parkin's tour uncertain and Annie's situation even worse, since it delayed Parkin's return. Annie needed to decide between staying with friends, and renting accommodations. Henry Ketchum, their railway promoter friend from Fredericton, was in England raising money for a ship canal he was building across the Isthmus of Chignecto—this plan was later dubbed "Ketchum's Folly," although it was a bold plan, one suited to the era all the same. Parkin was borrowing more and more money from him, and approached him about a possible house. Ketchum offered two possibilities. One house was in Amherst, Nova Scotia, which might prove too remote. Another in Sackville, New Brunswick, was less attractive, since its furnace probably needed replacing. Others options might prove more practical, Parkin suggested. Living in Fredericton and taking in a boarder was a possibility. He urged her to remember that he was increasingly coming into contact with minds and men of the first calibre, and that improved his future prospects. He sent her £5 to help tide her over and suggested that she could borrow more if she ran short. The uncertainty of the Australian venture was very troubling, but it offered such an improvement in their future prospects that he urged her to think of the long term.

While Parkin was waiting for a response, Lord Rosebery wrote to ask if he could speak at a meeting in Edinburgh at the beginning of November. In the meantime, Parkin spent some time in London. A visit to the Mission House opened his eyes to the squalor and degradation that lay behind the great capital, vice so bold and degradation "so frightful in its openness that one's belief in human nature's sacredness is terribly shattered." A few days later, he went to "a gloomy looking street and a gloomy looking house," the streets full of wretched little children all in rags and dirt, where he visited a hostel for little girls who might have grown up "bad and half-starved and half-naked, unless they had been brought into the mission home."

It was a combination of Parkin's moral earnestness together with his colonial background that made Parkin conscious of the social decay that he encountered in the great cities of England. He was far from sharing the belief in the inevitability of material and moral progress that motivated some of his contemporaries. For him, England was a country poised dangerously on a precipice, and decline was the inevitable consequence of failing to meet the challenge securely. He was not a naïve or romantic conservative who merely wanted to preserve the imagined past of the United Empire Loyalists. He looked to the future and thought that major reforms were necessary both to the imperial structure and to the United Kingdom itself.

On his way to Edinburgh, Parkin stayed with Rosebery at his Scottish estate, Dalmeny. Rich in his own right and immensely rich after he married a Rothschild heiress, Rosebery was a powerful political figure in the late 1880s and 1890s. A successful foreign secretary under Gladstone, he briefly became prime minister, in part because of his great talents, but also because he seemed so little interested in the post. Rather than clinging to power, he decided that the Liberals needed a period in opposition. His government died, as it were, of natural causes and Rosebery spent much of the rest of his life causing trouble for his successors from the sidelines. It was entirely consistent behaviour for the young Oxford student who, when told that he was not allowed to keep a racehorse as an undergraduate, immediately left university.

When Parkin met Rosebery, the latter was already showing signs of discontent with the routine of English party politics and, as he told Parkin, "he was half disposed to give up party politics and devote himself to the wider national idea." Parkin was overwhelmed with Rosebery's charm, wealth, social position, and political influence. Rosebery himself seems to have marked Parkin out as someone who could be useful to him in the future and hinted that he might give Parkin financial or other support should he find himself "in a position to represent Canadian opinion." In a speech Rosebery gave at Leeds soon after his meeting with Parkin, Rosebery described imperial federation as "the dominant passion of his public life," and added that this was a cause that "one might be content to live for and if needs be, content to die for too." Parkin believed that their talk had influenced Rosebery's views. "Is it not interesting to feel that one is influencing in a small degree at any rate, the men who influence the world?" On his way back to London, he stopped in to visit his cousin Barbara in Yorkshire. The same people who had once taken him as an Oxford student, he now described, slightly patronizingly, as "simple people and most kind." Although they supplemented their modest income by taking in lodgers in the summer, he said they did it "in a nice way."

While he was in England, Parkin had been offered the position as head of a boarding school in Windsor. Although there might have been some money in it, and "it might have been a temptation once," for now his passion lay with imperial federation and he wanted to try his hand at promoting his grand idea. Parkin's English trip had helped to clarify some of his ideas on imperial federation. Meetings in Glasgow and Leeds had convinced him that the idea of increased trade between England and the colonies was a practical proposal that appealed to "clear-headed" businessmen. But the real drive behind imperial federation was the belief that the consolidation of England's oceanic empire would be favourable to the world's peace, not least because it would strengthen and deepen sympathy between the United Kingdom and America.[8] Canada could best contribute to this cause by maintaining a separate identity in North America. The American continent would profit from the existence of two different forms of government and society, each learning from the experience of the other.

On the question of the form of imperial organization, Parkin now inclined toward a scheme in which the self-governing colonies would contribute toward imperial defence and would have input in decisions through an imperial council of state, the size and influence of their contributions increasing with their financial contributions.[9]

Gilder, meanwhile, had accepted the piece on federation that Parkin had previously discussed with him. In it, Parkin had tried to persuade his American readers that closer ties between England and her colonies was not a threat to American interests. Rather, they represented a natural line of development built on the lessons learned from American Revolution and their separation of the colonies from the United Kingdom.[10] In particular, the United Kingdom had learned from the American experience of federalism that it was possible under modern conditions to govern an immense territory. As the colonies grew in wealth and maturity, even "the slow British imagination" was beginning to draw the conclusion that England would have to concede a greater role in the administration of imperial affairs if the British Empire that had developed after American independence were not to suffer the same fate as the first.[11] Moreover, England found itself, with its possessions in Africa and Asia, with vast responsibilities towards "weak and alien races," obligations that it could not abandon without "a loss of national honour." Without continued British rule, these dependencies would degenerate into widespread anarchy.[12] The ultimate justification of the British Empire was its success in extending Christian civilization throughout the world.

While Parkin was in England, Denison and McCarthy continued

to organize in Ontario. The free trade forces were beginning to flex their muscles as well. On 18 September 1888, Senator John Sherman, chairman of the United States Senate Committee of Foreign Affairs, had declared that Canada should have followed the other British colonies out of the empire in 1783.[13] Goldwin Smith reiterated his position, arguing that a continental union would put a permanent end to commercial disputes and economic retaliation, and would lead to permanent peace both within North America and between the United States and England.[14] In the United States, annexationist forces were becoming more assertive. General Benjamin Butler argued in the *North American Review* that union would come "peacefully we hope; forcefully, if we must." And another former general and prominent railway manager warned that the British possessions presented a "continuous and growing menace to our peace and security, and ... they should be brought under the constitution and laws of our country as soon as possible, peacefully if it can be so arranged, but forcibly if it must."[15]

Parkin set sail for home on 3 November. The passage was very stormy and the ship ran aground on the Bar above Sandy Hook outside New York harbour, and it took some hours before they were freed. He arrived home on the 14th. Once home, Parkin finalized the arrangements for his antipodean tour. He approached his old pupil Bliss Carman to substitute for him as acting headmaster and classics instructor until someone permanent could be found. Carman assumed his new position at the beginning of January 1889.[16]

On 14 January, Parkin wrote to Miss Erskine that arrangements were finally in place for him to arrive in New Zealand in April, and from there to proceed to all the Australian colonies and to Tasmania. He had made the decision to burn his bridges in Fredericton and make a comprehensive study of the empire's greatest political problem. This trip would also open up literary prospects of some importance in the future. Annie and the girls were to meet him in England in the winter, though he was not looking forward to tearing himself up by the roots after such a short time back at home. His friend replied that he should not let home ties influence his decision. "'To help and not to hinder' is the motto of all good wives, as Mrs. Parkin will prove to you, no doubt," opined Miss Erskine, who didn't have to look after four small children.

A more critical letter came from Thomas Raleigh. As a lawyer, Raleigh was much concerned with the practical institutional aspects of imperial federation, which he thought had to date been finessed by its supporters. The creation of an imperial executive, not dependent on the result of English elections, would involve a complete change in the principles of responsible government and would furthermore entail the abolition of the House of Lords. These were no small changes to expect the English to accept. Moreover, if the colonies were to have a role in the formulation of defence policy, the local legislatures would have to abandon some of their autonomy in raising taxes. "These difficulties are not insurmountable, but until you begin to tell us how they are to be surmounted, Federation is only a formula, like Gladstone's Home Rule." However, as Raleigh understood, these details, important as they were, were not central to Parkin's current mission, which was to "spread the conviction that each part of the Empire has a direct interest in preserving the unity of the whole."

On 3 February, Parkin took the train to Salisbury to say goodbye to his brothers and sisters. Then, after lectures in Halifax and Saint John, he returned to Fredericton for an emotional farewell at the school. The students presented him with a formal and heartfelt address which thanked him for his years of constant and unselfish care, not undertaken for the sake of gain, but out of love. He had given his heart to the school through many changes and had brought "to manhood and womanhood many boys and girls whom we do not know even by name…." For his trip, they presented him with field glasses and the following lines of verse:

> Languor is not in your heart,
> Weakness is not in your word,
> Weariness not on your brow.
> You move through the ranks, recall
> The stragglers, refresh the outworn,
> Praise, you inspire the brave.
> Order, courage, return;
> Eyes rekindling, and prayers,
> Follow your steps as you go.

These comments were as fair as they were sincere and touching. For the previous seventeen years Parkin had served his school with dedication and enthusiasm. To the better students such as Bliss Carman and Charles Roberts, Parkin conveyed his love of poetry and literature. His mastery of the finer points of Greek and Latin grammar may have been weak, but his aim was to fire the imagination and to give his students some glimmering of the great world that lay beyond Fredericton.

However, Parkin's years in Fredericton were not a complete success, and Parkin left with a bitter taste in his mouth. Neither the university senate, the trustees, parents, nor the Old Boys said anything publicly about his departure. Parkin decided that he had probably overestimated the regard in which he had been held. "I am quite content to look for recognition in wider fields, or go without it, if that is the best training for me." If Parkin felt some unhappiness at his farewell, it is also likely that Parkin's preoccupation with outside interests in the previous couple of years combined with the precipitous circumstances of his departure left his associates in Fredericton with the feeling that he had let the school down.

On the day after the ceremony at the school, Parkin celebrated his forty-third birthday and left for his trip around the world. Annie accompanied him on the first leg to Ontario. It was, as Parkin put it, the beginning of the life of a "wandering Evangelist of empire."

The Canadian branch of the IFL had asked Parkin to make a speaking tour through Canada as the first leg of his trip. They raised $500 as a contribution towards his expenses, of which Leonard Tilley, who had been instrumental in persuading him to leave Fredericton, personally contributed $50. Sanford Fleming, the railway engineer whom Parkin had first met in Bathurst, and who understood as well as anyone the connection between the integrity of the empire and the financial well-being of the Canadian Pacific Railway, secured free passage for Parkin on the railway across the country.[17]

Parkin's first stop was in Ottawa, where he lectured to a large audience and met with Sir John A. Macdonald and Wilfrid Laurier. Laurier told Parkin "without reserve or hesitation" that Quebec was firmly attached to continued membership in the British Empire. In a continent that was mainly Anglo-Saxon, Laurier continued, the Quebec

Act provided French-Canadians with an equivalent of a Magna Carta. Annexation to the United States would put Quebeckers in the same risk of assimilation as they had suffered in Louisiana.[18]

Parkin then went to spend the night of 14 February with the chain-smoking Principal Grant, and spoke to a large meeting for an hour and a half, in spite of a bad cold. On the 16th he was in Belleville, on the 17th in Toronto, and on the 18th in St. Thomas. On the 20th, he travelled to Montreal for another large crowd, and returned to Toronto by the night train. After yet another large meeting at Convocation Hall at the University of Toronto, he left directly for Vancouver where he had more speaking engagements on 2 March. As the trained rolled across northern Ontario, he felt invigorated by the clear air and the dazzling whiteness of the snow. He chatted pleasantly with his fellow Pullman car passengers, but he spent most of his time reading the Bible. It did him good and made him wiser. "I feel as if I wanted to soak my mind with Bible thoughts," he told Annie. When he arrived in British Columbia, he was struck by the presence of the Chinese who had come to help build the railway. Unlike Principal Grant, who had returned from his ocean-to-ocean trip in 1872 to mount a campaign on behalf the indentured Chinese labourers, Parkin contented himself with the observation that they were "very nice and clean, and make good servants."

On 5 March, Parkin left Canada for San Francisco and his living conditions deteriorated rapidly. Porridge was described on the menu as "oat meal mush" and supper was a race with the cockroaches for the food. Western American ways were not his ways, he reflected, "and I hope they never will be." America, he concluded after his journey, was totally given up to things material and grossly material. On 9 March 1889 he sailed on the *Mariposa*.

7

The Knight-Errant

On 28 March 1889, Parkin crossed the equator and two days later landed at Auckland. In the pleasant autumn weather, he found a land of plenty, with shops full of newly picked grapes, peaches, pears, figs, and apples. The gardens were still bright with the last summer flowers. He found the climate was warmer than northern Italy, but the city was an English town transferred to a southern climate, though more democratic than its original.

New Zealand was a fitting place for him to begin his foreign adventure, since New Zealand's great Bishop Selwyn, whom Parkin had met through Bishop Medley, was the man who had opened Parkin's imagination to the moral possibilities of the empire. One of his first visits was to Selwyn's old church. "It was delightful again to hear our dear old service, with all its tender memories, and great consolations."

Parkin recalled Selwyn's comment that it was a race impertinence to regard the Maori as inferiors. They were, intellectually, in his words, the ablest type of "savages" with whom the European had come into contact, displaying mathematical ability, oratorical power, poetic imagination, adaptability, and military skill. He observed with pleasure the progress the Maori had made. Their property rights were recognized; they enjoyed the franchise, and sent representatives to the legislature. "He becomes a farmer, a sailor, a shepherd; he sends his children to school, builds churches, supports in places native clergy and lives in peace with his white neighbours. He has not done all that was hoped for him, but he has done more than other savages." The progress of the Maori was evidence for Parkin's the empire could be an educational and civilizing force.

The cause of imperial federation was another matter. There was no equivalent of the French-Canadians to give New Zealanders a focus for pro-British expressions of patriotic zeal, or a Goldwin Smith trenchantly pushing them to leave the empire. New Zealanders took the empire largely for granted. They relied on the British fleet for protection, and that factor was enough in itself, for the moment, to prevent any thought of nascent New Zealand nationalism. Although Parkin was initially pleased with the pro-imperial sentiment he encountered, he faced apathy in his attempts to rouse New Zealanders to take an active interest in the imperial federation cause. In his speeches, he pointed out the symbiotic relationship between New Zealand and the empire. England was a market for New Zealand wool, butter, and mutton, and a source of immigrants to the growing colony. New Zealand's ports and coaling stations provided vital support for the fleet. But there was little in this analysis that was not obvious either to New Zealand's colonial elite or to its farmers.

There were no branches of the Imperial Federation League in New Zealand. Parkin set about organizing. His splendid speaking skills attracted public attention and doubtless provided a pleasant evening's entertainment in some of the smaller centres. The meetings in Auckland and Dunedin went off well but did not attract sufficient members to found branches, and the capital, Wellington, displayed even less interest. Christchurch proved less lethargic. Parkin found it was like a miniature England, a reproduction of a college or cathedral town: beautiful chapel, quad, cricket and football grounds, but its branch disappeared from the records of the IFL after its second meeting. New Zealand had powerful ties of culture and economics with the United Kingdom. Parkin was asking New Zealanders to be less insular, to see themselves in a world context. They weren't interested, and in the 125 years since Parkin's visit, their relationship with the United Kingdom has slowly evolved rather than radically changed. Parkin's vision had little appeal for them.[1]

Parkin left New Zealand on 3 May for Tasmania and was seasick during the four days of the trip. As he wrote in verse for his daughter:

> Dearest Little Alice Parkin,
> I am sure that you will hearken
> While your papa tells you how he gets along;
> For the winds are in commotion,
> And there's trouble on the ocean,
> So he thinks he'll tell his sorrows in a song.
> On my back I'm now reclining,
> Without any hopes of dining,
> Till I reach again the far distant shore,
> For our stout old ship is heaving,
> And it's almost past believing
> How the winds and billows join to make a roar.

Soon after his arrival, he set about generating the publicity that he would need to make a success of his visit. The techniques became more refined as he became better known and knew more people, but he was extremely effective even from the beginning. Generally, he would make sure that he had letters of introduction to some of the prominent men of the locality. He sought advice from sympathetic political leaders, in Tasmania's case the governor, Sir Robert Hamilton, whom Parkin found "a very shrewd, cautious man, and a valuable friend at such as time," and Mr. Bird, the treasurer of Tasmania, who was able to provide a railway pass. There was already a branch of the IFL in Hobart, which assisted with organizational details. Thanks to his initial contacts, he was able to secure further local introductions. Chambers of commerce were special favourites for Parkin, since they regularly hosted public meetings and gave him access to many key decision-makers and solid citizens of the community. In Hobart, the chamber invited him to deliver an address under its auspices at the town hall on "The Commercial Relations of the Colonies with Europe and Canada."

The initial meeting established Parkin's reputation as an exciting platform speaker who provided a good evening of entertainment and instruction, and it attracted the attention of the local press, a vehicle Parkin quickly learned to exploit to the full. He was eager to grant interviews, and equally quick to fire off letters to the editor in response to the initial report of his speech. A critical editorial would find Parkin dropping by the newspaper's office the next day wondering if he might have a moment of the editor's time to talk over the matter.

His first address in Hobart produced sufficient interest that he was invited to return for a debate with some prominent local figures, some of whom were against imperial federation. His opposition made some strong points. They asked about the difficult question of colonial representation in the imperial parliament, the differing fiscal policies of the various units of the empire, and the geographical isolation of Tasmania. Another theme, which became more controversial in Sydney with its large population of Irish immigrants, was the history of England's relations to Ireland. If England had behaved in such a repressive fashion to an internal part of the United Kingdom, why should distant colonies expect better?[2] The chairman declared that Parkin had the better of the argument and the support of the crowd.

His speech at Launceston took him to a new level as an orator. It was the first time in his life, he told Annie, that he had been able to create such absolute conviction in his audience. When he returned to Hobart, Parkin found that his opponents had ganged up against him. The hall was densely packed. They had come to see Parkin take on not one or two opponents, but seven. Parkin opened for fifteen minutes, and then each of the speakers was allotted the same amount of time. Parkin concentrated intensely on every word and every argument, the lines of a response forming as the evening moved along. Then the chairman called on him and he spoke for almost an hour. He sat down and the applause and cheering began, and roared on and on. Then the crowd exploded with three loud cheers. "Will you sing 'God Save the Queen'?" Parkin asked them, and the evening ended with the strains of the familiar melody.

Launceston sent him a telegram. There was a great public desire to hear him speak again. Would he return? His public meeting at Launceston attracted a crowd of seven or eight hundred, one hundred and fifty of whom had to stand for the two hours of his speech. After the meeting he was surrounded by well-wishers. "Many look upon me as the Champion of a cause that they think their own." Or as he put it in another chivalric metaphor, "There is a feeling of knight-errantry about the thing which keeps me up wonderfully."[3] Before his first visit even the most ardent supporters of imperial federation thought that to hold a public meeting was to court disaster. Parkin's success had exceeded anything he could have hoped for.

Parkin was quite self-conscious as a speaker, concerned about the quality of his voice and learning to exercise more subtle control over it. He spoke best, he thought, when he was frightened, and he constantly critiqued his speeches in his letters home to Annie. As he spoke, he leaned his body toward his audience, left foot forward, left hand resting on the table, his right arm behind his back. When he raised the intensity of his speech, he gesticulated wildly with his arms, but then returned to his previous posture and developed his arguments with a gentle rocking motion of his body. He rarely enlivened his speeches with jokes. The effect he achieved was that of someone with a complete mastery of his subject and entire confidence in the rightness of his cause. The subject seemed to envelop him as he spoke, thoughts rushing to him faster than he could speak them; cold facts emerged from his lips warm, alive, and coloured.[4] It is estimated that he spoke at roughly 220 words a minute, so quickly that experienced reporters had difficulty recording his remarks exactly. In some sense, this was a bonus, since Parkin rarely spoke from notes, and consequently, when he was not at top form, errors of fact and repetition would mar his speeches. However, he often was focused and full of fire, and seasoned observers were as impressed with his delivery as general audiences. A reporter from the Leeds *Mercury* described him as one of "the living masters of persuasive oratory."[5] After one meeting, a man came up to him and said that he had heard all the great speakers of the past fifty years, but no one better than Parkin. High praise indeed.

While he was in Tasmania, a letter arrived from Annie that told of her financial difficulties in Parkin's absence. Parkin assured Annie that his trip was very important in advancing the league's propaganda, but that when they were reunited in England, it was important for them to get out of debt and put a little aside. He apologized for not sending her more money. It turned out that Downes did not have the money in hand when he made his invitation and was counting on raising it during Parkin's tour. It was not flowing in as rapidly as he hoped, and his expenses were greater than he had foreseen.

In Australia, he was living more or less from hand to mouth. He was never quite certain how much his supporters would raise and he did not like to seem overly concerned with money. He lived as frugally as possible, staying at private homes wherever he could and, if not, at clubs, which were cheaper than hotels. When he did stay at hotels, they were often of the cruder sort. In one, the proprietor posted a notice that warned his guests to hang up their boots so that they would not be eaten by rats.

"I sometimes wonder whether you will ever feel any confidence in me about practical things," Parkin confessed to Annie. If the sums she received from the trustees or the board of education or from selling the family furniture did not suffice, Parkin suggested that she borrow from relatives or from Mr. Ketchum to makes ends meet until his return. Their current sacrifices would pay dividends, he told her. Parkin was being invited to meet with, and speak to, influential people. How long, he wondered, would he have had to stay in New Brunswick before a chamber of commerce gave a dinner in his honour? "This may seem to you a cold business-like letter, but my heart is full of love for you and the dear girls always.... We must buoy ourselves up with the thought that the work is a great and good one, and that God seems to bless it." But Annie's humiliation and worry back home in Fredericton with her three daughters, living on the edge of poverty, must have been very great.

God's blessing was less evident in Sydney, the capital of New South Wales. Parkin knew that when he got there, he would be in for a rough ride. Unlike Canada, the six Australian colonies were still separate and didn't federate until 1901. One of the leading newspapers, the *Bulletin*, was the spearhead of a campaign to unite them, and the Young Australia movement was a vocal proponent of the cause. Sydney also had extensive Irish immigration. For the expatriate Irish, any imperial question was inextricably intertwined with the Irish nationalist drive for a separate state.

Parkin arrived in Sydney on 4 June 1889 but had to wait two weeks before the first public meeting. He did manage a long talk with the governor, Lord Carrington, whom he found generally unsympathetic to imperial federation. Although Parkin was by this point quite used to scepticism and concern about aspects of federation, he had never faced active hostility before. Generally when he spoke to an audience, even one critical of imperial federation, his rhetoric was able, at a minimum, to evoke feelings of warm patriotism. In Sydney, hecklers in the crowd caught him off guard from the very beginning. When Parkin introduced his Greater Britain theme and told the audience it was British, several voices shouted in response, "No, it's Australian." "You say Canada for the Canadians and Australia for the Australians," he replied (great and continued applause). He scorned the words and the thought (applause and groans). "Was the first voice of the Colonies going to be the voice of selfishness? (applause and interruption). Was it going to be the mistaken voice of limitation? (applause and interruption)."[6]

The meeting, Parkin decided, was "not a success, nor yet a failure." There were, however, sneering articles in a few of the opposition newspapers. He reminded himself that part of the reason for his trip was to learn about colonial affairs, and this meeting had been an important learning experience, though a trying one. "I have had many ups and downs. You know how susceptible I am to surrounding influences. I suppose it is part of the speaking temperament." However, a successful meeting at the Australia Economic Association and the Sydney University Union soon cheered his spirits.

On balance, Parkin's visit to Sydney was a failure. Press comment was unkind. The *Australian Star* called him a "very silly man" and dismissed his arguments as "outrageous nonsense." The *Evening News* declared that his arguments were "decidedly feeble, if not entirely false and misleading."[7] From his public meetings and his interviews with leading New South Wales politicians and journalists, though, Parkin drew the conclusion that moderate opinion in the colony favoured continued loyalty to the empire rather than separation.

The Knight-Errant

Parkin's experience in Sydney caused him to make subtle changes in his rhetoric. Instead of speaking of imperial federation, he started to describe his goal as a fostering of national sentiment. By "national," he meant British and the nation to which he referred was the British of the homeland and the diaspora. National unity meant an enhanced awareness of the common bonds of sentiment, trade, and political institutions that the self-governing colonies shared. It was closer to what he stood for, although it finessed important rhetorical and political differences within the movement. Parkin believed in what has been called Britannic idealism. Its origins lay in the writers of the mid-nineteenth century such as Thomas Carlyle, J.A. Froude, and John Ruskin. These writers, especially Froude, were immensely popular in their age. From them, Parkin came to see his era as one in which modern human beings were being ground down by those who accumulated wealth, and by the increasing dominance of machinery. In the face of this, Parkin sought a more chivalrous life that acknowledged the poetic beauty of existence, a heroic greatness of soul, courage, and self-sacrifice. One of the ways to achieve this end was patriotism, a love of the whole that was greater than the parts and that led Britons beyond their petty economic and politics interests. Although these ideas had always driven Parkin, it was in Australia that they jelled into the concept that he called "national unity." Others might, and did, see it as a customs union or a military alliance. For Parkin, it meant nothing more, and nothing less, than the spiritual unity of the English-speaking peoples as a force for good in the world.

While he was in Sydney, Parkin made friends with Gilbert Parker. Parker had lectured at Trinity College in Ontario before he immigrated to Australia, where he began a successful career as a writer and in 1886 became associate editor of the Sydney *Morning Herald*. He was twenty-five when Parkin met him. The two men struck up an instant friendship. Parker was considering moving back to Canada and setting himself up as a journalist in Toronto if there was a chance that he could make a reasonable income. Parkin toyed with the idea of joining him. They pledged to work "with tongue and pen" for Canada. "You have a husband with much of the Bohemian in him," Parkin wrote to his wife, but he pledged that he would try to be practical. Annie must have shuddered at the prospect of her husband even contemplating a venture more quixotic than his current one. Parker renewed his acquaintance with Parkin in England the next year and, when he returned to Canada for a short visit to investigate the possibilities he had talked about in Australia, Parkin sent a letter of introduction to his Canadian imperial federation friend Dalton McCarthy. Nothing immediate came of this encounter with Parker, but a decade and a half later, after many twists and turns in each man's career, they would become political allies in London.

Parkin left Sydney on 3 July and set out for the far more congenial atmosphere of Melbourne, 440 miles away. He could not get a sleeper and had to spend the night in a compartment, but four members of the Melbourne IFL were waiting for him at the station and installed him in a comfortable room at a club. Here he was reunited with Downes Carter, who had first proposed the Australia tour. At Melbourne, he heard good news from Annie. She had overcome her reluctance and had approached Parkin's former student Bliss Carman, who lent her enough money to tide her over until Parkin could send more. However, Parkin had bad news for her. His work was taking longer than he anticipated and he would not arrive in England until near the end of October.

Parkin's meeting in Melbourne drew two thousand. He spoke for an hour and three-quarters and, in his view, held them all the time. He was, he said, the most talked-about person in Melbourne for a day or two. Press reports were favourable. The *Telegraph* raved about it, and even the most hostile paper, *The Age*, had been forced to modify its opposition. There was a large dinner party for him one evening at the Masonic Club and another at the Athenaeum that the premier was expected to attend. There were also plans to print his speech and circulate it as a pamphlet. "People here appear to believe in me, and in my mission," he told Annie.

After his success in Melbourne he set out for the 500-mile train trip to Adelaide, where the chief justice, Sir Samuel Way, had arranged his stay; then to Ballarat, Melbourne again, Brisbane, Rockhampton, then back to Adelaide and Brisbane. Parkin's tour was a modest success. He learned that support for imperial federation was confined to pockets such as Melbourne, Adelaide, and Tasmania, and that those powerful elements in the various Australian colonies such as the Irish and the free traders were resolute opponents. Still he had learned a great deal and collected a considerable amount of material that would serve him well when he returned to England.

Parkin's judgment of the Anglo-Saxon in the southern hemisphere was equivocal. He wrote three articles on his trip for the *Century Magazine*, which published the two on Australia, but passed on Parkin's analysis of New Zealand. However, it did pay him for all three at $250 each. The $750 he received went a considerable way towards justifying his belief that there would be substantial spin-off benefits to his trip. To put the amount in perspective, Parkin had talked about an annual income of around $1500 as enough to tempt him into a literary venture with Gilbert Parker.

Australia, Parkin concluded, was a social experiment in a transitional phase and it was not clear whether it would succeed. The Australian colonies had been settled by Anglo-Saxons, and they brought with them as part of their cultural inheritance their energy and their commitment to hard work. But, Parkin worried, these British virtues were in danger. Tropical countries were thought unsuited to prosperity and free government because it was too easy to acquire the basic necessities and people became soft and lazy. An arctic climate was just as inimical because the conditions were too harsh and all effort was devote to mere survival. Only in a temperate climate was the necessity of labour balanced with the rewards of effort. These conditions produced a hearty and energetic race. In Parkin's words: "A New Englander, a Canadian, or an Englishman may come away from luxuriating in the sunny influences of the best Australian season without losing respect for his own more rigorous or even unpleasant climate. The east wind, the cold drenching rain, the northern blast, drive men back on home life, on work, on more rigid views of their relations to things. After all, the environment which makes a people most effective is the best. Great will be the glory of the Australian if he retains in the south that inherited energy which was bred in the north and which has made his country what it is."[8] Australia, in Parkin's view, faced another problem: its origins lay in its gold rush. Compared with Canada, settled by the noble-minded loyalists, Australia could look back only to a history based on the pursuit of material wealth. This factor, in Parkin's estimation, accounted for Australians' lack of moral strenuousness and their selfishness.

Politically, Australia had experimented with what Parkin called state socialism. It was a more democratic and egalitarian society than was found in England or Canada, and this difference had generated certain benefits. In the towns, there were "excellent museums, splendid libraries, free reading-rooms, parks, botanical gardens, manifold places of interest or amusement" for the multitude, and "music, the theatre, and clubs as expensive and almost as luxurious as those of Pall Mall or Piccadilly" for the rich. The existence of good transportation made these facilities accessible and also supported healthy and spacious suburbs that avoided the overcrowding common in European cities.[9]

However, these facilities were provided centrally, and there was not the same local support and control of schools and roads common in Canada and the United States that provided strong training in citizenship and provided a sound social basis for expanding democracy. The Australian experiment had demonstrated the flexibility of British political institutions and their adaptability to new conditions.

Australia's final handicap, to Parkin's way of thinking, was that it had not faced opposition, as had New Zealand, from a vigorous aboriginal population. Those in Australia, Parkin wrote, were one of "the lowest types of the human race," capable only of "acts of savage cunning" in waging "a fitful guerrilla warfare along the advancing fringe of civilization." Parkin incorrectly predicted that they would disappear like the natives of Tasmania, who had already been annihilated, but he was unfortunately right that the interaction between the aboriginal peoples and the white settlers largely marginalized the former.

Was Parkin a racist? He certainly was by modern standards. He had one standard—the idea of Britishness (call it British idealism) by which he judged all people and all peoples. Few measured up. Some like French-Canadians were close, and might with effort become British. Others like the Maori surprised him. He originally put them into the category of primitives of savages but Selwyn's testimony and his own experience led him to conclude that there was the possibility over a long period that they could attain to a British state of civilization. He considered that a very high compliment. From what he had learned of the Australian aboriginals, he did not think that the same was true of them.

At heart Parkin respected no culture other than his own, but he didn't exempt his own people from the need to live up to the standard he set for them. He was disappointed in the Australians, and came to the conclusion that the various Australian colonies were too divided among themselves to focus on the goal of imperial federation. Until the colonies formed a federal union there would be little sympathy for Parkin's greater ideal of "national unity." Tactically, then, he shifted ground. He wrote a series of articles for the Melbourne *Argus*, Sydney *Morning Herald*, Adelaide *Register*, and Hobart *Mercury* in which he tried to persuade the Australian colonies to adopt the Canadian model of a federal state.[10]

His return trip to England on the British India line took six weeks and covered 13,000 miles. The ship stopped briefly in India and Aden, passed through the Suez Canal, and then continued on to Plymouth, where Parkin landed on 25 October to discover that he had become a minor celebrity. Charles Dilke, whose own travels through Greater Britain had inspired the young Parkin, devoted several pages in his new work, *Problems of Greater Britain*, to Parkin's trip. The *Pall Mall Gazette* praised him for not only visiting the colonies, but stumping through them. He had become the "peripatetic prophet of Federation."[11]

Parkin capped his tour with a speech in the opulent surroundings of London's Mansion House, where Lord Rosebery praised the Canadian who had "indefinitely enlarged our sphere of influence by his magnetic sympathy and by his vivid eloquence." Convinced that Parkin was a useful instrument for their cause, Rosebery, Lord (Thomas) Brassey, a wealthy supporter of the movement, A.H. Loring, president of the IFL, Hugh Arnold-Foster, an author and book editor, and Sir Frederick Young, one of the early pioneers of imperial federation, offered him £300 plus expenses if he would spend the next six months campaigning for the league in England, with the understanding that he could supplement this income with writing and other speaking engagements. Since his payment from the league exceeded his teacher's salary, he hoped that, with the addition of his freelance income, he would begin to climb out of debt.

At the beginning of November, Annie and the children joined him in England. They rented a modest house in Putney in southwest London, and Parkin began preparations for meetings and lectures in England and Scotland.

Parkin had written to Annie on their wedding anniversary from Australia: "Looking back all through life I can say sincerely that the day of our marriage was to me of all others that which had in it the most pure and perfect happiness that I have ever known. The tender grace of it not only thrills my memory yet from time to time, but stays there as a constant force. I think it will do so as long as I live. Life has always since had a new meaning for me, that does not mean, I suppose, that you were or are so wonderful as compared with other women. But it means that you did, and do satisfy the inner want in me."

There is little doubt that Parkin's marriage provide the emotional sustenance that he needed. He genuinely seems to have loved Annie and his letters to her are consistently warm and sentimental. But he talked better than he delivered. Eventually words weren't enough and, as we'll see, she would break under the strain.

8

Colouring the Empire Red

No one could complain that Parkin did not give his backers value for money; he promoted what he now increasingly called national unity with enthusiasm and vigour. In late January and early February 1890, he was stomping the Midlands. He spoke at chambers of commerce and workingmen's clubs and made, he thought, a real impression on the Yorkshire mind. His tours of the Midlands and Scotland showed positive results. Financial contributions to the IFL increased, new branches were formed, and press opinion was sympathetic. "The heather is on fire," the league's *Journal* proclaimed. Parkin proved particularly popular in Leeds, where he spoke at least a dozen times and he was satisfied that, even if he had not overcome all opposition, he had helped put the question of imperial relations on the political agenda.

At this time, Parkin also began to explore other means of attracting support. Sometimes he addressed a small group of people—say a dozen or so—in a supporter's drawing room where he would talk privately with them and answer questions. Under such circumstances, he could be particularly charming. On another occasion, Lord Brassey invited him to speak to two hundred delegates to the Trades Unions

Council at his Park Lane mansion. Parkin would also buttonhole members of parliament at luncheons or when he encountered them at a club, with the hope of persuading some of the younger backbenchers to form a parliamentary group devoted to the promotion of imperial federation ideas.

The imperial federation cause was making good progress in Canada. In Toronto, Denison hit on an idea to promote patriotic sentiment. He learned that in the United States the Stars and Stripes flew over every school and he decided that this was one American practice that it would be good to follow in Canada. He organized a deputation to wait on the minister of education, who agreed that "to display the national emblem in some such way as to impress upon the children the fact that we are a country and have a flag and a place in it."[1]

These symbolic gestures were taking on a renewed urgency because, during 1888 and 1889, a movement for commercial union or unrestricted reciprocity, in effect a free trade agreement between Canada and the USA, was gaining force and was being harnessed by the Liberals under their new leader, Wilfrid Laurier, who had succeeded Edward Blake in 1887. By 1890, it looked increasingly as if the next election would be fought on this question. On 29 January, William Mulock, a Liberal MP, broke with his party and introduced a resolution in the House of Commons, which he intended as a pre-emptive strike against the free trade forces: "We desire, therefore, to assure Your Majesty that such statements are wholly incorrect representations of the sentiment and aspirations of the people of Canada, who are among Your Majesty's most loyal subjects, devotedly attached to the political union existing between Canada and the Mother Country, and earnestly desire its continuance."[2] Denison added his support for the resolution in a letter to the *Globe* in which he explained that the forces clamouring for independence consisted of two groups, one loyal to Canada, the other trying to separate Canada from the empire in order to attach it to the United States.[3]

The day after Mulock introduced his resolution, the annual meeting of the Canadian branch of the IFL took place and the discussion revolved around proposals for preferential tariffs between the various countries of the empire as an alternative to commercial union. It also urged the government to press ahead with the plan to introduce an inexpensive uniform rate of one British penny for letters sent within the empire to encourage closer ties between the English-speaking peoples.[4]

In February 1890, Denison wrote to Macdonald to express his view that the next election would be fought on the loyalty issue and that it should take place sooner rather than later and certainly before the next session of parliament. As evidence for the seriousness of the developing pro-American sentiment, Denison quoted a statement from the Toronto *Globe* that Canadians found the colonial yoke galling and that the time was long past when Canadian patriotism was synonymous with loyalty to the British connection.[5]

Denison sailed to England to promote the cause of imperial preference, arriving in Liverpool on 27 April. He was invited to speak the following evening at a rally where Parkin was to give the main address, but he was specifically instructed to avoid the divisive tariff issue.[6] The meeting took place in the People's Palace, a working-class area of East London. The meeting had a special cachet since Queen Victoria's son, the Duke of Cambridge, was in the chair, and Rosebery and Sir John Colomb, other heavyweights in the imperial federation cause were, along with Denison, to speak.

At the annual meeting of the IFL in London on 22 May 1891, Lord Rosebery endorsed Parkin's new term "national unity." It expressed well the aims of the movement, which was to base the empire on co-operative principles, and not on the current haphazard and inconsequential arrangements.[7] However, Rosebery's and Parkin's views were by no means universally shared, and it was the Canadian contingent, enthusiastically, if not always ably, led by Denison, that created problems both for the league and for the British government. Denison was a hard man to restrain indefinitely. At the general meeting of the IFL he called for the creation of a "discriminating tariff" that would give Canadian manufacturers an advantage in the British market against their American rivals. The creation of closer economic ties would give England an outlet for its surplus population "to a country under your own flag, with your own institutions, and with those law-abiding and God-fearing principles, which we are trying to spread through the northern half of the continent."[8] Denison also met privately with Lord Salisbury and tried to persuade the prime minister to issue a public statement that he favoured some sort of commercial union within the empire as a means of influencing public opinion in the forthcoming Canadian election.[9]

Parkin too was aware of the growing strength of annexationist forces in Canada. His speeches tried to raise English awareness of the problem. England, he argued, could not compete with the growing power of Russia, the United States, and Germany unless she retained her empire, but the self-governing colonies, especially Canada and Australia, were insistent that they have a voice in the direction of imperial affairs. Although many in England found it inconceivable that she would voluntarily yield her absolute control over foreign policy, Parkin responded that such intransigence was short-sighted. "Suppose the old American Colonies had remained in the same friendly relations to the United Kingdom as they formerly were in, suppose the population had grown to its present dimensions, or double the population of this country, can you imagine that 70,000,000 people would allow their foreign policy to be controlled by those 30,000,000 at home, or that those at home would consent to pay the whole cost of the consular and diplomatic services? I say that you cannot imagine it, and we are now face to face with a similar problem. The Colonies are increasing in power and in strength, and to-day the British Empire has to choose between two roads. Is it the road to separation or is it the road to permanent unity?" Parkin also began to develop a line of argument addressed to the growing power of the working class. Consolidation of the empire was in their favour, he told them, because, for comfort and job security, they, more than any other group, depended on cheap and safe imports of food and other raw materials, and also guaranteed markets for their manufactured exports. The widespread hardship that Lancashire suffered from the American boycott on cotton goods during the American Civil War was proof of this dependency.[10]

By July, Denison was safely back in Canada. Parkin, exhausted from his exertions on behalf of the league, took time off to rest and recuperate. Leaving Annie with the children in London, he set off with some friends on a walking tour and then installed himself at the Prince of Wales Pensions in a room on the top storey at 30 shillings a week for board and lodgings. After relaxing for a while with Alexander Dumas's *The Three Musketeers*, he set to work on some of the writing he meant to do to raise extra funds. "I am trying to make myself really and entirely trust in God's guidance, but it is hard work to give up one's own strength. I fear that is where the mistake has been made."

Much of Parkin's summer were spent in the time-consuming work of the Thring biography. Other than Annie, he had no secretarial assistance, and the publisher's advance of £25 was not large enough to allow him to hire anyone. Yet he had to transcribe letters by hand, copy Thring's diary, and bring some order to the papers at Uppingham. Not only was he out of pocket because of the work, he also had to turn down potentially profitable invitations such as one from Cambridge University Press to write a history of Canada. "Had I been unhampered with this large task," Parkin complained to Carman, "my uphill struggle here would not have been so severe." Instead of getting him out of debt, his other writing merely served to subsidize the Thring project. In some ways, it was a pity that he had not handed the project over to Skrine, who wanted it so desperately and would have been prepared to devote his entire time and his own resources to it.

In the 1880s, the USA was taking the first strong steps that would, within half a century, make its economy the most powerful in the world. The Republican election victory of 1888 signalled higher tariffs, which were established in the McKinley Bill of 1890; these tariffs were followed by the even higher rates of the Wilson-Gorman Tariff of 1894 and the Dingley Tariff of 1897. Under the circumstances, there seemed two alternative economic strategies a Canadian government could adopt. It is probably fair to say that no Canadian government, Liberal or Conservative, would have rejected a free trade deal with the United States if it could have negotiated one on reasonable terms. The size of the American market, combined with the attractiveness of north-south trade, made this always the preferred position. However, there were Canadian economics interests, such as the Canadian Pacific Railway, for whom trade with the United States was not attractive. Macdonald's government's interests and the CPR's had, over the previous two decades, been intertwined, often in dubious or unsavoury ways.

At this time, there was a small but vocal group in the United States who favoured closer economic and political ties with Canada. A leading member of this group was Erastus Wiman, who contributed to the *North American Review* a provocatively titled article "The Capture of Canada." Although Wiman's name was anathema to people like Denison, he seemed genuinely concerned about the impact of the McKinley tariff on Canada, a measure adopted against "people of the same lineage, the same language, the same literature, and governed by the same laws."[11]

It is not clear, even if Laurier had been successful in the election of 1891, that he would have been able to negotiate a free trade agreement. There were powerful protectionist forces in the United States that would have fought competition from Canadian manufacturers or resource producers. There was also the danger that the removal of tariff barriers, even if such a thing had been politically possible within the United States, might not make Canadian exports competitive. In such a case, a commercial union would have made Canada more politically dependent on the United States, without providing any compensating advantages.

The counter position advanced by the imperial federationists such as Denison was to persuade the United Kingdom, in effect, to levy higher tariffs on American than on Canadian imports. This appeared to be the more promising strategy. The British market was at least as important as the American, and Canada produced some of the same natural resources as the Americans. Therefore a British preferential tariff in favour of Canadian imports might, if sufficiently large, allow Canada to compete successfully against the Americans in the British domestic market. The problem, to put it bluntly, was: What was in it for the British?

Manufacturers in England wanted access to cheap raw materials and did not much care where they came from. They would be happy with free trade with the United States, which would give them cheaper inputs and would also allow them to compete more successfully in the large American market. Farmers, on the other hand, feared competition from cheap imports and did not care whether their competition came from the United States or from Canada. The success of Cobden and Bright's free trade movement earlier in the century had been a victory for the manufacturing interests over the farmers, because lower food prices meant that manufacturers could pay their workers less.

Denison accepted that the United Kingdom would have to make

small sacrifices for the sake of preferential tariffs, but he thought those sacrifices would be accepted for the sake of maintaining the integrity of the empire, and Sir Howard Vincent, a protectionist in British politics, formed the United Empire Trade League in early 1891 to co-operate with the colonials who sought imperial preferences.[12] The one thing that Canada might give the United Kingdom in return for imperial preferences was greater military aid, but as Principal Grant had acknowledged at the founding of the Canadian branch of the IFL, Canada's one consistent foreign policy seemed to be a resolute refusal to contribute anything whatsoever towards its own defence. It preferred to rely entirely on British naval forces, and to make a token commitment to the militia in conjunction with British regular troops, for its defence. In return, it expected the United Kingdom to sacrifice its own relations with the United States to protect Canadian economic interests and it was outraged, in a matter such as the Alaska boundary dispute, when the British decided to pursue their own interests rather than blindly supporting the Canadian position. There was a lot of British *quid*, but there was not much Canadian *pro quo*.

In Britain, meanwhile, Parkin continued to lecture on behalf of the cause while also trying to complete his biography of Thring. However, in spite of Parkin's hard work, the family's financial position was not improving. If anything, it was deteriorating. In the spring of 1891 they decided to leave London and take cheaper accommodation at Harwich, a town of about 15,000 on the North Sea coast. Even there, they couldn't afford a place large enough to allow Parkin a separate study, so that he had to work at the dining-room table. When the family did go on an outing to London, they usually chose to visit a museum or art gallery, or take in a free concert or play. Even so, Parkin had nothing left over to reduce his debts. When his hectic schedule of travel and meetings allowed, he enjoyed his moments with his family. The landscape was flat and dreary, but the sea wind was bracing and helped shake him out the mental paralysis that London induced. In his holidays he played tennis and badminton and went with his daughters for family picnics on the beach.

One of Parkin's friends suggested to him that he might think of writing a book about imperial federation and proposed that they try to put together "a little syndicate of believers in the cause" who would contribute about £500 so that Parkin might have a quiet year to devote to the project. Before that could happen, Lord Brassey, more to Parkin's amazement than to his delight, in June offered £300 on his own account, against royalties, on the strict condition that Parkin deliver the finished manuscript to the publisher by the end of October, four months later. If Parkin failed to deliver on deadline, Brassey said that he would not be responsible for the payment. Thomas Allnutt Brassey was about twenty-nine. He had position and wealth. He was literally in a position to lord it over his forty-five-year-old colleague in the imperial federation movement. If Parkin wanted the money, he had better focus on this project. Brassey made him sign a formal agreement on the terms.

Try as he might, Parkin could not make steady progress with the book. He was interrupted constantly by the need to travel, to sort out affairs at Uppingham, and to write his freelance pieces that earned the extra income. By the end of October, he noted in his diary that he was behind schedule on the book and still needed another month to complete the first draft. He approached Brassey, pleading the work he had done for the IFL in Scotland as extenuation. Brassey replied testily that he would agree to an extension until Christmas, but in future would consider himself bound only "by the exact details of our agreement." In spite of the pressure of the deadline, Parkin still spoke regularly to meetings about imperial federation, usually in London. His comments on these meeting usually ran along the line "good crowd, very attentive, good debate afterwards."

In November, Parkin became increasingly desperate about the progress he was making on the book. He approached the publisher, George Macmillan, to see whether they would be prepared to make a decision regarding publication on the basis of eighty per cent of the manuscript and a sketch of the rest. The publisher was agreeable but Brassey would not budge. "If I consent to your proposal, the whole object of limiting the time will be lost, as there will be no guarantee as to the time when the remainder of the book may be completed." As the December deadline loomed, Parkin was stricken with a severe toothache. When he went to the dentist to have the tooth out, the ether wore off long before the operation was finished, and he had ten very uncomfortable minutes. With the effects of the opiates he took to kill the pain, he was not able to work much on his book. On 17 December he received another unsettling letter from Brassey, who found parts of the manuscript satisfactory, but insisted on improvements to other chapters.[13] As it happened, he missed the deadline by a few days, but Brassey was in a forgiving mood. On Christmas Eve, Annie had given birth to another daughter, Christine Marjorie Randolph.

In Canada, Denison had been at his conspiratorial worst in the last few months of 1890. He had heard that one of the leading Liberals, Sir Richard Cartwright, had made a secret trip to Washington and concluded that there was a plot afoot to annex Canada.[14] Thirteen copies of a secret pamphlet were printed, but the printer recognized the author's handwriting and passed the news to Sir John A. Macdonald. According to Denison, Macdonald, anxious to see him, paid a clandestine visit in Toronto and asked about the timing of the election. "What Sir John," Denison exclaimed, jumping up from his chair; "in the face of all you know and all I know, can you hesitate an instant? You must bring the election on at once. If you wait till your enemies are ready, and the pipes are laid to distribute the money which will in time be given from the States, you will incur the greatest danger, and no one can tell where the trouble will end."[15]

Macdonald was seventy-six when the election took place. Wilfrid Laurier ran on the platform of unrestricted reciprocity with the United States. Macdonald had one of the great campaign slogans in Canadian history: the Old Man, the Old Flag, the Old Policy. Macdonald won, but worn out by almost half a century of political life, he died three months after the election. Politically, though, the issue of free trade was settled for twenty years, until Laurier raised it again, equally unsuccessfully, in the 1911 election against Robert Borden. Denison triumphantly declared that the Conservative victory "practically finished the attempt to entrap Canada into annexation through the means of tariff entanglements."[16] Parkin was characteristically more cautious. "Sir John A. Macdonald successful and so the Annexation and commercial union people set back for the time," he wrote in his diary.

Although the election had been won and the policy of free trade defeated, Denison had no intention of relaxing his guard. There was a viper in the midst of Toronto, a snake with whom Denison had once been friends. That man was Goldwin Smith. "If the tolerance now extended to traitors and conspirators be much further prolonged, you will see an armed body of men making for the top of John Street, sacking the Grange [Smith's house] and destroying that splendid library which has made its master mad with too much learning." Treason, Colonel Denison blustered, "could not be handled with kid gloves." Although Smith might think he could discuss such matters in a detached academic spirit, Denison, the old cavalry officer and winner of the Czar's prize for a book on cavalry tactics "would only seriously discuss annexation or independence with my sword." Denison never tired of harassing Smith, even in petty ways. In 1893 he introduced a motion at the St. George Society, a social group and benevolent society, which demanded Smith's resignation on the grounds of his "treason to his Sovereign of England and to Canada."

It is sometimes said that people get the enemies they deserve. This was not true in Smith's case. Other than by Denison, he was generally either respected or admired. When Parkin reviewed Smith's *Canada and the Canadian Question* (1891), a work that infuriated Denison, he wrote in the Leeds *Mercury*: "A book from the pen of so distinguished a writer as Mr. Goldwin Smith is at any time a considerable literary event."[17] In *Canada and the Canadian Question*, Smith argued that Macdonald's national policy had been a national disaster. Its railways and tariffs created trade that was "unnatural, forced and profitless," since trade more sensibly should go north-south for each of the four regions of Canada to their neighbouring regions of the United States.[18] As a whole, the system put the country in the thrall of powerful vested interests, who in turn corrupted its political system to maintain its artificial economy. "Before a general election the Prime Minister calls these men together in the parlour of a Toronto hotel, receives their contributions to his election fund, and pledges the commercial policy of the country." Instead of a system that promoted this kind of corruption, Smith proposed that Canada follow the English example. Before 1846, England had imposed tariffs on the import of wheat. When this duty was abolished and England moved increasingly to a free trade regime, it also moved into a period of unprecedented prosperity.

Canada, Smith went on, was an unnatural country. In his report, Lord Durham had spoken of two nations warring within the bosom

Parkin remembered his mother, Elizabeth, as a woman of high ideals and marked mental force. To his father, John (below), he attributed his powers of endurance.

Library and Archives Canada

Parkin as a young man. He worked in relative obscurity for many years as a New Brunswick teacher and high school principal until his skills as an orator, his innovative ideas on education, and his zeal for uniting English-speaking people world-wide thrust him onto the national and world stage.

Library and Archives Canada

Above, the University of New Brunswick in Fredericton, about 1870. Below, from Parkin's UNB days (left to right): Madame d'Avray, Professor d'Avray, Laurestine Marie d'Avray Bailey (daughter), and Loring Woart Bailey (professor). The identity of the woman in the chair is unknown.
Archives and Special Collections, Harriet Irving Library, UNB

Bishop John Medley of Fredericton was the first person to recognize Parkin's potential. He financed the young teacher for a year of study at Oxford—an experience that proved pivotal in Parkin's life.

New Brunswick Archives

Bliss Carman, a student of Parkin's in Fredericton, became one of Canada's most important poets. He freely acknowledged Parkin's influence in shaping him as an artist and as a man.

Library of Congress, Washington, D.C.

Parkin formed a life-long association with Balliol College at Oxford. The friends he made here deeply affected his life and career, and his son and grandson later attended.

Reproduced by kind permission of the Master and Fellows of Balliol College, Oxford; Balliol College, Archives PHOT 11

Edward Thring, headmaster of Uppingham school in England, inspired Parkin's ideas on education. Parkin was introduced to him during the year he studied at Oxford, and later wrote his biography.

Uppingham School Archive

Alfred Milner was one of the dominant figures of imperial Britain. He was proconsul at the time of the Boer War, and became Colonial Secretary during the First World War. He shared Parkin's belief in imperial federation.

Library of Congress, Washington, D.C.

Lord Rosebery, a wealthy and influential British politician, shared Parkin's passion for imperial federation. He served briefly as prime minister of Great Britain.

Library of Congress, Washington, D.C.

Vehemently at odds with Parkin's advocacy of imperial federation, Goldwin Smith, Canada's leading journalist, believed that Canada should seek closer ties with the United States rather than becoming part of a unified British Empire.

Library of Congress, Washington, D.C.

Parkin and his wife, Annie Connell Fisher. She was a former student of his, many years his junior. Although he loved her deeply, his pursuit of his dreams left her with crushing family responsibilities that at times she was unable to handle alone.

Library and Archives Canada

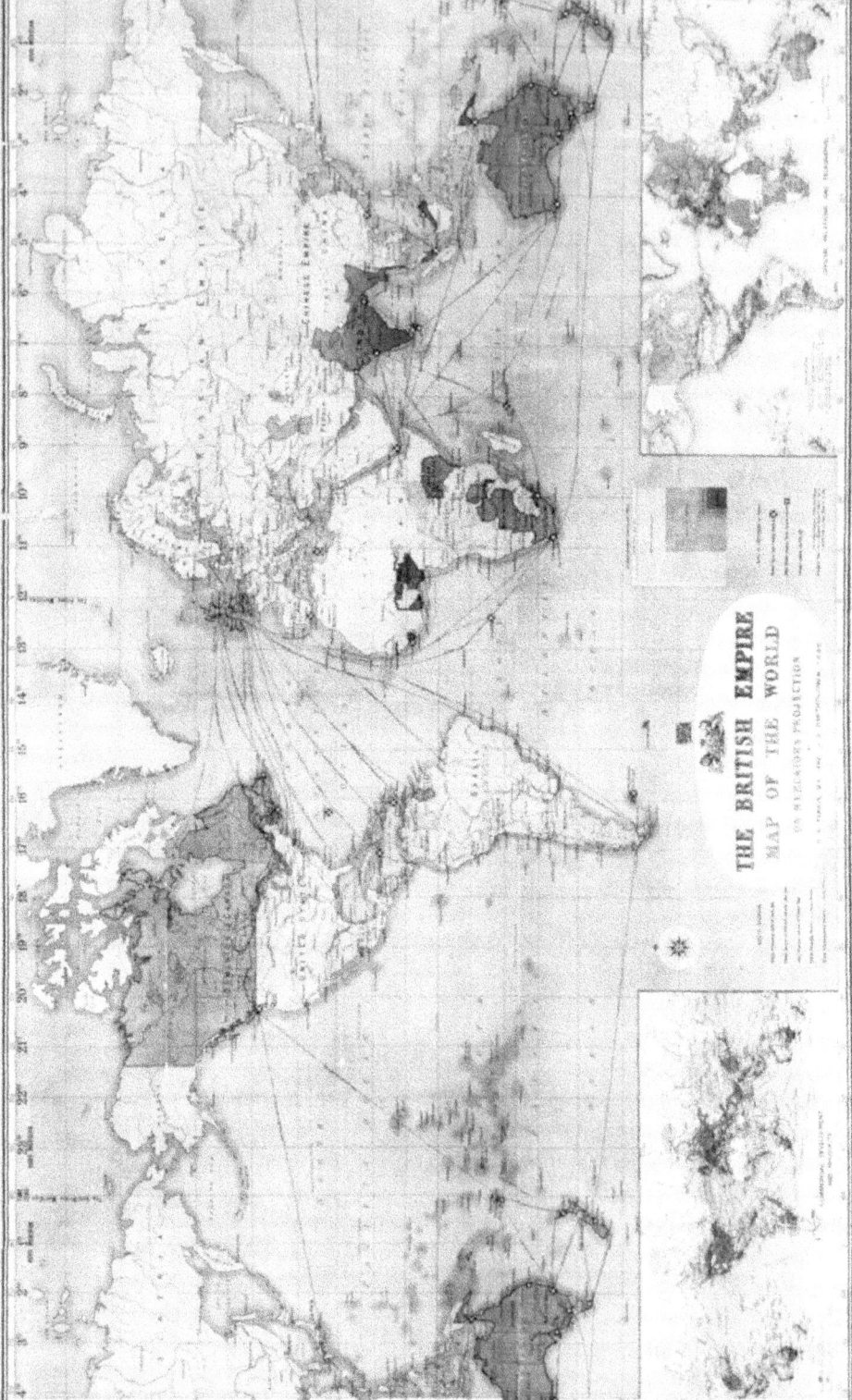

Parkin's famous 1893 world map showed the British Empire in glorious red (dark grey in this black-and-white reproduction). Parkin agreed with critics who argued that the Mercator projection that the map used distorted the size of countries like Canada. He replied: "If the sole object of a map were to reproduce countries in accurate proportion as to the size this criticism would be unanswerable. But I have specially undertaken to indicate the 'great lines of international commerce.' Anticipating this it could not be done effectively on the old Hemisphere maps." Steamboat routes between the United Kingdom and the many outposts of the Empire are prominently marked, as well as coaling stations.

Library and Archives Canada / NMC-16992

Parkin's British Empire map formed the basis of the first "penny post" stamp, issued by Canada in 1898. Parkin advocated inexpensive postage to help bind English-speaking people world-wide. The Government of Canada issued a commemorative stamp on the 100th anniversary of the penny post.

Library and Archives Canada

Parkin was appointed headmaster of Upper Canada College in Toronto in 1895. He instituted Arbor Day to plant trees and shrubs to beautify the campus. This picture was taken in 1902, the year he left.

Upper Canada College Archives

Upper Canada College class of 1897. Parkin assembled an outstanding collection of teachers at UCC, including Edward Peacock, who went on to become a governor of the Bank of England and earn a knighthood, and William Grant, who himself served as principal after the Great War. Stephen Leacock (seventh from the left) taught languages and literature. He later become professor of political economy at McGill, but is best known for his humorous writing with its embedded social criticism.

Upper Canada College Archives

Parkin in his study at Upper Canada College. The school was ailing in 1895 when he took over as headmaster, but with hard work and a clear vision about the character-building nature of education, he launched it on the course that made it one of the elite private schools in Canada.

Upper Canada College Archives

of a single state. Smith would have been happy had he thought the French-Canadians capable of warring. They lived, he suggested, in a mediaeval theocracy, a people "simple, ignorant, submissive, credulous, unprogressive, but kindly, courteous, and probably, as his wants are few, not unhappy."[19] Politically, the Roman Catholic Church was reactionary: the province was full of Jesuits, and the anti-clerical forces who favoured liberal social and political measures (the *Rouges*) were weak. Worst of all, wrote Smith, the "digestive forces of Canada have been too weak to assimilate the French element even politically as those of the great mass of American Englishry have assimilated, sufficiently at least for the purposes of political union, the French population of Louisiana."[20]

If Quebec seemed destined to remain a political and economic swamp, Ontario, Smith contended, had possibilities. "Rich by nature, poor by policy," might be written over Canada's door. It had minerals whose wealth could be unlocked by free trade. Its farmers were moral and honest; its social system, egalitarian; its spirit, democratic, though free from revolutionary resentment.[21] In education, the public school system resembled that of the United States and provided the basis for democracy.[22] The problem with Canada was its inability, just as with French-Canadians, to assimilate immigrants. Immigrants, Smith thought, retained much of their original identity, and the Tory tolerance of Britishness did not produce homogeneity. In one of his most famous pronouncements of liberal universalism, Smith wrote, "Nationalities are not so easily ground down in a small community as they are when thrown into the hopper of the mighty American mill."[23]

According to Smith, there were, at heart, two sections of one English-speaking race on the continent. Their state of fusion, Smith contended, was daily becoming more complete. Although a small number of the elite continued to maintain a connection with the United Kingdom, for most "Ontario is an American State of the Northern type, cut off from its sisters by a customs line, under a separate government and flag."[24]

Canada and the Canadian Question was the fountainhead of continentalist arguments and is still one of the most radical. Few have followed Smith in his belief that the destruction of the French-Canadian identity would be an unrelieved good or that little of value would be lost if Canada were assimilated with the United States politically, economically, and culturally.

If Smith wanted Canada's destiny tied to the United States, Parkin wanted Canada open to the world. Macmillan accepted Parkin's book quickly, offering Parkin half the profits of the book. Brassey was rather testy that Parkin had signed the contract without making provision that the first £300 be paid to him and held back Parkin's money until the oversight had been corrected. Parkin sent copies to some of his friends for comments, including, of course, the irascible Brassey. Brassey had criticism in detail and of organization, but he pronounced the "central idea a noble one." The book appeared 3 May 1892 under the title *Imperial Federation: The Problem of National Unity* by George Parkin, M.A.

Imperial Federation was not solely, or even primarily, a response to Goldwin Smith or to any of the other proponents of closer economic ties between the United States and Canada, such as Andrew Carnegie, an American industrialist, and Erastus Wiman. However, it and the other two projects that Parkin completed that year, a school text and an influential map of the British Empire, were all of a piece. They were all expressions of the idea that Parkin had been slowly developing throughout his adult life: "the completion of a closer and permanent political unity between the British communities scattered throughout the world should be a first aim of national statesmanship, and might become, if its advantages were clearly understood, a supreme object of popular desire."[25] Whether he meant to speak with false modesty or not, though, he said nothing short of the truth when he wrote that in stating "the case for British Unity I have constantly found myself merely linking together arguments already used by thinkers in many parts of the Empire."[26]

Parkin introduced his argument by observing that, with responsible government, the white colonies had taken great strides towards creating cohesive national units. Canada had become a federation 4,000 miles wide and the Australian colonies were taking courageous steps towards closer union. Even South Africa and the West Indies showed some progress, although Parkin observed that their progress was less, because of the presence of "coloured races." It was true that the American colonies has departed in the eighteenth century, but the rest of the British peoples remained united, and that unity, Parkin contended, was the indisputable political fact upon which his argument was based: "Not the creation, but the preservation of national unity, is the task which thus confronts British people, which they must accept or refuse. Unity already exists; it is the necessary starting-point of every discussion."[27]

If this unity were to be maintained, it would have to be on a new footing. Virtually all the imperial federationists objected to the fact that Canada was more than happy to allow the United Kingdom to bear virtually the full cost of Canada's defence. Political equality, they argued, entailed that the dominions pull their weight militarily. "Yearly the vast expense necessary to provide adequately for national responsibilities increased, and added itself to the weight of taxation incident to an advanced civilization and complex social system. While forced to bear the chief burden of the taxation required for national defence, the people of the British Islands could see that the mass of the colonists benefited by this protection already possessed, or were likely before long to possess a higher average of wealth and comfort than the mass of the people who bestowed the benefit."[28]

On this, the difference between Parkin and Smith is clear. Parkin wanted to maintain the transcontinental Canadian nation, admitted that it was costly, and wanted Canada to shoulder the financial burden instead of the United Kingdom. Smith saw no reason to maintain the political unit if it involved significant costs. Parkin had a vision of a new connection among the English-speaking peoples, a spiritual bond, held together by a transportation and communication network. There was, he said, a community of industrial interests buttressed by a community of thought. Emigrants left England not in fear of persecution but in search of opportunities, taking their culture and their love of their homeland with them.[29] Once there, they were bound together by cheap ocean transport, postage, and telegraph rates. Inexpensive editions of books brought English culture even to the Canadian prairies. Church societies helped to keep people in close touch, as did scientific academies. Even sporting societies contributed to the unity of the empire. Most of all, these emigrants took with them their passionate affection for Shakespeare, Milton, Scott, and Burns, the common imaginative heritage that held the British peoples together.[30]

Those were the facts that made for unity, but Parkin hoped for more. Just as when he was young, his dream was that to be British was to be noble and pure and to strive for the just and the good: "It is because I believe that in all the noblest and truest among British people there is this strong faith in our national integrity, and in the greatness of the moral work our race has yet to do, that I anticipate that the whole weight of Christian and philanthropic sentiment will ultimately be thrown on the side of national unity, as opening up the widest possible career of usefulness for us in the future; inasmuch as it will give us the security which is necessary for working out our great national purposes."[31]

Smith disagreed entirely. Culturally and socially he thought that Canadians were much closer to Americans of the northern states than they were to the British. British immigrants had not prospered as farmers. "Young Englishmen as a class have not done well; they have energy and pluck, but not steady industry, self-denial, or the habit of saving. The jesters of the North-West call 'remittances from home' the Englishman's harvest...."

The question is not so much why imperial federation arguments in favour of preferential tariffs did not prevail, but why they got any hearing at all. Part of the answer lies in a book by an American naval lieutenant, A.T. Mahan. *The Influence of Sea Power upon History, 1660–1783*, which went through twelve editions from its publication in 1890 to the end of the First World War and had a major influence on British and American military policy.

Mahan argued that the change in naval technology from sail to steam created a need not just for safe harbours but also for secure sources of coal that would allow the fleet to refuel abroad without returning to its home port.[32] England's success as a naval power arose from the synergies it developed. Its manufacturing generated products to exchange abroad. Its marine provided the means to carry on the trade, and its colonies promoted the expansion of that trade. The British Empire had developed in a stable and self-sustaining way. The English might be a nation of shopkeepers, but they were no less bold, enterprising, or patient than their rivals, and the fact that they sought wealth by developing the local economy rather than by plunder meant that their empire was more enduring than their rivals'.[33] Colonies grew best when they grew naturally and England's colonists were happy to emigrate and make new homes in their adopted lands, while retaining an affection for their land of origin.[34]

However, Mahan expressed concerns about the future strength of England's sea power that provided arrows for the bows of the imperial federationists. The initial establishment of the United Kingdom's overseas empire had been undertaken largely under the auspices of an aristocratic government that was, to a considerable extent, insulated from the economic effects of the wars it undertook. However, since 1815, England had become increasingly democratized, and it was not clear that democracies were willing to spend the money necessary to maintain military strength in times of peace.[35] Colonies attached to the mother country were, Mahan argued, the surest way of supporting the sea power of a country. It was therefore of the highest importance that the English government promote "by all means a warmth of attachment and a unity of interest which [would] make the welfare of one the welfare of all, or rather for war, by inducing such measures or organization and defence as [should] be felt by all to be a fair distribution of a burden of which each reaps the benefit."

Mahan's book arrived at just the right time for the proponents of preferential tariffs and Parkin immediately grasped the significance of Mahan's argument. As well as a cultural unity, Parkin conceptualized the British Empire as a global communication and transportation network. There had been very few people such as he and Charles Dilke who had travelled extensively throughout the English-speaking world (to date, Parkin had missed South Africa) on specifically political fact-finding missions. That experience allowed him to understand implications of Mahan's theory. The free trade enthusiasts at chambers of commerce meetings completely missed the point, he told them. In the new global world, safe trade rather than free trade was essential if England was to defend her far-flung commercial empire and, in an increasingly hostile world, the slight price of preferential tariffs became a genuine bargain. And safe trade required that the geopolitical unity of the empire remain intact. Break one link, and the whole collapses.

The argument drew its strength from the change from sailing ships to coal-powered steam ships. "Now it has become chiefly a question of coal endurance. Removed from the means of renewing its supplies of coal, the most powerful ship afloat within a very limited number of days becomes a helpless hulk. 'The striking distance of a ship of war is now on an average two thousand miles,' are the words used by Lord Salisbury not long since to indicate the nature and extent of this change in the conditions of naval defence."[36]

For Parkin, then, Great Britain, Canada, South Africa, India, New Zealand, Australia, and lesser colonies were more than independent places. They formed a system. Remove one and the system fell apart. Keep them intact and the British navy could defend the trade routes of the empire without having to rely on foreign powers. For Smith, Parkin's concept of free trade was largely a fantasy. Since Canada already did a large part of its trade with the United States and would do a great deal more if the artificial barriers to trade were removed, Canada had no need to spend vast sums of money maintaining a global system of trade when it could engage in north-south trade for almost nothing.

When it came to discussing the question of union or annexation, Parkin and Smith were both reduced to subjective impression about the opinions of Canadians. Many of Parkin's objections were racist. The United States accepted too many non-British immigrants, he felt,[37] and the enfranchisement of Negroes after the Civil War created a voting weight that would balance Canada's.[38] Although Parkin agreed with Smith that French-Canadians were "unprogressive," and narrow in political outlook, he was unwilling, unlike Smith, to see them destroyed in a union with the United States, although he doubted their ability to survive even in Canada.[39] It was Canada's destiny, he thought, to belong to the "the sturdy races of the North—Saxon and Celt, Scandinavian, Dane, and Northern German, fighting their way under conditions sometimes rather more severe than those to which they have been accustomed in their old homes. Selection implies less rapid increment; quality is balanced against quantity."[40]

How was imperial federation to come about? Like most of its proponents, Parkin was vague, but the details were far less important to him than they were to others. He liked the idea of a supreme council with some sort of proportional representation from the self-governing parts of the empire, but avoided working out the details, which was just as well, since any detailed plan seemed to come to grief, one way or the other, as his old friends Thomas Raleigh and Lord Thring told him. Parkin's aim was different. He wanted to maintain and enhance an imperial culture, common intellectual, social, and political attitudes that would hold the empire together. He did not object to imperial councils, as Milner favoured, or the preferential tariffs for which Tupper and Denison agitated. But he thought it was more important to provide the cheapest possible postal and telegraph facilities. Surely if people communicate they will bond together. Parkin felt that it was essential to create a "trained and intelligent public opinion" through well-equipped public reading rooms and working men's clubs "with maps specially designed to stimulate geographical imagination, and books to furnish accurate geographical information about the Empire...." It was also necessary to mould the young mind. "In schools there is an immense work to be done. The cultivation of national sentiment in the minds of the young, on the basis of sound knowledge, historical, geographical and industrial, is not only a legitimate work, but a primary duty for the schools of a country."[41] The educational tools for this task were lacking and he created them.

At the end of January 1892, Parkin wrote to George Macmillan to see if the publisher would consider including a map of coaling stations in *Imperial Federation* to help readers visualize the argument he made about the unity of the empire in the age of steam. Parkin had been in contact with J.G. Bartholomew, a Scottish cartographer and founder of the Royal Scottish Geographical Society. Bartholomew worked in the family cartographic business and was sympathetic to the imperial federation cause. He adapted an existing map as an insert for the book as Macmillan had agreed, but a larger idea began to grow in Parkin's mind: a much bigger map. Bartholomew and he worked together on the project. He proposed to present the empire and the world at large "from a commercial and economic standpoint." It would show the trade routes and the coaling stations, but it would also show "the character of the governments in the various countries of the Empire...." They needed to find a publisher, but initially no one was interesting in producing 1000 copies of this leviathan, eight feet by five feet, that would sell for twenty-five shillings.

By June 1892, Parkin still had not found a publisher for his map.

Macmillan's was willing, but only if Parkin bore the initial cost of £237. Parkin approached Lord Rosebery, who was uninterested: "It always distresses me not to cooperate with you, but I can find no more for Imperial Federation this year... and my budget, sorely strained in other ways, will bear no more. Were it otherwise I need not say how pleased I should be to help...." Fortunately, Parkin was lucky that some of his less aristocratic friends were more positive. Lord Brassey, Joe Haley, a young Yorkshire manufacturer, and Peter Redpath, a wealthy Montréal businessman, contributed £50 each to the cost.

The map appeared late in 1892 in its planned large format. It was based on Mercator's projection, which had the advantage, from a Canadian point of view, of making Canada seem not only enormous but also the centre of the world, with all communication and transportation routes flowing to and from it. British possessions were red and pink, as was surely right, while the rest of the world was consigned to drabness, as was also surely right. Bartholomew proposed that the title should read: Parkin's Imperial Federation Map of the BRITISH EMPIRE by J.G. Bartholomew G.R.C.E., Dedicated to Her Majesty the Queen by G.R. Parkin M.A. '

Like many authors, Parkin found his publisher's promotion of his map less zealous than he hoped, so he promoted it wherever he could. He persuaded the New South Wales government to take 400 copies; he recouped his costs with that transaction alone. Denison pushed sales in Ontario schools, so all in all, Parkin made a small profit, though, as usual, probably not enough to reward the effort that went into the project.

The most successful of Parkin's projects was a geography textbook for school use, *Round the Empire*; its themes were intimately tied to the map and the arguments for imperial federation, or Parkin's other term, national unity. One of his imperialist friends, Hugh Arnold-Foster, an editor with the London publishing firm of Cassells, approached him to write the text. Parkin complied, in the hope that it would give "the small English boy a better chance than he [had] hitherto had to get a connected idea of the Empire." Lord Rosebery, whose association with the book lent it status, agreed to contribute a two-page preface. Rosebery's preface was not addressed to the children who would read the book, but to the teachers who might consider its adoption. The British

Empire, he suggested, was a broad collection of states, united by a single flag and a single head. It faced an uncertain future. One possibility was parochialism and factiousness; the other was a growing sense of responsibility and inheritance of a sense of communion with British people scattered around the globe. Parkin's book would, he hoped, contribute to a sense of mission.[42]

The book was clearly directed at the English schoolboy. There is little about the United Kingdom in it, and the first chapter is titled "Leaving the Old Country." The British Empire, Parkin tells them, clearly and simply, is an oceanic empire. You could think of oceans as large bodies of water that divide peoples, but in the case of the British Empire, that would be wrong. Oceans, Parkins tells the schoolboys, as he has been trying to persuade their parents, are communications networks that unite the various colonies. With steamships, they shorten the time it takes to transport goods and people. The telegraph makes the same news possible the same day in Melbourne and Montréal.[43] Nor does the British colonist flee from his homeland to escape persecution; he emigrates to live under the same laws, similar forms of government and culture.

Parkin enlivened the book with descriptions of maple sugar production in Canada, gold mining in Australia, sheep in their millions in New Zealand, and ostrich farming in the Cape colony, where the visitor to a farm has to exercise supreme care lest he be felled by the mighty kick of a cock ostrich. The book also subjects the student, as we might expect by now, to disquisitions on naval fortifications and coaling stations. Parts of it are a miscellaneous jumble, since it was hard to fit places like Ascension Island and the Falklands into any coherent plan. At its heart, though, it is an imaginative school text, not a work of propaganda. It is only at the very end that Parkin lets his true feelings show, the feelings that motivated all his work. When all was said and done, for the settlers abroad, the British Isles were home. "Not only the emigrant, but his children and children's children, speak of coming 'home' to England, or Scotland, or Ireland. The great history of our country belongs as much to them as it does to us."[44]

Round the Empire was well-received. Parkin's friend, William Peterson, later principal of McGill University, found it admirable and declared that his two sons would be taught from it. Another correspondent praised the great usefulness it would to the next generation and hoped that it would soon become a "household word" both at home and abroad. The Leeds *Mercury* thought that it was a book that father and son could peruse with equal pleasure, and Lord Grey paid it the high compliment of suggesting that it should be used at Eton.[45] It was Parkin's most successful book, going through five editions and remaining in print until 1924, by which time it had sold a total of 190,000 copies.[46] His royalties may have been as much as £20 a year, a useful contribution to his budget. *Imperial Federation*, on the other hand, was not so fortunate. Macmillan's printed 5000 copies in June 1892, of which 2000 were in a cheaper edition intended for sales in the colonies. At the beginning of January 1893 Macmillan wrote to Parkin to say that he still had 1600 copies of the British edition and 800 copies of the colonial edition left. Total sales, then, had been 2600, and Brassey's £300 had not yet been returned.

As is clear from his publishing activity alone, Parkin was a busy man. Indeed, according to Parkin's son, Raleigh, his mother used to complain that it was not easy to be married to the tail end of a comet. The metaphor might be slightly muddled, but it is clear what she meant. However, despite Parkin's frenetic work schedule, the family continued to endure financial hardship. It is hard to estimate Parkin's financial position in 1892. It always was, though it could be summed up in two words: in debt. How did that happen? There is no adequate record of his income because it came from so many diverse sources. He planned a speaking trip to Canada later in the year. That would likely turn a profit. There was his regular and his freelance journalism. Brassey had given him £300 as an advance towards the royalties of *Imperial Federation*, but presumably much of that had been spent. It is probably pushing the upper limit to estimate his income in 1892 at £600.

The problem was that he travelled constantly in support of the imperial federation cause and was constantly away from home. We know that he got gifts from supporters, but it is quite reasonable to assume that Parkin made no clear distinction between the funds he received and the funds he needed to promote the cause. On the contrary, he seems to have treated his personal finances as what was left over after he had paid his hotel bills, his railways fares, and his meals while away from home, though he affected no grand style. "The Scotsman would take a column from me on the Ship Railway, and I am going to try to work that off with Ketchum as well as a magazine article when I come to town. My trip will now apparently cover 5 addresses.... The Sec. here sent me yesterday a cheque for ten pounds, 'to defray travelling expenses.' Of course I wrote Loring that I considered this a contribution to the League's work, and it will count on my pay, but it is valuable, as helping to make the thing remunerative, and not end in financial failure...." That meant, when all was said and done, there was little left over for Annie and the children.

Parkin's only extravagance, if it can be called that, since he really couldn't afford to pay for it, was to send his daughters to Switzerland to school. When she was about twelve, Alice went to Tannegg, a school in Toleure, run by Alise Hentschy. She had been governess to the Thrings' children and Parkin had come to know her during his visits to the Thring home. After her service to the Thrings was finished, she returned to her native Switzerland and established a boarding school. Parkin, who did not like the local state-supported schools in his area and couldn't afford an English public school, decided that Tennegg was the best solution.

Tannegg was a fee-paying school, and the cost of having Alice there overburdened the family's precarious finances. Parkin proposed to save money by sending his whole family, including Annie, off to Switzerland, and at one point everyone, minus Parkin, took up residence there. This idea was strongly opposed by Miss Hentschy. Toleure, she told Parkin, was not a tourist town. It might be possible to find accommodation and to send Maude to one of the local schools where she could learn French and German, but Hentschy believed that Alice should remain in the boarding school, "as she would not learn much, being rather slow, which disadvantage would be doubled by her difficulty for the language and sending her with a much younger class would be a pity."

In May 1892, Parkin proposed another plan that he thought might prove affordable. The girls might live with their mother in town and go to the school as day pupils. That scheme would not work either, came the reply. She refused to take day pupils even from the town and the girls were allowed only one Sunday a month away from the school, so they would see their mother very little.

By August, Parkin's finances had deteriorated so far that he had exchanged letters with Miss Hentschy suggesting that Alice remain at the school during the summer vacation. If he had to pay the costs of her return trip, he could only afford her school fees until Christmas. The reply was sincere and compassionate. It would break Alice's heart not to see her parents and to be left behind when the other girls set off to visit their families. Since money was the problem, she offered, in effect, to add herself to the list of Parkin's creditors. "You think you may not be able to send her to us longer than till Christmas for money reasons. Well then, send her to us till Christmas and then let her stay on as my guest, till next summer. She has only made a 'start' in so many things and if she can stay another year with us, she will have achieved something real for life. Besides, she is so dear to me I should miss her very much indeed.... P.S. I know you will not mention what I am writing to-day any more than I shall speak of it to anybody whatever." By the next year, either Parkin's finances had improved or Elise Hentschy's generosity had further expanded, since Maude was now studying with her sister. Maude was the bright one in the family. Alice, Hentschy thought, should content herself with domestic life, for which her abilities were "quite good enough ... in an ordinary way." By contrast, Hentschy thought that Maude "[would] do very well indeed in any higher course of English study and her knowledge of French and German [would] come in very useful."

These financial difficulties were wearing Parkin down. Around August 1892, he approached Peter Redpath to help find a job in Canada "in some important educational institution." Redpath wrote to Sir Donald Smith (later Lord Strathcona), a Montreal financier and one of the principal shareholders of the Canadian Pacific Railway, to ask for his help. Parkin's imperial federation ideas fitted neatly with Smith's financial interests, since the CPR was the instrument that carried freight and troops from Halifax to Vancouver. Annexation to the United States, with the diversion of trade to a north-south axis, would spell ruin.

Parkin's journalistic talents also brought him into contact with George Buckle, editor of the (London) *Times*. Previously, Parkin had written for provincial newspapers, some of which were quite respectable, but the *Times* offered Parkin a wider audience and paid a good deal more. Parkin was arranging a speaking tour of Canada, and Buckle commissioned a series of articles on Canada. Parkin sailed for Canada on 9 September 1892, arriving in Halifax on the 20th. So long as Parkin's interest in the imperial federation movement continued, it was important for him to continue to travel. In one sense, he was the movement. Although there were vastly more important individuals, such as Lord Rosebery, Parkin was the one who tied the whole thing together. He knew everyone, travelled everywhere, and made contacts. What's more, he was genuinely nice; he got along well with people.

While in Toronto, Parkin stayed with Denison at his home, Heydon Villa. The Colonel and Parkin became good friends during this stay, but the hyperactive cavalryman sometimes wore his guest down. If there wasn't a meeting to attend or guests to entertain, Denison bombarded him with conversation from dawn to dusk and beyond. "I have no mental rest with the colonel," Parkin told Annie, "except when I shut myself up in my room. I never knew of such relentless energy...."

Parkin was out of touch with his native land. It was good to be back in Canada preaching the message of imperial unity, especially since annexationist sentiment had only been defeated but not crushed the previous year. His itinerary took on some aspects of an author's tour. He was promoting *Imperial Federation, Round the Empire*, and his map. Wherever possible, he spoke to public meetings as a way of raising some ready cash, and he addressed crowded gatherings from coast to coast: Victoria, Vancouver, New Westminster, Calgary, Winnipeg, Port Arthur, Toronto, Ingersoll, London, Windsor, Woodstock, Montreal, Saint John, Sackville, and Halifax. He was always a good evening's entertainment. At the same time he was collecting material for his articles for the *Times*.

Parkin's meetings were generally well-received. Denison thought that the Toronto speech was powerful and convincing. On the west coast, the *Daily Columbian* of New Westminster declared that Parkin, whose speech—which had led to the formation of a local branch of the Imperial Federeation League—was "able, brilliant and intensely interesting.... No person of ordinary, or extraordinary, intelligence could listen to the lecturer without being convinced that the various parts of the great British Empire were natural correlatives of each other, in the widest and every sense...."

Yet there was just as much opposition and criticism. John Willison, editor-in-chief of the Toronto *Globe*, complained that Parkin and people like him seemed only to see the failings of the United States and not its brilliant past and magnificent prospects. The Montreal *Herald* objected to Parkin's geopolitical theories that saw Canada as a link in a chain with "the unclean natives of the Indian Empire" rather than "their blood brethren in the United States." The whole scheme smelled of little more than a device for getting promotion for a few Canadian militia colonels, it sneered.

As D'Alton McCarthy wrote to the secretary of the Imperial Federation League in England, "Parkin has addressed several meetings with very considerable effect in the different localities where he has spoken, but I do not think that the views that we entertain are looked upon by the mass of people as practical, and there is in their minds more or less the feeling that the advocates of Imperial Federation are connected with the aristocratic and privileged classes." When it came right down to it, then, most Canadians took a position somewhere between Smith's and Parkin's. They didn't like the British and they didn't particularly want to remain part of the empire if they had to pay for it. They didn't much mind whom they traded with, as long as it was profitable. They wanted to keep the emphasis on their neighbour; in spite of Denison's paranoia, they wanted none of Smith's annexation. Although there were differing opinions, some quite strong, most Canadians wanted things to continue on more or less as they were.

Parkin wanted changes, in more ways than one. By late November, he had reached Winnipeg and was staying with the lieutenant-governor. Annie wrote to him that she was running out of money once again and that she was having trouble coping emotionally with her financial position. Parkin wrote to a friend asking for a loan of £20 to be put in Annie's bank account. Parkin apologized for the miscalculation and his inability to manage the family finances. "Against all this separation and trial," he consoled her, "I can only place the feeling that one is trying to do the best he can in the line of apparent duty, and that one has many proofs that his weight and consideration in the world are increasing. If only things may so work out that I can make life easier and brighter for you."

9

Money Troubles and the Death of the IFL

In August 1892, just prior to Parkin's departure for Canada, William Gladstone became, to Queen Victoria's disgust, prime minister of the United Kingdom for the fourth time. She thought his election so greatly contrary to her wishes that she briefly considered ignoring the conventions of responsible government on the grounds that they couldn't possibly be right if they insisted that she do such a distasteful thing as meet with him regularly. Many lesser mortals, including Thring, felt the same way about Gladstone. A religious enthusiast and classical scholar who translated Homer for recreation while he was in office, Gladstone was widely regarded as a supreme political genius, one of the greatest political figures to lead the United Kingdom or indeed any other country. Like him or not, the Queen-Empress was stuck with him.

So, too, were men like Sir Charles Tupper, Canada's high commissioner in London at the time, who dreamed of uniting the empire around a series of reciprocal preferential tariffs. Gladstone, however, was a staunch believer in free trade. The United Kingdom had prospered since the abolition of the Corn Laws in the mid-nineteenth century—a move that allowed free trade in agricultural products. It was a policy that, on balance, helped manufacturing and the cities, since it lowered the price of food and, in effect, lowered the price of labour. It was widely perceived as the foundation of the United Kingdom's supremacy as the world's leading power. Free trade for many in the United Kingdom was more than an economic policy; it was a fundamental cornerstone of national identity and prosperity, and tinkering with it was anathema to powerful economic forces.

Canada favoured preferential tariffs so that it would have an advantage competing with American agricultural products in British markets. This of course ran directly into the face of the dominant British belief in free trade: that is, that there should be no tariffs of any kind. British manufacturing interests saw no benefit in preferential tariffs if they raised the price of food and consequently would lead to demands for higher wages. Canadian and Argentinean produce had already begun to take the place of grain and meat from small home farms.[1] In the summer of 1892, at a meeting of chambers of commerce in London, a proposal for preferential tariffs was soundly defeated, in spite of the fact that nineteen of the twenty-two Canadian chambers of commerce voted in favour. Only seven other colonial chambers supported the idea.[2]

The British economy was certainly not in crisis. It was one of the greatest in the world, but its agriculture was suffering from cheap foreign imports. In the decade between 1890 and 1900, the number of acres producing wheat declined by half a million. Industrially, the United Kingdom continued to grow, but at a much slower pace. More seriously, in sectors such as textiles, coal, steel, and shipbuilding, it was actually falling behind Germany, and possibly also the United States.[3]

Gladstone had no intention of altering the United Kingdom's policy of free trade. Tupper's attempts to identify the imperial federation movement and the Imperial Federation League with the policy of preferential tariffs worried other members of the organization. The IFL began to feel that it needed to dissociate itself from one of its sister organizations, the United Empire Trade League, if it were not going to lose the sympathy of the new Liberal government or stave off a division between pro-empire supporters in the United Kingdom versus those in the overseas dominions.

In November, a committee of the various organizations presented a compromise report to the cabinet. The report contained the elements of its view of a united empire: "That the voice of the Empire in peace when dealing with foreign powers, shall be as far as possible the united voice of all its autonomous parts...That the defence of the Empire in war shall be the common defence of all its interests and all its parts, by the united force and resources of all its members." The report added that there was a need for closer consultation and suggested that after the Australian and South African colonies had been made into federations, they should be represented in London as Canada was already, by a high commissioner, and that these officials should be available to consult with the imperial cabinet when colonial interests were involved in any foreign negotiation.[4]

Gladstone met with them and assured them that he would gladly entertain a more active contribution to imperial defence by the colonies if that was their wish. The other matter was not negotiable. England's policy of free trade had served it well. No good, in his view, would be accomplished by a meeting between him and the colonial prime ministers.[5] And that, as long as he was prime minister, was that.

Tupper was a member of the committee and signed the compromise document. On 10 January 1893, he wrote privately to Casimir Dickson, secretary of the Canadian branch, to express his profound dissatisfaction with it. "When you remember that the Council of the Imperial Federation League embraces many strong Free Traders, you will see how impossible it must be at once to obtain unanimity in a proposal for preferential duties within the Empire, and how important it was to obtain from all the committee what is contained in sections 36–37 of the Report. The policy of the United Empire Trade League, which has received the support of the House of Commons and your branch, is making very steady and great progress in this country, and will, I believe, be adopted at no distant day. It is impossible to effect such a revolution in public opinion in this conservative country without much time and patience."[6]

Parkin, in Tupper's view, did not understand where Canada's true interests lay. "Knowing as I do that the most active members of the Imperial Federation League were mainly interested in levying a large contribution on the revenues of the Colonies for the support of the Army and Navy of Great Britain, I am delighted to have been able almost single-handed to obtain such a report from such a committee. Unfortunately they captured Mr. Parkin, and having used him here are now using him in Canada to create the false impression that we do nothing to maintain the defence of the Empire, instead of showing you, as he truthfully could, that we have entitled ourselves to the gratitude of every man who has the interest of the Empire at heart."[7]

Tupper intended this letter to be confidential but Dickson read it to the annual meeting of the Canadian league and news of its content reached the press and was reported back to London. Colonel Denison immediately investigated Dickson, who was a lieutenant in Denison's corps and president of the band committee. Dickson, he alleged, was a scoundrel. He was a proven liar and he had misappropriated funds. He might be an officer, but he was no gentleman. Denison suspected gambling was the source of the wrongdoing and his resignation was now in hand.

Dickson's handling of the league's finances was just as dodgy. It appeared that he had sent no money to the parent branch since 1891. His claims to the contrary were not backed up with receipts and, when Denison checked with the parent organization and the bank that handled the league's transactions, there was no evidence that might exonerate him. The Canadian league was almost penniless and Denison set about a fund-raising campaign to put it back on a sound footing. Denison speculated that Dickson released the letter as a means of reassuring his creditors and others that he was still in good standing with the league.[8] In England the quarrels between the various factions within the league became more heated. On 9 April, Parkin noted in his diary that he was worried about the state of the league and met with Tupper on 6 May with the satisfactory result that Tupper issued a public withdrawal of some of his statements.

In early April, Parkin's friend Bartholomew put him in touch with George Brown, who was the manager of Nelson, a publishing house. Parkin dined with him in Edinburgh. Brown was sufficiently impressed that he wanted to know if Parkin might consider a position with the firm at a salary of £500. Parkin expressed interest, but asked for time to consider. He wanted to finish the Thring biography and his remaining federation work, tasks he estimated would take the rest of the year. Although Annie desperately wanted him to take the position for the sake of the family's financial security (and Parkin agreed that in principle it was the right thing to do), by the end of April or the beginning of May, he had decided not to pursue the opportunity for the moment.[9]

On 23 April 1893, with the league's future very much in doubt, Milner made Parkin a proposal. In the twenty years since Milner and Parkin first met, Milner had shown a genius in many areas of public life, including finance, and in the process he had made a considerable fortune for himself.[10] Parkin, he said, was the imperial federation movement's best weapon. Although he didn't agree with him on every point, Milner thought that above all else Parkin should keep travelling and speaking to carefully chosen audiences, so that he would not waste his efforts and tire himself as he was so prone to do. He was prepared to back his words with action. "If there were 20 men in England prepared to put their hands in their pockets in order to endow you [illegible] as a professor of this subject, I should be willing to be one of the 20. If there were only 10, I should still make an effort to be one of 10." He invited Parkin to meet with him to discuss the matter in more detail.

The next day Milner wrote to Parkin again to clarify where they disagreed. Ever since his Australian tour, Parkin had tried to finesse the difficulties of political, economic, and military arrangements by concentrating more on matters of national spirit and common bonds of sentiment. The best strategy, he felt, was to educate public opinion on the practical, sentimental, and spiritual benefits of imperial unity. If done successfully, Parkin was sure a groundswell of popular support would soon create the atmosphere in which statesmen could readily draft a formal scheme of union.[11] The "race" also shared cultural traditions. Parkin claimed that there was a sense of common and equal ownership of great national memories and names. The people of the great colonies had never broken with national traditions. "Who," he asked, "that reads our history but is not thrilled with the story of Waterloo and Trafalgar...."[12] Tennyson, Burns, and Shakespeare were the cultural glue that held the British peoples together. Economic forces might wax and wane, but the English-speaking peoples stemmed from the same cultural stock and, given time, in the true British way, federated political institutions would, he believed, emerge.

For Milner, imperial federation meant just that: federation. He explained his views to Parkin in the following way:

> The ideal of Federation which naturally presents itself to the mind is one which provides a supreme Parliament or Council, national not merely in name but in reality, because containing in just proportion representatives of all the self-governing communities of the Empire. Such a body, relegating the management of local affairs to local Governments, and devoting its attention to a clearly defined range of purely Imperial concerns, would seem to satisfy a great national necessity. It would secure representation for all the great interests of the Empire, it would bring together those best fitted to give advice on Imperial matters, and it would be free from that overwhelming responsibility for petty administration which now paralyses, and at times renders ridiculous, the supreme council of the greatest nation in the world.

Five days later Parkin noted in his diary that he had an "important talk with Alfred Milner about my future arrangements," and he spoke with him again on 5 May. The latter, an emergency meeting at 11:45 at night, led to a £75 loan from Milner, which Parkin desperately needed. "I don't need any thanks for so small a favour, & it shall be quite sufficiently rewarded if it enables you to carry on your work for the next six weeks with a quiet mind," Milner wrote to him, but he did ask, gently, for a receipt, "not formal—but simply that I may know you have it safely."

Milner probably didn't find ten men, but he did raise enough money and on 27 May he sent Parkin word that he had secured £500 for each of the next three years to allow him to carry on. With funding secure, Parkin was convinced he could complete a great deal more work. On 1 June he met with Milner and Brassey, another member of the syndicate (it included Rosebery and George Houstoun, an enthusiastic Glasgow supporter) that was prepared to finance him. They worked out the terms in a memorandum of agreement. Parkin was to receive a minimum of £450 or £500, if the funds could be raised, for a period of three years beginning 1 July 1893. The generous arrangement allowed Parkin to make any other financial arrangement he might like during the period, and to keep all his speaking and freelance fees "subject to the general condition of using his best energies to promote the unity of the Empire...." Parkin asked for a week to consider the matter. On 6 June, he met with Brown again to discuss the publishing offer. After the meeting, Parkin noted in his diary: "Decided not to take it." By the end of June Parkin was able to pay Milner back at least £50 of the loan and Milner was offering him the use of a sitting-room in his house from which to conduct business.

The executive of the British league met on 23 June to consider its future and appointed a committee to consider options. It recommended that the league be dissolved. The executive committee was divided on this course of action and appointed a second committee. Loring reported what was happening to Denison in vague and general terms. He himself believed that Tupper's determined focus on preferential tariffs to the exclusion of any other interests that league members shared was largely to blame.[13]

Although Parkin was well aware that there was division within the league, he didn't want to see it wound up. It was not because he thought the head office particularly valuable in itself, but it was the link that tied all the local branches together. For years Parkin had travelled throughout Great Britain, Canada, Australia, and New Zealand trying, generally to little effect, to establish vibrant local organizations. His work was just beginning to show some results, and the disappearance of the league would likely check any further growth.[14] However, after concluding that the report laid before Gladstone had "represented the maximum of political principles and opinions attainable, as a homogeneous body, by all the numerous and diverse elements of which the League was composed," the committee recommended that the operations of the league be brought to a close. On 24 November 1893, the Imperial Federation League was officially dissolved.[15] Parkin wrote to Denison describing the league proceedings as a puzzle. What appeared to have happened is that the free trade faction, in alliance with the defence faction, engineered a coup which saw them emerge with the office, address, records, and emblem of the league, but minus the members who supported imperial preference. Led by three council members who had voted to dissolve the old organization, they created a new Imperial Federation (Defence) League.[16] None of these arrangements and re-arrangements directly affected Parkin. Milner and his friends had retained Parkin's services as the spokesman for an idea, not the employee for an organization.

The Milner fund money was a particular godsend because Buckle at the *Times* had decided that he did not have space at the moment to print Parkin's articles on Canada because of the Irish Home Rule crisis. He would use them, he promised, but not just then, and until he did, Parkin would not be paid.

Parkin still had the burden of the Thring biography hanging over him. Unexpected, unasked for, unwanted, it was a duty he was determined to fulfil. He bought a new typewriter, buoyed by his new-found financial stability, and faced his work full of hopefulness: "What a mercy not to have the sharpest whip of necessity over one's back this year. The relief just came in time." He started back on the biography and the work went well, he thought, "thanks to air and exercise."

The money also allowed him to continue his other writing, as the contract allowed. He had a weekly column in the Leeds *Mercury*. He wrote freelance articles for Manchester *Examiner*, the *Scotsman*, and the *National Observer*.[17] Although he lobbied MPs, his main aim was to influence public opinion directly. He used his considerable oratorical abilities at debating societies and spoke whenever he could to workingmen's organizations.

Parkin's efforts took him throughout Britain, where he made use of contacts, old and new, to help him find audiences. Scotland was Rosebery's political base. It was also the home of Thomas Raleigh, Parkin's Oxford friend, J.G. Bartholomew, Robert Duncan, and George Houstoun, all strong financial supporters of the cause, as well as the home of John Webster, a young doctor who became a close friend. In the industrial Midlands, Parkin formed a close working and personal relationship with Talbot Baines, editor of the Leeds *Mercury*, Sir Henry Doulton, a china manufacturer, Cyril Ransom, a widely read historian, and Joe Haley, a manufacturer, willing to give financial support to Parkin and his projects.

In London, Parkin took a different approach. In the spirit of his

Britannic idealism, Parkin brought together about twenty Oxbridge graduates, with the aim that they would serve as missionaries among the working class. The hope was that they would serve as a pool of lecturers willing to speak to any club or organization on the topic of the empire. John Seeley issued a national manifesto, and they became known as the Seeley lecturers. Parkin was vice-president. Other members included Rider Haggart,[18] a popular novelist, James Bryce, an MP and later ambassador to the United States, and Spencer Wilkinson, a journalist.[19] It was their aim to bring home to all minds the importance of the British Empire; to tell the story of British enterprise in every part of the world; to recall those achievements of order and justice which had put a crown of glory on the British power in India and elsewhere; to show that upon co-operation throughout the empire depended the continuance of that supremacy at sea, without which commerce, the life-blood of the whole, could not be permanently secured; and finally, to impress upon the public conscience the greatness of the responsibility now confronting the British race in its imperial inheritance, as well as to discuss the means whereby this joint responsibility could be best discharged.

Parkin hit upon another way of moulding public opinion: forming the minds of the youth. So he went to the great public schools—Uppingham, Marlborough, King's at Canterbury, Clifton, Wellington, Haileybury, Sherborne, Rugby, Harrow, and others—where he had a captive audience of several hundred boys from the social classes who would likely lead the nation in the next generation. He had printed thousands of small versions of his map, which he distributed. On stage, working from his large version, he wove his magic spell: the empire was one. Take away any part and it disappeared. The unity of the British people must be nurtured. It was something sacred and precious.

More than most visiting speakers, Parkin genuinely inspired. Winston Churchill, who probably would have preferred tea with Hitler than to revisit his own schooldays, with their wasted years studying Latin and Greek, recalled that some of the few redeeming moments were the eminent visiting speakers. When Churchill met Parkin during the Boer War, about eleven years after his talk, he was able to recollect a passage from it, which Parkin thought "about as good a compliment as one man could pay to another. I have always thought that the work I did among the schools at one time was very useful in suggesting ideas to young fellows. I have had a great many proofs that the seed was not sown on stony ground." Parkin might have been even more flattered if he had been able to read Churchill's *My Early Life*. Writing in 1930, Churchill reminisced about Parkin's lecture on imperial federation. "He told us how at Trafalgar, Nelson's signal 'England expects that every man will do his duty' ran down the line of battle, and how if we and our Colonies all held together, a day would come when such a signal would run not merely along a line of ships, but along a line of nations. We lived to see this come true, and I was able to remind the aged Mr. Parkin of it, when in the last year of his life he attended some great banquet in celebration of our victorious emergence from the Great War."

In December, Parkin received an interesting feeler. John Usher, treasurer of the East and North of Scotland Liberal Unionist Association, sounded him out on his interest in running for parliament in the next general election in a Scottish constituency. It is possible that Rosebery, who was a grandee in Scottish politics, was behind the idea. The offer he put to Parkin was that the association would pay his election expenses because a place in parliament would give him a better platform from which to preach imperial ideas. The practical problem was that, at the time, British MPs weren't paid. As Parkin explained to Denison: "You know enough about the hard struggle I have had merely to find the means of existence here to know that the acceptance of such a proposition would under my circumstances be absurd, but the fact of the offer being made ... is very significant as showing a trend of thought."

Parkin, of course, immediately contacted Milner, only to find out that Usher had previously discussed the idea with him. Milner agreed that Parkin was not in a financial state to accept the position. The group who had contributed to Parkin's activities as a non-partisan lecturer would not agree to support a partisan politician. Milner himself had run unsuccessfully in 1885; he told Parkin that he had found it a thoroughly unsatisfactory experience. He had been asked to stand for the seat himself and had rejected the idea. "I see that a man can do any amount of good public work, and be of the greatest service, without joining in the party—can, in fact, be of greater service because he keeps himself in the background." He also chided Parkin for allowing himself to get run down again from overwork. "For the time being the great question for you seems to be a question of health. I was very sorry to hear of your attack of influenza, and I beg you most earnestly to take the greatest care that you effect a complete recovery and to give yourself a thorough rest well into the new year. Do not trouble yourself about the work at all. The work will come all right, & be quite easy to you, if you can recover bodily, and therefore mental, spring."

On 24 January 1894, Usher renewed the offer, this time accompanying it with a financial equivalent of Milner and Brassey's support, £500 a year for three years. The seat on offer was South Aberdeen, one Usher confessed Parkin would likely lose, but after paying his dues, he would be found a more promising one. After consultations in early February, Parkin was leaning towards acceptance. By the middle of February, Usher was becoming impatient. He wrote to Parkin saying that he understood the reasons for his indecision, but since there might be an election at any time, he needed an answer. He also mentioned, for the first time in the correspondence, that the incumbent, James Bryce, might decide (as he did) to continue his distinguished career and run again. On 24 February, Usher wrote that he was prepared to give Parkin time to talk to his friends, which he finally did on 27 February after another long consultation with Milner. Another friend whom he had consulted, Thomas Raleigh, said that he personally had felt compromised when he allowed the party to cover his election expenses, though he would still like to see Parkin in the House of Commons. Indeed, a diary entry of 26 March suggests that there was still some possibility that Parkin might stand for a different constituency under more satisfactory financial arrangements. Parkin's refusal to stand for parliament certainly did not reflect a belief that he would be sullied by involvement with partisan politics.[20] He would almost certainly have attempted to enter parliament if his means had permitted.[21] In July 1894 his Australian friend, Judge Samuel Way, commiserated with him that a lack of money had prevented his entry into parliament.

Parkin rarely took anyone's advice, even Milner's, about resting. In spite of lingering illness, he continued to accept speaking invitations, including one at Uppingham, which at least led to the sale of a wall map. The really good news was that Buckle started running Parkin's long, analytical articles on Canada in the *Times* on 31 January 1894, accompanied with an editorial. It had been more than a year since Parkin had made his trip, but over the next month the *Times* printed five articles, two on the Northwest, and one each on coal, the CPR, and trade. In the house style of the newspaper, they were signed "Our correspondent" but it was widely known that Parkin was the author and the newspaper received requests for thousands of reprints. Buckle commissioned more pieces from a very pleased Parkin.

Moberley Bell also told Parkin that he very much liked the articles. The approval of Bell and Buckle was important, because they stood at the centre of English journalism. Bell was roughly Parkin's age. Born in Egypt, he became the *Times*' correspondent there in 1875. In 1890, A.F. Walter, the newspaper's chief proprietor, recruited him to play a senior managerial role, especially with regard to the foreign department. He was largely responsible for managing foreign correspondents, so his goodwill was key to Parkin's relations with the paper. As well as his good wishes, he sent a cheque for £46.

From these articles, a number of opportunities arose. "We must take courage and go on," he wrote to Annie in Harwich. Parkin was invited to write a history of Canada, a proposal that very much appealed to him. Arnold-Foster suggested that he prepare a Canadian edition of *Round the Empire* and citizen readers for Canada and the United States. The most interesting proposal arose from his article on the Canadian Pacific Railway, which had particularly pleased Parkin, since he noted in his diary that it reads very well. "You see," he wrote to his wife on another occasion, "I'm full of plans."

In March he received a letter from his old friend Sanford Fleming. According to Fleming, William Van Horne, the American-born president of the Canadian Pacific Railway, had read his articles, and was impressed. He had inquired about the author and Fleming told him it was Parkin. Van Horne asked Fleming to approach Parkin with a business proposition. The CPR was, in his view, a much maligned institution. It was often attacked and it could use someone of Parkin's calibre to defend it. It had another need, which was to present a persuasive case to government about its business matters as they might occur from time to time. Van Horne wanted to explore the possibility that Parkin would join the CPR to undertake those roles. If the position interested him, and he was willing to start without much delay, Fleming intimated that Van Horne was prepared to consider a generous salary. Parkin replied by sending a draft copy of his and Bartholomew's map, accompanied with "the most seductive letter that I could manage to compose." On 18 April, Van Horne himself wrote to congratulate Parkin on the articles and make personal contact. Parkin met personally with Van Horne on 18 June and wrote in his diary that he agreed to consider the matter carefully.

Parkin's face-to-face visit with Van Horne took place during an assignment to Canada on behalf of the *Times* to cover the colonial conference in Ottawa. He had left for Canada on 8 June. A week before, on 31 May, his alma mater, the University of New Brunswick, awarded him an honorary LL.D. It was now Dr. Parkin who set out for Canada. Van Horne had asked Parkin to name his expected salary. Parkin told Carman that the friends he trusted most advised him to take the position at the CPR, and he had practically decided to accept, since it was not incompatible with the kind of work he had previously been doing. He asked for a salary of $5000. On reflection, Van Horne decided the price was too high. Citing a business downturn that was leading to "dropping everybody not absolutely necessary to the everyday running of the [rail]road," he suggested that Parkin's appointment would have to wait until business picked up.

Disappointed with the loss of possible employment with the CPR, Parkin, nevertheless, continued to research and write his articles. Parkin wanted to turn his *Times* articles into a book, but he wanted the exercise to yield a profit, rather than leave him scrambling to make ends meet. He talked to his old friend George Foster, the dominion finance minister, who put him in touch with T.C. Daly, the minister of the interior. Daly agreed to give Parkin a $500 grant to help him complete his work. That allowed him to stay in Canada until 12 August to research, write, speak, and make contacts. His dedication to his work was total. Yet, like many people deeply committed to a cause, he didn't seem to be sensitive to the possibility that taking a significant sum of money from an interested party, such as a government minister, might compromise his integrity or impartiality.

He wrote virtually every morning, almost always without exception. Over many weeks he notes that he is "not very well," "ill," "not feeling well" and even "distinctly unwell." And yet the very next phrase is "writing went very well today."

Just before he returned to London, Parkin visited his brothers and sisters, who still lived modestly in Salisbury. At roughly the same time, Bryce sent him a letter asking him if he would like his name put down for the exclusive men's club, the Athenaeum, though since the waiting list was fifteen years long, the matter was scarcely urgent. That was just as well, since in October he received a letter from former student and friend Bliss Carman that began to make him face financial reality for the first time in years. The poet wrote to say he had financial problems of his own. He was in debt himself to the extent of $600 to $700 and was paying interest on it at seven per cent. He had given his life insurance policy as collateral. Would Parkin be able to take over the interest payments on the part of the debt that he owed to Carman and assume that part of the debt? How degrading it is, Carman wrote, to have to deal with those two sticks with a snake wrapped round them, "$".

If Milner could sort out the finances of a bankrupt Egypt and help manage England's, perhaps he could do something for Parkin, and it was to him that Parkin turned. Milner asked, in a very businesslike way, for: 1. A statement for all of Parkin's liabilities; 2. A statement of his certain receipts, probable expenditures, and cash on hand, other than the £450 guaranteed by the Milner fund. He proposed to try to find the following: "1. A system for the regular & gradual extinction of your debts. 2. Equilibrium of expenditure & income consistent with your not overwhelming yourself (for example, I should like, if possible, to see you provided for during next year without engaging now to write another laborious book)."

Parkin replied on 24 October. Milner didn't ask for an explanation and was the sort of man who didn't particularly want one. Parkin had asked him to solve a financial problem, not listen to a tale of woe, but Milner heard one anyway. The cost of living in England was twice that of Fredericton. Even so, Parkin claimed that he and his family had enough to live on, provided no one fell ill (a fairly unreasonable assumption, since Parkin was always working himself into ill health). There was the girls' education to take into account, though there were various means of economizing, such as moving to an urban area with a good fee-paying high school, so that the girls could live at home, rather than living in Harwich and sending them to an expensive boarding school. As for himself, he would raise additional money by working on a proposed history of Canada.

As for his debts, he estimated that £508 were attributable to either money he had spent on the Thring biography so far, or to foregone income. Another £300 to £400 he thought had been acquired in his early days "of struggle in getting a hearing on federation ideas here in England when [his] income was very small. Well it has been a heavy and anxious burden but to tell you the honest truth both these things have been so large a part of my life and have been undertaken with such concoction of sound purpose that I am not quite ashamed of the result...." Some of Parkin's creditors were: Carman £60; Raleigh £45; Milner £25; Arnold-Foster £165. There were also the unpaid fees at the girls' boarding school. In general, the debt was divided between old Fredericton friends and English supporters of imperial federation. All told, it amounted to between £800 and £900, or about a year and a half's income. It says something about his charm and his capacity for friendship that he could run up debts of that magnitude without any apparent assets, or any immediate prospects of repayment. Parkin had been passing out far more of those two sticks of wood with a snake round them than had been coming in.

Another day, another debt. Often he stayed with friends or governemnt officials. He got free travel from the CPR, but any costs that weren't covered by someone else were covered by Parkin. If he had a head for business, he might have been a wealthy man, but the more energy and determination he put into his quixotic cause, the more he was out of pocket. There is a story, possibly apocryphal, that someone once said to Parkin that if he had exploited all the gossip he heard from his contacts in high places, he might have been a wealthy man. "You know, that never occurred to me," he is supposed to have replied.

Milner's advice was that Parkin should not attempt to pay back any of his debt immediately. His income for the forthcoming year would be between £650 and £750. Over the year, Parkin should spend the bulk of his energies completing the Thring biography and engaging in his imperial federation activities. The idea of writing a Canadian history was, Milner felt, a poor one in economical terms, unwise because it postponed finishing Thring; it was also inconsistent with the spirit of the agreement that Parkin devote the bulk of his time promoting imperial federation, though Milner would not forbid it. He would leave it to Parkin to make that decision. Why not consolidate his debts by borrowing against a life insurance policy, Milner asked? If necessary, Milner was prepared to consider acting as guarantor. He asked Parkin to come to London and spend the night so they could discuss his finances more fully. Parkin, however, was also thinking of returning to Canada, which he thought might help him restore his financial equilibrium.

Parkin's financial position suffered further shocks. Early in November, Parkin went to the dentist. The dentist decided that Parkin needed seventeen teeth extracted, and performed the procedure then and there. Then, an apologetic letter from Carman arrived at the beginning of December, outlining possible arrangements for loan repayment, which suggests that Parkin had not managed to make immediate progress on his debt consolidation.

Just before Christmas, when the children were in the midst of their Christmas preparations, the Parkins' cook left, "in a most selfish and thoughtless way," Parkin wrote to Maude in Switzerland. "I think she must have been a little bit out of her head from the way she acted. Mother is rather tired out." Over Christmas, Annie's condition deteriorated. He wrote to Maude that she and the other girls were going to have to assume more responsibility for running the house and looking after their mother as they grew up. The strain of being left alone for long periods and finding her family chronically in debt was proving too much. To Parkin's credit, he belatedly responded to his family's financial crisis and to the toll it was taking on Annie. He finally and firmly rejected the possibility of writing a Canadian history, though there were other practical reasons for doing do.

On 25 January 1895, another blow fell. Parkin received a letter from Van Horne, arranging a meeting, but warning him that business still had not picked up enough for him to renew his offer. It seems that Parkin had decided that working for the CPR was the way out of his financial morass, but Van Horne no longer wanted him. As his friend George Foster put it: "The C.P.R. arrangement would have suited you to a tee and given you great opportunities of studying Canadian matters from your own point of view which course is the best possible preparation for public life."

Like Dickens' McCawber, though, Parkin never doubted that something eventually would turn up.

10

Home Again

In September 1892, Bishop Medley died. His widow thought that his successor neglected her shamefully. "I see by the newspapers that the Bishop has gone to England, but he neither inquires for me nor came in to say good bye! He shows but little gratitude to my dear husband's memory, who did so much for him." Parkin, on the other hand, wrote a generous memorial to his mentor, the man who changed his life. In return, Margaret Medley took care of a task that, oddly, hadn't been attended to earlier. She arranged for the engraving of the tombstones of the Parkins' daughters. "Would this do?" she wrote.

Muriel Thring
&
Annie Connell
Dearly beloved children of
George R. Parkin
&
Annie C.
In Peace

Home Again

Margaret Medley wrote to him from time to time about Fredericton matters, keeping him up to date about deaths and visitors. Carman also exchanged pleasant and playful letters with his former teacher, as did Charles Roberts. Through the Thring biography, he kept in close touch with that family, especially Marie.

In September 1894, Parkin decided that he couldn't afford three children at Toleure, and that he should send the intellectually more promising Grace instead of Alice. By the beginning of December, Parkin's health was again poor, either because of his teeth, as he suspected, or overwork, as was everyone else's opinion. In any event, he always bounced back. Now forty-nine, he told Maude his aim was to grow old gracefully. He became more attentive to Annie. They went skating and took up badminton. A deeply religious man, Parkin tried to supervise his children's moral upbringing. While she was away at school, Parkin counselled Maude to be careful among continental girls and continental influences. She should read from the Bible, he told her, and observe Sunday, and religious things generally. "You may be certain that there is nothing so good for the life and character as reverence for all that the Bible tells us to reverence—that we cannot try too hard to live simple Christian lives. And wherever one is placed in life there is some struggle involved in doing this."

He hadn't been in one place long enough since Fredericton to become involved in the life of a parish church, but he got elected church warden in Harwich, telling Maude that his stern eye would frighten the parishioners into doubling their contributions. He set about cleaning up the burial grounds, and jokingly said that he soon expected to see the police hauling off to prison members of the congregation who refused to pay the church rate that he and the other church warden had imposed to clear off the church's £400 debt, and to make improvements to the exterior that he pretended to Maude were being made for her arrival in the summer. Private pews were also abolished at the same time, eliminating the physical division between rich and poor.[1] Whether it was in the church or the state or the school, spiritual bonds were primary.

In February 1895, Parkin published the *Great Dominion*. It was a substantially revised version of the essays on Canada that originally appeared in the *Times*, supplemented by the additional research he had undertaken the previous year. His brother Watson had already read it by April and the copy Parkin had sent them was being passed around the members of the family. Charles G.D. Roberts wrote to him about the *Great Dominion*, saying that it revealed "a personality which...should win the utmost heights of its aspiration.... What endless force and impulse you have in you! Your work always has life, and the power of awakening life." And his other protégé, Carman, wrote: "To say it is worthy of you, is to give it the highest praise.... Your rub to the slow Maritime provinces for their over-devotion to politics rather than business was well deserved....Then too I smile to see the 'wild man of the cloister' knocked down once more into Goldwin-Smithereens."[2]

It is not surprising that a book subsidized by the Ministry of the Interior and the CPR reads in places like a sophisticated immigration brochure, though Parkin was sincere in the opinions he expressed. So, when Parkin wrote, "It is...fortunate that a powerful and progressive railway company, with immense interests at stake, is at hand to take a vigorous lead in promoting the settlement of the country," it is certain to have pleased Sir William Van Horne.[3]

Parkin particularly emphasized the importance of the settlement of the West. Writing just before Clifford Sifton, Laurier's minister of the interior, turned to Eastern Europe for immigrants to settle the West, Parkin praised the 10,000 Icelanders who had successfully settled in Manitoba and the Northwest.[4] Avoid, Parkin warned, the Latin races, like the Italians. They will, he suggested, naturally gravitate towards the warmer climate of the United States. Russian Jews too are a poor choice, since they are not inclined to agricultural pursuits.[5] Neither are Englishmen of a certain class. A public school provides good training for martial pursuits; its graduates make excellent soldiers for the empire. But they don't have the steady endurance of a workhorse necessary for the hard work on Canadian farm.[6]

However, the majority of the people, Parkin thought, were inward-looking, with an exclusiveness "in race and religion as was ever that of the Hebrews."[7] In Parkin's view, the average Quebecker was isolated, refused to learn English, and was dependent on his priest. He needed to learn English if he was going to join the progressive, industrial world.[8]

"One has no hesitation in discussing frankly this question of race inertia in Quebec. The most clear-sighted men of the province admit and deplore it."[9] Parkin hoped that the French-Canadians would see that their future lay within the dominion as a whole, but he was afraid that their excitable nature might get the better of them. "The average Frenchman of Canada can no more be calm than the Frenchman of France: under excitement he is apt to lose his head...."[10]

Canada's two solitudes had deep roots. Parkin, Smith, Dilke, and others never penetrated beneath the surface of French society. They were right, though not in the way they thought. Quebeckers were very much like the Jews. Like them, they believed that they had a historic mission—though in the case of Quebeckers, it was to preserve true French Catholicism and to resist the pressures of English-speaking Protestantism. They were a tiny minority in North America, and they were not prepared to risk that sacred and precious thing that it was their destiny to cherish, certainly not for material rewards.

The *Times* described Parkin's book as presenting an alternative vision of Canada. Smith says the country has "four great portions, hopelessly separated from each other by natural conditions." Parkin's picture was a nation "composed of four great portions, closely united and essential each to the well-being and development of the whole." The reviewer shared Parkin's sense of the ingratitude of the French-Canadians, who enjoyed the same benefits and freedoms "as that of the Chinese and other foreigners in Canada" and more, and still were not satisfied. Parkin's book was praised as a "well-written and thoroughly interesting" rejoinder to Smith's "brilliant pessimism." The *Canadian Gazette* also described Smith's work as "more brilliant and hopelessly pessimistic." It found Parkin's book "a sympathetic and yet scrupulously accurate and impartial survey." The *Morning Chronicle* declared it "interesting and valuable" for prospective emigrants to the Canadian Northwest. The *Daily Telegraph* acknowledged the gravity of the French-Canadian problem, but thought that the lack of immigrants from France combined with "the increase in the English-speaking population both by new births and immigration is likely to make that element vastly more preponderant in the future than it is in the present." Only the reviewer for the *Nation* noticed similarities between Parkin's ideas and Smith's.

This similarity, the reviewer thought, when combined with Parkin's inherent good temper, helped to explain why Parkin could maintain reasonably good relations with Smith when Denison could not:

> The chief of these are the fossilizing character of race isolation, the retarding effects of primitive modes of agriculture, the decadence of Quebec now the English have left it, the reckless and corrupt system of provincial administration, and the migration of masses of the people to the factories of New England. The sinister influence of French-Canadian parties in Dominion affairs, and the separatist aspirations of the French race in an English colony, Mr. Parkin appears to treat lightly, though he counsels moderation and liberality in both elements of the population and adds complacently that the English provinces can afford to be calm under all conditions.... Here, as in many other instances, Mr. Parkin, so far from disagreeing with Goldwin Smith, apparently agrees with him, and takes up parable against the things which Mr. Smith censures and has been deemed disloyal for censuring.

Smith himself described the book as an inflated panegyric. What good purpose is served, he asked, to say that Canada covers forty per cent of the British Empire or more than fifty per cent of North America, when Canada's population is only five million out of 350 million in the empire and one-sixteenth of North America's? In what sense, he asked, is Canada really part of the British Empire at all? It is not subject to British law, nor does it contribute to British defence. It levies duties on British goods and claims the right to make its own commercial treaties. There is an upper social class in Toronto that feels close to Great Britain, "but between the English-speaking people in general on the north and those on the south of the line there is no difference whatever. The two populations are in a state of actual fusion, save in the political and fiscal line. There is, therefore, nothing in the way of British peculiarities of character for the existing system to guard."

Parkin had made significant progress on his life of Thring over the winter. His arrangement with Macmillan anticipated a book about 400 to 450 pages in length. Parkin was to receive £100—a payment of £50 when the work was half done, the rest on completion, a miserable return on his labours. On 15 March 1895, Macmillan acknowledged that Parkin was more or less at the halfway stage and agreed to send the cheque. He also agreed that Parkin should have no fear about introducing the religious side of the great headmaster's life: "...the spiritual side of his character was so strong and so genuine that it will interest those who care for such biographies and they are many."

Working on Thring and Uppingham allowed Parkin to continue to develop as an educational theorist despite the seven-year interlude since his role as headmaster in Fredericton. His Canadian tours and writings had also made him a well-known figure. As a consequence, when two of Canada's leading educational institutions were in chaos, and looking for new leaders, Parkin was mentioned as a possible successor. One case was King's University, Nova Scotia, where the Rev. Dr. Charles Willets was in the midst of a bitter quarrel with the governors and subsequently resigned. The other was Upper Canada College, in Toronto, where the governors were trying to dismiss their principal, George Dickson, who most emphatically did not want to resign.[11]

Dickson, whom some people thought had come close to destroying the school, was trying to turn his dismissal into a partisan political issue, a not impossible move since there were close institutional ties between the provincial government and the school. However, the government backed the board of trustees, and Dickson was out by May 1895. Charles G.D. Roberts told Parkin that Willets was the unanimous choice of the trustees as the new principal at UCC, but that Sir Oliver Mowat, the Ontario premier, thought that Willets' appointment might prove politically controversial and vetoed it. That left the UCC position open and Parkin was considered a distinguished and acceptable alternative by the both trustees and the politicians.

John T. Small, an Old Boy who was also a member of the British Empire League (the Canadian successor of the Imperial Federation League), suggested Parkin's name. The formal offer was sent on 3 June. His salary was to start at £500, to be increased when the college finances were set in proper order. Parkin was also provided with a residence and utilities. Parkin had a long talk with Milner and decided to pursue the matter.

"Before I can give you an answer," Thring's biographer and disciple told the trustees, "I need the answer to some important questions.

"Has the Head Master a decisive voice in all matters of internal discipline, in the appointment or dismissal of subordinates, and in making expulsions, when he deems that necessary?

"Does the Head Master determine the course of study?

"In a school which takes the place of home for the majority of its pupils, I look upon a strong religious tone and a sufficient religious training as essential.

"Does the school provide for its own Sunday services? If so, will the Head Master have a free hand in dealing with these? If not, are there Churches of different denominations near enough for boys to attend?"

Parkin didn't forget the practical aspects of the position. Was the residence furnished? And by how much would his salary be increased if he turned the school into a success? "I ought to say that the salary you mention seems to me inadequate in view of what I believe a Head Master would have to do to make the College a success. The mistake, so common in Canada, has evidently been made, of thinking more of appliances than of the men who after all make the school."

Parkin rejected the idea that he might go to King's because he still did not want to preside over a denominational school. He had absorbed Thring's educational ideals by living with them all the time he was writing the biography. Now he wanted to put them into practice, adapt them to Canadian circumstances, avoiding the mistakes he made at Reka Dom. There had to be a strong religious spirit at the heart of the school, because the school took the place of home, but it had to be a generalized Christian teaching. How to achieve this in practice was a problem that had never been resolved even in the large English public schools. Planning to attempt it at Upper Canada, he needed assurances that he would have the trustees' support.

They needed someone in place for the next school year. Toward the end of July they were pressing him to give them a decision. On 22 July, Parkin went to London to meet again with Mowat, Small, and another trustee. He also visited Buckle and Moberley Bell in the *Times* office. They asked him to delay his decision for a few days. The next day he talked with Sir Donald Smith and Sir Charles Tupper and again with Milner. George Foster took the train to London, where he told Parkin that he believed the idea was, on balance, a good one. Foster thought that Parkin might be able to build a political base in Toronto, and "that in the course of five or ten years you might slip into the political arena," though he noted that "five or ten years, however, is a good deal of life taken from a man at your age." On 26 July, Parkin met with Moberley Bell who offered him an assignment as the *Times* South Africa correspondent, but not a permanent job. If he went to Canada, though, Moberley Bell thought he might be a stringer and file monthly columns. For once in his life, Parkin opted for certainty. On 1 August, he accepted the UCC post.

Parkin's British supporters were very generous. There was about £112 left in the Milner trust fund. Several of the contributor's told Milner that they did not want their donations returned and Milner thought that there would be about £100 remaining that Parkin could have. Parkin paid £20 towards the girls' school fees, £10 to A.H. Randolph, a merchant and banker he knew from Fredericton, £15 to Raleigh, and an undisclosed amount to Arnold-Foster and likely to other creditors as well. It appears that when he knew he had a secure source of income, he adopted Milner's plan, since he borrowed £600, probably against security of his life insurance.

Parkin got letters of congratulation from Bartholomew, who hoped that someday soon he would become minister of education so that he could get geography added to the school curriculum. Milner wrote, hoping they could have one last meeting before Parkin sailed; Macmillan, his publisher, sent his view that the appointment was in Parkin's best interest. Principal Grant was more cautious. "[T]he mismanagement of the Government and of the Board has reduced it [UCC] almost to extinction," he wrote ominously. "You cannot afford to fail. You will therefore succeed, and you can do a great work for Canada in this...restricted sphere which you have chosen." Others didn't agree that Parkin had chosen a restricted sphere. Another friend wrote encouragingly that Parkin now had an important position where he could "influence the future and mould the thoughts of a new generation." The fact that someone who had stood so strongly for imperial unity was chosen was a sign of the times, he thought. Lord Thring, Edward's seventy-seven-year-old brother, thought that Parkin might have decided to leave England just when the cause was on the upswing.

August 10/95

Dear Parkin,
I am very glad to see in the Times **of Thursday that you have been appointed Principal of Upper Canada College at Toronto. I have no doubt that your ambitious soul is somewhat cast down at subsiding into a quiet life however great the post... "Big England" and "Imperial Federation" are sure to loom large on the programme of our present rulers...**
Ever Yours,
Thring

There had been an election in the summer of 1895. Lord Rosebery became Liberal prime pinister in March 1894, but after a desultory and ineffective year in office, handed power to Lord Salisbury, leader of the Conservative opposition. This period, in effect, marked the end of Rosebery as a major political figure. James Bryce ran again and won the Scottish seat that had for a while been held before Parkin as a temptation. The Conservatives and Liberal Unionists, Joseph Chamberlain's political group, formed the government with a considerably increased majority. Parkin's friend, Sir Harry Wilson, became private secretary to Chamberlain at the colonial office, and wrote: "I know you will understand what a congenial post it will be to me, and I only hope I shall be able to turn the opportunity to good account for the furtherance of our cause. I can see already what sound views my chief has formed on the question and I shall look to you to let me have the benefit of any new ideas of your own. I owe a great deal to you, and to Loring, as I told him yesterday, & never shall be sufficiently grateful that my energies have been turned by these better(?) means into their practical channel." Milner received a knighthood from the new government as a mark of favour, and in 1897 was given the momentous appointment as high commissioner to South Africa. Had Parkin taken the *Times'* offer his life would certainly have become even more intricately involved with Milner's.

Lord Thring was wrong. Parkin returned to Canada quite happily. "[H]ere it was really a choice between a Canadian as against an Empire sphere of work. I have no doubt about the decision being a right one. To be called back to Canada to carry on an important bit of work will not diminish one's weight in other parts of the Empire. And perhaps the day may come again when one will want and will have an opportunity to say his say." Rosebery made part of that Canadian work very specific: "I cannot doubt that you are right in your resolution, though we cannot but be sorry to lose you. You have done a great work here.... But it may well be that you have a not less important task in Canada, if only to keep an eye on Goldwin Smith!"

11

Principal Parkin

------♦------

From the opening till the Xmas holidays almost every hour and every thought has been spent upon the school. I now feel that people are beginning to have confidence in this place. God has blessed us in many ways, and we should begin the New Year with stronger resolutions to serve Him faithfully. May I have sound judgement to carry on with work wisely. May I be kept simple and humble and true. And may God bless my dear ones through this coming year.

PARKIN'S DIARY
New Years Eve 1895, Upper Canada College

When Parkin left Fredericton seven year earlier to become the St. Paul of imperial federation, he was an obscure New Brunswick schoolmaster. Now there was a grain of truth in Stephen Leacock's arch response to William Grant's exasperated complaint: "Has he no friends below the rank of Viscount?" "Plenty, back on the farm." Not everyone was as critical. A Montreal reporter described Parkin with admiration as "a writer of world-wide fame." Parkin was the author of several books,

Principal Parkin

with another on the way, the creator of a well-known map, a journalist whose work was respected by the editor of the *Times* and, most important, a natural orator, one of the most compelling of his era, in an age when television did not exist and an hour-long speech, even on politics, was considered a good evening's entertainment. Now almost fifty, a tall, spare man with a scholarly countenance, Parkin stood out in a crowd. Usually dressed in plain grey and black, his top hat tilted slightly to the back of his head, he looked very much the English professional man.

To celebrate Parkin's arrival in Toronto, the treasurer of the National Club wrote to invite Parkin, as someone who had worked for the patriotic cause, to a banquet in his honour on assuming the principalship. Before he had a chance to respond, Colonel Denison stepped in and, "as next senior officer," took command, making the arrangement for him. Parkin would stay with Denison, who invited the trustees for dinner to meet him. "I thought it would be a pleasanter way for you to meet the Board for the first time than to be paraded for inspection at a Board meeting in military style. I hope this will be satisfactory to you." He also accepted the invitation of the National Club on Parkin's behalf, and agreed that he'd give an after dinner speech so that the newspapers could report his general philosophy of education. And that took care of that.

The relationship between Parkin's educational and political activities during this period was intimate on many levels. Many of the people on whom he relied to rebuild the school were also his political associates. Yet his educational ideals and his political ideals were different. They were both ideals; they were both dedicated to making the world a better and nobler place through the improvement of spiritual bonds. And Parkin never held back about telling his schoolboys about the glorious civilizing mission of the English-speaking peoples. But Parkin's strictly political activities overlapped only tangentially with his attempts to rebuild Upper Canada College. To keep the focus clear, this chapter deals with his educational reforms, while the next two cover his political activities in the same period. Don't think that Parkin was doing nothing more than quietly refounding UCC between 1895 and 1902. Politically, he was creating quite a ruckus.

Upper Canada College was almost seventy years old when Parkin assumed control. Founded in 1829 by Sir John Colbourne, it had been a successful institution until Egerton Ryerson's long campaign for educational reform culminated in the School Act of 1871. Ryerson believed that education should be universal and compulsory. The creation of a strong public school sector weakened UCC, a private, fee-based school. It seemed an increasingly irrelevant, largely Anglican, institution. In 1887, the provincial government proposed to abolish it, sell its land, and use the proceeds to support the province's secular university in Toronto. The school's Old Boys worked out a compromise, which led to the province and the school splitting the endowment.[1] In 1891, UCC moved north of the city to an area known as Deer Park, about two miles beyond the built-up limits of Toronto. There were large grounds around the school. Avenue Road led directly to the city from the main entrance gates. There were only two houses within half a mile.

The school cost $500,000 and consisted of one large brick building, five storeys high, 274 feet across with a prominent central tower, creating, Parkin thought, a striking effect on an excellent site, with classrooms, sleeping rooms, great hall, all the appliances, such as baths, laboratory, laundry superior to those in an English school. Some of these facilities, he wrote Milner, were very noble and useful pedagogically; others, from an educational point of view, were absolute folly.

The headmaster's house occupied three floors in the south-east corner. It had a typically Victorian drawing room, a large hall with an imposing staircase leading up to the bedrooms, and a spacious study, where each year the family had a Christmas tree decorated with candies and candles. Upstairs there was a day and a night nursery. Every day began with the family and the domestic staff gathered in the dining room. Parkin read a short passage from the Bible, then everyone knelt at the dining room chairs to say the Lord's Prayer and the General Confession from the Anglican Book of Common Prayer, followed by another short prayer.

Parkin could have been forgiven if the last prayer was occasionally for the financial health of the school. Rather than rescuing the school, the move to Deer Park was rapidly destroying it. In the first three years, its operating deficits consumed half of the endowment. The interest on the remainder barely covered the pensions to faculty and maintenance on the facilities. Student fees had to provide for salaries and operating costs such as food and the other necessities in a boarding school, and enrolment was steadily declining from 300 in the 1870s to 120 in 1895. The trustees fired the principal and all the staff, some of whom they hired back at reduced salaries, abolished scholarships, and cut costs. The deficit stood at $16,000. At that point they turned to Parkin.[2]

Parkin's strategy for the running of the school was outlined in a speech he gave on Prize Day, a day that brought together parents, teachers, and trustees.[3] Parkin ensured that Judge John Kingsmill, chairman of the trustees, was present, for this was the new principal's opportunity to lay out his vision for the school. It was partly Reka Dom, but mostly Thring. It is striking how modern his address was. There were many reasons why modern society needed boarding schools, Parkin said. Some fathers travelled on business. Other families lived in isolated communities. Some children were orphans. But all too often, Parkin argued in his Britannic idealistic way, boarding schools were needed for a different reason. How, for instance, could the homes of the rich, with their luxury, their environment of servants, their social excitements and distractions, be a suitable place for steady discipline and the simple life demanded by the young? Life on a farm might be challenging, Parkin said, as he himself knew, but a lad on a quiet Canadian farm had an infinite advantage over another who has to fight against the temptations and distractions of a rich home, say in Toronto or Montreal. What could be done so that these scions of the rich did not grow to be decadent men unworthy of their country? They needed a spartan and egalitarian life that they could never achieve in their comfortable homes. Their character had to be moulded so that they could become the solid leaders that would be so badly needed in an age of democracy. The wealthy would pay to send their sons to a school which would inoculate them against the wealth of their parents.

Upper Canada College under Parkin would have three goals: produce Christian gentlemen; set the standard for academic excellence for secondary education in Canada; and, the one that made it most like Uppingham, give adequate training to each boy according to his capacity, dealing with the slow and weak, and even with the indifferent, as carefully and intelligently as with the clever and brilliant. It would not foster prize winners and neglect ordinary, or even stupid, boys. A school that did that was neither honest nor true to its vocation.[4]

How was this goal to be achieved? Parkin needed a music teacher, manual training, a good library, and a reading room. His teachers could no longer be poorly paid. He had to compete with the best English public schools. He appealed to the Old Boys to raise between three and four thousand dollars a year with the ultimate aim that UCC cut its ties completely from government. Parkin circulated his address widely. It was well received by the newspapers and by the trustees, who were doubtless glad that someone seemed to have a plan to get out of the morass. Privately, Parkin wasn't entirely sure that it was him. It was his first really big job of administration and he didn't know where to begin, he confided to Milner; it was consuming all his time and energy. Milner returned a comforting reply. At the beginning, the great administrator counselled, "you are probably quite right to bring your whole might to bear upon this big machine which you have to drive until you have once got it to start. When it is started, & has got some momentum, it should not be necessary for you personally to spend so much energy on it....I firmly believe, myself, that you will make the thing a very great success. I do not think 'administration', such as you describe, will prove a real difficulty to you, when once you turn your mind to it, though it may be more or less a new subject." In spite of Milner's friendly reassurance, the question of whether or not Parkin could actually make it as an administrator remained to be decided. On the basis of his private finances, he might not be the first person one might choose.

Friends were concerned about Parkin's inability to relax. Milner told him: "My only fear is that you will push more energy into the thing than it absolutely requires—waste strength in fact." Charles G.D. Roberts said much the same. "I hope you like your new undertaking, and that you won't go using yourself up with your too strenuous devotion to the boys. That is what I dread for you, in a position where you will be so continuously in contact with your work."[5]

At the beginning of January 1896 Parkin could write in his diary that there were seven new boys in the house and six new day boys, and progress had been made with the endowment fund. The morale of the masters was improving as they saw hope for the future. By 14 January, the number of boarders had increased to twelve, a seventeen per cent increase over September. Mr. Brock and Mr. Beatty donated $1000 and there were several donations of $500. Parkin also received the substantial contribution of £100 from his English imperial federation colleague Lord Brassey, who made his donation with the hope that it might encourage Canadians to help.

In April, Parkin began one of his more interesting projects. He regularly kept a vegetable garden, with a lot of tomatoes, and chickens—useful in itself and a reminder of his days on the farm. Then he began the planting of an alley of trees from the college down to the gates. This was the first of a series of Arbor Days. Parkin declared a half-holiday (half a day), the boys collected sixty dollars, and they planted three hundred trees and shrubs.[6] Parkin also built an attractive lodge at the end of the college lane, which, combined with the trees, gave a very pleasing approach to visitors. On 25 February 1896, the boys had enjoyed another "half-hol" with no tree planting, in celebration of the birth of their principal's son, George Raleigh, named after Parkin's Oxford and imperial federation friend, Thomas Raleigh. The college continued to prosper. The number of boarders increased, but there were difficulties attracting day boys, since the school was too far away from the city. The Belt Line railway, which had run close to the college grounds, was defunct, and the closest streetcar line was at Dupont, a mile away.[7] Another perennial threat to the college was sickness—a problem that had also threatened Uppingham. At Uppingham, Thring had had to resolve more than his share of practical problems, but he had once faced a mortal crisis that threatened to kill first his pupils, then his school. That event was so pivotal that Parkin opened volume two of his biography with the title "The Valley of the Shadow of Death." Bringing together boys always runs the risk of epidemic illness, though Uppingham's location was an unusually healthy one. Thring had been prudent in his sanitation arrangements, but the town had not; the drainage and the water supply was inadequate. Cases of scarlet fever broke out in the town early one February and by the middle of the month the situation worsened.

The situation abated but in October two of the boys fell dangerously ill. "Thou didst turn thy face from me and I was troubled," Thring wrote in his diary. Some of the parents began to panic and wanted to withdraw their children from the school. Thring's first impulse was to resist and stay to fight the disease. He spoke of "the cowardly panic" and of "deserters." On 15 October deaths began. Thring was reluctant to let the boys depart for fear of spreading the disease. He called in sanitary engineers to see if they could resolve the problem. The town refused to accept responsibility and blamed Thring. When the boys returned after Christmas, much worse happened. One of the boys showed symptoms of typhoid. Thring tried mechanical solutions, such as flushing the sewers, but these yielded little by way of results. The destruction of the school seemed imminent. Thring acted with the decisiveness for which he was renowned. He moved the boys away from the danger. He rented a hotel in Borth, North Wales, and reconvened the school there until the sanitary conditions at Uppingham could be addressed.[8] He saved the boys under his trust, and the school.

Parkin learned from Thring's experience that an epidemic must be avoided at all cost. He made it one of his priorities to raise funds to build a hospital on the college grounds and hire a resident doctor and nurse.[9] He privately raised five thousand dollars to which the trustees added another five hundred The large brick building, completed in 1898, was able to isolate boys who showed symptoms of the contagious diseases that might spread through the school and cause panic among the parents. He also fitted the school with fire escapes and ladders and hired a night watchman, although with his long experience of school boys he wasn't sure that the fire escapes weren't a mixed blessing and that the night watchman didn't have to be equally alert about youngsters sneaking out as about adults breaking in.[10] He also replaced the oil lamps with electricity and bought new linen and dishes for the dining hall.

Providing for the safety and security of the students' bodies was one thing. Tending their souls was central to Parkin's vision. Each boy had to attend the church of his choice whether he chose to or not. Parkin's spiritual mission met resistance from some of his staff members, for not all of them shared Parkin's vision of the school, and some of them resisted his idea that it was their responsibility to take an active role in Christian education of their students.[11] "Can I be true to any one's feelings and principles and lead such men?" he asked himself. It wasn't, he reflected, that they were bad people. On the contrary. "Good fellows they are too, and in their crude way trying to be serious—but they little saw the impossible situation they create from their attitude. I hope I am serious when I say that I see no point in working in forming out one's life here—if it be not for the Christian ideal. To what will this day's revelations lead one? I know not, but I pray to something higher and better. I feel as if the atmosphere had been cleared around us—as if I saw my way and when all was vapours and mist."

Parkin himself usually took charge of the Sunday evening sessions, which sought to create citizens for the empire. He taught his charges about the greatness of the empire, the majesty of the Queen, the tales of British daring on land and sea, things that ennobled the spirit and created a strong national feeling, for he felt that a deep national loyalty seemed to be one of the most powerful forces which God used to carry out his great purposes in the world. As his colleague William Grant said, Parkin never managed to keep God, Oxford, and the empire wholly separated.[12] Sometimes Parkin's addresses rambled and left the boys more mystified than enlightened. On one occasion Parkin kept the boys in chapel a long time, while the duty-master was waiting impatiently for them in another part of the school. When the boys finally emerged the following dialogue ensued:

Master: Why didn't you come straight from prayers?
Boy: Please, sir, we did.
What kept you so long then?
Please, sir, the Principal was speaking to us.
Oh, indeed, what about?
Please, sir, I don't know.
You don't know?
No, sir; please, sir, he didn't tell us.

Parkin, who as a visiting speaker so much impressed boys at others schools, brought in a variety of people to address UCC. George Monro Grant of Queen's; the Reverend Dyson Hague, a well-known clergyman and author; the Reverend Louis Jordan; Professor J.F. McCurdy of the Oriental language department at the University of Toronto; a military historian from Royal Military College; a professor of architecture from McGill; R.F. Stupart, who had lived with the Inuit; and Parkin himself spoke about his trip around the world.[13] Parkin also hired a drill instructor from Stanley Barracks once or twice a week to train the college rifle corps. He created a school cap with the college crest for boarders (optional for day boys) and a hat band, also with the college crest, for use on summer hats. It was clear UCC was not a school that would centre around sport. The "animal courage and brutal spirit of a prize fighter" counted for nothing, in Parkin's view. If boys played football or hockey or cricket, or even if they excelled in Latin or mathematics, the one thing needful was "love for your kindred or your fellow men." Sports and academic excellence were good; being of pure mind was better.

By 1899, he had increased fees by twenty-five per cent and the number of students again reached three hundred. There were 140 boarders, twice the number as when Parkin came. Instead of a small and demoralized staff of teachers, he had fourteen university graduates. Of the masters, three are particularly worthy of note for the role they played in Parkin's life.

William Grant was the son of Parkin's old friend Principal George Grant of Queen's. Willy made contact when he was studying Greats (Classics) at Oxford, where he is reputed to be the first Canadian to win first-class honours, a very high distinction. G.M. Grant wrote on behalf of his son who was about to finish his degree. He had the opportunity of a temporary job at Queen's, but the principal would rather he had some teaching experience before hiring him. William Grant became the first head of history and geography.[14]

Edward Peacock, who taught English for seven years, proved to have an uncanny knack for the financial world. He left teaching to join Dominion Securities, a firm in Toronto. From there he rose to become a director of the Bank of England and later of Baring Brothers, a bank. He became a wealthy man and received a knighthood in 1934.

Although Stephen Leacock became well-known as humorist, his university training was in languages and literatures. These subjects he taught at UCC for nine years, before he left to take a doctorate in political economy, after which he took a position at McGill University in Montreal. Money was certainly a problem at UCC, but lack of it did not affect Leacock's wit. Once a colleague taunted Leacock to draft a let-

Principal Parkin

ter about his salary to the governors. Leacock wrote: "Unless you can see your way to increasing my stipend immediately, I shall reluctantly be forced to—" and then the next page began "—continue working for the same figure." When Parkin said to him, "Leacock, I wish I could break this pernicious habit of smoking and swearing in the school," Leacock replied, "I know it's a difficult habit to break oneself of, Dr. Parkin, but if you will put all your energies into breaking yourself of it, I am sure that grace will be given you." Parkin had every reason to be proud of the group of teachers he assembled out of the wreckage of 1895.[15]

Parkin and his staff didn't always see eye to eye on how to run the school. Early in June 1896, for example, a lad named Franchot struck one of the masters. Parkin telegraphed his father and they agreed that the boy would be suspended for six months rather than expelled. Many of the masters vigorously opposed Parkin's decision. However, Parkin was not opposed to expulsion when he thought the case demanded it, and he was selective in those students he accepted. The boarding school at UCC was not going to become a dumping ground for the problem children of Ontario's upper classes.

Like most other private schools of its day, UCC enforced its discipline by caning, fines, and depriving students of privileges.[16] The boys were also exhorted. Colonel Alexander Dunn, a graduate of the school, won a Victoria Cross for the courage he showed during the famous Charge of the Light Brigade during the Crimean War. Parkin persuaded Dunn's family to donate the medal and his sword to the school and the relics were brought out on high occasions.[17]

Parkin's constant worry was money. He had to persuade all the stakeholders—government, trustees, the Old Boys, and the parents—that he needed it, and he had to persuade them to give it. On balance, he was generally successfully. To make the school a real success he had to reach beyond UCC's immediate circle into the broader community. Parkin put ads in the newspapers asking the public for $7000 to $10,000 a year.

Parkin had no experience in delegating authority. His school in Fredericton was small and he had operated largely independently in his imperial federation activities. His workload was beginning to take a toll on himself and on Annie. His friends had warned that he was exhausting himself. Parkin wrote in his diary at the beginning of 1897 that the old year had closed with great weariness for Annie and himself. Never had their strength been lower or their courage weaker, he noted. They were overworked and under great stress, and he was not sure that he could succeed in the work he had undertaken. Parkin was too dedicated to just abandon his current responsibilities and move on, but he needed an adequate income to live on, and adequate resources to do a minimally satisfactory job. Although he cut down as much as he could on non-academic activities at the school, he believed that some were necessary. He sponsored and paid for a dance out of his own pocket at a cost of $60, more than a week's salary.

These strains were creating a crisis in his personal life. He had made the major career decisions, but Annie, twelve years his junior, remained emotionally his former pupil. He had a personality that charmed almost everyone he met, and he was devoted to a cause in which she shared. In the years she had been married to Parkin, she had often been left penniless, alone, and in debt, looking after the children. At Upper Canada College, Parkin now expected her to slip seamlessly into the role as his hostess. It was not that easy for her. He had spent the past twenty years in the presence of the rich and famous, while she was a housewife. Her daughters might have been sent to Switzerland to learn foreign languages, but she was just Annie Parkin, a woman whose life had largely been restricted to New Brunsick, a small seaside town in England, and to hearing tales of her husband's adventures. She was not ready to move into the heart of smart society.

Thring's sister, whom the Parkin family called "Aunt" Anna, wrote to Parkin, expressing her concerns about Annie two years after they arrived at UCC. "I am so grieved to hear that dearest Annie is still far from strong but on the other hand I am not surprised at it. I must confess, the strain of her life in England was, I always feared at the time, too great and long for her and for that reason...I thought and hoped that the life in her own country would be less hard, less of a strain and more comfortable for her. I am greatly troubled that that is not the case as yet but I do hope, as your Trustees are so satisfied with your work, they will raise your salary soon now, so that the money cares will no longer be so pressing on you and Annie." By late 1897, Annie's nervous condition had deteriorated. In January 1898, she left Toronto for

Fredericton and stayed with Margaret Medley. Mrs. Medley reported that Annie had responded well to rest and seemed quiet and cheerful. Her sleep and appetite were more or less normal "but more than the rest here is needed to get rid of the nervous weakness which from time to time overtakes her." After consultation with the local doctor and Mary Pearson, Parkin's niece and a trained nurse, it was decided that Annie should set out as soon as possible for New York for one of the hospitals that treated nervous illnesses.

The New York specialist was hopeful. Annie's general health was good, and, as Medley wrote to Parkin, he "has put a definite time before her, and she accepts it, and will submit to the prolonged discipline with the hope of permanent restoration," though it might be years before she fully recovered. "I am thankful for what you say about purposing to live as quietly as possible on her return," Margaret Medley wrote to Parkin. "She needs great care and is worthy of all the care and expense which must now be incurred." In March, Thomas Raleigh wrote to commiserate that Annie's illness was more serious than first thought, and urged him to "see that she is not sacrificed to the College, however important the College may be."

In May, Parkin had a chance at a job with higher pay and few demands on his wife. Van Horne finally offered him a position with the CPR at a very generous salary of $8000–$9000, "with very considerable possibilities beyond this." In addition, Parkin would be allowed to continue with his freelance work. He found the temptation "very considerable." On the other hand, he felt that he was doing good work. The school was prospering and donations were up, "chiefly on the ground that I am in charge here." The position was also providing him a platform from which to speak. "In my own opinion there is scarcely any better in Canada." "The labourer is worthy of his hire, & a man like you, though he may never be rich, ought not to be poor. The community owes you a sufficient maintenance, & both for your sake & that of your family you are bound to take it, wherever you can honourably get it." Milner's observation was that a soldier of the empire like Parkin should pursue the higher career as long as the salary was sufficient. A British friend, Vaughan Morgan, gave Parkin similar advice, though like Milner he seemed to be giving Parkin the advice he wanted to hear. "No doubt the C.P.R. offer is an excellent one but I say resist the temptation, and as years go on, if you keep your health and do not overdo yourself, your financial position should be fairly good." Arnold-Foster, an English friend from the imperial federation movement days, also advised staying with Upper Canada, though he described the CPR as "better pay, and in some ways the more attractive post." It had, he thought, fewer long-term prospects. So Parkin stayed where he was. There is no evidence in Parkin's correspondence or diary to show that Annie's well-being played any part in his decision.

By November 1898, Parkin had come to the conclusion that he was in a position to negotiate a better salary from UCC. Over the past three years, his expenditures had, in total, he contended, exceeded his income by $2300, and he was not prepared to continue to incur debt for the college as he had for imperial federation. These expenditures, in his view, were not frivolous, but essential. He had done what he thought was necessary, but the costs to himself and to Annie's health had been high. His salary already had increased from its initial $2500 to $4000. Parkin now demanded $5000, of which $4000 would come from the trustees and $1000 from the Old Boys' Association, a sum he reached in 1900.

By 1899, pressure on the school's physical facilities was growing. Parkin had never liked the arrangement of one large building. Uppingham was intentionally arranged around a number of small houses, each with its own master, and Parkin wanted, as much as was possible with the existing physical plant, to approach that model. One advantage of this decentralized model, he argued, was that the quasi-autonomy of the house system would ensure that an ineffective principal could not destroy the school. In his Prize Day speech that year Parkin addressed the fact that he had met with little success in raising funds from the public and again offered his resignation if more public support was not forthcoming. He submitted a plan to the trustees.[18]

Parkin's vision for UCC was a school with 350 boarders and no day boys. The existing building would become the classroom block, and satellite buildings would be created as houses for boys and masters, creating a strong sense of community. Within five years, Parkin envisaged, UCC would become a great public school on the English model. He proposed that the principal's salary be set at $6000, but his most striking recommendation was that there be a new board of governors, to consist entirely of Old Boys and ex officio members. Henceforth, Parkin hoped, UCC would be completely independent of government control; that meant that it would also have to be financially independent.[19]

Parkin met with the premier on 17 November 1899, and he received an enthusiastic note from Van Horne promising a contribution "because I think you are going the right way towards making UC College the most successful educational institution in the country and that you will make it an object lesson for McGill...." By early 1900 enough progress had been made that the governor-general, Lord Minto, was invited to lay the cornerstone for a new building meant for sixty resident and forty day students. "By building these homes; by decreasing the number of pupils in our main college building; by gradually limiting the number of day boys; by striving in every way to make the surroundings of school life here beautiful, healthful, and efficient; by aiming to make it the home of Christian teaching, we believe that we shall be building up on sound lines an institution which may have a profound influence on the future of the country. Upper Canada College has had a past of which we are proud, and especially through the patriotic services which her Old Boys have rendered to Canada and the Empire."[20]

A committee headed by A.R. Creelman drew up lists of suggestions for the future of the school that Parkin forwarded to the minister of education. The centrepiece was a proposal for an endowment of $100,000, of which the province would provide half on the condition that UCC raise the other half by 1 October 1900. The bill was introduced in April and Parkin raised fifty per cent of his required share of the money; then he went to Europe for the summer. This absence was injudicious and, on his return, Principal Grant, whose own fund-raising skills were legendary, told him that he had to devote himself to raising the money, because a failure would be ignominious. He squeaked in just before the deadline. Grant told him frankly that he had not thought that he would make it, and had he failed, he would have had to resign. However, his success was greater than it might have been. Parkin raised $50,496 from 185 donors. The largest donation was $2,500, and the average about $275.[21] Grant commented: "Now that you have succeeded, I can tell you that you have done a [greater?]

work than you imagined. Now that you have proved that you can do without the rich man, they will come to you."

Goldwin Smith was appalled by the transfer of the school entirely into private hands. There was no opposition to the reform in the legislature, but the newspaper *Farmers' Sun*, one of Smith's outlets, expressed outrage. First, UCC had been entrusted to the leading spokesman for the new imperialism. Now, the government had given it away to be used as a propaganda vehicle for the Tory party and the Anglican Church.[22] Frank Arnoldi, an early historian of the college, defended the change in status on the grounds that the absence of public funding encouraged private donations, and the college was able to choose teachers and books and establish curricula superior to the public system.[23]

Parkin continued to work himself to the point of exhaustion. As he wrote to his daughter Maude, who was studying at McGill: "This month I have more to get through than in any month I remember for a long while: a chapter of a book, two Encyclopaedia articles, a *Times* column or two, my Prize day address, a Saint Andrew's Cross mass meeting in Massey Hall, my Sunday evening talks to the boys and so on, to say nothing of the school—endowments, plans for buildings and a probable visit to Ottawa." In Ottawa he was to hold one of his regular political discussions with the governor-general.

When Parkin arrived in Ottawa in the first week of January 1901, he found the celebrated twenty-six-year-old war hero, MP, and journalist Winston Churchill as one of his fellow guests at Government House, along with Ian Malcolm, another British MP, and Pamela Plowden, a friend of the governor-general, recently arrived from England. At breakfast on Sunday, Churchill was absent, and Miss Plowden offered a prize if anyone could make him talk or think of anything but himself for more than five minutes. After lunch, Parkin claimed success, which led to a slight row between the two. Parkin found Churchill pleasant, but brash, and doubted that he would ever be a success. As a fellow journalist, Parkin also resented the fact that Churchill got twenty-five cents a word for his journalism, far more than Parkin was paid. He hated to erase anything he wrote, Churchill had joked, because each word was worth so much.

There was drama that weekend. Winston proposed to Pamela and

Principal Parkin

had been refused. Parkin, as he so often did, had become the confidant of someone after a brief acquaintance. It appears that Plowden wrote him a letter which contained a penetrating analysis of Churchill's character. He was too impetuous, too much of an adventurer, too certain of himself to have solid judgment. In short, she thought that she could do better. Churchill thought differently about her. "[S]he is the only woman I could ever lively happily with," Churchill wrote to his mother from Ottawa.[24] He had met her at the age of twenty-one when he was a serving officer in India and she was the daughter of the governor of Bengal.

All of Parkin's hard work paid off, however. His total remuneration (salary plus accommodation) was increased to about $7250 or £1450, a considerable improvement over the approximately £600 he was earning when he left England, although his masters were less well paid than their counterparts in the public school system. Parkin's fundraising efforts and sound financial management allowed him to not only raise their salaries, but also turn the school's deficit into a modest surplus.

Parkin's professional success had been considerable. Six years of incessant work at the school, combined with his political activities, had made Parkin into a major force in Canadian public life. However, his personal life was clearly not a success. Annie's nerves had not recovered after her hospital stay in New York, and the demands on her had not diminished. At the beginning of the autumn term 1901, she made a decision she knew she had to make to save herself from total collapse: She packed her bags, took the younger children, and walked out, an extraordinary action for a woman in 1901 and one that was still talked about in hushed tones in the family decades later. She had good reason. Although Parkin's salary had steadily improved, the family remained in debt. She had five children, including young Raleigh, but she was expected to act as Lady Matron of the school and entertain Parkin's endless run of political associates and school benefactors, an activity she despised, in a city where she had no roots. She loved her husband, but she could no longer face life as the wife of the principal of Upper Canada College.

With Grace, Marjorie, and Raleigh, she sailed back to England and took a house in the West Kensington district of London, where she immediately experienced a sense of freedom she hadn't known for years. "G[race]. and I have been enjoying [Rudyard Kipling's] *Kim* so much. Get it. I quite feel at times like Kim, and feel now the sense of freedom he longed for. He is longing after school to get 'on the Road.' Read it and you will see what I mean. I don't mean of course getting away from you, but the other things, visits and teas and endless people...." Alice, who had been trained in household management after she left Toleure, took over her mother's role at the school.

Despite Annie's departure, Parkin continued to devote himself to his work. He was still not satisfied that the school was moulded into its proper form. It needed a preparatory school, where the young boys could be better looked after and kept separate from the bullying and the vices of older boys. The board had formally called for tenders for the construction of a preparatory school in April 1901, and the cornerstone had been laid in June. Since the building was not ready for the fall intake, however, Parkin took seven or eight of the smallest boys into his own residence so that they could have "all the comforts and advantages of home life, and the personal care which is so important in the management of boys of tender years away from their parents." Alice looked after them until the prep school was completed. Parkin pried another ten thousand dollars from the board to buy ten acres north of the school and another ten acres to the west in anticipation of future growth, and spoke of a further ten thousand for the construction of a gymnasium and a recreation room.[25] He also dreamed that one day the school would have a chapel.[26] In the summer of 1902 he planned a tour of the country to explore the possibility of establishing a nation-wide system of prep schools, which would send their students to UCC before they entered university. He saw this as an effort to create a homogenous national political sentiment.[27]

Although his wife and younger children were now gone, Parkin still travelled to the Maritimes to visit his brothers and sisters, and, at the beginning of the new century, seemed entirely responsible for them. Over Christmas 1901, he went for a sad visit. His sister Alice was failing, her mind "quite gone." He arranged for her to be put in an asylum. She died unexpectedly at the end of January. He telegraphed instructions for her burial to the institution in Saint John and to his brother Watson, and gave instructions for her to be laid to rest near the family home in Salisbury. "What a pathos there is about all life," he reflected. Still, in spite of the fact that his lumbago was giving him problems, he came back from his Christmas holidays "much refreshed." In March, Annie's Uncle Fred died suddenly of pneumonia, but Parkin was so worried about his wife's emotional fragility that he withheld the news.

Although he was severely overworked, Parkin resisted when the board urged him to get assistance in the form of a vice-principal.[28] This decision was unfortunate because, as the board likely knew, an administrative second-in-command was just what he needed. William Grant's mature criticism of Parkin as an administrator, written when he himself was principal of UCC, pictured him as weak and vacillating, unwilling to offend, even over small matters such as the school caps. Meetings would stretch on for hours and never reach a conclusion. Parkin lived and thought at the level of his national ideal. "He gave inspiring pep talks, to vision out a great scheme in his mind, to feel the glow of it, and then to leave us poor underpaid devils to do the drudgery."[29] His great crisis as principal came toward the end of his tenure in 1902, when it was necessary to appoint a headmaster for the prep school. Parkin had great difficulty making up his mind, but appears to have offered it to Edward Peacock. The board objected, and Parkin yielded to the pressure. Peacock resigned and was joined by William Grant and four other masters.[30] The loss of a third of the teaching staff was a very serious blow, though the school slowly recovered.

In the opinion of UCC historian Richard Howard, "Parkin's impact on Upper Canada College was profound. He arrived when the College was on the brink of disaster and left it with enlarged and beautiful grounds, several new buildings, sound finances, a dynamic games program, increased enrolment, and an enhanced reputation."[31] Howard especially praised Parkin's creation of a dynamic Old Boys' Association, which raised an endowment and assumed effective government of the school.[32]

Parkin's failures were more difficult to measure. Parkin would have preferred to have more boys proceed to university studies, rather than to go into business. He also wanted to address the quality of teaching in the province, which he believed had declined. Previously, those who had entered the teaching profession were clergy, moved by religious motives, and thus teaching attracted some of the best minds. Now, Parkin felt, teaching was secularized and poorly paid, so the brightest people went where the money was. In the best English public schools, it was possible to get a good education because the headmasters and the teachers were paid on par with other professionals. Parkin had hoped to achieve that at UCC, but failed.[33]

Parkin may have failed in the details, but he had finally brought his and Thring's vision of education to reality in Canada. In the opinion of Dr. Jim Power, who was principal of Upper Canada in 2006, Parkin's achievements were exceptional: "In challenging times, George Parkin launched initiatives that continue to benefit Upper Canada College students more than a century later, including establishing the first endowment to secure UCC's future. In addition, Parkin's creation of a designated Preparatory School planted the seed for the nurturing, exciting learning environment that UCC's younger students enjoy today."[34]

12

Canada's Imperial Mission

When Parkin returned to Canada in September 1895 to take control of Upper Canada College, he was as enthusiastic about the growth of imperial sentiment in his native country as he was about his new job as a schoolmaster. If there was political support for his appointment, there was also opposition. The *Weekly Sun* headed a story "Captured by a Party." Although UCC supporters were, it claimed, respectable men in their way, they were all prominent Tories; the school had been captured by a political party and was being used as a political seminary. This criticism counted for little to Parkin. The distinguished gathering at the National Club that welcomed him to Toronto toasted his brilliant career as "a teacher of boys and as a lecturer on Imperial Federation, and welcomed him as a public man, as a writer and as a man the want of whom we had felt and as a man for whom there was a place." These sentiments were widely shared. Glasses were raised to toast the educator, imperialist, and public man. The guests sang "He's a Jolly Good Fellow," and when Parkin rose, the cheering and applause were redoubled, and it was some time before he could speak. Those who had hired him, it seems, didn't think that the one calling precluded the other.

Imperial federation described a movement, however, not an ideology—and there were differences of opinion about many issues amongst supporters of the movement. The British branch of the Imperial Federation League, for instance, had collapsed, in part because of differences of opinion as to whether closer political, economic, or defence ties should be the primary aim of the movement. There were differences among the Canadian members too. G.M. Grant was perhaps the most nationalistic. According to his biographers, Frederick Hamilton and his son, William Grant, G.M. Grant "stood for the fullest and most complete national independence, with the responsibilities and dangers therein implied." Although he was alive to the glories of his British heritage, he was not naïve about the policies of English statecraft. "To the faults of England and of the English he was not blind. He saw the superciliousness of the British globe-trotter, the ignorance of the colonies, and the contempt for their interests shown by many British statesmen. He well knew that, thanks to British diplomats, Canada had been 'sorely despoiled in the east, the centre, and the west by treaties,' and he bitterly assailed, in public and in private, the self-complacent insularity which had traced the boundary of Maine, and given up our rightful claims on the Pacific."

Denison was less forthrightly nationalistic, but he too made it clear that membership in the British Empire League was not incompatible with putting Canadian interests ahead of the United Kingdom's on occasions when the two might conflict. He praised Rudyard Kipling's poem "Our Lady of the Snows" in his memoirs, *The Struggle for Imperial Unity*, and quoted the lines: "Daughter am I in my mother's house,/ But mistress in my own./The gates are mine to open/As the gates are mine to close,/And I set my house in order/Said Our Lady of the Snows." Certain treaties that Great Britain had made, Denison said, "never should have been made" and were "an absolutely indefensible restriction on the great colonies."

Parkin's perspective was different. He wrote to his young friend Wilson about "the community of the empire." "Oceans," he reflected, "do not divide our little band of fellow workers. We must hold fast to this truth, especially in regard to each other." Although he was now called to Canada "as against an Empire sphere of work," his influence would not necessarily diminish in other parts of the empire. People had to keep a broad perspective. Parkin pushed for a fast Atlantic service to Canada, or Sandford Fleming's project, a Pacific cable. These might not prove profitable, Parkin told Wilson, but they were still overwhelmingly worthwhile from a national, that is imperial, point of view. By increasing the value of the whole, strengthened imperial ties increased the worth of each of its constituent parts. By April 1896, Parkin was able to report to Wilson that his new position entailed a lot of public work, chairing public meetings, attending banquets, "and generally, mak[ing] himself more or less a voice of the community." It gave him plenty of opportunity to speak about educational questions and "national talk" too.

In Canada, there were significant domestic developments. On 23 June 1896, there was a dominion general election. A cabinet revolt against Mackenzie Bowell brought Sir Charles Tupper into power in 1896, but by then Denison was prepared to pronounce the Conservative party moribund. Denison's own brother, a Conservative member of parliament, thought his party was going to lose the forthcoming election and also said that he hoped it would. He believed that the Liberals, once in office, would drop all their coquettish flirting with the United States and would prove thoroughly loyal to a country which they themselves were governing.

Laurier won the 1896 election and formed a strong government. Oliver Mowat stepped down as premier of Ontario, accepted an appointment to the Senate, and became minister of justice. Perhaps more important in light of his later aggressive stance on tariffs, Laurier persuaded W.S. Fielding, the premier of Nova Scotia, to take the finance portfolio. Israel Tarte, the Quebec party boss, was made minister of public works; Clifford Sifton was appointed minister of the interior; F.W. Borden was minister of militia and defence; and William Mulock took the position of postmaster-general. Milner was encouraged by the change. On balance, Milner wrote to Parkin in June 1896, he liked the new government. It had run on a platform of free trade and, in itself, he thought, debate over tariff policy was healthy "because it keeps the pot boiling on the subject of unity—i.e. habituates people to the idea that we are one nation, & that the only question is, not whether we are to remain so, but how we can make our common power most effective."

It was Fielding who found the effective way: the preferential tariff or, as it came to be known, the Fielding tariff. If the Yankees wouldn't trade with Canada from behind their high tariff walls, Canada would trade with the United Kingdom. In his 1897 budget, Fielding imposed a twelve and one-half per cent additional tariff to those who applied tariffs on Canadian goods and in 1898 it rose to twenty-five percent. This, he told Ontario, was an imperial preference, but it was a made-in-Canada policy. He didn't consult anyone in Great Britain, and certainly not the Colonial Office, before adopting the measure. Unfortunately, before Fielding's tariffs could take effect the United Kingdom had to renounce treaties it had with Belgium and Germany. Parkin did little to press Great Britain to take this action, but Denison was extremely active: "Great Britain was going along half asleep. Canada has awakened her, and made her sit up and think. She has been jostled out of the rut she has been following, and is now in a position to proceed in the direction that may be in her own interest and in that of the Empire."[1]

The year after the election, 1897, saw the celebration of Victoria's Diamond Jubilee, sixty years since the young princess had ascended to the throne of the United Kingdom. Victoria was now the Queen-Empress, and throughout the empire there were celebrations. Lady Aberdeen, wife of the governor-general, founded the Victorian Order of Nurses as a permanent memorial in Canada. She asked Parkin to sit on the governing council. She also wanted to host a gala ball in Toronto and sought Parkin's advice. What should the theme be? A ball that represented the whole Victorian era, he replied, an extravaganza with costumed dancers representing individuals or symbolizing art, drama, literature, sport, or—the empire. The ball came complete with a splendid souvenir program, edited by Parkin and Professor James Mavor, which testified to the brilliant spectacle, patriotic spirit, and celebration of progress it manifested. The Jubilee celebrations in London culminated with a service of thanksgiving on 22 June. On 26 June the Queen reviewed the fleet at Spithead and watched as 50,000 troops from around the empire marched past her reviewing stand.

For Parkin, "our British nation" was the central and conspicuous dominating world movement of the nineteenth century. Human knowledge and power had expanded rapidly and would continue to expand, and Queen Victoria headed an empire greater in extent and power "than any that preceded it...." In an article he wrote reflecting on the monarch's long reign, he reflected that the British nation had exercised "a more decisive influence on the world's civilization than any other." Other empires, he argued, dominated through force; the Victorian age was known for its simplicity, sincerity, and devotion to duty. It produced a tender and gracious womanhood, a manhood true and strong. Victoria, as a constitutional monarch, presided over a system that allowed the colonies a natural process of evolution. The settler dominions became the most democratic communities in the world, without any break in their traditions. The queen's greatest contribution, for Parkin, was to set an example of simplicity and purity in her life. The beauty and power of her home life was the example upon which the greatness of the nation must ultimately rest. She stood as the resolute defence against the influx of social evils that accompany wealth and power. The Jubilee celebrations were the splendour of her reign, the climax of a life with a romantic interest without parallel.

The spiritual vision of Kipling's poem "Recessional," written to celebrate the Jubilee, moved Parkin deeply.

> The tumult and the shouting dies—
> The Captains and the Kings depart—
> Still stands Thine ancient sacrifice,
> An humble and a contrite heart.
> Lord God of Hosts, be with us yet,
> Lest we forget—lest we forget!

Parkin also found his own ideals expressed in the poetry of Alfred, Lord Tennyson. Tennyson's son, who was a close friend of Parkin, wrote his father's biography, and in a review of that book, Parkin praised the poet as an "imperialist in the broader and nobler sense of the word." Tennyson, Parkin suggested, was a very political poet. His verse, more than once, influenced naval estimates and his poem "Form, Form, Riflemen Form" helped rally support for a stronger army. But, most of all, his poetry provided the imaginative basis for those who wanted a British empire, held together by the strongest political bonds. "[T]he cement which gives their work stability comes in no small measure from the men of imagination."[2]

> Sons, be welded, each and all
> Into one Imperial whole,
> One with Britain, heart and soul!
> One life, one flag, one fleet, one Throne!
> Britons, hold your own!

When Laurier arrived in England for the Jubilee celebrations, he quickly became extremely popular. For many people, such as Parkin, Laurier represented the civilizing or transcending qualities of the British Empire. It had taken a conquered people, the French-Canadians, and given an opportunity for the best of them to progress in civilization and participate fully in imperial citizenship. He was also the leader of the senior and largest dominion and the man whom Joseph Chamberlain needed to persuade if his colonial conference, a major political thrust of the Jubilee celebrations, was going to be a success. Laurier was made a privy councillor and, against his will, knighted. Laurier had not wanted a knighthood, and had previously rejected one. When he arrived in London, however, Laurier discovered that it had been publicly announced that one would be bestowed on him. He tried to refuse it too, but was told that it would be a serious breach of protocol to do so. Reluctantly he became Rt. Hon. Sir Wilfrid Laurier.

After many meetings, speeches, honorary degrees, and a meeting with William Gladstone, Laurier attended a dinner on 2 July 1897 at the Colonial Institute. In reply to the Duke of Connaught's toast, "The United Empire," Laurier replied, praising the British Empire: "It was to the eternal credit of the English nation that wherever they have extended their Empire, they have always respected the religion of their new subjects and, when the concession of political freedom was made, it was made freely and generously." The next day, in a committee room in the House of Commons, he declared that the time had come for the self-governing colonies like Canada to elect members to the British Parliament, or "in some grand national council or federal legislative body genuinely representative of the Empire as an organized entity."[3] But, if anyone thought that Laurier was prepared to give away the shop, they were very much mistaken.

At the Colonial Conference, chaired by Chamberlain between 24 June and 29 July, Laurier rejected the idea that the conference formed the basis for an imperial cabinet. There was no desire for any sort of federal council, and Laurier expressed no interest in military co-operation or contributing to British naval expenses. As for an empire-wide free trade area, he pronounced himself quite happy with the preferential tariff. In short, Chamberlain came away empty-handed. Laurier had managed to sound sympathetic to the imperialists in Ontario without actually doing anything to offend his supporters in Quebec. Denison didn't blame Laurier for the failure to secure mutual preferential tariffs: "The other colonies were not ready for it, the Imperial Government was not ready for it, nor were the people...."[4]

Unlike Denison, Parkin did not play an active role in the Colonial Conference. Problems with Thring's biography consumed much of his time. There was difficulty getting access to important letters, and once he had them there were requests for excisions. The problems with the map continued. As usual, Bartholomew was complaining that their publisher, Cassells, was doing nothing to promote it. Costs for the new edition had increased, but the selling price remained the same. Parkin, he counselled, should find an agent for it in every colony—and two in India. On a more positive note, the *Times* had again sounded Parkin out about the possibility of taking a position with them. Moberley Bell, wrote Parkin, "wondered whether they could make it worth my while to work for them. I did not encourage the idea for the present." According to Parkin's diary entry for 10 August, Bell then offered Parkin £50 to £100 towards his expenses if he would travel within Canada to gather information. Parkin returned to Canada on 3 September 1897.

On 8 November, the governor-general wrote to Parkin from Government House. Lord and Lady Aberdeen were coming to Toronto. Lady Aberdeen wanted a few words about the Victorian Ball. His Excellency had been invited to a meeting of the National Club on the Saturday evening and asked Parkin to join him there. After the toasts to the Parliament of Canada and the Legislative Assembly of Ontario,

Frank Arnoldi proposed, "Canada, the Empire and Mr. Blake." Edward Blake was warmly received when he he rose to speak, as was appropriate for one of Canada's best-known public figures. He was a formidable intellectual and had been a magnificent parliamentarian in his day.

Years before, Blake had almost single-handedly brought down Macdonald's government, which had come under increasing attack because of allegations it had taken large sums of money from contractors who wished to build a transcontinental railway. The Liberals picked away at the Pacific Scandal, as it was known, for months, and Macdonald's government began to waver. On 3 November 1873, Macdonald got up in the House of Commons for one last-ditch effort to defend his government. He finished at two o'clock on the morning of 4 November. Blake rose in his place, and spoke for half an hour. When the house resumed, Blake spoke for four more. Remorselessly, he tore apart Macdonald's defence. His speech destroyed any shred of legitimacy remaining to Macdonald's government. It was one of the greatest displays in Canadian parliamentary history, before or since.

Blake had resigned as Liberal leader in 1887. In 1892 he received an invitation to sit in the British House of Commons as an Irish Nationalist during the Home Rule crisis, an offer he accepted, and which may have been an entirely satisfactory solution to the tensions between Laurier and himself. In the opinion of his biographer, he was "the distinguished Canadian whose views deserved to be heard."[5]

Speaking now in "severe and measured eloquence," Blake solemnly declared for home rule for Canada.[6] Separate habits of thoughts, policies, and mutual relations had developed and the common interest of the two countries had gradually diverged. Although there remained considerable and deep-rooted popular sympathy for the United Kingdom, Blake argued that this sympathy was inversely related to Canadian independence, not to a higher level of imperial integration. The time for setting up any sort of imperial parliament was past. Geographical considerations made it impractical, but the lack of common interests between the various units in the empire was the decisive argument against. "I sympathize with the grand ideal of Imperial Federation," he said; "I disapprove of any plan to implement it." Many competent and influential men had tried. "But I have seen, I regret to say, no new gleam of light from their labours."

If it succeeded, Blake said, waving a red flag in the faces of Denison and Parkin, it would foolishly harm Canada's relations with the United States. Once the economic interests of the two countries had diverged; now they coincided to a large extent. "In every subject we are too close to each other to be indifferent." Defence was another decisive issue. Militarism was on the rise and England had a world-wide empire. Would Canada support England if she pursued might over justice? More important, if conflict came between England and the United States, where would Canada stand? What would become of Canada? The United Kingdom, a great naval power, could not defend Canada's 4000-mile land frontier with the United States. Could Canada, with six million citizens against sixty million to the South? "Great Britain has, by her own deliberate acts, by intimations conveyed again and again by her statesmen to ours, shown Canada that were she to come into collision with the United States she must trust to herself, must defend herself as best she can.... Our present position appears to be at once humiliating to us and dangerous to England."

Shortly after Blake began to speak, Denison leaned over and said to Parkin: "As a former president of this club and president of the British Empire League, I will not let Blake's remarks pass without comment." Then he leaned over and told the chairman that he intended to speak for a few minutes after Blake finished. McNaught objected because of the lateness of the evening. "I must speak," insisted Denison, and the governor-general agreed to stay for a further fifteen minutes. Denison told Parkin they would divide the time and, when Blake finished, rose to speak.

"Mr. Blake can see no gleam of light in the direction of imperial unity," Denison said. "This is not surprising, since he has been away from Canada for some years, and he does not seem to know that in those years the whole tide of public sentiment has altered, and that the Canadian people are united in their attachment to British institutions, and full of hope as to the future unification of the empire. Blake is simply out of touch. He began his political career thirty years ago, and his ideas have not evolved. What we have listened to to-night is a remnant of the past. Certainly we hope to live in peace with the Americans, but we aren't going to beg for reciprocity. Canada has its own policy of preferential tariffs and, as for an American invasion, let them come if they will. I believe we could hold our own in spite of the odds against us, as our fathers did in days gone by, when the outlook was much more gloomy."

Shouts for "Parkin" brought the principal of Upper Canada College to his feet. What could Parkin do, extemporaneously, in six or seven minutes against one of the finest legal minds of his age, the gifted politician whose four-hour speech brought down Macdonald's corrupt government, who had spoken from a carefully crafted, prepared text? Denison had begun: "I wish to say a few words.... I have been a member of this club... for some years its president."

Parkin was more subtle. "I had no intention of speaking tonight." He spoke to gratify the members of the club and especially to join in honouring the governor-general, whose office was the keystone of Canada's political system. By chance, that very day, Parkin noted, he had read a letter pointing to the dangers of the American system, where the contest for the head of state was put up for auction. In Canada, by way of contrast, he noted that the governor-general was a model of impartiality and fairness, the representative of that woman, good and true, who sat on the throne of England. This passion of loyalty to a common sovereign, Parkin felt, drew British and Canadians together, with ties that were strong yet kindly. "And yet we are told there is no gleam of hope."

"No progress, no gleam of hope!" Now Parkin moved to the personal. Seven years ago he had said to his friend Justice Samuel Way of Australia that he expected to see him on the Judicial Committee of the Privy Council. "Now he's there. The premier of Cape Colony has contributed a ship to the navy. And yet we are told there is no sign of hope.

"Mr. Blake raises distinctions and splits hairs, but he ignores the passions of the Canadian people. Canadians have friendly feelings for the United States, but the Americans have more problems to deal with than any other nation on earth. Canada, under British institutions, is the most democratic on earth. Canadians can move forward into the future with confidence."

It was a perfectly crafted speech to the perfect audience. The National Club erupted in cheers. Lord Aberdeen privately thanked Parkin for saving the club's honour: Blake was "rather a wind-bag." Milner wrote to Parkin from Cape Town at the end of January 1898 that it had been good that Parkin was there to make an immediate reply. "There are very few people, who can do that sort of thing, & it is so much more effective than a laboured reply later."

Press reaction to Blake's speech was devastating. Blake had given the text of his National Club speech in advance to John Willison, editor at the *Globe*, in the hope that he might get fair coverage if the newspaper had the full version and didn't have to rely on a reporter's notes. From a combination of errors, the *Globe* did not carry the complete text, as Blake hoped. The Toronto *World* thought it a "doleful, dispiriting tale" by a "peace-at-any-price Little Englander, of a disbeliever in that great wave of imperial unity now sweeping over the Empire." The *Evening Star* accused Blake of preaching "blue ruin." According to the *Evening Telegram*, if you listened carefully enough, you might not go far wrong to suppose him "a sour and disgruntled partisan going about in search of a hole through which he can crawl to the leadership of some Canadian party." The Hamilton *Spectator* was perhaps the cruellest. The carpetbagger deserted Canada for Ireland in 1891. Why didn't he slink off there again? It was left to Goldwin Smith, who generally shared Blake's views, to grumble in the *Weekly Sun* that the principal of UCC should confine his efforts to earning his salary.

During his time as an imperial lecturer in England, Parkin frequently lectured at working men's clubs. He wanted, then and as his speech in reply to Blake indicated, to change the heart and soul. From those interior changes, changes in institutions would necessarily flow. He now knew the working class better than he had in New Brunswick or when he was touring Australia and New Zealand and speaking to largely middle-class audiences. He came to believe that the problems of the working class needed to be addressed. They lived in fever-stricken districts, filthy slums, whole families herded together in a single room. Vice, ignorance, and crime were rampant. They needed labour legislation, open spaces, healthy amusements, better hospitals, and improved education.

It was no surprise, then, that when the issue of Sunday streetcar service arose in 1897, Parkin sided with the working classes. The 1892 contract required a vote before Sunday service could commence, and the city was divided between those in favour and the strict sabbatarians. Parkin used his rhetorical powers to address several large rallies and wrote a pamphlet. A quiet Sunday such as the farmer enjoyed was, he said, his ideal; but Toronto was no farm. Poor families had few opportunities to spend time together at beaches or parks, and Sunday was usually their only opportunity. Those with more money could drive their own carriages, hire cabs, or even use one of the new bicycles. Would they deny the poor the only form of transportation they could afford? Some people said that it was bad for streetcar operators to work on the Sabbath. Would those same people not answer their telephones because the operators would have to work, or read the Monday paper?

It was at this local level, too, that Parkin and his fellow imperialists continued to have success. One was the creation of Empire Day in 1898, a grassroots idea originated by Celementine Fessenden of the Wentworth Historical Society. She persuaded George Ross, Ontario's education minister, to adopt the idea. He chose the name because "it suggested that larger British sentiment...the most stirring, which we can put into the minds and hearts of our children... 'Civis Britannicus sum.' Canada's prosperity can with greater certainty be assured as a part of the British Empire, than in any other way...."[7] Celebration of Empire Day spread to other provinces as well, including Quebec, and eventually throughout the empire. In Ontario, the Department of Education issued a circular instructing teachers to discuss matters such as the unity of the empire and its advantages, the privileges of membership, and to read from Canadian and British authors. They might also have patriotic recitations and songs, or invite guest speakers. At some point during the day the British flag or the Canadian ensign should be hoisted over the school building.

Another significant achievement was the "Christmas" stamp of 1898. From 1840, when Sir Rowland Hill created penny postage in Great Britain, postal reformers had agitated for comparable overseas treatment.[8] Significant progress was made with the establishment of the Universal Postal Union in 1875, and in 1890 with the celebration of the half-century of the penny post. Early in 1898, the Canadian postmaster-general, William Mulock, announced that he would unilaterally implement the policy the British Empire League had been lobbying actively for. From the league's perspective, low postage rates were an important element in maintaining a free flow of communication that would keep the bonds of empire strong. All letters bearing a three-cent stamp, the ordinary domestic rate, would be carried to the United Kingdom. The problem was that there was no requirement for the British government to carry them beyond the ports, so an Imperial Conference on Postal Rates met in London in July 1898. It finally agreed to the rate of one penny for a half-ounce letter between Canada, the United Kingdom, Newfoundland, Milner's Cape Colony, Natal, and any other colony that might later chose to sign on.[9] When Mulock returned home, a large deputation of the league was waiting to greet him at the station and a National Club banquet attended by Sir Oliver Mowat, Principal Grant, and Sandford Fleming was held in his honour. Denison was in the chair and praised the double aims of preserving the empire and securing better communication between its parts.

Mulock had a second reform. He wanted to reduce the Canadian rate to the equivalent of the American domestic rate, which was two cents, and on 13 June 1898 the necessary legislation was passed. Now he needed an appropriate stamp to celebrate this achievement. He had been upset when he was in England that many people he met did not understand the importance of the unity of the British Empire, and especially that they did not understand the significance of Canada. He wanted a stamp that would, in effect, serve as Canadian and imperial federation propaganda. When he returned to Canada, he asked for draft submissions from a few artists, but received nothing satisfactory. He consulted others, including Parkin, and decided to accept a simplified version of Parkin's map of the British Empire on the Mercator projection, with Canada front, centre, dominant, oversized, and like the rest of the empire, coloured a bright red. In case anyone missed the point, above the map was a crown, and below, a bunch of oak and maples leaves, and to drive the idea home, along the bottom ran the words: "We hold a vaster empire than has been." Finally, Parkin had his map printed and distributed en masse at someone else's cost. Goldwin Smith grumpily called the stamp a painted lie.

The question of communication, in this case secure communication, was pushed to the fore in the Spanish-American war. On 15 February 1898, the American battleship *Maine* was sunk in Havana harbour and the American newspapers actively agitated for war against Spain, which the USA declared on 25 April. The war led to the virtual annexation of Cuba, Puerto Rico, and the Philippines. Any remaining pretence on Spain's part to be a significant colonial power disappeared and the United States openly became one.

Kipling welcomed the USA to the imperialist club and lectured its leaders on their new responsibilities as colonial masters: They must sacrifice themselves to improve the well-being of their charges, just as the British did. For Kipling, imperialism was not about exploitation and power; it was about service. If the language and the undeniably condescending attitude in the poem he wrote on the subject is objectionable to modern readers, its general message should be understood in the context of the British idealism that motivated it.

> Take up the White Man's burden—
> Send forth the best ye breed—
> Go bind your sons to exile
> To serve your captives' need;
> To wait in heavy harness,
> On fluttered folk and wild—
> Your new-caught, sullen peoples,
> Half-devil and half-child.[10]

For Parkin, the war provided a salutary lesson. The Americans cut the Spanish cable to Cuba. Just as he had warned for years, safe communication and safe transportation were critical to guarding the safety and security of the empire. As long as the empire depended on a cable that ran through territory that belonged to potential enemies, it was not safe. A Pacific cable was essential. Parkin wrote to all the Toronto newspapers, and sent copies to Laurier. He provoked editorials on the subject. Fleming contacted Parkin's Australian friends to begin agitation at that end, and Grant, Parkin, Denison, and Fleming used all the resources at their disposal, writing furiously and lobbying MPs vigorously. The primary opposition came from private Australian cable interests, who would see their profits cut by a rival,[11] and the Colonial Office, which wrote on 28 October 1898: "...in the various communications which from time to time have been addressed to the Colonial Governments on this subject, Her Majesty's Government have never concealed their opinion that the construction of a Pacific Cable is a matter of much greater importance to Australia and Canada than to the United Kingdom."[12] However, by 1899 the governments of Canada, Australia, and New Zealand were behind the project and it was completed in 1902. Parkin's vision of an empire linked by culture, transport, and communication was a step closer to fulfilment.

13

The Most Delightful Man in Canada

On *21 May 1898*, Parkin wrote a short, but very satisfying, note in his diary. "Heard in morning that among the Birthday honours the Queen has made me a CMG. Telegrams of congratulations from Lord Aberdeen, Lord Strathcona and others." Wits said that "CMG" meant "Call Me God,"[1] but in fact it meant that Parkin had been appointed a Companion of the Order of St. Michael and St. George, a British honour created in 1818 and given to civilians "who may hold, or have held high and confidential offices, or may render or have rendered extraordinary and important services (other than military) within or in relation to any part of the British Dominions or Territories under British Protection or Administration, and in reward for important and loyal services in relation to foreign affairs." There was only one available that year for a Canadian and it was Parkin's. Parkin believed that Aberdeen had secured it for him. The evidence is ambiguous. Aberdeen certainly knew about the award before it was publicly announced,[2] but others such as Harry Wilson, Parkin's young friend newly appointed to the Colonial Office, might conceivably have been involved. The process was opaque, as Parkin later explained to Denison, who was perplexed that he had been continually passed over.

Milner, like most, courteously suggested in a letter that Parkin deserved the higher honour of the knighthood, but unlike most, he shrewdly noted that Parkin's achievement was all the greater since he did not actually hold any formal office, and that was usually the requirement for the award. The Royal Society of Canada was quick to jump on the bandwagon; within four days they unanimously elected him a fellow of this distinguished body. Parkin also had the honour of having a township in northern Ontario named after him. The pleasure others took in Parkin's honours was genuine. Mary Minto, wife of the new governor-general, described him as "so full of enthusiasm and so simple with all his cleverness." He was, she wrote to Milner, the "most delightful man in Canada." Her husband agreed. "By far the best man in Canada...a delightful man...the most level headed man I know of Canadian affairs."[3]

The Earl of Minto was fifty-three when he became Canada's new governor-general, just slightly older than Parkin. As a young man, Minto had been passionate about horse-racing, and spent six years racing under the name Mr. Rolly, riding twice as a jockey in England's premier steeplechase event, the Grand National. After that, he settled down to a military career, which involved a stint in Canada serving under General Middleton in the Northwest Rebellion of 1885. When he learned that Aberdeen was leaving office, Minton lobbied to replace him. Although Minto wasn't Chamberlain's first choice, he was awarded the position when the more politically skilled candidates the colonial secretary preferred turned it down.[4] Milner described him as a "straight and trustworthy gentleman," and Lady Minto, although not Lady Aberdeen's intellectual equal, "a particularly charming woman all the same."

Soon Parkin was spending weekends at Rideau Hall in Ottawa, which Minto, who didn't find the house grand enough for an English gentleman, was in the process of enlarging. Lady Minto was reading Parkin's biography of Thring, which had finally come out in December. Response to the book was generally favourable. It was a labour of love, sensitively and thoughtfully done, a solid piece of work about a formidable man whose thought had, more than any other, influenced Parkin. Thring was certainly the source of Parkin's core ideas on education, and he had reinforced Parkin's views on imperial federation. The main criticisms of the somewhat weighty two volumes were that there were far too many letters and that it was lacking in life. It was a criticism Parkin thought fair. "The fact that Skrine and Rawnsley had both thought it necessary to write a book about him made it difficult for me to use much material which would have lightened the volumes, and given them a more popular side. I was perhaps too sensitive about saying over again what had been said before, and Skrine has written to reproach me for not using as material everything he has written." The book sold well. Parkin was approached about producing a one-volume edition for the American market that concentrated less on Thring's life and more on his ideals and teaching methods.[5]

One imperial addition Parkin made at UCC was the creation of a cadet corps. Imperialists such as he and Denison were concerned that Canada should be able to help in the event of an imperial crisis, and the pitiful state of Canada's militia was a cause for concern. This concern was brought close to home by the Venezuela affair of 1896, which had reminded Canadians that their southern neighbour was not harmless. In a border dispute between Venezuela and the British colony of Guiana, President Cleveland had sent a message to the United Kingdom "couched in hostile terms, and ... almost insolent in its character." According to Denison, nearly all the governors of the states offered the services of their militias for an invasion of Canada. Many political and military figures in Canada believed that Cleveland seriously intended to invade, or at least to seize control of the Great Lakes and the St. Lawrence River unless Great Britain accepted arbitration of the border. The Spanish-American war soon revealed the United States as a country prepared to use military force to achieve its diplomatic ends. This was a worry to a country like Canada that was involved in a dispute over the Alaska boundary and over the seal hunt in the Pacific.

At the same time, British military concerns farther afield were also causing concern. Writing from shipboard, Milner, now the governor of Cape Colony and high commissioner to South Africa, wrote to Parkin. "[M]y poor little Cape Colony (the most backward of all the self-governing colonies) has done rather well" in learning the imperial spirit, he said. If it were not for that "eternal sore the Transvaal, which continues to get worse, S. Africa would be quite loyal." "Ever Your Faithful Friend, A. Milner."

The political situation Milner had inherited in South Africa was extremely volatile. The Boer government of the Transvaal refused to extend political rights to English-speaking settlers. Cecil Rhodes, a British-born entrepreneur who made a fortune in the diamond-mining industry, was prime minister of Cape Colony. Together with Leander Jameson, the administrator of Rhodesia, he conspired to overthrow the government of Transvaal. The "Jameson raid" was a fiasco, easily defeated by the forces of the government of the Boer Republic. Jameson was arrested and Rhodes driven from office. The Select Committee Report of the British House of Commons cleared Joseph Chamberlain and placed the blame on Rhodes, though many Liberal MPs suspected a whitewash or a cover-up.[6]

After the Jameson raid, Paul Kruger, the Boer leader, concluded that war was the only way for the Boers to retain their independence and identity. The Boers began to arm with modern weapons and on 11 October 1899 the Orange Free State and the South African Republic (Transvaal Republic) declared war on the United Kingdom. The initial stages of the war were a brilliant success for the Boers, especially against one of the best-trained and most successful armies in the world. The Boer irregulars defeated the British general, Redvers Bullers, and besieged the towns of Ladysmith, Kimberley, and Mafeking, whose defence was mounted by Robert Baden-Powell (later founder of the Boy Scout movement). These early reverses shocked a public who believed that British arms were invincible.

An old principle of international law said that when the Queen was at war, all the Queen's subjects were legally at war; but it could not compel any of them to fight with enthusiasm, and it was impossible to get some of Her Majesty's subjects to fight at all. Canada did not have a standing professional army. The Militia Act of 1868 formed the basis of Canada's military structure. A small unit under the command of a British professional soldier (in 1899, Lieutenant-General Edward Hutton) was stationed in Halifax. In July, Joseph Chamberlain wrote Minto to discover if the Act would permit the use of the Canadian militia outside Canada. Laurier said that Canadian troops were legally allowed to serve only in Canada. Minto requested him to revise the legislation so that the country could send troops immediately to South Africa. Laurier, fearing a split in his party and in the country, merely moved a resolution in support of the war in the House of Commons and, when it passed, stood to lead MPs in singing "God Save the Queen." He wasn't going to escape that easily.[7]

Laurier's French-Canadian colleagues, especially his most senior ones such as Israel Tarte and Henri Bourassa, were totally opposed to sending troops, and certainly not at the cost of the Canadian taxpayer. They raised no objection, they said, if Canadians wanted to raise money and send troops and pay for it out of their own pockets. For some French-Canadians, the position was more principled; they identified with Boers as victims of British domination. Principal Grant was one of the few in English-speaking Canada who shared this view. He deeply admired the Boers, sympathized with their struggles and the sacrifices, as he saw it, they had made for liberty. Although Grant had previously admired Rhodes, after the Jameson raid, Grant made it known that he hoped to live to see him hanged. "God keep us from a war of aggression on the Dutch," he wrote to Parkin on 7 June 1899, "who would be fighting for an independence sanctioned by solemn treaty."[8] When war finally broke out, Grant accepted the war, because it had been thrust on the empire. "The upward progress of humanity has always been accompanied with blunders and crimes on all sides," he wrote again to Parkin in February 1900, "and in trying to strike a balance the British Empire is fairly clean, or at any rate, less dirty than others. But when I cease to sympathize with a people struggling for independence, may I die."[9]

Grant's sympathy for the Boers was not widely shared in English-speaking Canada. There was widespread support for sending troops. The cabinet itself was deadlocked. In October, General Hutton printed a provocative article in the *Canadian Military Gazette* that promised a Canadian contingent of troops for South Africa, and he outlined a contingency plan to provide them.[10] Hutton and Parkin had known one another for some time (they had met, possibly as early as 1892), and Parkin was in close contact with Hutton during this period. It appears that Hutton sent Parkin a version of this report in advance, and Parkin offered to promote Hutton's views in one of his *Times* columns.

The Most Delightful Man in Canada

In Ontario, pressure to send troops continued to mount. Laurier needed to relieve the pressure, but he was determined to do as little as possible to appease Ontario. On 30 October a token force of a thousand specially recruited infantry sailed for South Africa. Early in November, the Canadian Club of Toronto organized a rally in Massey Music Hall, a new 4000-seat concert hall in the heart of the city. If there was any doubt about Tory Toronto's support for the war effort before the rally, there wasn't after. Every seat was taken. The hall was awash with Union Jacks as a 500-voice choir sang patriotic standards. The platform party was a political Who's Who. But the only man fit to address such a meeting was the apostle of empire: Parkin. He spoke for an hour and then revealed his *coup de théâtre*. Seated in one of the stage boxes was Clara Butt. A stunning woman, six foot, two inches in height, and one of the great contraltos of her age, she followed Parkin's oratory with booming rendition of "God Save the Queen." The cumulative effect was electric and the evening closed with a "mighty British cheer."

The Massey Hall speech was a triumph, he wrote to his daughter Maude. It was widely reported in the English papers and invitations to speak had come from all over Canada. Parkin's aim, he had told Hutton, was to make "patriotic enthusiasm coherent and intelligent." His protégé, Arthur Lee, a British military attaché with the British embassy in Washington, wrote to Parkin, asking if it were possible for the two of them to get together at the Royal Military College in Kingston so they could "have an Imperial, Anglo-American, 'Down-with-all-Dagoes,' pow-wow."

Public enthusiasm about the war convinced Parkin that something was amiss with the government. He approached Hutton and Minto to co-ordinate tactics. Unless someone says differently, people will assume that the government is pursuing the right course. Clearly, that was not the case. Should "quiet working" suffice, or should "the public mind show that it is on the alert"? Parkin clearly felt that there had been enough behind-the-scenes manoeuvring; it was time for him to work his magic. He would stomp the country, speak in all the major cities, create a public sentiment that the prime minister could not resist. Canada would take her place as the leading colony of the empire. This was no time for hesitation or indecision, he argued. Out of the crucible of war, a new British people would arise, great and unified. Colonial cooperation on the battlefield would advance the dream of imperial unity. Out of the war graves of South Africa, "where Englishmen, New Zealanders, Australians, South Africans, and Canadians died side by side," the nation's self-conscious would be aroused and it would become a living entity.

On Christmas Day 1899, Parkin wrote to General Hutton: "The question is whether some further popular demonstration is needed or not to brace up our political people. We had an enthusiastic meeting of the Board of Trade—and they passed a fairly good resolution—the only difficulty being some lack of skill in concentrating its meaning. But the feeling was all that one could wish for. When consulted about it I strongly urged that it should lead up to a mass meeting for popular endorsement.... I don't not know if a big mass meeting could now be managed successfully or not, but I would hope so." Colonel Gerald Kitson, a British regular military officer serving as commandant of Royal Military College, wanted more demonstrations. Parkin supported that tactic. He was not prepared to tolerate a Canadian government at odds with his imperial ideal.

Two days after Christmas, Minto replied to Parkin in a letter marked "Private." What Minto called racial difference within Canada, he felt, hindered Canada's relationship with the empire. The British policy of tolerance, Minto thought, had most likely been wrong. "Very possibly I think it might have been better if the conquered race had been required to [sink?] more of its identity than has been the case," the governor-general wrote. However, he concluded, what was done was done. The British, he said, had a right to assert their devotion to the empire, and thinking French-Canadians agreed that they must throw their lot in with the get-ahead Anglo-Saxon race, though they would not be enthusiastic about a British war. The lower classes were even worse.

By January 1900, Laurier had had enough of the efforts of Minto, Hutton, and their supporters to force an alternative South African policy on him. As early as December 1898, Minto had been supporting Hutton's proposed militia reforms, and Minto defended his intrusions into politics. Laurier decided to dismiss Hutton as the general officer commanding on a charge of insubordination, but Minto fought vigorously to protect him. His efforts came close to provoking a constitutional crisis; Laurier's government was on the point of resignation, but, instead, Chamberlain and the Colonial Office arranged for Hutton's recall.[11] The formal pretext was a dispute over a contract for the purchase of horses.

Parkin was determined to support his friends and their policies. His first impulse was to write a critical article in the *Times*, as Minto and Kitson wanted. Their position was that if the government of Canada were not ultimately in charge of the army, the army would become a political instrument. Parkin restrained himself for a time, but he couldn't hold his tongue forever. Buoyed by the mood of a St. George's Day meeting in Hamilton at which Sir Frederick Borden, the minister of militia, was present, Parkin gave the minister a piece of his mind. Parkin praised Hutton's work to loud cheers. This set him off on what was a recurring theme for his next years: the pettiness of politicians at a time when great men of vision were needed. "The lion's blood was up," as the Hamilton *Times* reported, "and the feeling was just as strong in the remotest colonies as it was in the beating heart of the great metropolis itself. Would posterity ever justify statesmen if they did not try to crystallize into some concrete form one of the greatest developments that had ever occurred in national history [Colonial co-operation in imperial defence]? The problems had to be firmly faced, with the feeling of statesmen and not with the feeling of politicians pursuing a do-nothing policy."

In South Africa, 5500 British troops who had been besieged for 118 days by Boer forces were rescued by a force led by General Bullers. On 1 March 1900, news of the "relief of Ladysmith," as the breaking of the siege was generally known, reached Canada. In Montreal, offices, factories, and McGill University celebrated with a half-holiday, and "God Save the Queen" was heard everywhere on the streets. A crowd proceeded to Israel Tarte's newspaper and hoisted the Union Jack over its building. More pro-British activity followed. French-Canadian students were quick to retaliate. Singing the "Marseillaise" and waving the French flag, they counterattacked. Tensions increased the next day in the press and continued in the House of Commons.[12]

Conservative leader Sir Charles Tupper tried to fight the November 1900 election on the issue of South Africa. However, the military situation had begun to improve earlier in the year, and Laurier was able to defuse the issue. Tupper gained seventeen seats in Ontario, but Laurier gained in the rest of Canada and, from Parkin's perspective, made disturbing gains in Quebec. Any exacerbation of the "race cleavage," he feared, would weaken the cause of imperialism by tying Laurier's hands and making him less willing to enter into new imperialist ventures.

In the view of Minto's biographer, the earl's association with Hutton, Kitson, and Parkin so soon after he came to Canada had proved a grave liability. It isolated him from the main currents of Canadian public life and reinforced his prejudices.[13] However, the recall of Hutton and the posting of Kitson to the British embassy in Washington left only Parkin, and Minto began to develop a more nuanced understanding of Canadian political life.[14] Early in March 1900, Chamberlain asked Minto to test Canadian public opinion on the possibility of an imperial advisory council, with its members possibly holding titles and sitting in the House of Lords. Minto consulted widely—Laurier, Tupper, Foster, Mulock, Parkin, George Drummond (a senator from Montreal), Grant, and J.S. Willison—then reported that there was little Canadian enthusiasm for the idea and that opposition did not arise solely from French Canada. There were, he pointed out to Chamberlain, many in Canada who loved England, liked "God Save the Queen," and didn't want a federated empire.[15] In particular, for the most part, they didn't want to pay for the empire. Lord Strathcona might be prepared single-handedly to finance a contingent, Strathcona's Horse. The British paid most of the cost of the Canadian troops sent to South Africa; Canada kept its own contribution to less than three million dollars.

If Minto consulted widely, Parkin too had a network of informants across the empire. In South Africa, of course, he had Milner, who was at the very centre of events. General Hutton, too, served in South Africa, and then transferred to Australia, where he is considered the creator of the Australian army. Sir Samuel Way, chief justice and lieutenant-governor of South Australia, was a regular correspondent, as was Parkin's long-standing associate in the imperial federation movement, Henry D'Estère Taylor. Parkin could count on Arthur Lee to pass on information he gained from Teddy Roosevelt (Lee was, among other things, an honorary member of the Roosevelt's Rough-riders, since he had been military attaché to the United States army in Cuba during the Spanish American War). Kitson also kept an eye on things in Washington. Harry Wilson knew what was going on in the Colonial Office. Parkin had other contacts too: Hugh Arnold-Foster was financial secretary to the Admiralty; there was also Parkin's rich Scottish supporter George Houstoun; the Mintos; Moberley Bell and W.L. Monneypenny from the *Times*; Sandford Fleming; and Denison. Parkin even had the odd interview with the prime minister, and he encountered countless businessmen and politicians at social events and political rallies, such as the one he spoke at in the small town of Orillia that attracted a crowd of five or six hundred people who were, in Parkin's estimation, sympathetic to his national idea.

Sympathy for the national idea was not growing as quickly as the imperial federationists wanted, however. Parkin found politicians a frustrating barrier. They stood in the way, he felt, rather than advancing the ideal. "I am not happy over the attitude of the politicians now in power towards national questions," he wrote to Milner. Public opinion was favourable and they could have raised more money for imperial defence. Instead, "they take the politician's point of view, not the statesman's." This leaves the responsibility to others, outside parliament, to educate the public, he wrote to Milner.

Writing from the Transvaal, the newly ennobled Lord Milner praised the heart of the nation, but condemned its antiquated institutions. Existing parliaments were too small, and with rare exceptions, produced politicians who were not fit to deal with big issues. "Until we get a real Imperial Council, not merely a consultative but first a constituent and then an executive Council, with conduct of all our world business we shall get nothing."

Other friends were sending Parkin the same message. Kitson told him that the Canadian government still was not pulling its weight in imperial defence. Loring warned that he doubted the United Kingdom government's ability to hold the empire together. It's no wonder that when Sir Frederick Young visited Canada and addressed a meeting of the British Empire League, he complained of Canadian apathy, and praised the Englishmen, Australians, and New Zealanders who were to do the fighting. Parkin was outraged that the government was not taking a leadership role in forging tighter imperial ties and making active contributions to imperial defence. There must be, he wrote almost in despair to Hutton, "some definite plan of organisation for Imperial defence. Why should the force which these countries can contribute to the national strength depend on outbursts of public opinion rather than on some carefully thought out scheme?" As Arthur Lee summed it up: "[A]ll the Military Forces of the Empire must be re-organised on an Imperial basis."

By 1902, Parkin was the only figure of substance in Canada pursing the "national" cause. Hutton and Kitson had, in effect, been sent packing by Laurier for their attempts to interfere in Canadian affairs. According to his biographer, Carman Millar, Minto had been domesticated: "By the end of his term Minto had become an experienced, capable, and judicious governor."[16] Sir Charles Tupper left politics after his defeat by Laurier in 1900, and in any event he was nearly eighty. Denison was still active, but he was a Laurier supporter and more than happy to work with him. On 13 May 1902, George Monro Grant's body was laid to rest near Sir John A. Macdonald's in Cataraqui Cemetery in Kingston. Parkin attended the funeral and was deeply moved by the tributes his old friend received, not just from his peers, but from the citizens of Kingston.

In January, Parkin met with Laurier for two hours, and found him "entirely colourless" on imperial matters. The prime minister could only touch on what Parkin insisted on calling "national" questions "as they became practical." That meant that the rest of us had to create public opinion, Parkin told him, and make politicians act. The dual nature of the country was a permanent drag on the movement towards imperial unity. As Lee put it in a letter to Parkin: "I know too much about the real quality of French-Canadian loyalty to ever wish to repeat the experience."

Queen Victoria's death the previous January had unleashed an outpouring of imperial sentimentality, and Joseph Chamberlain hoped to take advantage of it by inviting the colonial leaders to a conference to coincide with King Edward's coronation in June 1902. "The basis upon which the British Empire rests," Laurier told the House of Commons, "the basis upon which it has grown, has been the local autonomy of all its constituent parts, and I do not see that anything can be done at the present time which would warrant a change in that basis in any way whatever." Departing from his customary sunny ways, he warned the House that this was a particularly dangerous time to become entangled with Europe, even with England. Canada did not want to be drawn into a vortex of militarism.

Parkin was outraged by such nonsense. His friend, Edward Hutton, now a major-general, had written to him from shipboard off the coast of Ceylon. Australia became a federated dominion like Canada in 1901 and he was on his way to create the new Australian army. "My task will be to create a military system and organization which will satisfy the recently developed requirement of Australian and of Imperial Defence, and at the same time meet the demands of our modern Constitution, form of government, and of our complicated social system." Few people outside England understood the significance of the task, and one of those who did, in whom Hutton confided, was Parkin.

To Parkin, Canada seemed foolish compared to Australia. Nothing since he had returned to Canada, Parkin wrote to Minto, had been as petty and small as Laurier's attitude, nor had so diminished Canada's place in imperial affairs. Of course the attitude was largely the result of Quebec's influence, but equally distressing was the lack of outrage from English-speaking Canada. In this struggle Parkin worked largely alone and was the only opponent Laurier and his circle respected. "The rest are children," Laurier observed.

Parkin opened his attack on the government with a stinging letter to the *Globe* on 20 March 1902:

> I believe the day is not far off when this country will be heartily ashamed of the niggardly attitude it has taken in the matter of paying for the brave fellows we have lately sent to fight and die in the nation's cause in South Africa. If this attitude represents the real and permanent feeling of the Canadian people many of us may be compelled to change deeply cherished views. I for one would prefer that Canada should be outside the empire than holding a contemptible position within it.
>
> If Canada were poor, there might be an excuse; but Canada shirks a burden that other colonies are prepared to assume.
>
> In a time when our own prosperity is at its greatest height,

but when the severest strain is laid upon the generous old motherland, we contentedly allow the shoulders which have so long borne the burden to continue doing so. We do this with the eyes of the world fixed closely upon us. We even decline to discuss the question of defending the empire with that motherland after she has for more than a century guaranteed security to Canadians, as to other colonists, in every corner of the globe. As she now bravely braces herself up to bear the tremendous weight of responsibility thus thrown upon her, few more harmful blows could be struck at the nation's prestige than a lukewarm message from her greatest colony.... Let us not blame our politicians; as usual, they are, on both sides, thinking of the next election, and await the direction of the people's voice. Meanwhile the people make no definite sign. In my judgement self-respect means more for Canada than a surplus."

It was a letter, Parkin told his daughter Maude, "in which I attack all politicians violently. I have a slight idea that it may have some influence in the world." The tone of the letter reflected Parkin's belief, which he had held since the 1870s, that imperial federation was not mainly about ships and soldiers and money, but about moral and ethical positions. It was about how a nation should act and what made a nation great, namely accepting its responsibilities rather than hiding from them.

Willison, the *Globe*'s editor and an ardent Laurier supporter, replied in an editorial. "Very extreme," he called it; it was reckless, even if it was sincere. Instead of criticizing Laurier for what he wasn't accomplishing, shouldn't the imperialists be grateful for what he had accomplished? There was no crisis, no need for haste. Let imperial affairs evolve naturally; there was no need to force matters at some conference or other. "Responsible statesmen may not rush into a revolution of our whole political, financial and military position. If Dr. Parkin will remember what Sir Wilfrid Laurier and his colleagues have done during their five years of office in the way of strengthening the bonds of empire, we feel sure he will admit there can be no real anxiety about their attitude at the approaching conference, and that if from any source comes any feasible, practical plans for further strengthening the empire and enabling Canada to bear her part therein with dignity, while she is yet left freehanded to do her own work, that plan will meet with the heartiest support from Sir Wilfrid. But the whole edifice of Imperialism will be in danger of coming down with a crash if we are pushed hastily into some ill-considered project."

Parkin continued his busy round of public meetings, speaking one night at Brantford about fifty miles from Toronto, a few days later in Toronto. At the end of February he spoke to undergraduates at McGill University in Montreal and polished his remarks for publication. Canada was the foremost colony; it had come of age. With maturity, though, came responsibility and a need for choice. Annexation to the United States was out of the question. Canada's whole history stood against it. Independence was not an absurd option, but it was a lesser one than maintaining membership in a great and integrated empire. That empire protected Canada's trade; so it was only fair that Canada should contribute her share of that defence. Just as we voted at the municipal level, at the provincial level and at the dominion level, so soon we would also vote at the imperial level and take our place as full citizens in the empire. In an address at the end of February 1902, he argued: "We are members of a nation [in] whose affairs we are profoundly interested—in matters of peace and war, diplomacy, postal and telegraph communication, consular service, a hundred other things common to the nation at large. When we leave the final control of all these matters to one section of our nation we abdicate our right of equal citizenship; we voluntarily take a position of inferiority." Then on St. George's Day he was in Hamilton. On the day honouring England's patron saint, as was fitting, the hall was decorated with flags and bunting. The platform guests included Willison, the new Conservative leader Robert Borden, and Parkin. All reiterated their positions, but later Minto encouraged Parkin to continue his campaign to put as much pressure as possible on Laurier.

On 3 May, Parkin addressed the Canadian Club. His theme was that defence issues were now at the forefront and Canada needed to play its part. Willison ran the story on page thirty-two. In his editorial, he reminded Parkin and his audience of a few basic truths. There was no doubt that Parkin was a "clever and practised orator," and some of what he said was undoubtedly true. Canada cannot rely on another country for its defence. As for the idea that Canada should join some scheme of imperial government together with imperial defence, it was just as reasonable and just as Canadian to insist that self-government be retained. Parkin, Willison said, likes to mock parliamentarians. Well, Willison continued, he's someone who has only an academic knowledge of the matters about which he speaks and talks about them only to public meetings. As people say just before they are about to be rude, "to be frank without discourtesy, we think that the two hundred representatives of the people of Canada in Parliament are just as honest as he is, and, by the nature of their position, understand difficulties in government far better."

Parkin took Willison's attack as proof that he was making progress. The Toronto Board of Trade adopted a resolution favouring improved co-operation in imperial defence and trade. Borden hectored Laurier in the House. Public opinion was strongly with them, Parkin wrote Denison in May. He felt it in Hamilton and at the Canadian Club. To Parkin, at any rate, it was clear that they were destiny's children. "Some men are naturally built to drive the wheel forward; nature intended others to act as a drag. I do not think there is much question as to where our place is."

As Parkin pressed the issue of defence, Denison pursued his crusade on preferential tariffs. He proposed that the United Kingdom and the colonies place a duty of between five and ten per cent on all foreign imports, the proceeds to be devoted to imperial defence according to the decisions of a council on which the colonies would be represented.[17] Denison planned a speaking tour of England to soften public opinion there, prior to the colonial conference. Annie wrote to her husband, asking if Denison's speaking tour was advisable. The answer to her question was that the tour was, at least from the conference impresario's point of view, distinctly ill-advised. Chamberlain did not like Denison, and he especially did not like Denison messing about in his own back yard.

What Parkin only now learned was that Chamberlain had none too favourable an impression of him either. Indeed, he considered him "as a second Denison who was perhaps even more dangerously impulsive!" Parkin's young friend Lee, now a British MP, tried to reassure the colonial secretary about Parkin and arrange a meeting between the two when Parkin came over at the time of the coronation. If Parkin, in spite of all his expressed contempt for politicians, was even vaguely serious about entering British politics at this juncture (as some letters suggest), this should have put paid to the idea. Annie's instincts were sound: "I cannot go into it all now but my first impulse is against it. What do politics mean to a poor man? .... Haven't they nearly always as it were to sell their independence," she wrote to her husband, nearly in despair. Neither Parkin nor Denison sold their independence, but from the point of view of a shrewd practical politician such as Chamberlain, however, either of them seemed as likely to pop up at the wrong time and criticize him for not doing enough as they were to congratulate him on a job well done. In his eyes, they were the sort of men who would put the interests of the empire ahead of the interests of the United Kingdom. For Chamberlain, within broad limits, the interests of the United Kingdom and the empire simply coincided. The Colonial Conference of 1902 resulted in much talk but little action.

If Chamberlain was leery of Parkin's presence in England at this time, Annie was also unsure of the wisdom of a visit from him. In 1902, the Parkin family was still scattered. Annie continued to live in England with the younger children and when Parkin proposed to come to London for Edward VII's coronation, she wasn't enthusiastic. She asked him to think about the expense before he made the final decision. "I dread doing what is wrong and having it ruin one's peace of mind, and above all we must keep an independent position... a simple true, sincere life is what I wish for most, and I love the freedom and scope and the simplicity we might have or may have in life. I think I am seeing a good many things clearer and above all I pray to be kept loving and true," she wrote.

Annie went on to relate some of the freedom and simplicity she referred to. She had, she wrote, gone to the seaside with Raleigh, who had been ordered to take the sea air by his doctor for chest problems. They had picked up shells and played with a hoop she had bought. Another day he had built sandcastles, while she wrote letters and read without interruption. "How do you think money matters are going to look for the spring and summer?" the letter ended. "I fear from the tone of your last letter you did not feel very cheerful. Do think it out and don't let us be led into temptation...." In another letter the next day, Annie described how she had bought their son inexpensive toys, including a toy trombone, which he had his heart set on for some time. He had, Annie wrote, opened each present in bed that morning, said "How sweet," and kissed his mother. "Why should we sacrifice our duty for the sake of anything as great as that sight might be?" she wrote to her husband.

These criticisms stung Parkin, as they were meant to. Annie replied in a vaguely conciliatory way: "If I have anything to do with it there [would] be no more separation, but you must be patient and humour your old wife who loves you so much tho' you hurt her feelings by not believing it and calling her cold...." Two days later, on 28 February, she was back on the attack, insisting that Parkin for once give her priority over his career. "You are very dear to me darling and my love gets stronger and all the romance and beauty is there unless it gets crushed out for the time by weariness and worry...." Three days later, she was taxing him for his lack of attention to practical details. "My dearest one, I hope you will try to answer all my questions. You don't usually, you know, but these about a base if you come etc., are necessary...."

When she returned to London, all her frustrations came to a head.

90 Baron's Court Road
West Kensington
Friday evening, March 14th, 1902

Dearest,
Do you suppose I really ever want to leave you? Why you are my life, my everything. It is only as you know a corner that I wanted to work out of, forgive me if I have done wrong, only I beg of you don't let us go on doing wrong. I do want to be kept right, and above all things I don't want to get bitter or lose heart, for we have so much in each other... I didn't expect any magic in the year. It has done all I could expect. I did not expect it to be easy. I felt cornered absolutely with circumstances at home and in times of absolute weakness, desperate. You know why or ought to know. Alice and Maude know. This seemed to me a fair thing to try. It has taken much cour-

age, more perhaps than you think, has taught me much and I know done me great good. I have tried to be true about it and asked God's help and want to be with you...
   Your own
   Annie

On 7 June, Parkin sailed for England in spite of Annie's concern about the expense. Minto and four provincial premiers were aboard the same ship. Chamberlain had suggested that the premiers might consider common tariff, political, and defence questions. Laurier, as premier of the senior dominion, elegantly but firmly announced that he was prepared only to discuss economic, trade, and communication matters. He thought that the empire's current defence and political arrangements were entirely satisfactory as they stood. In Minto's view, Laurier single-handedly destroyed the conference. The governor-general did not want to see contributions of men and money from the colonies to imperial defence, but he thought that Laurier should have been more accommodating. He regretted that even Parkin's "magic pen"[18] and passionate eloquence had not shifted Laurier's course. When G.M. Grant first addressed the inaugural meeting of the Imperial Federation League in 1885, he made the same complaint about Canada's failure to make its proper contribution to imperial defence. Seventeen years later, little had changed. French-Canadians were unlikely ever to give money to British imperialists and most English-speaking Canadians, much as they enjoyed Parkin's rhetoric, weren't going to insist on paying for something that they got for free.

14

I, Cecil Rhodes

"I walked between earth and sky and when I looked down I said 'This earth should be English' and when I looked up, I said 'England should rule the earth.'"[1]

Cecil Rhodes, an entrepreneur of genius, a successful politician, a visionary who named a country after himself, and a philanthropist whose extraordinary gifts to Rhodesia (now Zimbabwe) and South Africa are now more resented than prized, created scholarships that have become a symbol of academic and all-round excellence.

On his estate, Rhodes built Groote Schuur, a great house in which he intended to live for the rest of his life. After that, it would become the official residence of the prime ministers of South Africa. It was alive with wild animals—a lion, zebras, even emus and a llama, since Rhodes imported flora and fauna to add biodiversity. In front of the house lay a plain of fifteen miles of pine trees leading the eye to the foothills beyond.

Rhodes built another house on the estate, "The Woolsack." Smaller, it lay in the heart of a shaded oak grove. According to Rudyard Kipling's biographer, "A heavy mixed scent came from the pine and eucalyptus grove, while flowering shrubs grew like weeds in the garden, and myrtle and plumbago hedges, and oleander. Behind all towered the flank of Table Mountain and its copses of silver trees flanking scarred raines, the mountain of which he had written as he saw it throbbing in the heat."[2] The path to Groote Schuur from The Woolsack was through a ravine overflowing with hydrangeas.

Kipling and his American-born wife, Caroline, lived in the Woolsack for long periods. Kipling and Rhodes were great friends, and for Kipling, Rhodes had achieved semi-divine status. "I don't think that anyone who did not actually come across him with some intimacy of detail can ever realize what he was. It was his presence that had the power."[3] When Rhodes wasn't away on business, Kipling and Caroline often dined with Rhodes, and discussed Rhodes's latest vision, his last will and testament. For Rhodes, his legacy, literally and figuratively, was something of an obsession.

Rhodes's first will, written in 1877 when he had only £10,000, has fascinated conspiracy theorists around the world, but especially those in the United States, many of whom believe that this document reveals clearly what the scholarship scheme conceals more subtly. He had joined the Masonic Lodge, and although impressed with the wealth it had accumulated and the power it exercised, he realized the organization, and its rites and ceremonies, existed largely without any meaningful rationale. Why not follow their model, he thought, but for a worthy purpose: form a secret society to restore the United States to the British Empire. Once re-united, the Anglo-Saxon race would bring the whole uncivilized world under its rule. The aim of the enterprise was the entirely desirable goal of rendering war impossible and promoting the best interest of humanity.

The secrecy Rhodes proposed was romantic, since most of its aims were relatively straightforward and largely reasonable.[4] One was to find talented young men who wanted to serve their country, and support them out of the society's funds. Another was to promote the cause of imperial federation, to support closer ties between England and its colonies, and actively oppose secession movements. To these ends it would try to influence the press, and if necessary, buy newspapers.

Finally, it would engage in active fundraising. Since Rhodes made the secretary of state for the colonies one of the trustees of his estate, it is not obvious how he expected keep his plan out of the public domain.

The will that Rhodes discussed with the Kiplings was his seventh. By 1900, he had changed his means if not his dream. Rhodes was among those, like Sir Charles Dilke and later Winston Churchill, who thought that the division of the English-speaking peoples by the American Revolution was nothing less than a tragedy. Rhodes realized, naturally, that the United States was never going to return to a position of subservience, nor did he want it to. Like Kipling, he thought that it was the destiny of the English-speaking peoples to rule the world and that it would be good for humanity if they did so. The question remained: How could he best use the great wealth he had amassed from South Africa's and Rhodesia's gold and diamond mines to bring about this end? It was over long dinners with the Kiplings that Rhodes worked through his last effort at will-making.

On 26 March 1902, Cecil Rhodes died. His will was published on 8 April. He had been kicked about a fair bit politically in the last few years of his life, after the failed Jameson raid. Driven from office as premier of Cape Colony, he died aged forty-nine of a congenital heart defect. Rhodes was not wealthy on the vast scale of, say, a Rockefeller or a Carnegie, but his bequest of £4,000,000 (roughly $400,000,000 in current dollars), most of it intended to provide scholarships for Americans and colonial young men to study at Oxford, was still spectacular enough. Parkin had condemned the Jameson raid and held Rhodes partly responsible. However, Parkin thought that this generous and imaginative bequest redeemed him. In reply to a reporter, Parkin presciently commented in the Toronto *Globe* in April 1902 that the scholarships were "likely to have a profound and far-reaching effect....It is one of these germ ideas which will impress the imagination of the world and...will go a great distance towards promoting a closer relation between the two branches of the Anglo-Saxon race." He teased his daughter Maude: "Do you not wish that you were an athlete, and a person of good character, and a boy, and so with a chance to win a Rhodes Scholarship at Oxford?"

Rhodes was buried, as his will instructed, among the loneliness of the Matappos in Rhodesia in a square to be cut on the top of the

I, Cecil Rhodes

hill and covered with a plain brass plate bearing the words, "Here lie the remains of Cecil John Rhodes."[5] Among the trustees of his estate, Rhodes appointed Lord Rosebery; Lord Grey, a board member of Rhodes's company; Lord Milner, his executor; Leander Jameson, his physician and political ally; Alfred Beit, a partner in Rhodes's De Beers diamond company; and Bouchier Hawksley, Rhodes's lawyer. Rhodes made bequests not related to the scholarships, some of which involved financing political activity in South Africa, and he left £100,000 to his old Oxford College, Oriel.

The bulk of Rhodes's estate, however, was earmarked for his scholarships. He wanted to bring young men from the United States and the colonies to the United Kingdom, give them an education, and introduce them also to its way of life, in the hope that the friendships made at Oxford would foster greater understanding between the future leaders of the English-speaking world. This goal, he thought, was best achieved in a university where most of the students lived in a residential setting. He considered, and then rejected, the idea of giving scholarships of the University of Edinburgh, precisely because its students did not live in residence. He did not, he made clear, wish to turn the Americans who received the scholarships into imitation Englishmen. His hope, as he put it, was that they would form an attachment to Great Britain without "withdrawing them or their sympathies from the land of their adoption or birth." Although there is a myth that Rhodes provided scholarships for only thirteen states, representing the original American colonies, he in fact provided continuing funding for all the American states and territories.

The Rhodes Scholarships are famous for their selection criteria. His scholars were not to be merely bookworms. Although he fiddled with the weighting, Rhodes eventually decided that forty per cent should be given to scholarly accomplishments, twenty to fondness for sports and success in them, the next twenty to qualities of manhood, truth and courage; and to fill out the selection criteria, a likelihood to make a commitment at some later point to public life. The first marks were to be awarded on the basis on an examination; the next two by a student vote, and the last by the school principal. Section 24 stated: "No student shall be qualified or disqualified for election to a Scholarship on account of his race or religious opinions." It would soon become apparent that the will might be wise in the grand vision, but it was singularly flawed in its attention to detail.

The Trustees first met on 5 May 1902 at Lord Rosebery's comfortable London home in Berkley Square. Six trustees were there, but it was unusual later for so many to be present, since some of them normally resided in South Africa and, after 1904, Lord Grey was governor-general of Canada. Increasingly, Rosebery and Hawksley, Rhodes's London-based solicitor, managed the Trust's affairs.[6] One of their initial concerns seems to have been Rhodes's odd distribution of scholarships for Canada: although Canada had seven provinces, he allotted it only two, one each for Ontario and Quebec.

It was a stroke of luck that Parkin, as usual, had ignored Annie's concerns about money and come for the coronation, even if the coronation itself had to be postponed because of King Edward VII's bout of appendicitis. In early May, Lord Grey had written to Parkin that he wanted to discuss the question of the Canadian scholarships with him and intimated that there might be more funds available for Canada. On 18 June 1902, Lord Grey wrote again to Parkin to invite him to a breakfast meeting to discuss Canada's quota. Parkin replied, suggesting that perhaps they should also meet with Principal William Peterson of McGill University. Grey invited fellow trustees Jameson and Beit, and also asked Richard Haldane, a distinguished barrister who often appeared before the Judicial Committee of the Privy Council in Canadian cases. The Trustees eventually decided to increase the number of scholarships to eight each year.

Four days later, Grey wrote to Parkin again. "I want particularly to see you. Can you come here tomorrow...to breakfast 9 a.m. or before 11.30." The day following his meeting with Grey, Parkin was interviewed by Jameson, Beit, Bouchier Hawksley, Sir Lewis Mitchell, and lords Rosebery, Grey, and Milner. They made preliminary enquiries as to whether Parkin would be interested in implementing the scholarship plan. They promised him an adequate income, ample freedom of action, and a generous expense allowance. On 27 June, he wrote to Lord Grey saying that he looked on the proposal as a call to wider work and that he was inclined to accept the offer. In return, the Trustees wanted to know when they could expect a firm answer. Parkin equivocated; he couldn't give an exact reply. The board at UCC, he thought, had the right to six months' notice, though he didn't think that they would insist on more than four weeks if he stuck it out for the beginning of term, and felt an obligation at least to do that.

Parkin began to consult with friends such as James Bryce and Sir William Anson, warden of All Soul's College, Oxford. Increasingly, though, he was now turning to his daughter Maude as his confidante. Although she was only twenty-two, she was an extremely intelligent and cultured young woman. She had more than fulfilled Miss Hentschy's expectations for her. She was one of the first women to attend McGill, where she won a scholarship and graduated near the top of her class in 1903. He had been writing to her for years and could talk to her as to no one else in the family. "There are many difficulties and perplexities, and my own feeling at the present moment is that we are more likely than otherwise to come back to the old work, at any rate for some time. The whole thing is so new: it has such possibilities of great influence or great failure that no one is disposed to move without much reflection and least of all myself." Although Annie had been with him for a while, he continued to lead an quasi-independent existence and was scheduled to leave in five days for Canada. Parkin complained to Maude in a letter that he would "be afloat without a home advisor at one of the most critical periods of my life," but he had rarely taken Annie's opinions or interests into account in the past, and there is little indication that he did in making his decision about the Rhodes post.

His continuing lack of sensitivity to Annie's desires and needs was evident in a couple of events he recounted to Maude. On one occasion, Annie felt uncomfortable about attending fancy parties and had begged off a lavish reception at the home of Winston Churchill's aunt. Parkin went anyway. Another day they had a far more upscale event, an invitation from the Prince and Princess of Wales. Parkin wrote to Maude that he hoped "to keep Mother up to the scratch for it." His diary entry for that day reads: "At St. James Palace to a reception by the Prince and Princess of Wales. Very striking and interesting." Some of Parkin's friends could see that this life was grinding his wife down, even if he could not. "Aunt" Anna told him that the best reason for taking the new position was to help Annie: "I feel sure if dearest Annie is relieved of money cares her health is sure to improve much more rapidly again than it will if they continue."

In any event, Parkin's appointment was still very much a work-in-progress, rather than a done deal. Rosebery approached people in Oxford about the details and they balked at the £2000 salary that the Trustees were proposing for this new post. Academic positions at Oxford paid £1200–1300. The new appointment should be in the same range, though they agreed that an allowance for travel and entertainment would be appropriate. A man of tact was needed, they thought, one with wide sympathy and stimulating character. Rosebery asked if they could they suggest some names. They wanted some time to think about it. Rosebery mentioned Parkin. Parkin, they agreed, was well suited and did have his contacts throughout the empire, but it would be a pity to take him away from the good work he was doing in Canada. It was quite possible that an entirely suitable person could be found in Oxford. It is not clear from the memorandum whether the Oxford authorities did not want Parkin, or whether they were protecting their turf, but they certainly were not smoothing his way.

Neither did the Board of Governors at Upper Canada College, although they did not put any particular barriers in his way either. Just as in Fredericton, Parkin wanted to leave at fairly short notice. He was supposed to have been recruiting masters while he was in England, but the Rhodes business diverted him. He also wasn't entirely sure what he wanted from his board. The offer from the Rhodes Trustees was not a permanent position. It was only for two years. On 12 July he cabled to see if UCC would grant him a leave of absence. He would set the system for selecting Rhodes candidates in order and then return to Canada. His problem was there were too many board members on vacation for it to meet and give him a decision, and the Rhodes Trustees wanted an answer. He wasn't prepared to consider a compromise that he undertake the initial organization for a shorter period of time. "I have consulted two or three very clear-headed friends upon the matter (I mention Lord Strathcona as one) and they strongly advise me not to undertake a large task like this unless I have a fair prospect of carrying it forward to a successful conclusion, for which they think the time we spoke of quite inappropriate."

The Rhodes Trustees didn't seem clear exactly what they wanted from Parkin either. At one point, Parkin wrote to Maude in the middle of July, saying it looked like he wasn't going to get the job. At another point it did. "The only comfort is that I do not much care—entirely different as the decision must make one's line of life & work. But in either case there is full employment for one's best energies...." However, the Board of Governors allowed Parkin to resign effective 1 October 1902. With the Rhodes Trustees he agreed to what was in effect a generous two-year contract, the length of time the Trustees estimated it would take to put the scholarship scheme into effect. Parkin was happy with the arrangement. At £2000 he was receiving roughly twice his UCC salary—four years' income for two years' work, as he put it. He received a further £1000 for travel and hotel expenses.

It was generous, but if "Aunt" Anna Koch thought that a salary even that large would soothe Annie's problems, she was mistaken. Although Raleigh Parkin claimed that his father paid off all of his debts before his death, there must have been many who forgave debts incurred so many years earlier, though probably none so charmingly or a graciously as his former student early in 1902:

Many thanks for the cheque, of course! It seems an outrage to be taking your money when the favour was so long ago—and so infinitely small in comparison with all I have received at your good hands. You know I owe you nearly everything, over and above what a man always owes to his parents. I really think you ought not to send me any more. The thing must be discharged by this time, isn't it? I have not [kept] count. Bless your Heart!
With much love,
Bliss Carman

Discharging one debt didn't preclude him from assuming another. He decided that he would take up the debt on the family farm in Salisbury. He wanted the farm for Raleigh, so that he would have a connection to Canada when he grew up. "Mother does not believe in this a bit," he wrote to Maude, "but she does not understand some of my instincts. I think I can do it by some extra work here and there," he concluded with his usual optimism.

Parkin returned to UCC in late August. He was especially interested in supervising the opening of the prep school, which admitted forty-five boys. The board appointed George Spalding acting principal. "I shall miss my talks with you very much," Minto wrote in a farewell note. For the next eighteen years, until he was seventy-four, Parkin would have his perfect job, one where he didn't have to keep God, the empire, and Oxford separate.

Parkin was due in Oxford on 7 October 1902. He took the SS *Tunisian* of the Allan Line. Sea travel agreed with him. He read a lot, slept well, and sleep restored his mental balance. On shipboard, he could forget the petty worries of everyday life. He arrived restored and refreshed and, in this case, ready for a new challenge that might give him a "new mental start." Twenty-nine years earlier, on 11 October 1873, he had matriculated, coincidentally the same day as Rhodes, though there is no evidence that the two men had knowingly met. At that time Parkin couldn't afford to live in college, and used wax candles to economize. Now he was negotiating with the university authorities how to organize the £60,000 a year generated for the scholarships.

Rhodes's will provided for fifty-two scholarships each year. These were divided into two types: Colonial (British Empire) and the United States. Rhodesia received three each year. Each of the following received one scholarship each year, for a maximum at any one time of three: South Africa (awarded to graduates only of The South African College School, Cape of Good Hope; The Stellenbosch School, Cape of Good Hope; Diocesan School of Rondesbosch, Cape of Good Hope; St. Andrews College School Grahamstown, Cape of Good Hope); Natal; *Australia*: New South Wales, Victoria, Queensland, Western Australia, Tasmania; New Zealand; *Canada*: Ontario, Quebec; Newfoundland and its Dependencies; Bermuda; Jamaica.

Rhodes provided for thirty-two American scholarships. American states were not to receive one each year, but two every three years. Further, the scholarship plan was not centred on the United States as much as the total number of scholarships might suggest, since he provided in his will that, if there were insufficient funds to pay all the scholarships, the Rhodesian ones should have priority, the students from Rondebosch and St. Andrews schools next, the colonial scholarships third, and the Americans last. Rhodes added a further codicil to his will that created a third category. It gave the German Kaiser authority to nominate five scholars each year in hope that "an understanding between the three great powers will render war impossible and educational relations make the strongest tie." He made this additional provision because he believed that the Kaiser had made English language instruction compulsory in German schools. He didn't specify where these stood in the hierarchy of financing, but presumably they would have taken the last spot.

Tact, charm, and perseverance were in the job description of making this dream a reality. Parkin had these qualities and he needed them, particularly when dealing with Oxford. In one sense, Oxford University existed only as a sentiment or a state of mind. It was much like a mediaeval kingdom, with a very weak monarch. The university itself had little in the way of endowment, though some of the colleges were extremely rich. Rhodes, after all, had bequeathed a very large sum to Oriel College, not to Oxford University. The university's central administration was extraordinarily weak. It needed college approval for almost all important changes in university regulations. More particularly, Parkin needed the co-operation of the colleges because they were fundamental to Rhodes's vision. First, Oxford education depended almost exclusively on weekly, one-on-one meetings between a student and a don assigned by his college. There were lectures, but these were optional and often sparsely attended. More important, but closely connected, Rhodes made it clear in his will that he chose Oxford because it was a residential university. If the colleges would not admit the students who received the scholarships, Rhodes could not achieve his objective. It was not immediately obvious to all the dons at Oxford why it was to Oxford's benefit to have the university overrun by a bunch of colonials and Americans, rather than the usual batch from Eton and Harrow, and scholarship boys from some of the better grammar schools.

Parkin spent his first fortnight meeting with individual members of the university and with the university's governing body, the Hebdomadal Council. After some preliminary discussions, he had to meet with each of the individual colleges. Students had to apply to individual colleges for admission and it was necessary to find out which ones were prepared to accept applicants and how many. The other matter into which he needed to make preliminary enquiries was what courses of study were open to students. One of the many questions that had not been resolved was the age of the students and the stage of their academic career when they received the award. Oxford prided itself on its broad general education. For a student at Oxford, the highest achievement was a first in Greats, an undergraduate Classics degree. While some of the Ivy League universities followed the English model in pursuing general studies, most of the leading American universities were increasingly following the German practice of specialization, and many offered research degrees, such as a doctorate. This qualification increasingly was becoming necessary to teach in American institutions of higher education, but it was not necessary at Oxford, and Oxford dons deplored the level of specialization that it involved. Parkin spent a month negotiating with the various colleges.

In late November, Parkin sailed back to Canada to sever his ties with UCC completely. The governors still had not found a replacement for him and were counting on him to serve as their United Kingdom recruiter. He was no longer interested. "To tell the truth," he wrote to Maude, "anxious as I am to see the right man in the place I am not at all anxious to bear the responsibility of selecting him."

As usual, Parkin took the opportunity of the crossing, even at that time of year, to relax and refresh himself, reading novels such as George Meredith's *Diana of the Crossways* and a biography of Darwin. He found Darwin's ideas of "natural selection," "the survival of the fittest," and "the struggle for existence" were evidence that the universe was designed by an intelligent creator. "All this has been in a way familiar to me for years through reviews & quotations," he said, probably forgetting that it was just what Loring Bailey had taught him at the University of New Brunswick when he was an undergraduate.

As it happened, Parkin was en route to New Brunswick, via Toronto. While there, he convened the first of many conferences and meetings he held over the next two years in Sackville, site of Mount Allison University, about fifty miles or so from his boyhood home. He invited representatives from each of the Maritime provinces to discuss the administration of the Rhodes Scholarships. He followed with meetings in Montreal and Toronto.[7] There were some who wanted the competition to be open between all the institutions of higher learning in each province each year; and others who wanted the scholarships to alternate between the denominational and non-denominational schools. For example, the secular University of New Brunswick would get three appointments each seven years, as would the Methodist Mount Allison. St. Joseph's, a bilingual Roman Catholic institution in Memramcook, near Moncton, would be granted one.[8] In Quebec, Parkin's problem was to try to secure the co-operation of the Université de Laval. For Parkin and many of the other imperialists, the co-operation of the "better sort" of French-Canadian was important to create closer co-operation between Canada and the empire. However, Laval's rector was not convinced that he wanted to send the province's best and brightest francophone Roman Catholic to study in Oxford and he took a long while to be convinced.

On his way to Newfoundland, Parkin found himself only sixteen miles away from Guglielmo Marconi in Glace Bay. Bad weather had left him stranded, so he decided to pay Marconi a surprise visit. Parkin had met many interesting people in the course of his visits to Government House, but in January 1902 Minto introduced him to a uniquely fascinating young friend: his twenty-six-year-old protégé. Parkin liked the young man immediately; he found him simple and modest, "a most satisfactory kind of great man." Parkin also thought that Marconi's plan to transmit information by wireless telegraphy across the Atlantic at one-hundredth the cost of a cable fit perfectly into Parkin's ideas of using improved technology to bring the empire closer together.

In December 1901, Marconi had proven that it was possible to transmit over long distances when he sent three short beeps from Signal Hill in Newfoundland to Cornwall. Now he was prepared to try something far more ambitious. In October 1902, Marconi approached Moberley Bell at the *Times* and asked if he would like to be the recipient of the first Marconigram, as it later came to be known. Bell replied that he would contact his Canadian correspondent, Fred Cook, to see if Parkin could use his contacts to get the governor-general or the prime minister to send the first message. Minto agreed that the king should be the recipient. By December 1902, the various parties had negotiated a text, but Marconi had run into technical difficulties and wasn't quite ready to proceed. It was Parkin's good luck to turn up just when Marconi was ready.

On 20 December 1902, Marconi sent Lord Minto's message. The text, which was transmitted from Cape Breton and received in Cornwall, read:

> *To his Majesty the King, London—May I be permitted by means of this wireless message to congratulate your Majesty on success of Marconi's great invention connecting England and Canada?*
> *Minto*

Since he was there, Parkin took the liberty to send his own message:

> *Being Present at transmission in Marconi's Canadian station have honour send through Times inventor's first wireless transatlantic message of greeting to England and Italy*
> *Parkin*

Parkin's message was written in ink, except for the first word, "Being," which was in pencil. There were people who thought that Marconi's whole operation was nothing but smoke and mirrors deception. Parkin added "Being" at the very last minute to make sure that there could be no pre-arranged transmission of his note.

Early in 1903. Parkin's old friend William Peterson, principal of the University of McGill, informed him that he was being awarded an honorary doctorate, his second. It was recognition for his past accomplishments, but Parkin's new career was going to provide even more challenges that his previous ones. He was setting off on what were to prove virtually endless travels. Just as there was no reason automatically to expect Oxford colleges to participate in the Rhodes plan, there was equally no reason to assume that every American state and territory would want to send some of its most promising students to England to study. Rhodes's will caught the public's imagination and there was great interest, but there was no guarantee that would translate

I, Cecil Rhodes

into bodies in cabins on trans-Atlantic steamers. So on 3 January 1903 Parkin held a preliminary meeting with the Association of State Universities in Washington.

Rhodes had said that he wanted his scholars to taste British life, but not to be seduced from their native lands. That provision suggested that they should not be too young when they arrived in residence, and the association decided that the students should have completed at least two years of university, but that they not be more than two years beyond their degree, no more that twenty-four years old, and to enjoy college life, must be unmarried. They would also pursue the broad education at which Oxford excelled, and would not, except in special circumstances, pursue a research degree.

Oxford would send examinations which would determine students' eligibility for admission, though each state might add its own additional examination, and the states would bear the costs of the selections. Each scholar needed to be able to pass an Oxford test called Responsions. This requirement caused innumerable problems over the next decade and a half. Responsions tested basic competency in Latin and Greek. It was a test that any English public school boy of ordinary intelligence could pass without much effort, since it formed a large part of the his curriculum, but Greek wasn't necessarily part of the high school curriculum in South Carolina or Idaho. Yet, in 1903, success in Responsions was not a qualifying requirement that Oxford was prepared to waive for anyone.

A final question was harder to resolve: what state should a student candidate represent, the one in which he was at college, or where his home was? The problem was that the United States had some "national" universities such as Harvard and Yale, which attracted students from many states, and other state universities and colleges whose students were largely home-grown. Some of the latter wanted to restrict the competition to their own students. Others wanted students to have a choice of where they might compete, so that a Harvard student, say, could choose to compete either in Massachusetts or in his state of origin. Parkin preferred the latter option and strongly advocated it, but he would be prepared to sacrifice the principle if the result would be a functioning selection committee.[9]

Although access to the president of the United States was easier in

1903 than it is today, it was still an honour to visit the White House, and it was an indication of the interest the scholarships were generating that Arthur Lee could arrange for his two old friends, George Parkin and President Theodore Roosevelt, to lunch together on 5 January. According to Parkin's diary, Roosevelt advised him to keep politicians completely out of the selection process, since they could be counted on to use the scholarships to reward their relatives and cronies. After he met with Roosevelt, Parkin visited Baltimore, Philadelphia, Princeton, and New York, before finally leaving for Toronto. In Philadelphia he lunched with Andrew Carnegie, who told him that the best American young men would not attend Oxford because it would not prepare them for what they sought in life. Parkin asked what that was. "Dollars," Carnegie replied.

By the middle of January, Parkin was suffering from a short bout of illness that was partly exhaustion, and partly a bronchial infection. If Parkin wouldn't listen to his friends' advice that he needed to slow down occasionally, he couldn't ignore his body when it told him that it occasionally needed some rest, though that didn't stop him working from bed. Annie stayed in London with the children. She was worn out after the summer with her husband. "[A]fter you left she had a rest and felt so much better," Maude wrote to him. "I think she'll get rest now."

Annie took a long while to recover, but Parkin usually bounced back quickly. On 19 January he left for Atlantic City, New Jersey, and soon began to get a taste of the serious problems that were going to face the scholarship plan on the ground, one of the many that Rhodes never considered. The state of Delaware, he discovered on inspection, had no educational institution above high school level or "a very one horse college." The state was extremely corrupt, even in its elections to the United States Senate. There was simply nobody in Delaware that he could find who was fit to award the scholarship and nobody he could find who might even give him reasonable advice on the matter.

As he proceeded south, he increasingly realized the need to come to terms with what was called "the coloured question." When he was in Toronto in December, James Hughes, an inspector of the Toronto School Board, contacted him. Booker T. Washington, a prominent black American educator, had recently lectured there. He wanted the

I, Cecil Rhodes

Rhodes Scholarships to be "available for Colored as well as White men" and asked Parkin to contact him. He offered to serve on a committee to help deal with the problem. As Parkin headed south, he received a letter dated 21 January from W.E.B. DuBois, an economist and another leading black American educator. There were ten or twelve institutions for Americans of negro descent that were doing high-grade work, but unless a special effort was made, they might very well get left out. Would it be possible, DuBois asked Parkin, to organize a meeting between Parkin and representatives of those institutions to see how they might participate in the scholarships? Parkin thought that he had worked out an arrangements with the Southern white universities that would allow representatives of the better black universities to attend the initial organizing meeting, but Chancellor Hill of Georgia did not invite them to the conference because of what "he himself described as a technicality, viz., a slight difference in the amount of algebra required," he reported to the Trustees.

Some people who knew Rhodes were puzzled about why he included clause 24 in his will, a clause which stated that no student should be disqualified on account of his race. However, the Trustees took the position that the meaning of the phrase was clear as it stood, and they would apply its plain meaning. Parkin made a point of visiting Booker Washington at Tuskegee and dining with a dozen of his faculty. He also went to Atlanta where he met personally with DuBois. He found these meetings "all interesting to the highest degree," and since he said this in a letter to Maude, it undoubtedly represented his honest opinion. The black educators asked Parkin if the Trustees would set some of the scholarships aside specifically for blacks. He replied that to do so would as explicitly contradict section 24 of the will as to exclude blacks.

However, Parkin was not looking for trouble. He did not intend to use the Rhodes Scholarships as a means of social engineering. He told Washington directly that it was no part of the trust's responsibility to solve the racial problems of the south, and that in his view the Negro must rely for justice upon public opinion in their own country. As a correspondent from Tennessee warned Parkin, if blacks were allowed to compete for the examinations, it was more than likely that Southern whites would boycott the scholarships or simply absent themselves.

If a black Rhodes scholar ended up at Oxford, he would almost certainly be shunned by the Southerners. In 1904, the white universities in Georgia decided to rotate the scholarships among themselves. DuBois wrote to the Trustees in protest. Parkin promised to look into the matter and confided to Hawksley that he didn't see how the rotation could not progress to a black college after each of the white colleges had had a scholarship. The final decision was that any kind of rota system violated the fundamental principle of the will. When Tennessee also decided to go ahead with a rota system, regardless of the Trustees' views, he could not endorse it:

> Then again, in your Southern states there is behind the rotation system the question of the coloured Universities which the Trustees would prefer not to touch in any way. When we parted at Atlanta I could say with perfect truth that the students of coloured Universities were free to apply for examination. If a system of rotation is fixed, it will probably be urged that it is an indirect method of exclusion. The terms of Mr. Rhodes's Will are such that it would be well nigh impossible for the Trustees to formally endorse anything that looked like this.

On 5 February 1903, Parkin was at a conference in Kansas City and by 10 February he was back at Atlantic City, New Jersey, where Annie had been left to wait for him while he went on his travels. Rosebery sent him a telegram: "Think you are overtasking yourself. Pray be more careful." As usual Parkin paid no attention to such advice. On 16 February, he was in Minneapolis; from the 23rd to the 27th in Regina, Vancouver, and Victoria. On 3 March, he told Maude that he didn't think he could keep up the pace he had started. While Parkin was on the West Coast, Annie remained in a hotel in Atlantic City. Parkin had just paid off the last of his debt to Alise Hentschy for the girls' school fees, but Annie herself was once again short of money and a continent away from her husband. "I hope you haven't made any mistake about money. It does go so quickly tho' I try to be so careful. I shall be all right except for the passages and if they require much I can't pay it which is awkward."

Parkin spent 4–7 March in Spokane, Portland, and Oakland. Often he travelled overnight on the train. In San Francisco, he visited the State University and then Stanford, at both of which he addressed large numbers of students. Then he started back east, with his first stop as Salt Lake City in Utah.

"I must write you a few lines about my visit here before I resume my journey eastward tonight, as I am compelled to do to keep my engagement at Denver," he wrote to Hawksley on 14 March 1903. Parkin had just emerged from a meeting with the three presidents who constituted the inner councils of the Mormon Church. The tour, he said, was added to the experiences of his life in ways he had not expected. The Mormons impressed upon him their sect's keen interest in education, and expressed a strong desire that they should have an opportunity take advantage of the scholarships. The size of the Mormon population in Utah and the Mormon presence in education, Parkin pointed out, combined with section 24 of the will, would make it very hard to establish a selection committee that was not permanently dominated by Mormons and did not permanently choose Mormon candidates. "Between the 'nigger' in the South and the Mormon here, we shall not be allowed to forget that there are unsettled race and creed questions," Parkin reported back to Hawksley in London. Then he boarded a train for yet another stamina-testing twenty-four-hour run to Denver.

On 24 March he was in New York and in despair. The private universities there, such as Columbia, had reservations about meeting with the University of New York, but by 27 March Parkin's diplomatic abilities had smoothed things over. "I had found out many weeks ago that the conflicting elements were numerous and that it would require some skill to make things work in harmony." He even managed to make progress on the thorny question of Delaware. Many boys from the state went to Princeton, Pennsylvania University, and Johns Hopkins, he was told, so why not ask their presidents, along with the president of one institution from Delaware, to form the selection committee? "I think this will turn out very satisfactorily," Parkin concluded. And with that, he and Annie set off for Genoa, where they landed on 9 April, proceeded to Monte Carlo on the 11th, to Nice on the 13th, Marseilles on the 14th, and then to Paris, where he installed himself in the Villa St. Georges to write his report. Since the previous June he had crossed the Atlantic five times and travelled 17,000 miles by train.

15

Home and Away

The Oxford dons who were sceptical of Rhodes's bequest had some justification and it was no mere witticism that Parkin had trouble separating Oxford and the empire. To fulfil Rhodes's intentions, Parkin believed, Oxford needed to become a "great Imperial University."[1] That was not every Oxonian's understanding of the university's mission. It was fortunate that the Trustees decided that even Parkin could not handle all the work himself. They appointed Francis Wylie early in 1903 as the Trust's resident administrator with a salary of £1000 and an entertainment allowance of £250. Wylie was an Oxford man, a fellow of Brasenose College, who knew his way around the system better than Parkin. One of the conditions under which he accepted the appointment was that Parkin would not reside in Oxford. Wylie feared that the older, more senior man with the international reputation would overshadow him and undermine his authority. The Trustees agreed. Parkin was not to live in Oxford. They provided Wylie with a residence in South Parks Road near the centre of Oxford, where he could entertain the Rhodes scholars.[2] Douglas Brodie and Charles Boyd became London secretaries reporting to Hawksley. The first year, 1903, Wylie had the opportunity for a trial run, since only the five German scholars appointed by the kaiser and seven South Africans came into residence.³

Even after travelling 17,000 miles, Parkin had surveyed only half his domain. It was now time to organize the other half, and for better or worse, he took Annie with him. Now that she was free from her responsibilities as "wife of the Principal of Upper Canada College," Annie tentatively tried to rebuild her marriage. Parkin's generous salary meant that their money worries were diminished, but not eliminated. They had in effect two families, as a consequence of the tragedies of the child deaths and the still birth. When Parkin accepted the Rhodes position, Lal (Alice) was twenty-three. Maude, his heart's darling, was twenty-two, and Grace was twenty. The "babies," Marjorie and Raleigh, were eleven and seven. The older girls stayed with friends or took genteel positions such as lady's companion, all of which required parental subventions. When Annie and Parkin travelled, the younger two were left to stay with their nanny. It wasn't a very satisfactory arrangement and it wasn't common, even by Edwardian standards. The alternative was leaving Annie behind, but that would have meant, as always, finding somewhere for her and the children to live. Parkin was too romantic to be calculating. It just seemed best to him for them to be together. Annie liked the idea. Her experience of the trip was at best ambivalent.

They arrived at Cape Town, South Africa, on the SS *Norman* on 16 June 1903. Parkin hoped to spend some time with Milner, who was in charge of reconstructing South Africa after the Boers' defeat, along with a group of brilliant young men he had recruited—"Milner's Kindergarten," as they became known. Milner had been raised in the peerage to the rank of viscount for his services in South Africa during the war. Parkin acknowledged this achievement by addressing a letter to him as "My Lord." In response, Milner jokingly teased his friend's prissiness: "Please don't 'Lord' me, after 30 years!" and apologized that he would not have much time for socializing since Parkin had come at an especially busy time of the political year.

The truth was that Parkin's trip to South Africa was as much social as business. The choice of the South African scholars was in the hands of four designated schools, so there was little that Parkin needed to do except meet with Jameson, who was a Rhodes trustee, some of the other influential politicians, and then undertake some tourism at his usual gruelling pace. He and Annie left Cape Town on 19 June. From there they went to Colesburgh Junction, where, in Annie's words, they had a lovely tea with Lady Michels after the poisonous tea and coffee on the train. Then they moved on to Bloemfountain, Johannesburg, and Pretoria. On the 28th Annie found herself in a railway compartment meant for four people. They were provided with two bundles of old, grey bedding, and she worried that two other people might descend on the compartment. "Got ready—it was so cold I merely loosened my things and put on a dressing gown, fur coat, cloak, rug and by means of hot water bottles slept fairly well but I wish you could have seen us. I laughed till I cried almost. It is all very dirty and rough and really makes travelling here a good deal of a bother." June 30 was the date of the important conference regarding the scholarships, and then it was back travelling again. On 3 July they lost their luggage; on the 11th Annie wrote in her diary that they had to go a great distance out of their way; with all the dust, she says, she felt like a pig; "Travelling here is by no means reduced to a science—one has to learn by bitter experience. Sometimes the organization is very bad and the tipping expense ruinous." On 13 July, Parkin and Annie were in Bulawayo in Rhodesia and on the 16th at Rhodes's grave, which Annie found beyond words, surely the most wonderful burial place in the world, on top of a great granite hill. "The grave lies on the top—surrounded by huge boulders that seem to rest lightly but just surround it like huge sentinels." Early in August they visited Jameson at Groote Schuur. Annie was struck by the orchard and the wild animals roaming about. What Parkin liked about it was the fact that you could go in and order meals at any time. It was, as he described it, a perfect Liberty Hall. Parkin had an important talk with Jameson, who introduced him to the fine art of smoking, which Annie even encouraged. He didn't progress beyond cigarettes to cigars, but was inclined to think that taking up smoking was a good idea. It helped him sleep and it calmed his nerves—something to think seriously about, as he put it. They went to Kimberley in Rhodesia on the 20th to see the diamond mines that were the source of Rhodes's wealth, then to Grahamstown, King Williamstown, and back to Capetown.

On 9 August 1903, they boarded ship again. Parkin found the 6000-

mile trip desolate, devoid of sea life. No porpoises, whales or flying fish, scarcely even seaweed. There were gulls and sea pigeons aplenty, but he had been hoping for an albatross and was disappointed. At sea, Parkin seemed a different man to Annie. They built castles in the air, "very rural castles," dreaming of a comfortable farmhouse with orchard and arbours, chicken coops, dairy and Jersey cows.

In the past they had gone on holidays to Cap à l'Aigle on the north shore of the St. Lawrence River where they could tickle for trout with their children. "Sometimes I feel as if I had done enough work in the world to justify a good long rest; then when I see a Pope eleven years older than I am starting off cheerfully to rule over the Roman [Catholic] world I feel as if it would be a bit weak to shrink from anything that comes...." He and Annie spent the days walking the decks, talking, sleeping, and reading. On Sunday they went to all three church services.

By 26 August, Parkin and Annie were 11,000 miles from London, nearly halfway around the world. Parkin had just finished a book on whaling, and had started one on the history of civilization. He had read one of Thomas Hardy's novels on Annie's recommendation, another by one of his favourite authors, Robert Louis Stevenson, and some books about Africa and New Zealand. Annie, though, was already anxious to get home. According to Parkin, she rebelled against being a wife (by which he meant "dutiful wife") once in a while. They had two adjoining cabins; she made hers a reminder of home, with photographs of her children that he said she mooned over. "I have never felt quite sure that she would not some day spread her wings and fly homeward where her heart is a good deal of the time," he noted, not understsanding that he was dragging her away from where her heart lay.

At the next stage they suffered a setback. Parkin was due to meet with a delegation in Tasmania, but when the ship arrived in Hobart on 28 August, he found it couldn't land because of an outbreak of smallpox. Instead, they headed for New Zealand. They landed at Lyttleton on 10 September and caught a train for Christchurch. In New Zealand Parkin was widely interviewed in the press, and socialized extensively. He enjoyed these activities, especially meeting Mrs. Spencer Medley, daughter-in-law of his mentor, Bishop Medley. But he also saw these contacts as a way of popularizing and strengthening his central mission.

Although New Zealand had only one scholarship to award, Parkin, as usual, held a conference to discuss the selection criteria. Because New Zealand was much like the United Kingdom in education and culture, the conference decided that the candidates could be young, between nineteen and twenty-two, graduates or undergraduates with at least two years of university. The governor-general suggested that he should preside over a selection committee that consisted of the chancellor of the University of New Zealand and representatives of the university's four colleges.[4]

The Australian colonies had formed a federal state in 1901. Parkin hoped that they might hold a national conference under the governor-general, his friend Lord Tennyson.[5] It was not to be. Each state insisted on individual treatment. Tasmania sent delegates to meet with Parkin in Melbourne. Although Tasmania did not yet have a university, they wanted to use the scholarships to serve as a catalyst for the creation of one. They required that the university have a majority on the selection committee and that the Tasmanian candidate spend a minimum of two years enrolled at the institution.[6] Although Parkin did not think that the Rhodes Scholarships should be used for social engineering in racial or religious matters, he had no qualms whatever at using them to secure desirable educational reforms.

At Sydney, Parkin said he met the most difficult and delicate situation that he had yet encountered. Sir Normand MacLaurin, chancellor of the University of Sydney, had decided not only that the award should go exclusively to the graduates of his university, but that his university senate should make the decision. After widespread consultation, Parkin put enough pressure on the chancellor to persuade him to agree to a conference. While Parkin was waiting for it, he took the train to Queensland, where the educators wanted to send younger students. Parkin agreed, and it was a typical day at the office: "Fifteen hundred miles ride for a single day's work seems a good bit of distance, but I have never felt better repaid."[7]

If Queensland provided a satisfactory outcome, the Sydney conference didn't, but everything didn't always run smoothly. Parkin spoke for an hour, but then, as he saw it, the chancellor bullied the school masters into temporary silence and had everything his own way for a short while. "I think I told you in my last [letter] of the struggle at

Sydney, and how the one Chancellor there relentlessly squashed the school men; the most prominent of whom sat silent and seemed afraid to speak. Well, a few days later I saw in the papers that the school men had met, protested against the decision arrived at, and passed a resolution that I should be asked to return to Sydney. That would be absurd, as I could learn nothing by doing so beyond what I know now, but it vexes me to think that a bit of obstinacy baulked free discussion and the harmonious decision which was sure to follow." The schoolmasters pursued Parkin around Australia with letters trying to persuade him to change the procedures agreed on at the Sydney conference.[8]

In Melbourne, Parkin and Annie stayed with the Tennysons and were vice-regally entertained: races, a concert, the theatre, garden and dinner parties, all in swift succession. Parkin stayed up until one o'clock in the morning talking to his old friend, while Lady Tennyson diverted Annie. At Ballarat, they visited the gold mines, and in South Australia his old friend, Sir Samuel Way, the governor, took them to see the marvellous gardens at Marble Hill, the governor's summer home in the valleys behind Adelaide. Lady Way, he wrote to Maude, was "a woman who everybody admires and loves," and she and Annie became devoted to one another, Parkin told Maude. While they were there, Parkin received an honorary degree from the University of Adelaide. It was agreed that scholars should not be raw boys with no university training.

Next, in West Australia, which had no university and didn't want to see its youth sucked elsewhere, it was concluded with equal enthusiasm that a successful candidate could be as young as seventeen, though Parkin privately admitted that he had made a mistake in agreeing to this provision,[9] even though he was sympathetic to the principle that local circumstances should play an important role in determining selection criteria.

By the end of November, Parkin was more or less satisfied with the work he had done. He and Annie left Australia and were on their way home via the Suez Canal. They arrived back in London toward the end of December. Early in the new year, Parkin learned that he had received a very appropriate honour: to join Admiral Dewey, Mark Twain, William Van Horne, and other travellers as members of the Ends of the Earth Club.

With Annie left behind to look for permanent accommodation outside Oxford, Parkin set off on his travels once again, leaving Southampton on 16 March 1904 and landing in New York early in the morning of 23 March. He brought with him a package of sealed envelopes that had been prepared by Oxford for prospective Canadian and American Rhodes scholars.[10] Prior to his departure, Parkin had consulted Simon Newcomb, a world famous astronomer, whom Parkin had known as a child when Newcomb worked briefly as an apprentice to a herbalist in Salisbury. Parkin had been worried about how to prevent cheating if the exams were being held in different parts of the country. Newcomb suggested that the examinations be staggered across the times zones. That problem solved, on 11 April Parkin set sail for Bermuda, arriving on the 15th.

The Bermudan scholarship perplexed him. There were only 5000 whites on the island, some of whom Parkin described as poor whites. There were also "many self-respecting and progressive negroes." He brought together his usual committee of the great and the good, but it beggared his imagination how Bermuda could provide a qualified candidate each year. "Indeed almost everybody here wonders how Mr. Rhodes came to assign so small a population so great a prize," he wrote to Hawksley. The local inhabitants speculated that it might have been because Rhodes's brother had once been stationed there and had enjoyed himself, or that Rhodes simply had no real understanding of the colony.[11] In the event, the local citizens rose to the challenge. They raised funds to improve the leading local school. Nonetheless, many of the wealthier families sent their children to England or Canada, and if these boys were allowed to compete, they would normally defeat the local candidates. So, the legislature created two scholarships annually for study at a Canadian university. A winner, for example, might go to Mount Allison University, in Sackville, New Brunswick. After he completed a degree at a Canadian university, he would be able to compete on fair terms with the sons of richer parents who had been sent abroad.

Parkin then set off to the other problem Caribbean island, Jamaica. "The ship was poor—the food atrocious. If I get back from all these wanderings with unwrecked digestion it will be due to the tough internal fibre I have inherited from my yeoman ancestors in Yorkshire," he wrote to Hawksley. "I may be detained here for ten days or a fortnight, unless I charter a schooner, and at present season this means serious risk of being becalmed."

Unlike Bermuda and the southern United States, there was no "coloured problem" in Jamaica, since all of the local schools were mixed race. They were, like Bermuda, also unable to consistently provide Rhodes scholars, because anyone who could, sent their children away, not just to get a better education. The local schoolmasters were determined that only locally educated students should be allowed in the competition; the wealthier parents were equally anxious that their sons should qualify. The compromise was that the scholarship would be reserved to locally educated candidates every third year. In other years, any candidates who declared an intention to settle in Jamaica after completing his studies at Oxford was eligible.

Resolving that issue was relatively simple. Getting home wasn't. Since tourist season was finished, the boat to Santiago de Cuba no longer ran. There was some doubt whether he could cross to Cuba, but he saw his chance and arranged a passage on a Norwegian tramp steamer running from Port Antonio to the north coast of Cuba. The cattle ship had 300 loose oxen on board whose movements and moanings were intensified by a storm. With luck they made landfall. After several days, he managed to hitch a night-time ride on a banana car that took him thirty or forty miles, all the while pelted by a tropical storm. A day or two later he was able to board a local train that took him to Santiago. Santiago was the terminus of the railway Sir William Van Horne had built on the island. That train, in turn, wound its way 400 miles through virgin forests to Havana. From there, after misadventures with his laundry and luggage, he boarded a ferry to Key West, and eventually arrived by train in New York. The Manhattan Hotel probably never looked so good. He left Kingston, Jamaica, on 1 May 1904, Havana on the 12th, and arrived in New York on the 15th. He doesn't say that it was fifteen days well spent, but he didn't cool his heels either. Three day later he was on the road again, heading for St. John's, Newfoundland.

While Parkin was in North America, he had left Annie to find somewhere more permanent for them to live. His ties to Canada were becoming increasingly precarious. The previous year, when they were in

South Africa, he received news that the house he knew as a child and which he was buying for Raleigh burned down. His brother Watson, seventy-four, and sisters Lizzie, seventy-three, and Olive, seventy, were still living there and Watson was working the farm. He had to decide whether it was worthwhile rebuilding.

In London, Annie was at a loss as to what sort of accommodation she should get. Parkin's contract ran only until October 1905, so she didn't know whether she should buy or rent, and if she rented, whether it should be furnished or unfurnished. The other parts of her problem were fairly normal. Rents in attractive, fashionable areas were too high. Attractive, unfashionable areas were usually inconvenient. Or they could move farther out of London where the commuting cost would eat up part of the saving in rent. Maybe they should rent for a short period and plan on moving back to Canada. Would he please tell her what he wanted. Uncertainty didn't matter much to someone who went to Jamaica not knowing how he might get off the island, but it drove Annie crazy. "One thing certain we must not drift along but know what we are doing," she wrote, trying to get her husband to pay attention to his domestic affairs for a moment.

On 25 March 1904, Annie sent yet another letter to her husband, worrying about their financial situation. When they had left London in 1895, Milner's trust was giving him £500 a year. Now the Rhodes Trust was paying him £2000 a year with half that much again for expenses. Yet when Annie went over the accounts from the beginning of the year, she felt sick. Her estimates of their annual expenses were: rent, £300; servants, £250; housekeeping, £200; coal, £30; light, £30; education, £75; travelling, £100; recreation, £40; wine, etc., £20; repairs, £25; clothes for the family, £350; doctor, £50; postage, papers, £25; sundries, £55; church, £50. Their minimum budget ran to £1600; they had to get into a "settled way of living," she told her husband; "I beg of you consider it as much one of your duties as mine, at present I see nothing clearly." "I hope you will not pledge yourself to anything on the farm this year. I feel so strongly a home is the thing we need and ought to have first and it will not now be easy to get a suitable one."

Stress is one of the factors that triggers depression, and Annie's letters to Parkin show enough symptoms that earlier suspicions that she suffered from this illness are readily confirmed. On 30 March, after the letters about the house and her financial worries, she wrote: "I must be resting tho' sometimes I don't yet feel up to any thing and get often discouraged with myself in every way. Weak and stupid and not much good....I get so dead to everything and restless thinking, thinking and planning and yet it amounts to nothing." In a few sentences she expresses her low mood, feelings of lethargy, lack of energy, sense of personal worthlessness, and inability to concentrate. Persisting over two weeks, these symptoms would likely lead a doctor to a diagnosis of depression. Such depressions are likely to recur. Annie understood the sources of her problem, and she often told her husband. He was too busy to listen. "I have got too uprooted to have any growth. I feel like some plant or tree that had had much sunshine and care but had been transplanted too often and bore no fruit and only lived an artificial existence. Only as something torn up by the roots and lying in a corner is what I feel like just now." Annie complained that she could not get direction from him, but he was, as usual, in transit. However, in May she turned up a place at 40 Elvaston Place, a respectable address near the centre of London, for £300 a year.

Meanwhile, it had taken three days by rail and an overnight boat ride for Parkin to get to St. John's, Newfoundland. Had he come a year and a half earlier, he said he might have been too discouraged to carry on his work, but this was his seventy-first problem and he could cope with just about anything.[12] A large delegation met him at the station and they proceeded to wrangle from just before noon until midnight. The Rhodes Scholarships scheme had formed the basis of political manoeuvring on the island for much of the past year. The origin of the difficulty lay in Newfoundland's peculiar educational organization, which was based on several separate and competing Catholic and Protestant systems. The locals also wanted to exclude those who studied abroad. Parkin engineered a compromise similar to Bermuda's, so that the scholarship was reserved in alternate years for Newfoundland residents, though he thought that the local students would not be sufficiently prepared to profit from their experience at Oxford.[13]

At a meeting at the Royal Colonial Institute in December 1904, Parkin summarized his accomplishments over the previous two years:

Practically it has brought me in touch with almost every educational man of merit in the United States and in all our Colonies. In New York I met the heads of fifteen of the greatest American Universities, and in Washington the Presidents of the State Universities were assembled in conference. At Boston the Colleges and Schools of New England were represented. At Chicago nearly sixty heads of Colleges from the six neighbouring states, representing altogether between twenty and twenty-five millions of people, had been drawn together by President Harper. At Atlanta the nine Southern States were represented, the delegates coming 600 miles southward from Virginia and 500 miles northward from Louisiana. At Kansas City, Spokane, San Francisco, and Denver, the representatives of the Far West and Pacific Coast were collected. In the Maritime Provinces of Canada, at Montreal, Toronto, Winnipeg, Regina, and Vancouver, independent conferences were held, as also in each of the Australian States, in New Zealand, Bermuda, Jamaica and Newfoundland. In South Africa the consultation was chiefly with individual schools or the heads of educational departments.[14]

Sir Anthon Kenny, a former warden of Rhodes House, wrote that Parkin gave new meaning to the word "indefatigable." Parkin's exertions had, however, taken their toll on him once again, and in early December his doctor ordered him to stop work and take some rest at the seaside. Even at fifty-eight, Parkin must have realized that he had once more pushed himself to exhaustion, since he was even willing to forgo answering letters. There was no fear that Parkin's rest would prove a long one. He was heading back to North America on 4 January 1905. The Trust had made his position permanent effective 1 October 1904 on the same terms: £2000 salary and £1000 expenses.

No one could have done more than Parkin to set the scholarships going. He had dedication, energy, tact, charm, contacts, skill at bringing people together; and yet there remained so many unresolved problems. For example, Tennessee was still pressing for its rotation system as a way of avoiding the "coloured problem." On top of the other difficulties already raised, Parkin pointed out that in 1903, five American states failed to appoint any candidates and twelve appointed only one of the two to which they were entitled. To narrow down the pool of eligibility would exacerbate this problem.

Another problem was Quebec, which was supposed to alternate its candidate between McGill and Laval. After some effort to get Laval to nominate a candidate, its choice, a M. Belleau, rejected the scholarship on the grounds that he had two feet of different shape and that, after an operation, his feet were even weaker. He did not, in his own view, meet the athletic qualifications, and besides, he did not like violent sports. Parkin sailed again for New York on 4 January 1905 and headed immediately for Montreal to deal with this crisis. He despaired, as always, of the French-Canadians. "Our French Canadian friends had never really grasped what was expected of them," he complained to Hawksley. Since Laval's own candidate had withdrawn, there was a possible candidate at the Jesuit college, Loyola, but it wasn't clear whether Laval would sanction a successful Loyola candidate because of rivalry between the two institutions. As it happened, the Jesuit failed the qualifying examination and wasn't eligible. Parkin then threw the competition open to the province as a whole and consulted Peterson, McGill's principal, who thought he had turned up the perfect candidate, Talbot Papineau. This man, who was a descendant of the patriote who led the rebellion of 1837, Parkin hoped would exemplify the role the scholarships could play in bringing the two races together. Unfortunately, Lord Grey, the governor-general, told Parkin a little later that young Papineau was not the slightest interested in his family name, took after his American mother, and spoke barely a word of French.[15] Parkin's romantic dreams suffered a serious setback.

From Montreal, Parkin proceeded to Washington. He had missed dining with the American president the previous year, because it was an election year, and had to make do with a luncheon given by Mrs. Cowles, Roosevelt's sister, lunch at the embassy, and a scientific reception hosted by Alexander Graham Bell. The politicians were all busy "booming" candidates for the presidency. Since 1905 wasn't an election year, lunch with Roosevelt was possible. Parkin listened carefully as Roosevelt outlined his ideas of the merits of studying at Oxford. It would boost young men's careers when they returned to the United States, Roosevelt confirmed in what Parkin called "his simple and straightforward manner." They would gain an understanding of European affairs that would make them better diplomats, at least if they could attend to what was important in an Oxford education and avoid the trivial. Parkin also met Howard Taft and shrewdly picked him out as a potential president.

In Philadelphia, Parkin was taken to the home of a leading socialite where he met a gentleman who launched a violent tirade against the scholarships. Millionaires in general, and Mr. Rhodes in particular, imposed on the world things it did not want, opined the guest. Oxford should not be desecrated by an irruption of young barbarians from Kalamzaoo and Wallamarroo, Auckland, Arizona, and Africa, or the descendants of those Teutonic tribes whose barbarian virtues Tacitus described so glowingly. Parkin, for his part, was not prepared to take this assault lying down. "Perhaps I see the scholarships in a different light," he replied. (The other guests in the drawing room were delighted. They had not expected such an entertaining afternoon.) The effete civilization of Rome had been swept aside by hordes of Goths and Vandals to make room for something better. Even the gentleman's own America was being regenerated—perhaps he would say swamped—by Italians, Greeks, and Slavs coming in millions. It was only as they were leaving that Parkin discovered that his adversary was the celebrated Anglophile novelist Henry James. Parkin continued his trip through Canada, stopping very briefly in Salisbury to visit his relatives and the farm, before sailing back to England, where he arrived on 22 February.

Early in January, Annie sent Raleigh and Marjorie to stay with Tucken, the children's old nurse, while she and Maude set about furnishing their new house with what she called cheap furniture. She had also hired servants, though she doesn't say how many. She had never had such luxury or comfort, she told her husband. Such material comfort came despite Parkin's disappointment that year with the fact that Annie, along with the rest of her relatives, had been largely ignored in the will of Annie's wealthy uncle, Peter Fisher. Although he was worth about $470,000, he left almost the whole of his estate to charity, and virtually nothing to his relatives. "It was a cruel thing, one cannot help thinking," Parkin wrote to Maude. Undoubtedly there were others in the family who shared the view.

Maude, however, was not one to be fazed by such news. She continued comforting and assisting her mother, while at the same time she also began helping her father with some of his work. For several years Parkin had a work-in-progress, a life of Sir John A Macdonald, which was more a work-not-in-progress. Maude, who was currently at loose ends, decided that she would start working on it for him, an offer he was happy to take up. In the fall, she moved to Manchester and took a job as assistant dean of women in Ashburn College, part of the University of Manchester.

For the rest of the year, except for a vacation in France, Parkin attended to Rhodes matters from England and returned for a while to his other interests. On 18 May, he spoke to the Society for the Propagation of the Gospel with the Archbishop of Canterbury present, and the next day he responded to Lord Minto's toast, "The United Empire." "I was apparently right in thinking that I had some good points to make as I was much congratulated afterwards." Afterwards he went with Annie and Alice to a reception at the prime minister's Downing Street residence. Early in June he took the chair at a meeting of the Colonial Institute for a paper on the British Empire in the East, and the next evening he discussed Canada in connection with imperial organization. It was a rare week that at least one evening wasn't booked.

In August, there was a major change in the Trust. Milner returned from South Africa and attended his first meeting.[16] Soon he became its most active member. Parkin arranged a welcome lunch for sixty-eight of the Rhodes scholars at a stately home outside Oxford, the home of Lady Wantage: ten thousand acres, a thousand cattle, hundreds of horses, villages of charming cottages. They were able to get the entire party into the dining room.

16

Settling Down?

Although Parkin's employment by the Rhodes Trust took him into, as he called it, a different sphere of national work, he had only been the most visible member of the imperial federation movement, not its only member. Despite the absence of G.M. Grant, whose death in 1902 had been a serious blow, not just to the league, but to the intellectual life of Canada as a whole, the British Empire League in Canada continued its exertions after Parkin's departure.

At its meeting on 12 May 1903 in Toronto, it noted that it was making good progress towards another of its goals: reduced postage on newspapers and periodicals coming to Canada from Great Britain. The league expressed a strong desire to maintain freedom of action for Canada in setting tariff rates against other countries including, although it didn't say it explicitly, Great Britain. Canada, the league argued, also needed some sort of defence policy. Either it should raise forces for its own defence or contribute towards imperial defence. If Canada wanted the empire's support in case of war, it should give material support to the empire.

Other questions also plagued the imperial federation movement.

Settling Down?

In the nineteenth century, the supporters of imperial federation had never been able to overcome the most important theoretical and practical problems that might face this new form of political organization. Early in 1903 a distinguished Oxford law professor, Sir Frederick Pollock, began the most serious attempts to date to think through the meaning of a federated empire. Like Joseph Chamberlain, the colonial secretary, he was a Liberal Unionist, and politically and professionally he was interested in the constitutional and institutional changes that were necessary as the colonies moved to self-governing and independent status. In 1903, he convened a committee, which met in London and was chaired by him. Its structure was based on the old Imperial Federation (Defence) League, an institution that emerged from the 1893 coup that destroyed the Imperial Federation League. This structure proving unworkable, Pollock changed to a more informal format of intellectual dinner parties, usually at the fashionable Trocadero restaurant, where the participants could mix good food and company with serious papers and formal discussion on matters relating to imperial organization. The Pollock Committee then circulated these position papers to various public figures throughout the empire, where they increasingly formed the basis for public policy discussions. Membership expanded to include academics, lawyers, civil servants, senior politicians such as Winston Churchill and Arthur Balfour, and recognized experts such as Milner and Parkin.[1]

Lord Grey, who served as governor-general in Canada from 1904 to 1911, believed—in what was probably a serious misreading of Canadian public opinion—that Canadians were ashamed that they weren't paying the fair share of their own defence. Since, like many of his predecessors, he took an active view of his role, he also felt that he should help to change the situation. When he found that Stephen Leacock shared these views, he had his daughter arrange for Leacock to give a series of public lectures in Toronto, Hamilton, Winnipeg, and other places. Grey was impressed with Leacock's talks and persuaded the other Rhodes Trustees to send him in 1907 on a tour of Australia and New Zealand similar to Parkin's path-breaking trip of 1889 to do "imperial missionary work," though he was careful to suggest that Leacock go under the aegis of a university and not as an official spokesman for the Trust.

When he got to the southern hemisphere, however, Leacock quite dropped out of sight, rather to Parkin's surprise, and Parkin was shocked when his friend H.D'E. Taylor wrote that Leacock had spent only three days in Melbourne. "That means, in my judgment, a practical failure in the work he was trying to do. I cannot understand it at all. I impressed upon him as strongly as I could the importance of Melbourne as a centre of Australian thought." Parkin sat down to compose a note to rebuke his younger colleague. The passion that had driven him in those days still smouldered and the sacrifices he made had counted for something:

> I am afraid that I have grown garrulous in talking over those old Australian experiences. I was desperately in earnest in those days, and the circumstances of my journey burnt themselves into my mind. Not without reason, too, for I had a family to support, and £400 was the sum on which I foolishly agreed to make the whole trip. All the rest I had to work out with my pen as I went along, and you can understand that when my evangelical work was all over, I had more sympathy with St. Paul than ever before. But it was an experience that I would not have missed for anything, and looking back upon it now, with the life long friendships that I formed, it is an unmixed happiness. I feel sure that in the same way you will look back upon your adventures as among the valuable things of life.

In April 1908, Parkin wrote pointedly to ask whether Leacock intended to prepare a report on his tour for the Trust. Parkin wasn't alone in feeling that Leacock hadn't returned much value for money and had treated the whole affair as a paid vacation.

Parkin's passion for his cause had never diminished. Although Leacock made little use of his trip to Australia, Parkin was still drawing on friendships he had made thirty years later. In Sydney, he had met Gilbert Parker, a promising young journalist. After a successful literary career and an even more successful marriage, Parker became a British MP, and, as he and Parkin had pledged so many miles away, he was promoting the cause of imperial federation. Parkin and he used their

Cecil Rhodes, successful entrepreneur and politician, thought the earth should be English. When he died, he left a will directing that his fortune be used for scholarships at Oxford University. Parkin played a crucial role in implementing the Rhodes scholarships and making them the most prestigious in the world.

Library and Archives Canada

As prime minister of Canada, Wilfrid Laurier resolutely stood up for Canadian autonomy, putting him at odds with Parkin's vision of a united British Empire.

Library of Congress, Washington, D.C.

Charles Tupper was premier of Nova Scotia at Confederation and sixth prime minister of Canada 1895–6. As Canada's high commissioner to Great Britain 1883–95 he vigorously disagreed with fellow Maritimer Parkin on the meaning of imperial federation.

Library of Congress, Washington, D.C.

Rudyard Kipling was an ardent supporter of British imperialism.
His great poem "Recessional" moved Parkin deeply.

Library of Congress, Washington, D.C.

As a schoolboy Winston Churchill was impressed by a talk Parkin gave,
which inspired him about the ideals of the British Empire.

Library of Congress, Washington, D.C.

Booker T. Washington, prominent black American educator, looked to Parkin for fair treatment of black scholars in awarding Rhodes scholarships.

Library of Congress, Washington, D.C.

When Theodore Roosevelt was president of the United States, Parkin was a welcome guest at the White House.

Library of Congress, Washington, D.C.

Lord and Lady Minto skating on the Ottawa River in front of Rideau Falls, December 1901. While serving as governor-general of Canada, Lord Minto relied heavily on Parkin for advice.

Topley Studio / Library and Archives Canada / PA-0338030

Parkin spoke during the 1917 Canadian wartime election to help get Prime Minister Robert Borden re-elected.

Library of Congress, Washington, D.C.

Lord and Lady Aberdeen and family. From left: Dudley Gordon, Lord Aberdeen, Marjorie Gordon, Lady Aberdeen, Haddo Gordon (on sleigh), and Archie Gordon. Lord Aberdeen, who served as governor-general of Canada, and Lady Aberdeen were both friends of Parkin and held his opinions in high esteem.

Topley Studio / Library and Archives Canada / PA-027328

The Parkin children at Diablerets, Switzerland, about 1902. From left: Raleigh, Grace, Maude, Alice, and Marjorie. In debt as usual, Parkin sent his daughters to Switzerland to study at a school run by a former governess of Edward Thring's children. She let Parkin postpone payment of their school fees, thus becoming yet another of his creditors.

Library and Archives Canada

"The Cottage" at Goring-on-Thames, the Parkins' home in England during the years Parkin was secretary of the Rhodes scholarships. Parkin decorated the walls of his study with photographs of his heroes such as Bishop Medley and Edward Thring. The Parkins' older daughters, Maude and Alice, loved the comfort of their parents' home. Alice lived with them into her late twenties and Maude was a frequent visitor.

Library and Archives Canada

Parkin's son-in-law Vincent Massey became Canada's first native-born governor-general in 1952. Unfortunately Massey's wife, Alice Parkin, did not live to share this honour, having died two years earlier.

Library of Congress, Washington, D.C.

Parkin's daughter Maude and William Grant on their wedding day. William thought that his marriage to Maude would make Canada a better place. His father, G.M. Grant, principal of Queen's University, had been one of Canada's leading intellectuals. Maude was one of the first women to graduate from McGill University. Their son, George Parkin Grant, became famous for a book, *Lament for a Nation*, that explained, in part, why his grandfather's political dreams had failed.

Courtesy of Sheila Grant

Parkin and Annie with grandchildren. George Grant, affectionately embraced on Annie's lap, later recalled his grandmother as warm and loving.

Library and Archives Canada

Parkin visits for the last time with his family in Salisbury, New Brunswick, 1920. He always felt an attachment to the place of his childhood and visited whenever his travels returned him to North America.

Courtesy of Sheila Grant

A Parkin family gathering, 1920. The group includes Parkin and Annie, and families of their daughters Maude Grant, Alice Massey, and Marjorie Macdonnell.
Library and Archives Canada

A year before his death, Parkin had a little picnic with his two-and-half-year-old grandson George Grant. The event took on iconic significance in the family. Maude interpreted it as a symbolic handing on of the duty to promote Parkin's political vision of a unified empire espousing British ideals.

Courtesy of Sheila Grant

Sir George Parkin, 1921
F.H. Varley
Oil on canvas / 122.5 × 142.8 cm
National Gallery of Canada
Gift of Raleigh Parkin, Westmount, Quebec, 1960

Frederick Varley's place in Canadian history was established in 1920 when he exhibited as one of the founding members of the Group of Seven. The same year he was commissioned to paint another famous Canadian, Sir George Parkin.

Settling Down?

connections in the press behind the scenes to exert influence in favour of politicians and policies.

Parkin continued to speak regularly, and was quick to adopt new technology to make his point more effectively: "'Greater Britain: Its growth and meaning' illustrated by lantern slides," was the title of one lecture he gave. In May he spoke on one evening to an audience of two hundred at the Author's Society on a programme with Lord Curzon and Bernard Shaw. Two days later he addressed 1500–2000 at the Seamen's Mission, with the Bishop of Stepney in the chair. In June 1908 his audience was ten thousand in the Albert Hall.

Now in his sixties, Parkin found that his ceaseless activity was beginning to exact an emotional as well as a physical toll. "Energy has come back to me very slowly and when I have got through the day fairly well and done something almost every evening brought a return of depression which it seemed well nigh impossible to shake off, struggle as one might against it." Annie had been low-spirited too. Sometimes in the past he was able to cheer her up when she was down, but he didn't seem able to do that anymore, he lamented to Maude. "We have had so much happiness in life with each other that we don't want to have it knocked out of us in our later years. It is strange that neither of us have ever felt the problems of life quite as perplexing as they now are."

After much effort on Annie's part, they found a house they liked in Goring-on-Thames, on the railway line, about twenty-five miles from Oxford, almost midway between Oxford and London. It was the same house that Oscar Wilde had rented in the summer of 1893 in the hope of completing his new play, *An Ideal Husband*.[2]

The current owner was less flamboyant than the former tenants, a Dr. Fell, who was said to be descended from the clergyman satirized in the verse:

> I do not like thee, Doctor Fell,
> The reason why I cannot tell;
> But this I know, and know full well,
> I do not like thee, Doctor Fell.

If this were indeed the same family, then there may have been character traits that ran in it. According to Parkin, the good doctor was all business and courtesy on the exterior, but Parkin had found out through Wylie that he had made a mess of the family finances and caused no end of family feuding. Parkin took a thirty-year lease at £120 per annum, then built an addition at the cost of £600–£700 consisting of a dining room with two bedrooms above it. Parkin rented a house in the village while they supervised the construction. They got some of their furniture out of storage and their daughter Grace, who had a good eye for decorating, helped find pieces in second-hand shops and at auctions, especially eighteenth-century furniture, which was then out of fashion. Annie, as always worried about money, kept meticulous accounts. The total cost of the furnishings was £490.113.10½. They kept four permanent servants: a cook, a house-maid, a parlour maid, and a gardener. There was also often a scullery maid (a tweeny) and a boy to help the gardener, neither of whom lived in the house. On the walls were photos of G.M. Grant, Sandford Fleming, Bishop Medley, Lord Rosebery, and Edward Thring.

Just as at UCC, Parkin insisted on a vegetable garden, though he added fruits and flowers and had a full-time gardener to maintain it and a greenhouse to provide it with young plants. He also had a henhouse, and a few ducks that could swim in the Thames, on which the house backed. A boathouse held a rowboat and a punt, which served for quiet excursions on the river. Young Raleigh was away at boarding school. Parkin enjoyed sending him fresh walnuts from his tree. When Parkin was finally installed in his country retreat, he had a Christmas card engraved with an image of "The Cottage" and three lines from Horace, one his favourite authors.

> *Hoc erat in votis: modus agri non ita magnus,*
> *Hortus ubi et tecto vicinus jugis aquae fons*
> *Et paulum silvae super hit foret.*
> This used to be my wish: a bit of land,
> A house and garden with a spring at hand,
> and just a little wood

Parkin was able to get involved in the institutional life of the church again. Parkin's piety had never waned; he always attended divine service whenever he could. He was not dogmatic in his religious beliefs;

Settling Down?

his was a religion of the heart, and he still began the day with daily prayers with the family when he was at home. He started a branch of the Church of England Men's Society in his parish, and served as its first secretary. He spoke for the Society for the Propagation of the Gospel in neighbouring cities such as Oxford and Reading, and began a series of Bible lectures in Goring.

Parkin's ease in settling down was due to the fact that the Trustees had given him a vote of confidence. Partly that was because he was doing a good job. Another part was that he was the only one, other than Wylie, actively on the job: "My Trustees are all as slippery as eels. Lord Milner has got off to the Continent. Sir Lewis soon leaves for S. Africa, to which Jameson has gone, Lord R. is nowhere, Lord G. writes faithfully from Canada, but of course does not count here. Indeed I have to take almost everything off my own bat." The Trustees were now about to see if they were right.

To date, the quality of the scholars had varied. The German scholars had been almost exclusively of aristocratic background. They rarely stayed for their third year, since their military duties normally prevented it. They found Oxford's education lacking in rigour compared with German higher education and many of them looked on their two years as more fun than study. Some of the Canadian scholars acquitted themselves extremely well. One, J.G. Archibald, from McGill, took a first in Greats and secured a fellowship at All Soul's College. H.J. Rose, also from McGill, did even better, winning the Ireland and Craven prizes, among the highest achievements possible in the university, and a fellowship at Exeter College. Goldwin Smith had himself won the Ireland in his day. Lord Grey wrote to tease him that it was now in the hands of a Canadian. Another Canadian, Chester Martin, also won the first Beit prize to be awarded for an essay in colonial history.[3]

In 1907, the Rhodes Trustees faced their first major crisis, and it brought them face to face with the "coloured question." Pennsylvania elected a black Harvard graduate, A. LeRoy Locke: What were the Trustees going to do about it? One not unreasonable question was, what exactly had Rhodes meant by race?

It was not uncommon at the time to speak of the British race, or the Dutch race. Was it plausible, Parkin wrote to Hawksley, that he had "Dutch, English, Jew, and the rest in his mind," and that he was not thinking in terms of colour at all? This opinion was supported by Dr. Jameson, who had some claim to know Rhodes's mind best on a matter such as this. "Mr. Rhodes did not mean to include black men. He would turn in his grave to think of it." However, Milner's opinion prevailed and it was unequivocal. Milner didn't think the Locke selection was a particularly happy occurrence at this point for the scholarship scheme, but he thought that the result should stand for two reasons. First, the terms of Rhodes's will were clear and unequivocal: race was race. Second, the Trustees worked on the principle that local committees could decide their own criteria for selection. In any event, Milner sneered, why should it affect other Rhodes scholars? "They need have no contact with the 'untutored mind' or the black body of this American citizen. I do not see how he touches them in any way. They may regret his situation, just as they regret the general situation, but one is just as much an abstract question for them as the other."

Milner considered Parkin and Wylie naïve because they thought that Locke's appointment was a progressive development. Racial prejudice was just as strong in the North as in the South, he suggested. Rosebery shared Milner's view, but Wylie was afraid that reaction among Southern scholars, existing and prospective, would be so hostile that the harm might be irreparable. Milner agreed to ask the Pennsylvania committee to consider the consequences of its decision before making it final.

Pennsylvania held firm, so the next problem that faced Parkin and Wylie was getting Locke into a college. One of the central aspects of the scholarships was that candidates were supposed to experience collegiate life. The first three or four colleges to which they submitted his name declined to admit him on the grounds that there might be "friction" with other American scholars. Although Parkin thought that the "chivalric" side of the English often came out when they saw someone being trampled on, to be on the safe side, he was prepared to admit him as an unattached student.

They were right to be concerned about the American reaction. Some of the American students threatened to resign their scholarships if Locke was allowed to take his up, and a couple of newly elected American Southerners wrote to ask that they not be assigned to the same college. A delegation of three from North Carolina, West Vir-

Settling Down?

ginia, and Maryland met with the Trustees in London on 22 March 1907. They convinced Milner that Locke's appointment did impose a significant threat to the success of the scholarship scheme in the United States, even though Milner still dismissed the impact that Locke himself might have on Oxford. There was a general consensus that there would be less concern about the election of a black scholar from Jamaica.[4]

When Locke arrived, he was actively shunned by many Southern scholars. Fifteen refused to attend an annual dinner given by the Trustees because Locke accepted. There was a similar boycott of a luncheon hosted by the American ambassador. Locke's academic achievements had certainly been enough to merit the Pennsylvania committee's choice, but he didn't excel at Oxford. Wylie found him superficial and his mind unscholarly. Worse, he lacked a sense of responsibility, got himself into debt with his college, and was expelled. He was only to be allowed back when he was ready to take his examinations. It was not an experiment another American committee chose to revisit. No other American black was elected until 1963.[5] In spite of his hardships, Locke had a successful career. After Oxford, he studied at the University of Berlin, received his Ph.D. from Harvard in 1918, and taught at Howard University in Washington for almost forty years. He was a leader and interpreter of the Harlem Renaissance, a group of black writers after the First World War.

Other problems also plagued the administration of the American scholarships. In general, Rhodes's decision to give each American state the same number of scholarships had not been a wise one. It was "educationally naïve and administratively impractical."[6] States varied widely in their demography, their geography, and the quality of their education systems. New York had a superb university network and was densely populated. New Mexico was a sparsely populated frontier territory with no great likelihood of finding highly qualified candidates two years out of three.

The Oxford requirement of Responsions also posed a serious and continuing problem for Parkin and Wylie. As even Oxford students needed to pass Responsions in order to graduate, the Trustees decided that there was no point in accepting candidates who could not meet this standard. Hence they asked the university's authorities to create an examination comparable to Responsions, and that was the examination that Parkin brought to America. It consisted of an examination in either arithmetic or geometry, at the candidate's choice, and the requirement to read from specified Greek and Latin authors. In the first exam, barely half passed. In five states, no one passed, and in thirty-six states, three or fewer candidates were available for the selection board to interview.

It was the Greek requirement that was the main problem. Initially it is likely that it discouraged many otherwise qualified candidates from applying. Greek was not widely taught in American secondary schools, though Latin was. Parkin and Wylie decided in 1908 that they would allow students to be selected for the scholarship and then take their Greek examination in Oxford after they had spent the summer studying. The problem resolved itself when Oxford ended the requirement at the time of the Great War.[7] Responsions was a large part of the reason that, for the period from 1904 to 1914, there was no year in which the full quota of scholars was elected, and distant Montana managed only two in total.[8]

Australia presented problems too. In Australia, as in the other jurisdictions, Rhodes's requirement that character, leadership, and sport be criteria sometimes meant that the academically strongest candidate was passed over. For example, C.K. Allen, who was ironically later warden of Rhodes House, was passed over in New South Wales. Although Allen received the maximum possible score for academic achievement, he was rated middling for character and scored only two out of twenty for sports.[9] In Queensland, G.F.E. Hall, the son of a carter and gold miner, was head prefect, an excellent student, played six sports, and was enthusiastically supported by his whole school: He was Rhodes's ideal candidate, if Jameson were right, in all but one regard—he was black. However, the committee had no reservation about selecting him, and the Old Boys and the local businessmen raised £70 for his fare. Parkin mentored him in Oxford, where he earned second-class honours in engineering.[10] The Australians, though, found it especially difficult to penetrate British society. They were treated like colonials who knew nothing, but once they got over being awed they realized that they often knew much more about their subjects than their glib, patronizing Oxford colleagues.[11] It was a problem that in some ways continues into the present.

The following year proved another busy one for Parkin. On 13 January 1908, Parkin arrived in New York on the *Lusitania* with the dreaded examination papers. After the usual routine business, another visit to Roosevelt in Washington, Grey in Ottawa, his relatives in Salisbury, he was back in England by the end of February. At that time, he and Annie had dinner with a brilliant young scientist, Harry Wimperis, whom Parkin was helping get an appointment at Oxford. "It seems as though he knows many of the influential people," his son-in-law wrote in his diary with some understatement. Wimperis had married their twenty-five-year-old daughter Grace in 1907, and the Parkins' first grandchild was born on 14 August 1908. Parkin, as was common for major family events, was away abroad, this time in Halifax.

He had returned to Canada on 10 July 1908 for the tercentenary of the city of Quebec. The event itself was a whirl of balls, a royal reception on the terrace of the Chateau Frontenac, and fireworks and illuminations, "as fine as any that have been," he wrote.

The *Times* had wanted him to cover it, and he thought he could clear £200–£300 after expenses for six articles. It also gave him a chance to bring himself up to date on Canadian affairs, so he cleared a leave of absence with Milner and Hawksley, and set off for Canada with Maude. In the two months he was in Canada, he visited Sault Ste. Marie, Winnipeg, Prince Albert, Regina, Brandon, Winnipeg, Fort William, Guelph, Montreal, Bathurst, Chatham, Salisbury (relatives), Oakfield, Halifax, Truro, Charlottetown, and Moncton.

Once back in Britain, Parkin continued to promote his vision of Oxford. At an 1908 meeting of the Royal Colonial Institute in London on "Oxford and Empire," he spoke "passionately but practically about the role of Oxford as the great Imperial University."[12] Oxford should, he argued, teach the law of any man who comes to Oxford from any part of the empire: English, French, Dutch, Roman, or Islamic. It should establish a strong school of imperial geography, and improve the teaching of oriental and modern languages to remedy the linguistic weakness of the ruling class. A school of government could train students for service across the empire. "If Oxford were to accept the role of an Imperial University," he pleaded, "and say we are going to establish the best Imperial Law School, the best School of Geography and Language and Government the world has ever seen, I believe the British world would rise up to assist her forward with the ideal."[13] This was one further, and more sophisticated, development of Parkin's Britannic idealism.

For Parkin, the empire, Greater Britain, was a glorious lesson to the world in self-government. Because there were also challenges to this way of governing, the British Empire allowed a variety of forms to arise out of different conditions. It was a vast laboratory of political experiment. In New Zealand, "probably the most democratic country in the world," Parkin wrote, "it is testing bolder methods of franchise, land ownership, regulation of labour, control of pubic amenities and the State management of Insurance than have been tried elsewhere." Canada and Australia, Parkin noted, were experimenting with different ways of working out the federal principle with a constitutional monarchy. South Africa was trying to adapt the idea of self-government to a country in which a majority, the black population, was, according to Parkin, not yet ready to participate, but aspired to. Parkin understood that imperial federation could take on a symbolic form, that the empire could become a laboratory of experiments pointing toward the best development of the British race, and that each part could learn from the innovation and mistakes of the other.

The Colonial Conference of 1907, like the previous conferences, had been a failure in the eyes of those who wanted a united empire, with the wily Laurier avoiding any clear or costly commitments for Canada. Milner, however, was still determined to forge closer bonds between the dominions, as the former colonies were increasingly known. He persuaded L.S. Amery, one of the brilliant young associates who worked with Milner in the reconstruction of South Africa, to re-visit that country to help create imperial goodwill, and especially to charm the Boer leader, General Smuts. Amery also opened up a correspondence with leading Australian political figures such as Alfred Deakins and "Billy" Hughes, and important Canadian figures such as Robert Borden, Mackenzie King, Sam Hughes, and Sir George Drummond. Lord Grey believed that it was important to change Canadian public opinion toward the empire before the 1911 Colonial Conference, and he encouraged Milner to make a visit.[14] At Milner's urging, Arthur Glazebrook, a financier, and Ernest du Vernet, a lawyer, formed a club in Toronto to promote imperial feeling. Grey himself continued to put personal pressure on Laurier.[15]

Members of Milner's "Kindergarten" returned home between 1908 and 1909. They thought that the technique they learned in bringing unity to South Africa could profitably help the empire. In September 1909, they formed the Round Table movement, whose members agreed that it was necessary to move beyond occasional colonial conferences to some form of organic unity for the constituent states of the empire. Lionel Curtis, an English civil servant and prolific author, and Phillip Kerr (Lord Lothian) were the forces behind the movement. They sought to create an educated public opinion by means of conferences and journals that would establish the groundwork for later political action. After the Great War, Parkin's Canadian sons-in-law were the core of the Round Table movement in Canada.

Halford Mackinder, an eminent geographer, was also persuaded to devote his energies to the cause of promoting imperial unity and was guaranteed £850 a year for four years to allow him to do it full time. Mackinder, one of the most influential geographers of the twentieth century, is generally credited with creating the concept of geopolitics. His thesis was that there was a continuing struggle between world empires, or what he called world organisms. The eventual winner would be whichever empire used its manpower most efficiently.

Robert Baden-Powell, a hero of the Boer War, established the Boy Scouts in 1908. He was determined to address an analogous problem—the United Kingdom's moral, physical, and military weaknesses. He had become aware of these issues when he returned to England from South Africa and was shocked by what he considered the government's unwillingness to address them. The Scouts' motto, "Be Prepared," suggested a world of constant readiness for potential conflict and many of the scouting maxims were meant to promote good hygiene or train in survival techniques in case of war.[16] Kipling wrote the Boy Scouts' patrol song and much of the mythology of the movement was drawn from his Mowgli stories.[17]

Increasing military tension between Britain and Germany caused the concept of imperial federation to take on a new importance.

Toward the end of November 1908, Parkin's own direct knowledge of what Laurier called the vortex of militarism began to increase. He was invited to lunch at Downing Street with the prime minister and several members of the cabinet, and spent the following weekend at a social event sufficiently grand that even he normally would not rate an invitation. However, his host was Field Marshal Lord Roberts of Kandahar, hero of Afghanistan and South Africa, and a beloved national figure, made famous in the expression "Bob's your uncle." After the ladies had "withdrawn" following dinner, the gentlemen, left to to their port and cigars, had a serious discussion "of course about Anglo-German questions." The seventy-five-year-old former commander-in-chief of the British army, worried that the United Kingdom was not preparing itself for the next war, was campaigning for conscription, and had founded the National Service League.

It might be easy to conclude, from the well-known people with whom Parkin was associating at this time, that he had become a member of the establishment. This would probably be a mistake. Parkin was a very prominent figure, as was Kipling. Field Marshal Lord Roberts was a national hero, but he was retired, and Baden-Powell, also a hero form the Boer War, was in the process of setting up the Boy Scout movement. What they had in common, and shared with Parkin's other associates, is that they were critics of mainstream British social and economic policy. The establishment was happy with the existing relationship between the United Kingdom and its colonies. The Britannic idealists wanted to transform it. The Establishment was content with the social condition of the English worker. Parkin and his colleagues were social reformers who believed that immediate action was necessary both for the workers' sake and for the sake of the English-speaking peoples as a whole. They agitated for action that the government and the Establishment did not want to take.

Parkin's interest in education and reform was reflected in his many speeches and written works, and Parkin continued to turn out a steady stream of spoken and written words. "Dr. Parkin showed me many books for which he had written introductions," was one entry in Harry Wimperis's diary. Parkin accepted commissions for articles for the *Encyclopaedia Britannica*, which he was very good at completing, and also for the *Times*, because it paid so well. He liked the idea of writing books, and could always be tempted, but he never had the time. Indeed, before he even finished the Thring biography, he had accepted an offer to write Sir John A. Macdonald's biography for the Makers of Canada series. This offer was too prestigious to decline, he felt, but he had been unable to find the time when he was rebuilding a school, influencing public opinion, and then careening around North American on 17,000-mile rail journeys. Maude had started to help, but then she got a job of her own, and the project bogged down once more. It picked up again when Willie Grant, Principal Grant's son, was appointed first Beit lecturer in colonial history at Oxford. A regular visitor to the Parkins' house in Goring, he offered to help Maude and Parkin complete it.

Surprisingly, given its convoluted and prolonged route to light, Parkin's *Macdonald* received strong and positive reviews. The Toronto *Globe* praised it "as near a classic as could reasonably have been expected, in view of the short interval that had elapsed since the death of the illustrious statesman with whose long, varied, and prominent career it deals." The *News* said it was "animated and skilful" and that Parkin's grasp of his subject was "quick and accurate." The *Sentinel* thought it his most entertaining book, and praised him for his impartiality. The New York *Evening Post* said that this was easily the best of the Makers of Canada series to date and the prestigious *Times Literary Supplement* said that it gave "all that is essential to know of the various important questions in small compass without loading the question with unnecessary detail."

Although Parkin was forthright in his criticism of the corruption that marred Macdonald's whole political record and brought about his downfall in the Pacific Scandal of 1874, Parkin partly exonerated Macdonald because of the fractious and antagonistic electorate he had to manage. Although Macdonald governed autocratically, Parkin argued, Macdonald's strength of will, vision, and his supreme ability to understand both his colleagues and his opponents raised him ultimately to the level of a statesman. Macdonald had entered Canadian politics at a sordid and dreary period. By his death in 1891 he had turned Canada into a nation and left it strong, united, and vigorous. This was his achievement and his exoneration. It was generally thought that Parkin had handled the matter of Macdonald's heavy drinking delicately and tactfully.

By the end of the summer of 1909, however, it was clear that there would be no time for writing for a while. The Rhodes Scholarships required attention, and Parkin had arranged a lengthy tour of the United States. The quality of scholars being very uneven, he concluded that he needed to change the way the scholars were selected for the scholarships. There were too many cases in which schools were simply passing the scholarships between one another, a practice that was not generating good candidates. There were very few first-class American students at Oxford, and many poor ones. This should not have been the case when there were so many good students from which to choose and the scholarship itself was the most generous in the world. "We ought to, I think, achieve more marked results."

Another problem that Parkin always had to deal with was Quebec. In 1908, Laval selected a candidate named Lanctôt who was a year older than the maximum permitted age of twenty-five. This decision posed a real dilemma for Parkin and the Trustees. Of all the scholarships, Laval's was probably the one they most wanted to see awarded, a symbolic union of the two races, or at least the better sort of French-Canadian. However, Parkin and Hawksley were very reluctant to create a precedent by deviating from the rule:

> Monsignor Mathieu, the late Rector, has had charge of the selection from the first. I pointed out to him the necessity of guarding in the future against any irregularity such as occurred in 1909, as well as the need of giving full and early publicity to each election, and of securing open competition. He freely admitted the irregularity. He explained that he had faced difficulties over-coming the scruples of his French co-religionists about sending their young men to Oxford, and that they could conciliate the two sections of the Roman Catholic Church in Montreal and Quebec by alternating the scholarship between them.

After visiting Quebec City on 14 September 1909 to clear up problems with the scholarships there, Parkin headed south. At almost every university he not only spoke to administrators but addressed students as well, usually gatherings of several hundred or more. At the end of October he was at Princeton, where he met Woodrow Wilson, who

Settling Down?

much impressed him. "Another thing strikes one—the President of a University, Woodrow Wilson—has come within sight of nomination for the presidency of the United States. That is one of the results of yesterday's voting. It illustrates the wide difference between British and American politics. Here it is an extremely healthy sign," he reported back to Hawksley. He continued through the south, to Texas. On 3 December he was in Albequerque, New Mexico. On the 4th he left for Denver. By the 7th he boarded another train for Lincoln, Nebraska.

Writing to Hawksley from the train, he reported that he had never worked harder in his life. Half the nights and almost every Sunday he had been on the move and by his own estimate he averaged three hundred miles a day, including the stops for conferences. He visited thirty of the forty-eight states and territories; his longest single run was 800 miles from the University of Texas to Arizona. During this trip, he estimated that he spoke to 10,000 students, in groups averaging five hundred. Over the two-month period he took only one day off, to see the Grand Canyon, which he thought was the most impressive natural wonder he had ever seen or ever expected to see. Hawksley, Parkin told him, shouldn't expect to see any of the £250 he had advanced as expenses returned.

After he had written his report, he and Annie left for a vacation in Italy. Parkin wanted to show her the places that had so moved him when Bishop Medley's generous gift to him as a student had allowed him to travel during his term-break at Oxford, and when he had made Miss Erskine's acquaintance so many years before. They left on 21 February 1910. After visits to Milan and Florence, they reached Rome on 26 February, where they stayed at the Hotel D'Angleterra. Parkin was drawn to St. Peters where he heard a service. He wanted to soak his mind in the marvel of the place, try to feel the immensity of the Coliseum, absorb the general impression rather than analyse the details. Rome was much changed in the years since his first visit, he thought, but it had been a dream of his for twenty years to bring Annie there, and "I am more than satisfied with the impression it is making on her now that she is here," he wrote to his children. They continued south through Italy to Naples where they boarded ship, headed for South Africa.

He spent much of the trip south socializing with the other passengers and playing cards, euchre, and small stakes poker. On its way the ship called in at Port-Said, Suez, Manbosa, Zanzibar, Dar-es-Salaam, and Mozambique before it reached Rhodesia, where Parkin had to sort out certain Rhodes-related problems. While Parkin dealt with educational strategy in Umtali, where he believed that the school was wrong to try to prepare scholars for the Oxford matriculation, Annie was left to sort the luggage out at the hotel. This time, though, they did get to Victoria Falls, and it was an enchantment for them both. They brought a butterfly net and a killing bottle and captured over fifty specimens. They sat alone in a little summer house, surrounded by the steady roar of the falls, the smell of the wild animals, and the intense colour of the rainbow thrown up by the water. The mist, Parkin wrote in his diary, seemed like floating lace of the finest kind, always creating the wonderful arches of colour. For a moment all their cares and their depression was taken away—but it didn't last. Five days later they were at Bulawago. "Confusion at Station and all the rooms engaged... furious...drove off—not a room to be had anywhere," Annie wrote angrily in her diary. "Found Mr. MacDonald who sent over and tried to make it right. Mr. B and Mr. L (?) most kindly gave up room. Very poor one, altogether horrid. Hotel full and uncomfortable."

On the 16th Parkin walked the long, winding path up the hill to Rhodes's majestic tomb. He spent a long time there meditating: all his current work stemmed from the man who chose that silent place as his grave. In the high distance, there were rounded hills of granite; nearer were masses of rock and the twin boulders of a lighter colour. In a huge cleft like a railway cutting, baboons appeared and disappeared. Low-lying bits of green lay between hills. There was an effect of vast distance and he didn't want to leave. He was sixty-four and knew he would likely never visit this majestic spot again.

Parkin judged that Rhodesia was not ready to provide Rhodes scholars. Rhodesia was a place where the right kind of man who had a fairly free hand, someone like a Thring or an Arnold, or perhaps a Parkin, could profoundly influence the whole future of the country. As the situation now stood, Rhodesian whites, who came from educated social backgrounds, normally sent their children to England at a relatively early age. This separation caused anxiety for their parents and was socially undesirable. In Parkin's opinion it was mutually beneficial for the Rhodes Trust and the parents to establish good boarding schools in Rhodesia. Parkin toyed with the idea of trying to find wealthy Johannesburg businessmen who would take over the Rhodesian and South African scholarships and relieve the Trust of the responsibility, but nothing came of the idea.

Annie was very tired after the visit to Rhodesia, so Parkin left her behind in Kimberley to rest while he proceeded to Grahamstown on 24 April. Meeting with parents, politicians, and educators in South Africa, Parkin learned that there was considerable dissatisfaction with the scholarship scheme, though there was little that the Trustees could do to address the concerns, even though they might want to. Since the requirement was that the winner must be from each of four named schools, it meant that it was quite possible for a far superior candidate from another school to be passed over. However, Parkin speculated that perhaps Rhodes intended to use his scholarships to draw the best students to these particular schools.

Still very tired, Annie arrived in Johannesburg on 3 May 1910. On 18 May they boarded ship headed for England. On 3 June, her diary entry reads: "Joyful at the thought of home."

17

This Great Struggle for Humanity

Parkin once advised a Canadian Rhodes scholar always to travel first class "for the sake of the people one meets." In a way, this approach to life, along with his undoubted talents as an orator and journalist and his abundant charm, brought him far. He lunched with American presidents, British and Canadian prime ministers, governors-general, and on occasion, socialized with royalty. He had spent Ascot weekend with a field marshal, whom he also entertained to tea. A dinner at a leading London club hosted by the editor of the *Times* had found him between the Archbishop of Canterbury and Lord Northcliffe, owner of an important British newspaper.

If his public life rode the wave of his ambition, some of his family got left in his wake. Alice, or Lal as she was known in the family, turned thirty-one on 1 July 1910. She had accomplished little in her life. Unmarried, unhappy, and still living at home, she developed an affection for a gentleman, Stanley Buckmaster, a member of parliament she met while campaigning for him. Buckmaster was not at all the sort of man the Parkins had wished for their daughter, since she had no prospects with him: he was married, although his wife was an invalid.[1] The

Parkins relied on the traditional solution to an undesirable relationship of this sort. They packed Lal off to Europe—Switzerland, France, and Italy. Her mother tried to reassure her that she really would enjoy it once she got "into it" and kept happy and did not "strain after impossibilities." Such a cure is not infallible, and the next summer Lal went on what was described as "a fishing holiday with friends," of which Buckmaster was conveniently one, but the venue was discrete Norway rather than blatant Scotland. The following year her family retaliated with a vacation even farther away—1000 miles up the Nile. Still, what she really wanted was some purpose to her life. "If I were a man," she wrote to her father from Egypt, "how I should love to be earning a lot and lifting your load. Still perhaps the love and affection as well as the good will of a daughter may be of some comfort to you."

It could not have been much consolation to her that Maude, a year younger, had accepted William Grant's proposal and was to be married in June 1911. William Grant was almost eight years older than his fiancée. He knew her when she was a teenager and he taught at Upper Canada. He claimed to have felt an attraction for her then, but nothing came of their relationship and Maude moved to England with her family in 1902. But William, as Beit lecturer in colonial history at Oxford, visited "The Cottage" at Goring (and Maude) often, and helped with the Macdonald biography. He shared Parkin's general approach to imperial affairs.

Although Parkin and Annie liked to spend a vacation at Cap à l'Aigle on the north shore of the St. Lawrence River when they could, fishing was a common family passion, and in Scotland there were trout and salmon enough for everyone. In 1910, William joined the party, and although he intended to, never quite summoned up the courage to propose to Maude in person. Instead he wrote a sweet but somewhat priggish letter asking her to marry him so that, together, they could do great things for Canada. "With you beside me, I know that we can do ten times as much for Canada, can ten times as well fulfil whatever purpose it may be for which we came into the world, as I could alone." Over the next year, while he was in Kingston and she was in Manchester, they exchanged frequent letters. As the autumn progressed, he became increasingly concerned about Annie's condition.

He had seen his own mother's mental health decline. In turn that led to deterioration in her physical health and eventually to her death. Don't let that happen to your mother, he urged Maude. He thought that Maude herself was overworking. Take some time off, he suggested; look after your mother; both of you should rest. By March 1911, he had become seriously alarmed. Little rests, visits to friends, tours of South Africa, he said, didn't seem to be enough. Annie needed to go away to the seashore in France, where she would have no house-keeping worries. If not that, then she should consider a sanatorium.

Late in 1910 Parkin took another of his whirlwind tours of North America. He left the United Kingdom on 29 September on the SS *Royal Edward*. Just before he departed, he was able to assure Hawksley that Wylie and he had found places for the black Rhodes scholars from Jamaica and Queensland. Jesus and Lincoln colleges respectively accepted them, some of the others fearing that current scholars from the Southern states would make trouble as a matter of principle. Parkin invited them, as he did the other Rhodes scholars, to a reception at his house in Goring. Both the Jamaican and Queensland scholars turned out to be excellent athletes, and their achievements on the sporting field went a long way in neutralizing any bigotry against them.

As he often did, he docked at Montreal and stopped in Salisbury for a visit. Watson was eighty and still worked the farm. Parkin regularly sent his brother and sister money to help make ends meet. Then Parkin was off to Boston and New York, where he stayed, as usual, at the Manhattan Hotel. After a brief stay in those two cities, Parkin travelled to Ohio, Kentucky, Tennessee, Illinois, Wisconsin, South Dakota, Wyoming, and Salt Lake City, Utah, to deal with the Mormons, who caused him almost as much trouble as the French-Canadians. Following that came Nevada, California, Oregon, Portland, Seattle, Vancouver, Victoria, Calgary, Edmonton, and points in between. He sailed for England on 17 December.

Family events occupied Parkin for much of the spring and summer of 1911. William and Maude celebrated their wedding at the Goring parish church on 1 June 1911. Wedding announcements had appeared in the *Times* and the *Morning Post*. William had to respond to fifty letters of congratulation, but Maude had a hundred. Consistent with Parkin's first-class approach to life, Parkin had Harrod's, a swank London store, cater the event.

Annie made it through the strain of the wedding. She had not been well before, and by the end of June and the beginning of July she wrote "wretched" for many of her diary entries. On 10 July, her entry is "Things difficult." Over the summer, she slowly recovered, and she was feeling stronger after a vacation with their fourteen-year-old son, Raleigh.

Despite Parkin's efforts on behalf of the Rhodes Trust and the call of family obligations, he continued to proselytize for imperial federation. In recognition of his efforts, in November 1911 Oxford rewarded Parkin with an honorary doctorate for his unstinting labours. In an article, "True Imperialism," Parkin spelled out what his life's work had stood for. True imperialism, he contended, was not the result of a divided allegiance. For British people, it was the natural result of a true patriotism. Goldwin Smith had thought the colonies would pull the United Kingdom down; but they had not.

The British Empire was founded on democratic principles, Parkin argued, and the highest impulse of its various statesmen should be to work towards a permanent union. This union should recognize the autonomy of the dominions, while recognizing that each should contribute to imperial defence and have a say in the administration of the empire. The various national federations in Canada, Australia, and South Africa make such imperial co-operation more, rather than less likely. There were problems with this vision, he conceded. First, democracy put political power into the hands of people who did not understand the imperial and industrial questions upon which they were prepared to vote. Second, the United Kingdom's food supply was not secure. Third, the current imperial parliament could not deal effectively with the legislative burden that faced it. Fourth, the economic system created both idle and parasitic rich and poor, "who place pleasure before public service in their scheme of life." What must be remembered though, Parkin argued, was that above all, it was Christian imperialism that the British people pursued. "It has its foundation in our sense of Christian responsibility. I am one of those who believe that extended power and influence are not given to nations without some Divine purpose. I am convinced that when the moral energy of a nation does not rise to the fulfilment of that purpose the nation is doomed to decay."

Parkin received another honour when he was elected president of the Royal Geographical Society. On 13 January 1912 he delivered his presidential address. He could be quite generous about the "coloured problem" when it came to individuals, but it was not one that he thought nations should willingly suffer. Although he was tolerant of individuals because he was a gentleman, he shared all the prejudices of his age when it came to considering black people as a social group. Even in a scholarly address, he could seriously advance the proposition that Canada should take comfort in the fact that its temperature sometimes fell to minus thirty-five. "In the first place, an occasional thirty-five degrees below zero gets rid of the black problem altogether. You cannot get a Negro population permanently to stand thirty-five degrees below zero. That problem put a great strain on the whole of the Southern United States; it confronts our race in South Africa; and a colour problem threatens in a lesser degree Australia and New Zealand. In the second place, it keeps out that Mediterranean flow of population which is flooding across the whole of the centre of the United States."[2] By contrast, the cold attracts the strong northern races: the English, Irish, and Scots, the Scandinavians, North Germans, and Russians. Canada takes this kind of immigrant and faces him with the choice of becoming tough or dying. "What is the result? Within one generation you will see a half-submerged type of man with his backbone strengthened; he turns industrious, looks ahead, and may soon become a useful citizen. All that is a result of latitude."[3] The idea that there might be some connection between climate and politics was as old as the writings of the seventeenth French philosopher Charles de Secondat, baron de Montesquieu, but it was rarely advanced in such a simplified and vulgar form.

At the same time as Parkin was being honoured for his past efforts, contemporary political developments were offering hope for future success in achieving his goals. In the 1911 Canadian federal election, after a decade of effort, Robert Borden finally drove Sir Wilfrid Laurier from office. Laurier had run on a platform similar to that which Goldwin Smith defended in 1891, much freer trade with the United States. "Great excitement over Can. Election returns," Annie wrote in her diary. Borden's election seemed a perfect opportunity for the Round Table movement to present their case to the new Canadian prime minister, and perhaps make more headway than they had with the awkward Laurier. Borden came to London in July and August 1912 to meet with the Foreign Office and the Admiralty. Lionel Curtis arranged for Borden and Parkin's old college friend, Borden's minister of trade and commerce, George Foster, to spend the afternoon and evening with Starr Jameson, Milner, a former senior foreign editor of the *Times*, and a member of the Indian government. Early in August they were wined and dined at a country house weekend hosted by Waldorf and Nancy Astor, wealthy Americans who were well connected with the British elite.[4] A further development in the imperialist cause was the appointment of Geoffrey Dawson, one of Milner's protégés from South Africa, as editor of the *Times*. His editorial policy strongly promoted imperial unity. He gave Edward Grigg, a prominent member of the London Round Table group, a relatively free hand to write articles on the empire.[5]

Parkin, meanwhile, continued to travel, lecture, and work on behalf of the Rhodes Trust. Late in 1912, he set off on another visit to North America. Laval was upset because its students had to write the qualifying examination for Oxford in spite of the fact that their students had probably a better background in classical studies than most and they wanted an explanation and an exemption before they would participate again. Parkin had written to Dr. Kingsbury, the Mormon chairman of the selection committee in Utah, suggesting, at this point not so gently, that it might be nice if the committee's choices were more balanced. Kingsbury replied: "I do not know whether the criticism of me is that I favor the Mormons or the non-Mormons in voting for the Rhodes scholars. Occasionally some people say I favor the Mormons in my official position, and other people say I favor the non-Mormons," and then offered to step down.

In spite of these continuing conflicts, Parkin was pleased with the progress he had made over the years. He made a trip to Newfoundland—two days and three nights each way—to sort out a problem there. That was satisfying. He had also met in Washington with the Association of the Presidents of State Universities. Not only had he met a great many of the leading educators in the United States, but they adjourned their own business for a day to discuss the scholarships. Perhaps even more gratifying was a comment made over lunch by the chancellor of New York University. "You have no idea," he said, "the influence you are exerting on educational thought throughout America by the presentations you have made during your various trips of the ideals outlined by Rhodes and of the ideals that prevail in English education." He said he saw this in a hundred ways, intangible and not easy to put into definite shape, but very real. "I am myself often surprised at the way in which I am listened to, and the interest shown in my opinions." The Trustees agreed about the importance of Parkin's work and, after a decade on the job, increased his salary to £2500. He was sixty-six.

Annie had accompanied Parkin on this trip. She was growing tired yet again of the constant separations from her husband. There was the strain of managing the household if she stayed, the exhaustion of travelling with him if she went. She wanted to see Maude's baby, her new granddaughter, in Kingston. There was also the bonus that they could rent out "The Cottage" in Goring if she weren't there. Even with a substantial salary, Parkin's penchant for first class didn't come cheap and he still spent most, if not all, that he earned,

Toward the end of November, Parkin developed tonsillitis. Annie managed to keep him in bed until lunchtime, but he insisted on getting up and carrying on with his work. He went to his meetings in Washington and New York, but by 1 December he was feeling distinctly unwell. Annie gave him quinine and put him to bed. The next afternoon they went to Niagara Falls, but by the evening he had great trouble swallowing. He developed quinsy (peritonsillar abscess), a pus-filled swelling in the throat that is a rare complication of tonsillitis. The condition was difficult to treat before antibiotics and Parkin was fortunate that he did not need surgery. The abscess broke on 10 December and he began to recover.

The continued strain imperilled his recovery. Annie's emotional health was so poor that she broke off a letter to Maude that she began on 19 March, resuming it only on 2 April. "I feel worse and worse but I really could not help it. Your last letter makes me feel very sad deservedly—to have left you so long. Try & be patient. I start with such good resolutions but the days get very full & my strength gives out." Her husband's ill health contributed further to her stress. At six feet, he still towered over most of his contemporaries, though he was now slightly stooped. His moustache gave him a distinguished air, but his hair had turned grey and his face was furrowed. As she noted, "He sees himself he will have to be more careful. He really worked too hard after he got back & lately really finds he must stop." She knew he wouldn't and the responsibilities of being his wife overwhelmed her. She needed to keep well, watch over him, and take as much responsibility as she could away from him. That meant, most of all, that she could never let him go to America again without her, because when he travelled in North America, "he does such careless things." Parkin's decision to land on Jamaica on the off-chance that a Norwegian tramp steamer might get him as far as Cuba was probably an extreme example of such behaviour. If she went with him, though, their money problems would simply get worse. What would they do about their house when they were away? "[These problems] must be worked out some how & I am going to feel very cheerful & happy. But it has been a very hard time & I too am dead beat. It is my head and nerves, but I hope the hardest is over & I feel so thankful for all we have here."

Parkin's doctor ordered him "a complete change and rest," which he interpreted as a trip with his wife to Cologne, Frankfurt, Rottenbugh, Innesbruck, Venice (where they celebrated their thirty-fifth wedding anniversary), Verona, and Lucerne between 20 May and 27 June. It was scarcely the six months on the Riviera that William had prescribed for Annie's recovery, but it worked its magic for Parkin. By the end of July he was looking forward to another American trip to administer the examinations for the next crop of scholars.

Lal met them at the railway station on their return. She was still living in Goring and tending the garden, with no immediate prospects either for marriage or steady employment. Parkin decided to send Raleigh to the Royal Military College in Kingston, Ontario, where Maude could keep and eye over him and to put him in touch with his Canadian roots. He had done well on the written examination and was accepted, but he failed the physical. After he recovered from the initial shock, Parkin made use of his extensive contacts in the military, pulled a few strings, and got him in. In order to see that Raleigh made the trip to Kingston safely, and also to get Lal away from the unsavoury Mr. Buckmaster, she was delegated to accompany her younger brother on the trans-Atlantic voyage. Lal stayed in Canada, where she met and married Vincent Massey in Kingston on 5 June 1915. Parkin took a two-week vacation in Scotland visiting sites associated with literary figures such as Samuel Johnson, Burns, Carlyle and Ruskin, then left on 10 September for New York. The trip was relatively sedate. He had a brief visit with President Taft, took in some World Series baseball games, and visited family.

At the beginning of 1914, Parkin began to have trouble with appendicitis. He consulted London doctors, but decided to do nothing until he had talked to Sir William Osler. Osler saw no reason for an operation. As the illness receded, Parkin, rested and refreshed, plunged back into work. The Trustees had finally given Parkin permission to publish a short history of the scholarships and he was preparing it. Earlier thay had asked Parkin to delay publication because they didn't want to encourage too close scrutiny into its financial affairs before they had a chance to regularize them. Parkin and Wylie emphasized the duties that the scholarships conferred on the beneficiaries. Milner, to whom Parkin sent the draft for comment, replied that "Rhodes' permanent fame will rest on the scholarship's scheme as embodying the noblest form of Imperial aspirations."

Parkin was still not happy with the the selection of the Rhodes candidates in the United States. Some of the universities showed a distinct tendency to favour older candidates, and there was too great a concentration from certain universities such as Princeton and Yale. However, he thought that the scholarship scheme had two beneficial effects in the United States. First, it brought to the attention of Americans the defects in their high school system. Second, he thought they were beginning to see that the Oxford honours system was more rigorous than the German research style of post-graduate education they had previously admired.

Was a reform of the system of selection in order? There were forty-eight scholars elected each year from the United States and a maximum number of scholars in residence of ninety-six. Instead, a new proposal was to create three lists of sixteen states. In year one, states from lists A and B would elect scholars; in year two, states from lists A and C, and so forth. In the interests of fairness, Parkin proposed that the exams be administered in each state every year and that a candidate be allowed to write the exam, even if it were not that state's year for a scholarship. His proposal worked, for 1914 was the first year in which every eligible state selected a candidate.

Parkin's annual autumn tour of North America did not take place in 1914. As he wrote in his diary on 4 August: "War was declared with Germany today and the nation is committed to the greatest struggle in its history." A week later, he went to London to send an application in to the War Office in the hope of getting his eighteen-year-old son a commission as a junior officer in the First Hundred Thousand, Kitchener's Army. London was in the "full tide of wide excitement," he noted, and there were crowds surrounding the recruiting office. The war was expected to end quickly with a decisive allied victory, so in October he approached Lord Roberts to ask his help in speeding along his son's application. His own former student, Charles Roberts, wrote hoping that Parkin's influence might help him see active service.

Parkin never got to use the Field Marshal's influence. On a trip to France, the old hero died. His funeral took place in St. Paul's Cathedral on 20 November 1914, with Parkin among the mourners. He was as deeply moved as at any time in his life, he told Alice and Maude, by the notes of the "Last Post" sounding "in that vast Cathedral over the hero of so many fights." It had not been a good year for his friends. In January he attended Lord Strathcona's funeral in Westminster Abbey. He was, Parkin thought, the first Canadian buried there, and the quiet, unostentatious service was fitting for a great but simple man. In February Lord Minto died of cancer, and Wylie's eldest son died in May. Parkin himself was showing signs of age.

In early October, a policeman and a military officer approached Parkin after church and told him that his four barns were being requisitioned to stable three horses and two soldiers. Parkin voluntarily took responsibility for the soldiers' meals and looked for ways to make voluntary contributions to the war effort. At sixty-eight, he still knew how to move a crowd, and he was in frequent demand as a speaker on patriotic occasions. He wrote letters of condolence to those who lost sons at the front. And he tried to influence American public opinion in a way favourable to the British war effort by writing to many of the influential figures whom he knew through his many scholarship trips across the country. The German invasion of Belgium, he told an American university president, threatened the heart of Western civilization. The implicit claim that might is superior to right put the morality of states back in the Middle Ages. Americans, said Parkin, seemed not to think that their vital national interests were at stake, but if Germany took the war to the sea, they would be as much threatened as the United Kingdom was. That, however, was not the main issue. Would America throw her moral sympathy unhesitatingly on the side of right and justice between nations, or would it allow the best hopes of the world to be ruined by the arrogant claims of brute force?

By June 1915, he told the same correspondent that he must find the situation in America embarrassing, because of the country's incapacity to defend its own ships and its own people. Americans wanted to maintain the Anglo-Saxon form of civilization, and it was going to be very difficult for them to deal with Germans, externally, or even internally, after the war. To a British audience, however, Parkin's appeal was to idealism, purity, and sacrifice. For Parkin, the war represented in the most extreme form possible, the vision of the world he had been preaching almost from the time he left university. It is very hard for people who have lived after the Second World War to understand, but attitudes to the first and the second world wars at their beginnings were quite different from the way we view the wars in retrospect.

In 1939, British, Canadian, and American attitudes to Hitler were complex. There was little enthusiasm for war in Canada and there was a strong peace faction in the United Kingdom. The United States didn't declare war until 1941, after Germany declared war on it. It was only after the six years of devastation and the horrors of the Holocaust that Hitler's regime was universally recognized for what it was, and the Second World War retrospectively took on the character of a crusade.

The First World War was different. Germany was seen as the essence of militarism. Rhodes's bequest of five scholarships for German students was a modest recognition of the danger Germany was perceived to pose. Germany had invaded France as recently as 1870, and when it invaded neutral Belgium in 1914, the outrage of the people in the British Empire was real and intense. Horror stories of German atrocities were widespread, and the desire to save "brave little Belgium" became a symbol of everything that was good and noble. Men flocked to the colours because the cause was noble, though, like Parkin, they expected the war to be short. It was only once it became prolonged and the casualties mounted that criticism of conduct of the war became serious. But even to the end, few people on the allied side doubted the purity of the allied war aims.

So Parkin's plea to his British audience was entirely consistent both with the moral ideal with which he had lived his life and the general understanding of the nature of the war.

> First, it summons each one of us as individuals to brace up within himself the spiritual forces necessary to sustain the mightiest effort of sacrifice and suffering that our people have ever been called upon to make. We must cultivate courage to face great dangers, and endurance to bear a prolonged strain of unexampled adversity. We must fit ourselves by temperance, purity and unselfishness to be worthy champions of a cause which we know to be righteous.
>
> It summons us to forego luxury and ease—to shun idleness and indifference—to spare no effort to increase our efficiency for any work we are called upon to do for the common cause. It reminds us that we are bound by every instinct of patriotism to subject our private interests to those of the country—to be ready for any sacrifices, even that of life itself, to save the nation and the world from the dangers that threaten them.

Parkin's expanding family shared his values. Marjorie had married Jim Macdonnell, a former Canadian Rhodes scholar, on 23 July, five days before he shipped out for France. Parkin's other sons-in-law enlisted too: William Grant and Massey in the army, Harry Wimperis in the Royal Flying Corps. Macdonnell later won the Military Cross and the Croix de Guerre. Raleigh saw action in the bitter fighting at Suvla Bay in the Dardanelles, where half of his brigade was either killed or wounded.

When a German submarine torpedoed the liner that was carrying the fall examinations, Parkin wrote to an American correspondent to say that the United Kingdom was making a tremendous sacrifice, but it was doing so without hesitation because the cause was so important. Americans should consider the threat to their own democracy if Germany prevailed. We do not envy, he wrote to another, "your people who are compelled to look on as mere spectators in this great struggle for humanity."

When a second set of exam papers met the same fate, he sent a third, and told the president of the University of Wyoming: "The old fighting energy of this country is now aroused, and so much is at stake for ourselves and for the world at large that I think we are prepared to make the necessary sacrifices. We think, too, that we are fighting your battle as well as our own." On 5 August, the first anniversary of the declaration of war, he spoke to a packed meeting in Goring in support of a resolution that was simultaneously being passed throughout the empire: carry on until victory.

There was little work for Parkin in his official capacity. By his estimate more than 150 colonial Rhodes scholars were enlisted as of September 1915, and there were American Rhodes scholars serving in the Red Cross. There was little point for students to come to Oxford under wartime conditions. Eighty percent of its undergraduates had enlisted, including nearly all the colonial Rhodes scholars. Of the dozen who remained, six were medical students who had been advised to continue their studies so that they could help the war effort when they qualified as doctors.

Throughout 1916, Parkin continued his busy schedule of speaking engagements. As casualties mounted and Annie and his daughters waited anxiously for news from the front, Parkin saw deeper political meaning behind the military tragedies. He noted that the heavy Canadian casualties in France had stimulated national pride and encouraged enlistment. The same phenomenon had occurred in Australia and New Zealand. In spite of the horrors of war, of which he was fully aware, he found it inspiring that people from around the empire came together and were willing to lay down their lives for an ideal of justice. The ordeal of war, Parkin felt, was purifying and strengthening the British race. As he noted, public feeling in England powerfully emphasizes "sacrifice and suffering, and I feel sure that it is going to leave us a stronger nation and a greater one in the higher sense." He saw the sacrifice not as degrading, but as noble and spiritual.

For years, Parkin had used the word "nation" to mean the British Empire and had imagined that it would come together, not by artificial plans, but in an organic, spontaneous, natural way. Now, he imagined, it was all happening as he had dreamed. The unity of the British Empire was being forged on the battlefield as he watched.[6] He would not have been surprised, if he could have looked into the future, to learn that the sacrifices made by Australian soldiers and sailors at Gallipoli formed a defining moment in the history of that country, and that, to a lesser extent, the Battle of Vimy Ridge helped shape the Canadian nation.

Parkin would—and did—explicitly reject Laurier's view that Canada had been drawn into a vortex of militarism. Like Sir Robert Borden, who insisted that Canada had earned a place at the peace table by its exertions on the battlefield, Parkin saw a new and nobler political world arising from the carnage. Early in 1917, he wrote to an American recipient to condemn the closure of German ports to American ships. "That kind of thing is not compatible with our modern ideas of civilisation. What interests us most about the whole matter is that your American people are now learning what is really back of the whole struggle, and what is the nature of the enemy with which we are grappling."[7] After the Germans resumed their policy of unrestricted submarine warfare, the USA declared war on 6 April 1917.

Parkin's ability to visit America that year, he said, depended on how great a threat German U-boats posed to a trans-Atlantic crossing. Parkin's official contacts were always top grade. On 1 May he received a letter marked "SECRET" from the Admiralty. He was instructed to bring his luggage to Platform 6 at Euston Station, London, at thirty minutes after noon. Tickets were not required, but the letter of authorization would serve for him and his servants. On 6 May he and Annie boarded a liner whose other passengers included Robert Borden, from whom he had got the invitation to sail, and members of the Foreign Office. Their escort was a convoy of two gunboats and a destroyer. The trip was uneventful. They arrived safely in Quebec City and headed directly to stay with the Masseys at Victoria College, where Vincent was dean of men. When they were in Ottawa they heard of the Zeppelin (gas-filled airship) raids over the English coast. Maude was staying at the coastal town of Studland with the girls, and the raids were close enough that the Parkin's dog, Dick, lost sight in one eye from a bomb.

On 2 July 1917, Parkin wrote a letter that profoundly influenced the future of the scholarships in the United States. Parkin was seventy-one and still full of energy, though it was clear that he could not continue to administer the scholarships indefinitely. It seemed as if states like Utah could never be adequately controlled by even such an active hands-on administrator as he, who was living in the United Kingdom. So he wrote to Frank Aydelotte, a former Rhodes scholar who was one of Parkin's and Wylie's favourites, and told him that he had just had a very good idea. Would it be possible for Aydelotte to travel with him over the next few weeks and see the sort of work he did? Aydelotte accepted by telegram and for about five weeks he shadowed Parkin in his work.

In most ways, Aydelotte was Rhodes's dream. An Indiana farm boy, he played rugby at Oxford and was a member of an elite literary club. In 1914 he founded the *American Oxonian* and as a university teacher sought to infuse the curriculum with the Oxford approach to undergraduate teaching. Parkin had corresponded with him since 1907. He was sufficiently pleased with their collaboration on this tour that he recommended to the Trustees that Aydelotte become the administrator of the American scholarships as American secretary. The Trustees agreed to this proposal on 6 May 1918. The new secretary was to be responsible for liaison with the Trustees, managing the elections, and generally, aggressively promoting the scholarships in the United States to increase their prestige and the quality of the students sent to Oxford. He received an honorary knighthood for his services to the Trust in 1953.

Parkin had another successor of sorts. His son-in-law, William Grant, reached the rank of major and was serving at the front in the Canadian army at the age of forty-three. In August 1916, he was thrown from his horse, seriously injured, and invalided back to England. The principalship of Upper Canada College became open. He had influential connections such as his brother-in-law Vincent Massey who took steps to secure it for him. When Grant took the position in 1917, his inaugural address revealed that the ambiguous feelings about the principal he knew fifteen years earlier still lingered. Parkin, he said, had quickened and stimulated his vague ideals that it was his duty to work for the good of Canada, and that work, he felt, should be done with enthusiasm. For that, Grant was grateful. The ideals in which Grant believed owed much to Parkin "in their intensity," but, as

Grant noted, no principal is "a hero to his masters, and we were not slow to criticize." Under the circumstances, the comment was harsh, though probably fair.

Annie joined Parkin on his American tour, meeting him in Chicago in September. Together they left on a westward tour. Annie was never a good traveller. On the Grand Trunk Railway to Saskatoon she wrote in her diary that the heat was so great she felt "like a stewed rat." Her skin was dried up and rough and she longed for quiet and fresh air. She grumbled that Regina had reminded her of South Africa, "except for the absence of niggers." The women she met at Government House, she felt, were inferior to her normal company, with little interest in things, dull with poor-looking faces. They tried to copy the smart set in London, she thought, but without much success. Her years in England had slowly raised her sense of social place. She still wasn't comfortable in high society, but she knew that she was Parkin's wife and, consequently, had status and belonged to a privileged circle of cultured and sophisticated men and women.

This second leg of Parkin's journey was quite different from his first. Although he didn't quite become "007," he was a secret agent. Instead of reporting primarily to the Rhodes Trustees, Parkin now reported to H.L. Lyons at British Pictorial Services in New York. He spoke without any fees, refused to let the Rhodes Trust bear any of the cost, and offered to pay all of his expenses himself, which amounted to £538.5.0 as his own personal contribution to the war effort. However, the Rhodes Trustees negotiated with Colonel John Buchan, the senior official in charge of British propaganda (and later, as Lord Tweedsmuir, governor-general of Canada), and his office agreed to pick up the tab.

The British had realized early in the war that, although there was some sympathy for them in the United States, it was by no means wholehearted. There were several reasons for latent American hostility towards the United Kingdom. One was America's founding myth, a myth repeated in every school textbook, which portrayed George III and the British as a tyrannical people whom the American patriots had to defeat to gain their liberty. Other reasons for American antipathy to Britain included George Washington's farewell address as president and the Monroe Doctrine (1823), both of which made a sharp delineation between American interests and Europe's, and had suggested that the USA should remain neutral in the event of European conflicts unless American interests were clearly at stake.

This mainstream political suspicion of all things British was further complicated by the fact that there were large numbers of immigrants in America from central Europe, including Germany, all of whose home countries were fighting the United Kingdom. According to the 1910 census figures, there were almost 3.4 million immigrants from Austria, Germany, and Hungary, all of them belligerent powers fighting against France and Britain.[8] This was a large political constituency to contend with.

The propaganda unit of the British government set out on a conscious effort to change public attitudes. Sir Gilbert Parker, a British MP whom Parkin had met thirty years earlier during his first visit to Australia, was in charge of British propaganda, or as he preferred to called it, publicity.[9] Operating out of Wellington House in London, he was responsible for forming public opinion in the United States. As he described his activities: he advised and stimulated many people to write articles; utilized the friendly services and assistance of confidential friends; had reports from important Americans constantly; and established association by personal correspondence with influential and eminent people of every profession in the United States, beginning with university and college presidents, professors and scientific men, and running through all the ranges of the population.[10] Buchan decided that the primary need was to provide a flow of news to American and Canadian papers and to supply war films. Geoffrey Butler set up the British Information Bureau in New York, one of whose responsibilities was to provide lecturers.[11] However, they were anxious that the lecturers have adequate cover. Parkin, for example, was keen that the South African statesman Jan Smuts carry out speaking tour similar to his, but J.S. Amery in the offices of the War Cabinet rejected the idea because "the difficulty is to find a suitable excuse for his going beyond that of mere propaganda." After the war, the German General Ludendorf mentioned the superiority of British propaganda as a major reason for the allied victory.[12]

Parkin started the political side of his tour in Chicago. The leitmotif of his tour was the proposition that that the British Empire was not a mere land-grabbing octopus, but an association of free, democratic communities coupled with the most liberal and progressive form of government possible in those regions of the world where democratic self-government was not yet possible. The British Empire with all its disparate parts was not looking for further imperial expansion; it was fighting to defend democracy against German autocracy, tyranny, and militarism, J.S. Amery wrote to Parkin.

Parkin spoke to chambers of commerce, Rotary clubs, church groups, students—anybody who would listen. Given his fame and abilities, there were many. Only a minority of Americans were pro-German. A larger proportion of the population was sympathetic to the United Kingdom. The vast majority was indifferent. It was the aim of British propaganda, as Parkin had recognized from the first, to persuade the third group that the British cause was identified with the very survival of civilization.[13] This approach was working, Parkin told his old friend Lord Bryce, the British Ambassador in Washington. He discerned a growing tide of anti-German feeling in the American Midwest and Southwest.

One of Parkin's favourite topics for his talks was British and American democracy. Americans liked to think that their country was democratic and the United Kingdom wasn't, Parkin argued, but through slow and steady evolution, the great dominions and England had created a political system that allowed the popular will to work just as effectively as and even more speedily than it did in the United States. In fact, Parkin contended, although the two countries were democracies, the United Kingdom, contrary to American prejudices, was possibly even more democratic than America. Why? America had no members of Congress drawn directly from the working class, but the United Kingdom had sixty members of parliament, including the redoubtable prime minister, Lloyd George himself. Australia's prime minister was a labour leader and a working man. The prime minister of Canada came from a simple background, and General Smuts was a son of the velt. "Have you in this country anything more democratic than this?" When he spoke to a chamber of commerce, he was more likely to focus on the economic ties that the United States and Great Britain could develop once Germany was defeated.

Of course, there was also Rhodes business to transact in between the public meetings. As Annie observed in a letter, "Father seems as tough as a rhinoceros & I think enjoys the stimulus of it all." "[His] little typewriter is delightful. You see it is really a travelling office and two lines of work—scholarship and foreign office (political)."

Parkin and Annie returned to Toronto for Christmas. Early in the New Year a series of illnesses struck their grandchildren. Alison came down with chickenpox, Margaret, Charity, and Alison were in UCC's isolation ward with measles, and Lal's son Lionel was suffering from convulsions. The strain was too much for Annie, who had not yet recovered from her trip, and on 17 January 1918, she left for Clifton Springs, a cross between a sanatorium and hotel, in New York, where she received massage and a kind of electrical therapy until Parkin joined her a week later.

On 4 February, Parkin and Annie set out for a tour of the southern states. Parkin's many years in the United States had rid him of any residual suspicion he might have had of the Great Republic. He fully shared Rhodes's vision of a full reconciliation between all the English-speaking peoples: "Mutual understanding and trust between us has become almost essential."

Parkin believed that the great work he had begun more than thirty years previously, the unification of the British Empire, had been virtually completed by the forces generated by the war. At the time of greatest need, the outbreak of the Great War, the British race had not faltered. The dominions and the colonies had rallied to the flag. "Our right to possess that Empire, our power to organize and maintain it, our capacity to secure it for the highest results of civilisation, have been rudely challenged.... To that challenge our British nation is bound to give an answer. The victory on the field of battle to which we all look forward confidently will be a sufficient reply. Even the fuller realisation of what our Empire is and may be—that Empire which is at last in this time of stress and trial, finding itself as never before—will not be enough. The real answer must be in the things of the spirit—in deeper loyalty to our high and ever higher ideals— in fuller acceptance of the immense responsibilities that God's Providence in the course of history has laid upon us."

The empire was not perfect, but it was fundamentally sound. The evidence for this was the sight of soldiers from India fighting side by side on the plains of France with men from Britain and the dominions. This was the message he brought to Canadian voters during the general election of November 1917. One of the central issues in the Canadian general election of that year was conscription (compulsory military service). Borden's Union Government was campaigning on a platform in favour, while the Liberals, under Laurier, were bitterly opposed. The issue largely divided the country along French/English lines, and Parkin's speaking engagements in support of Borden's government had as their goal more Canadian troops in Europe.

Now that the United States had become the ally of Britain and the other English-speaking countries, Parkin saw his next problem as making real Rhodes's vision of a closer and more sympathetic understanding between the United States and the British Empire. The war was helping to accomplish that too. "A profound change is coming over the United States in the attitude of the people towards the British Empire....this question of a sympathetic understanding between our two great nations concerns the future of the world and the safety of civilization more than anything else."[14]

On his return, Parkin filed his official report of his sixth, and last, visit to North America. In it he recounted his itinerary:

> I crossed the country speaking at St. John, N.B., Toronto, Winnipeg, Saskatoon, Edmonton, Prince Rupert and Vancouver. On the Pacific Coast after leaving Vancouver my meetings were at Seattle; Eugene (University of Oregon); Portland, Oregon; Berkeley, California; Paolo Alto (Stanford University); Pasadena (near los Angeles); and Pomona. Coming from Los Angeles eastward I spoke at Albuquerque in New Mexico; the State University near Denver; Colorado Springs; Lawrence in Kansas.
>
> From Chicago, where I spoke to the Chamber of Commerce, the University Club, the University of Chicago and the British Empire Club, I made three separate excursions (1) northward to Minneapolis, Duluth, Fargo and Grand Forks in North Dakota, connecting up thence with Winnipeg; (2) southwest to St. Louis through Missouri (State University), to Oklahoma City and Norman (State University), returning to Chicago by Fayetteville in Arkansas; (3) Chicago southward to Champaign, Urbana (Illi-

nois State University); (4) Chicago to Alma (Central Michigan); Ann Arbor (University of Michigan); thence to Cleveland, Ohio; Clifton Springs, New York; Chautauqua, NY; Cornell University and Philadelphia. Southward from Philadelphia I visited Newark in Delaware; Washington (mostly interviews); Florida, where I spoke at Winter Park, Orlando, Deland, and Gainesville. Thence to Tuscaloosa in Alabama (State University) and on to New Orleans and Baton Rouge in Louisiana. From that North to Oxford, Mississippi; Atlanta and Athens in Georgia; and Asheville in North Carolina.

In the New England States, Boston; Cambridge; Concord, New Hampshire; Andover, Massachusetts; Hartford, Connecticut; were taken either in coming or going.

But, as Annie complained in her diary on another unpleasantly hot stop on this very long tour: "Father is wonderful. He too gets tired at times, but the feeling that he is influencing peoples' thought and doing good work. Then too he has the wonderful power of throwing people aside & not letting them bother him. And, too, he doesn't have to bother about his clothes." Parkin's successes still owed much to his wife.

18

A Radiant and Triumphant Personality

On 11 November 1918, Parkin went up to London from his home in Goring for the first time in over a week. A bout of influenza had kept him in bed, but he wanted to share the dramatic intensity of the Armistice, which ended World War 1. He was in the Rhodes office, dictating a letter, everything quiet, no sign of excitement. Suddenly, at eleven, a signal went off and within ten minutes London was in a state of delirium, which lasted all day and grew in intensity. Parkin went to his club, the Athenaeum. He found the men there thoughtful, filled with awe, or, as he described Buckle, a former editor of the *Times*, "almost unstrung by the greatness of it all." Their talk was less of the past than of the future that the war had made possible, "of all the vast consequences of what the day was bringing." Parkin's young son, Raleigh, had done his part and been spared. "Surely this will show that there is a Power that rules the world, and it is not one that abdicates," he told him.

Following the war, Raleigh went to Oxford, Jim Macdonnell returned to practise law in Canada, Harry Wimperis transferred to the newly formed Royal Air Force, and William Grant continued as principal of UCC. Vincent Massey entered the family manufacturing business. A few days after the Armistice, Parkin got a telegram from Maude. Just like her mother, she gave birth on 13 November to a son in the principal's apartment at Upper Canada College, and the students enjoyed a half-holiday in honour of the occasion. She named him George Parkin Grant. Her father wrote back: "It is good of you and William to wish for the combination of names which will carry onward the two family traditions. I hope he will prove a worthy descendant of the really great grandfather [George Monro Grant] as well as my humbler self.... I think the strongest wish I have in the world now is that all the grandchildren shall grow up to be earnest workers for all that is good."

That future, Parkin now thought, lay in an alliance between the United States and the British Empire. When Woodrow Wilson came to London in December, Parkin journeyed to the city from Goring to cheer him from the balcony of his club. Parkin had been lecturing large audiences on "The Relation of our British and American Democracies to the War and to each Other." Only co-operation, he told his audiences, between the two great English-speaking peoples could make the League of Nations an effective institution. America must not believe the myth that Britain is a tyrant with respect to Ireland or India. The truth was, Britain still was more democratic: the franchise was wider in Britain than it was in America. Together, Parkin thought, Britain and American must shoulder what Kipling had called "the white man's burden" in Asia and Africa. This would build mutual understanding and their joint effort would benefit humanity. Wilson's vision of the League of Nations mirrored Parkin's own ideals of an international order. Parkin had liked what he had seen when he had met Wilson a decade before. He recognized a fellow visionary.

Parkin, however, was now an old man, and his ability to work for those ideals was declining. So, too, were his friends. Whenever Parkin was in Oxford he tried to visit Tom Raleigh, his close friend for over forty years and his son's godfather. His was one of the finest minds of his generation—lawyer, academic, author, one of the viceroy of India's closest advisors—but now that superb intellect was gone, and he was dependant on a nurse to get through each day. When Parkin visited and talked about old times, Raleigh brightened up a bit, then sank back into silence. Parkin was of an age when his friends were ill or dying. He was well aware that he had come to Oxford as an older student and that Tom Raleigh was younger than he was. He also knew that his own war work, the fifteen-month propaganda tour around the United States and Canada had, at the age of seventy, exhausted him.

There were still scholarship problems in South Africa and Rhodesia that needed sorting out, and Parkin dreaded the prospect of the trip. Fortunately, his doctor ordered him to take a long vacation before the seventy-four-year-old Parkin undertook any more strenuous travel. Parkin had an understanding with the Trustees that he would continue as organizing secretary until the end of the war. He now asked that they find a successor and began to make arrangements for his retirement.

Milner was colonial secretary in Lloyd George's government and deeply involved in the peace treaty negotiations in Paris. He had no time for Trust business, so arrangements for Parkin's retirement were not finalized until October. The Trustees (or perhaps Milner) were generous. Parkin was to stay until 1 July 1920, when Edward Grigg, the Prince of Wales' private secretary, was to replace him. After his retirement, Parkin was to have £2000 a year for the rest of his life, and Annie, if she survived him, £1000. Milner also sent him a very kind letter, which he signed, "With kind regards from an old friend."

> Needless to say, no pecuniary arrangements, however liberal, & we are all anxious to act with liberality, can express the appreciation we feel for all that you have done for the Trust. You have simply created the Rhodes Scholarships as a great permanent institution, with an assured reputation &, as I believe, the promise of an ever greater future. The system, for all its great endowment might have been a lifeless thing, if you had not breathed a soul into it. The force of your inspiring personality, your tireless energy, your belief in what you were doing & contagious enthusiasm have given it an immense momentum, while the number of younger men, ex-Rhodes scholars, who have caught something of your spirit, may be trusted to 'spread the light' in ever-widening circles.
>
> You are indeed the father of a movement which may have an

immense influence for good on the future of the Empire & the Anglo-Saxon race."

Parkin's old friend didn't leave his gratitude at the financial level. He was right, of course, that no pecuniary arrangements could serve as a suitable reward for all Parkin had done for the Trust, and fortunately, Milner as colonial secretary had access to exactly the right sort of reward: the kind of knighthood that could be bestowed on a Canadian. So, on 28 November 1919, Dr. George Parkin, CMG, received a letter from the private secretary to the secretary of state. It announced that Lord Milner proposed to submit his name to the king for a KCMG in the New Years Honours List and wondered "if such an honour is acceptable to you." The honour was perfectly satisfactory and Parkin didn't have to give the matter much thought; he accepted by return mail. The investiture took place at Buckingham Palace at 10:30 on 5 March 1920. The only problem was what to wear, given the continuing post-war rationing, but Annie assured him that she knew a tailor who was turning pre-war suits with good cloth into most satisfactory modern ones. E.R. Peacock, Arthur Glazebrook, and other friends collected £300 as gift for Sir George and Lady Parkin with the suggestion they buy a car. A group of former Rhodes scholars asked him whether his would sit for a portrait by the Canadian painter and respected war artist F.H. Varley, which they could present to Lady Parkin as a gift.

Letters and telegrams poured in: from Kipling, "an auspicious beginning, too, to the first letter I write this New Year"; old Denison, "heartiest congratulations from us both should have come before"; General Sir Edward Hutton, Edward Peacock, and Vincent Massey's actor brother Raymond also sent their congratulations. A relative in Welsford, New Brunswick, passed on the good wishes of the family assured him that "the old folk"—Olivia, Lizzie, and Watson—were all keeping well. When the Grant children were told that their grandmother was now a lady, one of the girls remarked, "But I thought grandmother always was a lady."

When Lord Aberdeen sent his congratulations, he reminisced about the dinner in Toronto at the National Club almost twenty-five years earlier when Parkin had taken on Edward Blake. "Mr. Blake uttered a rather doleful remark regarding Imperial Federation to the effect that 'NOT A RAY OF LIGHT' had recently fallen upon that subject. You took up this phrase with characteristic vigour and effect, heading each separate passage with a repetition of the word 'NOT A RAY OF LIGHT?—NOT A RAY OF LIGHT.'" Parkin's better speeches certainly made a lasting impression.

With retirement in sight, Parkin began to make plans for new living arrangements. Early in the war, he had made an arrangement with the Wimperises. They had a smallish flat at 7 Chelsea Court, near the river in London, and he had "The Cottage" in Goring. It was agreed that they would swap accommodations on a regular basis each year. There was no reason for Sir George and Lady Parkin to stay in Goring any longer, so Parkin bought the lease on a London property and sold Goring to W.A. Linsday, a British MP, for £2250, of which the net proceeds were about £1200.

A momentary problem arose in his retirement plans. Parkin's successor, Colonel Grigg, was private secretary to the Prince of Wales, and the prince, who had agreed to several overseas tours in the next eighteen months, wanted him to remain in his post for that period. For a while it looked as if Parkin might have to stay, but the Trustees invited Geoffrey Dawson, a former editor of the *Times*, to serve as an interim secretary, and to Parkin's surprise, he accepted. Wylie agreed to sort out the problems in South Africa. For the first time in his life, Parkin was begging off an assignment because of poor health, congested boats and trains. His diary entry for 30 June 1920 read: "My last day as organizing Sec. of the Trust."

Retirement gave Parkin more time for involvement in church affairs. He was still not much interested in theological matters. From his earliest days in New Brunswick, he was concerned with the missionary activities of the church and its philanthropic activities. His Christianity was more practical than theoretical, and he objected to practices in the church that bolstered social distinctions, such as pew rents and the sale of advowsons (in effect private ownership of churches and the right to appoint their vicars).

Parkin also continued to campaign against the abuse of alcohol. "It seems to me clear then that the whole weight of our national influence as Christian men must be thrown against a national evil so intolerable and so disastrous as this. Whether we shall best exercise that influence as total abstainers, or in the practice of that same rigid temperance in drink that should control our use of food or our indulgence in amusement each man's conscience must decide. My personal experience is that the line of duty in this particular varies with the circumstances in which we are placed. There is not much danger of going astray on this point if Christian principle is kept steadily in view."

When Parkin stood for election for the House of Laity in the National Church Assembly of the Anglican Church in 1920, he was elected, standing fifth of the seven successful candidates. It was work that excited him: "At Oxford, the other speaker beside myself was the Bishop of St. Albans...." Among the interesting things he said was that he insisted on all candidates for the ministry in his diocese agreeing that they would accept calls to work as freely in the dominions and colonies as in England. "There are too many parsons in England. You couldn't throw a stone outside on the streets here without hitting a parson. That is good fresh talk. We are getting a new breath of life into the Church. The National Committee—the Dominion Conference—Parochial Councils, etc.—all show this."

"I have a busy two weeks ahead of me," he wrote to Alice in November, a major church meeting and speeches to give in Oxford, Reading, Cheltenham, and Liverpool. He had, though, lost some of his spring. Always at his best extemporaneously, and usually held back as the star speaker to the end of the evening, his technique often was to listen carefully to the preceding speakers, absorb what they said, then respond. He could no longer do this. After a major meeting at the Mansion House, when it came time for him to speak, he was too weary and couldn't do justice to his subject. From now on, he would have to be one of the opening acts.

Parkin was also able to indulge in a few leisurely trips. Harry Wimperis lent him his car from time to time and Parkin liked to drive to visit Mrs. Buck, a wealthy widow who lived in the Malvern Hills, near Wales. They would take in the sights, such as Tintern Abbey. Annie liked to visit the old furniture shops on the high streets. Parkin's greatest pleasure was to borrow an axe, go into the copse above the house, and cut wood for two or three hours. His energy level quickly returned and soon he found he was able to walk ten miles a day without difficulty.

A Radiant and Triumphant Personality

Despite the fact that he was now retired, Parkin remained an influential figure. In early 1921, he received a letter that would have sent Denison into paroxysms of bliss. Arnold Haultain, who had been for twenty years Goldwin Smith's private secretary, had been demobilized in 1919 and still had not been able to find work. He asked for Sir George's assistance. The line in the letter that might have given Denison satisfaction was the following: "Goldwin Smith appointed me his Literary Executor, and bequeathed me his royalties. But, as no one now buys his books, the Royalties now bring me nothing." Parkin was not a vindictive man; he generously sent a letter to the secretary of the Royal Literary Fund on Haultain's behalf. Parkin could easily afford to be generous. *Round the Empire* was still in print and selling well enough that there was talk of a new edition and even a proposal that he might adapt it for use in Canadian schools.

Smith wasn't the only figure from Parkin's past who intruded on his old age. Parkin was reading a biography of Disraeli, in which he was pleased to find that the sparring match in the House of Commons between him and Gladstone that Parkin had witnessed from the gallery in 1874 had been particularly mentioned.

Parkin also, belatedly, began to make more of an effort to mind family matters. On Maude's fortieth birthday, Parkin wrote to her to reminisce about his absence on the day she way born. He was at the synod in Montreal, he told her. He had had "great searching" about going away from Annie at such a time, but she had heroically insisted, "as it seemed a duty. For various reasons it had a good deal of influence in my life afterwards."

To Raleigh, Parkin talked about the numbing shock his mother felt when she went to her daughter Muriel's crib and found her lifeless and cold, and the subsequent loss of his other sister Annie, just a few weeks after her birth. "I was then on the ocean, half way across on my return, and the news met me in New York," Parkin recounted. He didn't feel a need to expiate, but he did feel a need to explain.

Raleigh had been a disappointment to Parkin, who was used to dealing with Rhodes scholars. Tom, as Raleigh was called when he was young, was just ordinary, on the sickly side. At Oxford, however, Raleigh got involved in founding an Anglo-American Club to discuss international relations and foster mutual understanding between the two countries. His father thought this initiative showed that his son was finally beginning to make a mark in the world, and, to help him out, Parkin wrote to Lord Bryce, the British ambassador to the United States, to ask Bryce to serve as co-president of the club.

Parkin's optimism about his son's future was shaken, however, when Raleigh became unexpectedly ill. In January 1921, the Parkins were renting a house in Seaford, Sussex. It had central heating, a sheltered beach, and they were given a low rent on the condition that they retain the services of the owners' principal maid. Another old friend had passed away, and Parkin was writing an obituary of Principal Peterson of McGill for the magazine *Nature*. Raleigh had come home after visiting friends down the coast and Brighton. He and his father were walking along the sea front. Suddenly, Raleigh panicked and became unable to walk. Even after a rest, he found it difficult to go more than a hundred yards. He could barely breathe. Raleigh leaned on his father, who supported him into town. The doctor, however, found no physical ailment. Over the next few days he began to show signs of agitation and irrational fears. His case was diagnosed as belated shellshock. Some people called it the Fisher nerves.

Parkin also had to contend with problems in Salisbury. By now, his brother Watson was ninety-one, Lizzie ninety, and Olive eighty-four. Parkin had appointed Joe, Lizzie's son, a railway clerk who lived in nearby Moncton, to manage the family's financial affairs. Watson continued in good health, but Olive and Lizzie were both ill and weak. Lizzie's trouble, indeed, was described as a nervous breakdown, induced by too much worry over her sister, Olive. Just about the same time that Parkin heard the diagnosis of his son, he received a letter from his nephew that Lizzie had passed away.

After Lizzie's death, Parkin began to receive letters from Jim, Olive's son, who had been gold mining in the Klondike where, in the view of some, he had acquired certain vices, and who had recently returned home to look after his mother. Jim wanted to receive money directly from Parkin and not through the intermediary of Joe. Parkin apparently gave his sister about forty dollars a month. Jim thought that sum too little. He outlined his expenses, such as thirty cords of wood at eight to ten dollars a cord, land oysters, eggs, bacon, fruit, everything their heart could wish for to keep them alive.

A Radiant and Triumphant Personality

In a letter to Parkin, Jim wrote: "I am writing plainly to you as I want you to know exactly how I feel about it. I don't want anything for nothing from nobody. I cannot leave here to go to work anywhere. I have not made a dollar since last October with an expensive family to support in an expensive place. I am determined to stay with mother while she is in such a frail condition...as for ready cash to run this place on I am now down to my last 5 dollars."

The budget item that was controversial was eight or nine bottles of brandy that amounted to over fifty dollars. Jim claimed that the brandy was medicinal, and was recommended by the doctor for the health of the elderly. Joe hinted that the brandy was recreational and was one of the vices Jim picked up gold mining.

In April, Parkin and Annie sailed for Canada. He had decided it was time to sell the farm. Whether it had to do with his aging siblings, his squabbling nephews, or his ailing son can't be said for certain. He made a quick trip to Salisbury, and sold, or thought he sold, the farm to another of his nephews, Blair Steeves. But shortly after the sale, Steeves welched on the deal, bought another property, and offered to rent Parkin's place instead. The offer was summarily rejected with recriminations and bad feeling on both sides. Joe and Jim then began to jockey for position to see who could extract three hundred dollars from Parkin to dyke the marshy land and hay it. Their activities seem very much like those of characters of a Russian novel exploiting one of the property-owning town dwellers. Parkin wanted to sell the farm for six thousand dollars, but settled for four thousand. He also got a request from his eldest brother's eldest daughter's daughter ("you don't know me but") asking if he would give her away at her marriage. Parkin had outgrown his ties to Salibury many years before, but connections and blood and sentiment meant that he never entirely severed them.

In mid-August, the Parkins went to Cap à l'Aigle. They meant to make this vacation a family affair: the Grants, the Masseys, and the Macdonnells came too. Annie spent much of the day with the Grant girls—Margaret, Charity, and Alison. In the evening, the adults sat in a circle around a crackling fire in the big fireplace talking about politics, literature, or the theatre. In the daytime they fished. Massey, who had a talent for it, took photographs. The last outdoor event was a formal picnic organized by Annie for the children. Each of the children and the three nurses were sent invitations on birch-bark rolls to meet in a meadow overlooking the river. After the food and ice cream, the picnic finished with "God Save the King." One day Parkin took his slightly chubby two-and-a-half-year-old namesake, George Parkin Grant, for a picnic all by himself on the beach. He later kept a framed photograph of the occasion in the dining room in London beside the chair where he read and smoked.

On 24 September, Annie and Parkin sailed from Quebec City on the SS *Empress of France*, arriving in Liverpool on the thirtieth. His Christmas letter from Denison contained sentiments with which he thoroughly agreed: "We have ... fought a good fight together, and have so far won out. There are practically no annexationists about now. Poor old G[oldwyn] S[mith] would turn in his grave if he knew how wrong he was." His old Scottish friend, George Houstoun, wrote him in a similar vein the previous year: "Perhaps those of us who almost were ourselves out preaching the doctrine of Imperial Federation and one Imperial Parliament were instruments which prevented, or helped to prevent, the breaking up of the Empire." And Buckle of the *Times* told him that "You are among the half-dozen men who have done most to advance the British Empire in my lifetime."

Parkin still read as widely as ever: a four-volume set of Cicero's letters, in English, "as fresh as if they were written last year"; another four volumes of Robert Louis Stevenson's letters; his friend Tom Raleigh's history of the Scottish church; and the five volumes of Sir Michael Sadler's *Report on Indian Education*, which was "as interesting as any novel." He had more time for his family. He spent time with Grace and Harry and their daughters combing the bays and coves of Studland in Dorset, and having their tea on the beach.

A very pleasant letter came from his old university in March 1922. The University of Padua was celebrating its seven hundredth anniversary. It had asked the University of New Brunswick to send a representative, but UNB had no funds for such a venture. Would Sir George represent them? Consistent with his principle that it's always better to travel first class (though not with Annie's that it's nice to know you have money in the bank), Parkin bought a ticket on the Simplon-

A Radiant and Triumphant Personality

Orient Express. The Oxford Union also asked him, as their ex-secretary, to bring greetings from them also.

In Padua he was met by a Chinese student who served as his guide. He took him to a cab, where another young man in period costume was waiting. As they drove through the crowed streets his guide shouted out "Viva Canada," and the crowd responded "Viva Canada." Parkin lifted his hat in response, feeling very much as if he were in a royal procession. When they arrived at the Great Hall of the university, the representatives were asked to separate themselves into nations to elect representative orators for the ceremony the next day. Parkin was chosen to chair the election.

The afternoon of the 15 April, the delegates of the various universities were marshalled into nations. Parkin chose to wear his Oxford DCL gown and walked with the Oxford delegation through the narrow streets to the vast hall. King Victor Emmanuel was greeted with continuing and deafening rings of "Viva," before the solemn proceedings moved on to three hours of speeches. To his surprise, like all the other delegates, he was awarded an honorary degree, so that now he was a doctor of the oldest university in the world. In fact, no one had told him in advance that the delegates were to receive degrees; he actually missed the official presentation of his, but he was given it later.

On 17 June, Parkin and Annie took the short train ride to Oxford for the annual Rhodes banquet Saturday night. Milner was in the chair, and Parkin, although asked to speak briefly, indulged himself with quite a long speech, and later mingled with the crowd of over three hundred. For the first time, he could relax and enjoy himself. Then they strolled back to the Wylies and stayed the night. On Sunday he and Annie returned to Chelsea Court.

On Thursday morning, Parkin suddenly began to show flu-like symptoms. Initially, these gave no cause for alarm, but he deteriorated rapidly. By noon the next day he was only semi-conscious. The family called in several specialists. Friday evening, he was tossing restlessly; then he fell into a coma. He never recovered consciousness. Maude, Grace, and Raleigh stayed with their mother. They were together in his bedroom when he quietly passed away at 10:30 a.m. on Sunday 25 June 1922, aged seventy-six.

Many tributes poured in after Parkin's death, but none was more sincere or heartfelt than the letter written by a former New Brunswich schoolboy whose pockets Parkin had stuffed with apples and to whom he recited Swinburne's "Atalanta in Calydon" while they tickled for trout.

August 22nd, 1922

My Dear Alice Massey,

I have almost written "Dear Lal Parkin." I can hear your blessed father's voice so plainly, clear and ringing as it was in those days at home when you were small. A very precious remembrance it is.... Your father was far and away the greatest influence in all my young years and early manhood. And indeed it can be truly said that that influence never faded or weakened. It had always a strange hold, so that it was impossible to think up any mean or unworthy conduct, without at once thinking how ashamed one would be to have it come to his knowledge. And along with this there has always been the most vivid and delightful visual memory of his look, his walk, his charming manner. Such a joyous, triumphant, radiant personality touches us with profound happiness even in our sorrow. It isn't possible to print all that I feel and recall. But I want you to know that I share with you this great beloved memory.

Bliss Carman

19

Epilogue and Legacy

When Parkin went he left a gap in the rhythm
Of the great song. His going was a loss
To chivalry, and the fine-mannered years
Stumbled into his sleep. On friend or foe
He cast no shadow of intolerance,
And took your way of thinking with a warmth,
Or differed with you as a gentleman.

"Sir George Parkin" BY WILSON MACDONALD[1]

A hearse bore Parkin's remains to the grey stone Norman parish church of St. Thomas of Canterbury in Goring on 28 June. The church, built originally about 1180 and still mostly unaltered, stood opposite the small post office and quite close to a bridge which is said to be built over a ford where the great Celtic queen, Boediceia, once crossed the Thames. The service was simple, dignified, and beautiful. Many friends came, especially from Goring and Oxford, along with Rhodes scholars who had not left for the summer. "The Cottage" bordered on the churchyard and Parkin was buried close to the church between the two. An elegant but simple memorial—a recumbent cross in Clipsham stone—was prepared by Edward Warren, a London architect; T.E. Jago, a sculptor, designed a memorial tablet for the interior of Goring Church. To accommodate his many London friends, a memorial service took place in the beautiful church of St. Martin-in-the-Fields in Trafalgar Square at noon on 3 July 1922. The lessons were Wisdom III 1–9 and Revelation VII 9–17 and the hymns "O God our help in ages past" and "The day Thou gavest, Lord, is ended." The year after the memorial service, the Dominion of Canada bought a gentlemen's club on the other side of the square, renovated it, and turned it into Canada House. A decade later, King George V and Queen Mary opened South Africa House, built just opposite St. Martin-in-the-Square and designed by Sir Herbert Baker, Rhodes's architect. What better signs could there be of the bonds of friendship between the British peoples and how pleased Parkin would have been with those developments.

To Annie, her husband died the young and vigorous man she had known and loved. "I never wanted him to grow old—to me he was always so young and full of life and happiness. I have been very anxious about his health these last four years...in some ways he was very frail—and then he seemed in other ways so vigorous, but the dread was often in my heart. I hoped he would be spared to us a few more years without feebleness, but it was not to be and I do thank God that he knew no failure of power, no suffering, nor the pain of parting." Earlier in the year, Parkin had reflected that he and Annie shared twenty-two years together in each of two centuries.

Parkin's friends, wanting to make a gesture in his honour, collected money to donate books to Oxford University. Shortly after Parkin's death, his colleague and friend Lord Milner also passed away. The Trustees wanted a fitting memorial to Milner, the man who had provided the Trust with its guidance almost from its inception. They eventually decided to build Rhodes House, a stunning piece of architecture, also designed by Baker, which served as a residence for the Oxford secretary, and included a library and meeting rooms. The imposing entrance rotunda memorializes the Rhodes scholars who gave their lives for their countries. As visitors pass through the entrance they step

Epilogue and Legacy

onto the marble "Parkin floor," paid for by the funds collected by his friends. If you stop and turn back toward the rotunda, you will see a white marble bust on a pedestal on each side of the entranceway. On the left is Alfred, Lord Milner;[2] on the right, Sir George Parkin.[3] If anyone asks, you can say that they are there together because Parkin gave a speech on imperial federalism to the Oxford Union in 1874 and Milner was so impressed that he invited him to his rooms for breakfast the next morning. "We met and talked, and I cannot but think that our discussions have had their influence in the world."

After Parkin's death, Annie had £1000 a year from the Rhodes Trustees as her residuary share of her husband's pension. To avoid the high income and other taxes to which she would have been liable in postwar Great Britain, Edward Peacock advised her to return to Canada. She bought a semi-detached red sandstone house at 7 Prince Arthur Avenue in Toronto, just north of Avenue Road and Bloor Street. As Lady Parkin, widow of the celebrated Sir George, she enjoyed a considerable social prominence in Toronto and knew most of the important families, at least from the time when Parkin was headmaster of Upper Canada College. Maude, William, her three granddaughters, and the young George Parkin Grant were a few miles up the road at Upper Canada. She spent summers with them at the cottage at Otter Lake near Parry Sound, and had Christmas with one of her children or another.

Her daughter Lal and Vincent Massey lived fairly close as well. Massey had a beautiful house, "Batterwood," near Port Hope, Ontario. There he and Alice made their home. After Massey made an unsuccessful run for parliament as a Liberal, Mackenzie King appointed him Canada's first ambassador to Washington in 1925. The Conservatives removed him from that post in 1930. He then served as national president of the Liberal Party until King was successfully returned to office in 1935. King then rewarded his Anglophile friend's efforts by sending him to London as Canada's high commissioner, a post he held throughout the war. Queen Elizabeth made him a Companion of Honour. Alice Massey was an ideal wife for her ambitious husband. She had been raised since childhood to mingle with the great and the good and her social skills more than compensated for her lack of intellectual accomplishments. In 1952 he became Canada's first native-born governor-general. Lal unfortunately did not share this honour; she died two years before.[4]

Marjorie had married Jim Macdonnell, who as Canadian secretary assumed responsibility for the Canadian business of the Rhodes Scholarships in 1921. He became president of National Trust and chairman of the Board of Trustees of Queen's University. Although comfortably well-off, he never became rich because his real love was politics. He was elected a Progressive Conservative member of parliament for Muskoka in Ontario in 1945, and then in the Greenwood constituency in central Toronto from 1949 until his defeat in 1962. When the Progressive Conservative Party came to power in 1957, John Diefenbaker felt obligated to put him in his cabinet as a minister without portfolio, but he didn't trust him and took the opportunity to drop the now elderly businessman in 1959. Macdonnell died in 1973.

Grace and Harry Wimperis continued to live in England. Harry combined his early scientific training with his experience in the RAF, and in 1935 become director of research at the Air Ministry, where he established a committee to examine whether "advances in scientific and technical knowledge can be used to strengthen the present methods of defence against hostile aircraft."[5] The committee's research led to the development of radar and its military application, without which England might very well have lost the next war with Germany. Grace was a woman with considerable taste and refinement, but she suffered even more than her mother from depression.

Raleigh Parkin married Louise Cockburn, sister of a British radical journalist and novelist, Claud Cockburn. Raleigh returned to Canada and worked for an insurance company. He and Louise were active in anglophone literary circles in Montreal. He spent much of his retirement collecting his family's papers for the Pubic Archives of Canada.

Toward the end of August 1931, George and Annie's grandson George Grant was at camp. That day's letters brought him news that his grandmother had died on the twentieth. She was seventy-three. "I am terribly sorry about dear Granmummy," the twelve-year-old wrote to his mother. "Dear Granny was so good and loving." In later life, he remembered her as soft and warm, the person he loved best when he was a child. "I liked a lot of kissing, I felt there was a great deal

Epilogue and Legacy

more...sensuality in Grandmother Parkin. I loved being hugged; I loved the wetness and the softness."[6]

What was George Parkin's legacy?

First of all, he was one of the most important Canadian educationalists of his age. As Thring's disciple and biographer, Parkin spread Thring's radical educational ideas throughout the United Kingdom and the United States. Thring admired Parkin's grasp of his aims and his lucid manner of expressing his ideals. This was the reason he chose him as his biographer. Although the experiment at Reka Dom was almost certainly destined to fail, when Parkin was given a second chance with Upper Canada College, he re-invigorated the school. He took a demoralized, almost bankrupt institution, and left it vigorous and financially well-endowed. The physical building he inherited prevented him from putting his educational ideals fully into practice, but he was beginning to create a prep school when he was hired by the Rhodes Trustees. His educational innovations at Upper Canada found imitators across the country.

As founding secretary of the Rhodes Scholarships, his primary responsibility was to find a way to choose the scholars. It was not a simple task and Parkin interpreted his remit very broadly. If a jurisdiction that Rhodes, wisely or not, had seen fit to give a scholarship to was not in a position to provide a scholar, then, by heavens, it would have its educational system re-organized in such a way that it could provide one. It is unlikely that there has ever been one tail wagging so many dogs over such a large tract of space. Through the scholarships, Parkin had an important influence on Oxford as well. Its dons initially weren't at all sure that they wanted a lot of foreigners treading their sacred halls, especially Yanks, but Parkin helped get around that prejudice. The Rhodes Scholarships were also responsible for Oxford, eventually, introducing a research degree that met the needs of North American students. They also led to the abolition of the requirement to pass Responsions, the Greek and Latin qualifying exam. In itself, this might seem like a small thing, but Responsions was a barrier not just to Rhodes scholars from Montana, but to working-class students from Birmingham.

Along with his educational activities, Parkin was also involved in numerous projects meant to tie the English-speaking peoples together, such as the Atlantic and Pacific cables and the penny post. No one would say that he was solely or mainly responsible for any of these endeavours, but he was actively involved. Parkin also created a magnificent visual construct of his concept of the unity of the British Empire: the map he developed in partnership with J.G. Bartholomew. It was a wonderful instrument for his lectures; it was the key image on the first penny post; and it created superb propaganda for Canada, since it created a map that showed that country at the centre of the world.

But what of his dream? His great mission in life tied the rest of his activities together. It was a dream he shared with Medley and Selwyn, with Carlyle, Ruskin, and Froude, and Miss Erskine and Thring, all those he admired and who thought that a spiritual union of the British peoples would be the greatest possible force for good in the world, a redemption from the degradation of the industrial cities, from the debased men and women that democratic society was throwing up, from ugliness and vulgarity.

Never for a minute did Parkin waver in holding to his idealistic faith. Politicians mostly wrote his ideas off as impractical, and they would have ignored him if he had not been such a powerful speaker, journalist, and author. His book on imperial federation was the finest statement of the ideals of the movement. His analysis of Canada in *The Great Dominion*, and the newspaper articles on which it was based, lucidly articulated a vision of Canada as a country whose destiny lay on an East-West axis. *Round the Empire* taught a generation of schoolchildren to see the empire as a unity. His biography of Sir John A. Macdonald portrayed the trajectory of Canada's greatest founding father from his origins as a corrupt deal-broker to a statesman, and was widely praised when it appeared.

Did Parkin's dreams come true? Yes and no. He died a happy man. Eighty years later, the Great War seems an unmitigated disaster. That's not how it seemed to Parkin. He had lived his entire life, and lived it intensely, as a great struggle for good. German militarism was a great evil, and he had seen all of the members of the British Empire fighting together against that evil. In that fight, he recognized the spiritual unity of the English-speaking peoples he had been preaching all his life. It's hard to say, but he probably would have been happy with the Statute of Westminster, which recognized the autonomy of the settler dominions in 1931, and would also have approved of the later creation of the British Commonwealth of Nations. The fact that not all of them were white would not have bothered him at all, since, at least when the Commonwealth was created, most members embodied key British values such a monarch, parliamentary government, and an independent judiciary.

Why, today, is Parkin unknown and why are the values he held so passionately so out of favour? No one answered that question better than his grandson, the great Canadian philosopher, George Parkin Grant. In 1965, Grant wrote one of Canada's most famous political books, *Lament for a Nation*. It celebrated the noble but failed vision of his grandfather. Parkin had wanted to create a Canada that was qualitatively different from the individualism and materialism of the United States, and he had wanted it to remain part of an empire that was a spiritual force for good in the world. This, George Grant argued, was no longer what the future held for Canada, and perhaps it had never been possible. Parkin's efforts to bring it about were noble, and Parkin's failure, Grant thought, was something to regret. *Lament for a Nation*, Grant wrote, was a "celebration of memory; in this case, the memory of that tenuous hope that was the principle of my ancestors."[7]

The man who lives on in the institutions he created, such as Upper Canada College and the Rhodes Scholarships, and was the source of the spiritual vision that is the basis of probably the greatest book ever written on Canada's political destiny, was once known to the English-speaking world by a single word: Parkin.

Parkin wrote to his grandson, George Grant, shortly before his death, and told him that it was his duty to carry on the work of advancing British ideals.

Courtesy of Sheila Grant

Timeline

8 Oct. 1783	Lewis Fisher family arrived in Fredericton as Loyalists from New Jersey.
2 Feb. 1788	Susannah Stephens Williams born (Annie's grandmother)
17 Mar. 1788	Lewis Fisher received "Heddon grant" in Nova Scotia because of his loyalty to Britain.
1795?	John Parkin born in Mickleton, North Riding of Yorkshire, England.
1802	Elizabeth McLean born in Nova Scotia, to a Loyalist family.
15 Aug. 1807	Peter Fisher married Susannah Williams.
13 Apr. 1816	Lewis Fisher died in Fredericton.
1817	John Parkin left England for Halifax, Nova Scotia.
1 Dec. 1818	Annie's father, William Fisher born, 5th child of Peter and Susannah Fisher.
1820	Parkin's parents, John Parkin and Elizabeth McLean, married at Hillsborough, N.B. (23 June or 21 Oct. depending on source).

1821	John Parkin received crown grant of 210 acres of farming land on a branch of the Coverdale River in Albert County, N.B., which later became known as Parkindale.
5 Aug. 1822	William Parkin born (first child of John and Elizabeth Parkin).
25 Nov. 1823	Ann Parkin born.
1824	Jane Parkin born.
1825	Mary Parkin born.
1827	Annie's mother, Charity Ann French, born.
8 July 1827	John Parkin obtained further grant of 89 acres.
28 Mar. 1828	John Parkin (son) born.
18 Mar. 1829	Alice Parkin born.
14 May 1830	Watson Parkin born.
28 Aug. 1831	Elizabeth Parkin born.
1833	Eliza Parkin born.
14 July 1835	Olivia Parkin born.
17 Sept 1836	John Parkin purchased 573 acres in the village of Salisbury; this becomes the family farm.
16 July 1837	Charlotte Parkin born.
1845	Parkin family moved north to Salisbury, N.B.
1845	James Parkin born.
8 Feb. 1846	**George Robert Parkin (GRP) born.**
15 Aug. 1848	Annie's grandfather, Peter Fisher, died.
23 Mar. 1854	Alfred Milner born.
10 Apr. 1856	Annie's parents, William Fisher and Charity Ann French, married (his second marriage).
13 June 1858	**Annie Connell Fisher born.**
20 May 1862	GRP's mother, Elizabeth Parkin died.
1862	GRP entered Normal School in Saint John.
1863	GRP received his teaching certificate. Taught first at Buctouche, N.B., then on Campobello Island in the Bay of Fundy.
1864–67	GRP attended University of New Brunswick. Graduated in 1867.
17 June 1867	GRP appointed headmaster of the Gloucester Grammar School at Bathurst, N.B.

Timeline

26 Mar. 1868	Eliza Parkin died.
1869	GRP took his first long trip—travelled by steamer up the St. Lawrence River to Quebec and Montreal, by train to Chicago, returned home through Niagara Falls
25 Sept. 1871	John Parkin (son) died.
13 Dec. 1871	GRP appointed headmaster of the Collegiate School at Fredericton.
May 1872	GRP received Master of Arts from UNB.
8 Apr. 1873	Jane Parkin died.
1873	GRP received a leave of absence for the 1873–74 school year to study abroad at Oxford University.
8 May 1874	GRP debates imperial federation at Oxford Union.
Sept. 1874	GRP resumed teaching at Collegiate School in Fredericton; taught and inspired Bliss Carman and Charles G.D. Roberts and influenced Fredericton School of Poetry.
20 July 1875	Charlotte Parkin died.
10 Oct. 1876	Charity Ann Fisher died.
Apr. 1877	GRP began Reka Dom educational experiment.
9 July 1878	GRP married Annie Connell Fisher in Christ Church Cathedral, Fredericton.
1 July 1879	Alice Stuart Parkin born.
14 Sept. 1880	Maude Erskine Parkin born.
1880	End of Reka Dom residential school experiment.
3 May 1881	John Parkin (father) died
23 Apr. 1882	Grace D'Avray Parkin born.
Apr. 1884	Baby boy stillborn.
1884	Imperial Federation League (IFL) created in United Kingdom.
9 May 1885	A Canadian branch of the IFL created.
7 Sept. 1885	Muriel Thring Parkin born.
21 July 1886	Muriel Thring Parkin died.
1886	GRP visited England to research Uppingham School and Edward Thring.
15 Feb. 1887	Annie Connell Parkin born.
1 Mar. 1887	Annie Connell Parkin died.

1888	GRP invited to make speaking tour of Australia on behalf of IFL; quit teaching post in Fredericton.
8 Feb. 1889	GRP left, visiting Canada, New Zealand, and Australia. Agreed to continue to lecture for IFL.
24 Dec. 1891	Marjorie Christine Randolph Parkin born (6th child).
Jan. 1892	GRP began discussing map of the British Empire with Bartholomew; talks continued for several months.
Spring 1892	GRP published *Round the Empire*, a successful school text.
3 June 1892	Macmillan published *Imperial Federation: The Problem of National Unity*.
Sept. 1892	*The Times* sent GRP to Canada to prepare a series of articles on the dominion.
May/June 1893	Lord Milner arranged for a private endowment for GRP of £450 annually.
Spring 1893	GRP's Map of the British Empire prepared and distributed; GRP used it as teaching aid to illustrate geopolitical unity of the British Empire.
24 Nov. 1893	Imperial Federation League officially dissolved.
1894	British Empire League formed.
Feb. 1895	GRP's third book, *The Great Dominion: Studies of Canada*, published by Macmillan.
Summer 1895	GRP returned to Canada and became principal of Upper Canada College, Toronto.
25 Feb. 1896	George Raleigh Parkin born (7th child).
8 Dec. 1897	GRP gives National Club speech.
May 1898	GRP received CMG.
Oct. 1898	GRP's work on the Thring biography finally completed, the two-volume work published.
Christmas 1898	Imperial penny postage inaugurated with world's first Christmas stamp, issued by Canada, based on Parkin's empire map and imperial slogan.
1 Oct. 1900	GRP successfully raised the $50,000 required to free UCC from political control.
Jan. 1902	Alice Parkin died.
26 Mar. 1902	Cecil Rhodes died, his primary bequest that he offer "inducements to Colonials and even Americans to

Timeline

	study on the banks of the Isis and to learn...to love [England]...and make it big and prosperous."
7 June 1902	GRP left Toronto for England.
25 June 1902	GRP approached by Lord Grey to undertake the organization of the Rhodes Scholarship system.
12 Aug. 1902	Agreement struck between Rhodes Trustees and GRP regarding salary to expire 1 Oct 1904.
late Aug. 1902	GRP returned to Canada and to UCC to settle his resignation, which was effective October 1.
Summer 1903	Home on Parkin family farm in Salisbury burned.
9 Aug. 1903	GRP began to organize scholarships.
Mar. 1904	GRP arrived in New York with the Rhodes Scholarships qualifying examination questions.
1905	GRP settled in England, making frequent trips to America.
1906	GRP purchased "The Cottage" at Goring-on-Thames, halfway between London and Oxford.
1907	Grace married Harry Egerton Wimperis.
1908	Parkin's fifth book, *John A. Macdonald*, published in the Makers of Canada Series
Oct.–Dec. 1909	GRP toured the USA, met Woodrow Wilson, visited universities.
16 Apr. 1910	GRP visited Rhodes's grave.
Oct.–Nov. 1910	GRP travelled extensively in USA, Western Canada.
Jan. 1911	GRP was back in England.
1911	Mary Parkin died.
1 June 1911	Maude married William Lawson Grant.
Nov. 1911	Honorary Doctor of Civil Law conferred upon GRP from Oxford.
1912	Parkin's sixth book, *The Rhodes Scholarships* (containing an extensive biography of Rhodes), published.
1915	Alice married (Charles)Vincent Massey.
23 July 1915	Marjorie married James M. Macdonnell.
16 Dec 1915	Ann Parkin died.
Late 1917– early 1918	GRP toured western USA on behalf of Rhodes Trust and the British propaganda unit.

1918	Namesake nephew George Parkin Grant born.
1 Jan 1920	GRP made Knight Commander of the Order of St. Michael and St. George.
30 June 1920	GRP retired as organizing secretary of the Rhodes Trust.
August 1920	"The Cottage" at Goring sold.
21 Feb. 1921	Elizabeth Parkin died.
5 Jan. 1922	Olivia Parkin died.
May 1922	GRP went to Padua for anniversary celebration.
25 June 1922	**Sir George Parkin died.**
29 Nov. 1926	Watson Parkin died.
1927	Raleigh Parkin married Margaret Louis Cockburn.
20 Aug. 1931	Annie Parkin died.
27 July 1950	Alice Massey died.
1961	Grace Wimperis died.
1 Feb. 1963	Maude Grant died.
1977	Raleigh Parkin died.

Notes

Chapter 1: A Farmer's Son (pp. 1–13)

1. W. Austin Spires, *History of Fredericton: The Last 200 Years* (Fredericton, New Brunswick: Centennial Print and Litho Ltd., 1980), 115
2. The following description is drawn largely from Sir Charles G.D. Roberts, "New Brunswick," in *Picturesque Canada: The Country as It was and Is*, ed. G.M. Grant (Toronto: James Clarke, nd), 760–8
3. Paul Bogaard, Mount Allison University, Sackville, N.B., telephone conversation, 12 July 1996
4. Terry Cook, "Apostle of Empire: Parkin and Imperial Federation" (unpublished Ph.D. thesis, Queen's University, Kingston, Ontario, 1977), 21
5. G.H. Mowat, "The Prank that Failed," *The Dalhousie Review*, 33, no. 2, 138–9
6. Spires, *History of Fredericton*, 112
7. Ibid.
8. W.S. MacNutt, *New Brunswick: A History 1784–1867* (Toronto: Macmillan of Canada, 1963), 307

9 Eugene Fairweather, "A Tractarian Patriarch: John Medley of Fredericton," *Canadian Journal of Theology*, VI (1960): 15–24
10 Paul Bogaard, telephone conversation 12 July 1996
11 Carl Berger, *Science, God and Nature in Victorian Canada* (Toronto: University of Toronto Press, 1983), 70
12 George Parkin, "The Presidential Address," *The Geographical Teacher* (1912): 190
13 W.S. Wallace, *The Memoirs of the Rt. Hon. Foster* (Toronto: The Macmillan Company of Canada Limited, 1933), 23
14 Roberts, "New Brunswick," 766

Chapter 2: *The Passionate Young Teacher (pp. 14–25)*

1 MacNaughton, *Development of the Theory and Practice of Education in New Brunswick*, 62–3, 70, 175–7, in Cook 26
2 Spires, *History of Fredericton*, 126
3 L.M.B. Maxwell, *The History of Central New Brunswick* (Sackville, N.B.: The Tribune Press, 1937), 165
4 John Willison, *Sir George Parkin: A Biography* (London: Macmillan, 1929), 27

Chapter 3: *The Magic of Oxford (pp. 26–42)*

1 A.R. Woolley, *The Clarendon Guide to Oxford* (Oxford: Oxford University Press, 1963), 102
2 John Jones, "On the Crest of a Wave: Jowett's Balliol," in *Balliol College: A History 1263–1939* (Oxford: Oxford University Press, 1988), 202
3 Richard Symonds, *Oxford and Empire: The Last Lost Cause?* (New York: St. Martin's Press, 1986), 26
4 See John Dixon Hunt, *The Wider Sea: A Life of John Ruskin* (London: J.M. Dent & sons, Ltd., 1982)
5 Alan Kadish, *The Oxford Economists in the Late Nineteenth Century* (Oxford: Clarendon Press, 1982), 173–4
6 LAC, MG 30 D44, vol. 9, "The Parkin Chronicles," 16

7   Kadish, *The Oxford Economists*, 174
8   Willison, *Parkin*, 33
9   Bliss Carman, "Edward Thring," *The Century Magazine*, XXXVI, no. 5 (Sept. 1888): 657
10 D. Leinster-Mackay, *The Educational World of Edward Thring: A Centenary Study* (New York: Falmer Press, 1987), 64
11 Christopher Hollis, *The Oxford Union* (London: Evans Bros Ltd., 1965), 98
12 Hollis, *The Oxford Union*, 117–21
13 He spoke at one later debate, on 11 June, when he moved a motion that "a part of the Public Revenue should be devoted to the establishment of a National Theatre." "The Parkin Chronicle," 25
14 Cook 95
15 Ibid. 96
16 Wrench, *Alfred Lord Milner*, 43
17 Charles Wentworth Dilke, *Greater Britain: A Record of Travel in English-Speaking Countries During 1866 and 1867* (New York: Harper and Brothers Publishers, 1869), A2
18 J.A. Froude, "England and Her Colonies," *Fraser's Magazine*, 1,1, 10
19 Ibid. 1,1, 13
20 Ibid. 1,1, 14
21 Symonds 49–50
22 Edward Jenkins, "An Imperial Confederation," *The Contemporary Review* 17 (April 1871): 60
23 J.E. Tyler, *The Struggle for Imperial Unity (1868–1895)* (London: Longmans, Green and Co., 1938), 100
24 Ibid. 1
25 Ibid. 6
26 Symonds, *Oxford and Empire*, 25–6
27 Ibid. 26
28 LAC, MG30 D44, Sir George Parkin Papers, vol. 61, 17390, diary of Sir George Parkin, 1873, entry of 4 November

Chapter 4: Reka Dom and Annie (pp. 43–55)

1. Spires, *History of Fredericton*, 132
2. Ibid. 140–50
3. Cook 119
4. E.M. Pomeroy, *Charles G.D. Roberts: A Biography* (Toronto: The Ryerson Press, 1943), 21–2; Q. Horatius Flaccus, *Odes* (ed. John Conington), 1, 2 [http://www.perseus.tufts.edu/cgi-bin/ptext?doc=Perseus:text:1999.02 accessed 9 December 2005]
5. Bliss Carman, "Parkin," *Daily Province*, Vancouver, 31 August 1922, in Cook, 40–1
6. John Coldwell Adams, *Charles God Damn: The Life of Charles G.D. Roberts* (Toronto: University of Toronto Press, 1986), 14–15
7. Bliss Carman, "Parkin," *Daily Province*, Vancouver, 31 August 1922, in Cook, 118–9
8. Charles G.D. Roberts, "Epistle to W. Bliss Carman," *Orion and Other Poems* (Philadelphia: Lippincott & Co., 1880), 110–11
9. Cook 127–8
10. Ibid. 108
11. Ibid. 109
12. The following information concerning the Fisher family is taken from Robert Fisher, "The Fishers of New Brunswick," unpublished typescript. I have this document thanks to the kindness of Rob Fisher and it is used with his permission. Since it is not in the public domain I have not cited page references.
13. Donald Creighton, *The Road to Confederation* (Toronto: Macmillan, 1964), 319
14. Cook 127
15. Denison, *Struggle for Imperial Unity*, 59
16. Ibid. 63
17. Cook 129

Notes to pages 57–64

Chapter 5: Imperial Federation (pp. 56–67)

1. It subsequently became the Art Gallery of Ontario and now has been restored and is open to the public in much the same period furnishings as when Smith lived there.
2. *Daily Telegraph*, St. John, 14 Dec. 1880, Sir George Parkin Papers, vol. 67, MS "The Future Relations of England and her Colonies"; in Cook 135
3. Ged Martin, *Britain and the Origins of Canadian Confederation, 1837–1867* (Vancouver: UBC Press, 1995)
4. Goldwin Smith, *Daily Telegraph*, 28 Dec. 1880, in Cook 135
5. William Clarke, "The Future of the Canadian Democracy," *Contemporary Review*, XXXVIII (Nov. 1880): 805
6. Clarke 805
7. Keith Sinclair, *Imperial Federation, A Study of New Zealand Policy and Opinion 1880–1914* (London: The Athlone Press, 1955), 15
8. Kendle, *Imperial Conferences*, 3
9. John Robert Seeley, *The Expansion of England* (Chicago: University of Chicago Press, 1971), 12
10. Parkin Papers, clipping, Parkin's speech at the Seeley Memorial Meeting, Cambridge University, 13 June 1895 in Cook, 13
11. Seeley, *Expansion of England*, 55
12. Ibid. 58
13. Ibid. 87–88
14. Ibid. 37
15. Imperial Federation, *Report of the Conference held July 29, 1884 at the Westminster Palace Hotel, The Right Hon. W.E. Foster, MP, in the chair* (London, Paris, New York: Cassel & Company Ltd., 1884), 26
16. Ibid. 30
17. Sir George Parkin Papers, vol. 2, 558–562, Thring to Parkin, 26 April 1884
18. Goldwin Smith, "The Expansion of England," *Contemporary Review*, XLV (Apr. 1884), 529
19. Smith, "The Expansion of England," 534

20 Sir George Parkin Papers, vol. 2, 566–569, Parkin to Thring, 16 May 1884
21 Sir GeorgeParkin Papers, MG30 D44, vol.2, 574–582
22 Imperial Federation League in Canada, "Resolutions adopted at the meeting in Montreal," 9 May 1885, 2
23 Ibid. 23
24 Ibid. 44
25 Ibid. 49
26 Ibid. 51–2

Chapter 6: Foreign Travels and Domestic Tragedies (pp. 68–87)

1 Parkin, "Uppingham", *The Century Magazine*, Vol. XXXVI, no. 5 (Sept. 1888): 643–57
2 He wasn't named and there is no record that he was buried.
3 Cook 149
4 Ibid. 151
5 Ibid. 153
6 George T. Denison, *Struggle*, 91–92
7 Denison 97
8 Parkin, "Imperial Federation," *The Nation*, 22 November 1888, 411
9 Ibid. 412
10 Parkin, "The Reorganization of the British Empire," *The Century Magazine*, XXXVII, Dec. 1888, 187
11 Parkin, "The Reorganization of the British Empire," 188
12 Ibid. 192
13 Denison 99
14 Ibid. 104–5
15 Ibid. 105
16 Muriel Miller, *Bliss Carman: Quest and Revolt* (St. John's, Newfoundland: Jesperson Press, 1985), 57
17 Cook 227
18 Parkin, *Imperial Federation: The Problem of National Unity* (London: Macmillan and Co., 1892), 160–2

Chapter 7: The Knight-Errant (pp. 88–100)

1. Keith Sinclair, *Imperial Federation, A Study of New Zealand Policy and Opinion 1880–1914* (London: The Athlone Press, 1955), 13
2. Hobart *Mercury*, *Tasmanian News*, and Launceston *Examiner*, cited in *IFL Journal*, IV (Aug. 1889): 180–181, 189–190, in Cook 233–4
3. Parkin to Bliss Carman, 3 September 1889, in Cook 247
4. The description of Parkin's oratorical techniques comes from an article in the Toronto *Globe*, quoted in Cook 258–9
5. Cook 261
6. Willison, *Parkin*, 67–8
7. *IFL Journal*, IV (Sept. 1889): 215–217, in Cook 236
8. Parkin, *Century Magazine*, XLI (March, 1891): 690
9. Ibid.
10. Cook 249
11. Ibid. 250

Chapter 8: Colouring the Empire Red (pp. 101–124)

1. Denison 134–5
2. Quoted in Denison 131–2
3. Denison 130–1
4. Ibid. 138–9
5. Ibid. 16
6. Ibid. 139–40
7. Ibid. 143–4
8. Ibid. 144–5
9. Ibid. 149–50
10. *IFL Journal*, V (May 1890), 119–120, in Cook 255–6
11. Erastus Wiman, "The Capture of Canada," *North American Review*, CLI (August 1890), 218
12. G.R. Maclean, "The imperial federation movement in Canada, 1884–1902," Ph.D., Duke University, 1958, 86–7
13. Macmillan's quick acceptance of the book for publication pleased Brassey, though he was annoyed that there was no formal provi-

sion in the first contract for the repayment of his £300. Parkin made arrangements with the publisher to rectify this oversight, and Brassey was finally satisfied.

14 Denison 163
15 Ibid. 165–6
16 Ibid. 167
17 Parkin, "Mr. Goldwin Smith's Book on Canada", Leeds *Mercury*, 31 March and 3 April 1891
18 Smith 166
19 Ibid. 9
20 Ibid. 10
21 Ibid. 26
22 Ibid. 29–30
23 Ibid. 35
24 Ibid. 47
25 George Parkin, *Imperial Federation: The Problem of National Unity* (London: Macmillan and Co., 1892), vi
26 Ibid. viii
27 Ibid. 14
28 Ibid. 20
29 Ibid. 37
30 Ibid. 38–40
31 Ibid. 49
32 A.T. Mahan, *The Influence of Sea Power upon History, 1660–1783* (Boston: Little, Brown and Company, 1890, 1918), 1
33 Ibid. 28
34 Ibid. 52
35 Ibid. 66–7, 119–120
36 Parkin, *Imperial Federation* 63
37 Ibid. 134–5
38 Ibid. 135
39 Ibid. 160–62
40 Ibid. 205
41 Ibid. 313
42 Lord Rosebery, "Preface," in George Parkin, *Round The Empire* (London: Cassell & Company, 1892), v–vi
43 Parkin, *Round the Empire*, 6

44 Ibid. 262
45 Cook 263
46 Ibid. 264

Chapter 9: Money Troubles and the Death of the IFL (pp. 125–141)

1 Roy Hattersley, *The Edwardians* (New York: St. Martin's Press, 2005), 69
2 Guy Robertson Maclean, "The imperial federation movement in Canada, 1844–1902" (Ph.D. thesis, Duke University, 1958), 89
3 Hattersley 15
4 Maclean 92
5 Ibid.
6 Ibid. 94
7 E.M. Saunders, ed., *The Life and Letters of the Rt. Hon. Charles Tupper* (Toronto: Cassell, 1916), Tupper to Dickson, 10 January 1893
8 David P. Gagan, "The Queen's Champion: The life of George Taylor Denison III, Soldier, Author, Magistrate and Canadian Tory Patriot" (Ph.D. dissertation, Duke University, 1969; University Microfilms, Inc, Ann Arbor Michigan, 1970)
9 Raleigh Parkin, "Parkin's Other Possible Careers," 6
10 He had just published England and Egypt in 1892 and was Chairman of the Board of Inland Revenue, the country's chief tax collection agency.
11 Cook 163
12 Proceedings RCI, XXXVII (1905–1906), 269; Parkin, *Imperial Federation*, 39–40, in Cook 187
13 Maclean 97
14 Ibid. 98
15 Kendle 17
16 Maclean 100
17 Cook 271
18 He was author of *She* and *King Solomon's Mine*, two extremely popular novels that fostered a romantic view of empire.
19 Cook 356
20 Cf. "The necessary compromises of politics, the threat to his intel-

lectual independence, and the worry that his imperial creed would be tainted in a partisan atmosphere led to his rejection of Usher's proposal, despite its promise of increased fortune and fame." Cook 355

21   Willison, *Parkin*, 207. Willison also suggests that Parkin once consulted his friend George Foster about the possibility of a seat in the Canadian parliament. A letter from his friend Foster is ambiguous and, on my reading, not terribly encouraging. One the one hand he says: "I should like very much to see you in Parliament and while there are difficulties to be met in taking what may be looked upon as an outside man and getting a constituency for him, it does not appear to me that this should be an insurmountable difficulty, I would do everything I could to assist you in accomplishing that end." But on the other: "It would, however, not be impossible if you went in this capacity [principal of Upper Canada] to Toronto and made a place for yourself, that in the course of five or ten years you might slip into the political arena. That five or ten years, however, is a good deal of life taken from a man at your age."

Chapter 10: Home Again (pp. 142–151)

1   Cook 347
2   Pearson Gundy, ed., *Letters of Bliss Carman* (Kingston and Montreal: McGill-Queen's University Press, 1981), 93
3   Parkin, *Great Dominion*, 59
4   G.R. Parkin, *The Great Dominion: Studies of Canada* (London: Macmillan and Co., 1895) 9
5   Ibid. 35
6   Ibid. 36
7   Ibid. 136
8   Ibid. 142
9   Ibid. 144
10 Ibid. 146
11 Richard B. Howard, *Upper Canada College 1829–1979* (Toronto: Macmillan of Canada, 1979), 127

Notes to pages 154–165

Chapter 11: Principal Parkin (pp. 152–170)

1. Willison, *Parkin*, 139
2. I owe this description of the problems of Upper Canada to Cook.
3. Goldwin Smith, who traditionally gave the prize for classics, was not present, because Denison prevented him from getting an invitation. (The next year, when Smith was invited, Denison denounced him and declared that he ought to be behind prison bars. There was a general consensus that, once again, he had exceeded the bounds of propriety.)
4. Parkin, "Principal's Prize Day Address," *College Times*, 1–11, in Cook 386
5. Laurel Boone, ed., *The Collected Letters of Sir Charles G.D. Roberts* (Fredericton, N.B.: Goose Lane Editions Ltd., 1989), 250.
6. Howard 130; the elms, unfortunately, did not survive the arrival of Dutch elm disease in the 1960s and 1970s.
7. Howard 131
8. George Parkin, *Edward Thring: Headmaster of Uppingham School* (London: Macmillan, 1898), II, Ch. 1
9. Sir George Parkin Papers, Vol. 13, pp. 3751–4, Parkin to Bell, 16 January 1899
10. University of Toronto Archives A-0003/049 (05), Parkin to Kingsmill, 26 October 1896,
11. Howard 131
12. Symonds, *Oxford*, 242–3
13. Howard 158
14. Ibid. 131–2; See William Christian, *George Grant: A Biography* (Toronto: University of Toronto Press, 1993), Ch. 1
15. Howard 156
16. Parkin, "Prize Day Address," *College Times*, 9, in Cook 390
17. Willison, *Parkin*, 144
18. Howard 132–3
19. Ibid. 133
20. John George Hodgins, *The Establishment of Schools and Colleges in Ontario, 1792–1910*, Vol. 11 (Toronto: L.K. Cameron, 1910), 201–2
21. Howard 133–4

Notes to pages 166-178

22 QUA, W.D. Gregory Papers, Goldwin Smith to Gregory, 29 November 1899, in Cook 396, Willison 142
24 Frank Arnoldi, *An Epoch in Canadian History, An Appreciation, 1829–1904* (Upper Canada College Old Boys' Association: Toronto, 1904), 29
25 The story does not appear in Randolph Churchill's biography because the letter to Parkin had disappeared, though two different people had seen it and remembered its contents clearly.
26 Much later, the extent of Churchill's relationship with Pamela Plowden became public. He continued to correspond to her for over half a century and his letters were auctioned off for very high sums in 2003. In 1950 Churchill reminisced that he had proposed fifty years earlier.
27 Howard 163
28 Willison, *Parkin*, 147
29 Cook 398
30 Howard 164
31 Grant, "Private Memo...", in Cook 410
32 Howard 165; Grant had also resigned June 1901 to study abroad, but withdrew his resignation in the autumn. University of Toronto, UCC Archives, 80–0006/001 (38), Parkin to Denison, 24 June 1901; Parkin to Denison, 4 December 1901
33 Howard 165
34 Ibid. 166
35 Ibid. 166–7
36 Dr. Jim Power, private communication, July 2007

Chapter 12: Canada's Imperial Mission (pp. 171–185)

1 Denison 231
2 Parkin, "Memoir" 170–1
3 LaPierre 243
4 Denison 232
5 Joseph Schull, *Edward Blake: Leader and Exile, 1881–1912* (Toronto: Macmillan, 1976), 214

Notes to pages 178-187

6 The account of Blake's speech is taken from "At the National Club," *The Globe*, 29 December 1897.
7 Quoted in Michihisa Hosokawa, "Making Imperial Canadians: Empire Day in Canada," unpublished paper, 10–12 July 2003, 2
8 C.A. Howes, *Canadian Postage Stamps and Stationary* (Lawrence, Mass.: Quarterman Publications, 1911, 1974), 179
9 Howes 180–1
10 Rudyard Kipling, "The White Man's Burden," 1899
11 Graham M. Thompson, "Sandford Fleming and the Pacific Cable: The Institutional Politics of Nineteenth-Century Imperial Telecommunications," www.cjc-online.ca/include/getdoc.php?id=1527&article=1060&mode=pdf 68 [accessed: 30 August 2005]
12 Thompson fn 12

Chapter 13: The Most Delightful Man in Canada (pp. 186–203).

1 The knighthood, KCMG, stood for "the King Calls Me God," and the highest level of the order, GCMG supposedly meant "God Calls Me God."
2 Willison 250
3 Frank Underhill, "Lord Minto on his Governor Generalship," *Canadian Historical Review* XL (June 1959): 121–131
4 Elliot, Gilbert John Murray-Kynynmound, Viscount Melgund and 4th Earl of Minto, Dictionary of Canadian Biography Online, http://www.biographi.ca/EN/ShowBio.asp?BioId=41478 [accessed: 30 August 2005]. A soldier, with a military man's distrust of politicians, Minto gave the impression that "he was little more than an imperial busybody, an autocratic proconsul and militarist out of touch with Canadian life." Some later Canadian historians have pictured him "as a man chosen by an aggressive Colonial Secretary, Joseph Chamberlain, to be the instrument of the Colonial Secretary's policy to entangle Canada in an expensive network of imperial obligations against which Laurier struggled heroically for six years in defence of Canadian autonomy." A more recent biographer has argued that Minto saw Canada as a country whose sur-

vival in a North American context required strong British military, economic, and cultural ties that should be buttressed by a combination of self-interest and sentiment.
5 Sir George Parkin Papers, vol. 13, 3758–61, Maurice Macmillan to Parkin, 23 January 1899
6 R.R. James, *Rosebery: A Biography of Archibald Philip Primrose, Fifth Earl of Rosebery* (London: Weidenfeld and Nicolson, 1963), 404
7 LaPierre 266
8 Hamilton and Grant 414
9 Ibid. 415
10 LaPierre 267
11 http://www.biographi.ca/EN/ShowBio.asp?BioId=41478&query=minto
12 LaPierre 269–70
13 Miller 64
14 Ibid. 120
15 Ibid. 122–4
16 http://www.biographi.ca/EN/ShowBio.asp?BioId=41478&query=minto
17 *The Globe*, January 20, 1902; Hopkins, *The Canadian Annual Review of Public Affairs, 1902*, 135–137; in Paul Stevens and John T. Saywell, eds., *Lord Minto's Canadian Papers 1898–1904*, vol. II (Toronto: The Champlain Society, 1981), 152
18 Miller 186

Chapter 14: I, Cecil Rhodes (pp. 204–221)

1 Quoted in Roy Hattersley, *The Edwardians* 85–6
2 Lord Birkenhead, *Rudyard Kipling* (Random House: New York, 1978) 231
3 Lord Birkenhead 232
4 Others were not. "To and for the establishment, promotion and development of a Secret Society, the true aim and object whereof shall be for the extension of British rule throughout the world, the perfecting of a system of emigration from the United Kingdom, and of colonisation by British subjects of all lands where the

means of livelihood are attainable by energy, labour and enterprise, and especially the occupation by British settlers of the entire Continent of Africa, the Holy Land, the Valley of the Euphrates, the Islands of Cyprus and Candia, the whole of South America, the Islands of the Pacific not heretofore possessed by Great Britain, the whole of the Malay Archipelago, the seaboard of China and Japan, the ultimate recovery of the United States of America as an integral part of the British Empire...."

5 Anthony Kenny, ed., *The History of the Rhodes Trust, 1902–1999*, "The Will of Cecil Rhodes" (Oxford: OUP, 2001), 568
6 Anthony Kenny, "The Rhodes Trust and Its Administration," *History of the Rhodes Trust, 1902–1999*, 2
7 Douglas McCalla, "Canada and Newfoundland," in Kenny 204–5
8 Ibid. 204
9 David Alexander, "The American Scholarships," in Kenny 106–7

Chapter 15: Home and Away (pp. 222–235)

1 Richard Symonds 127
2 Kenny, "The Rhodes Trust," 5
3 Ibid.
4 Anthony Kenny, "The Smaller Constituencies," in *The History of the Rhodes Trust 1902–1999*, 419
5 Poynter, "Scholarships in Australia," 317
6 Ibid.
7 Quoted in Poynter 317
8 Poynter 318
9 Ibid. 319
10 R.F. Scholtz and S.K. Hornbeck, *Oxford and the Rhodes Scholarships* (Toronto: Oxford University Press, 1907), 26–7
11 Kenny, "The Smaller Constituencies," 428
12 McCalla, "Canada and Newfoundland" 209
13 Ibid. 109
14 Scholtz and Hornbeck 23
15 McCalla 205–6
16 Marlow, Milner, 178

Chapter 16: Settling Down? (pp. 236–253)

1. John Edward Kendle, *1887–1911: A Study in Imperial Colonial and Imperial Conferences*, 57
2. McCalla 210
3. Alexander 110
4. Ibid. 112–3;
5. Ibid. 113
6. Ibid. 114–5
7. Ibid. 116–7
8. Poynter 320
9. Ibid. 324
10. Ibid.
11. Symonds, *Oxford and Empire*, 179
12. Ibid.
13. Kendle 127
14. Ibid. 131
15. Gearóid Ó Tuathail, *Critical Geopolitics: The Politics of Writing Global Space* (London: Routledge, 1996), 92
16. Birkenhead 257

Chapter 17: This Great Struggle for Humanity (pp. 254–274)

1. Just how serious Buckmaster was can be inferred from the fact that he bribed her young brother with such an expensive fishing rod that he treasured it to the end of his life.
2. Willison, *Parkin*, 242
3. Ibid. 243
4. Kendle, *Imperial Conferences*, 201
5. Ibid. 206
6. Yet Canada insisted on separate representation at the peace talks. In 1922 Canada refused to help the United Kingdom in the Chanak Crisis. In 1926 Mackenzie King successfully ran his campaign on the charge that the British were interfering in Canadian affairs

and the Statute of Westminster of 1931 established legal autonomy for the settler dominions.
7 RTA, file 1225 (Delaware), Parkin to Dr. Mitchell, 12 February 1917
8 www.census.gov/population/www/documentation/twps0029/tab04.html [accessed: 14 February 2006]
9 James Duane Squires, *British Propaganda at Home and in the United States From 1914 to 1917* (Cambridge: Harvard University Press: 1935) 50-1
10 Quoted in Charles Grant Miller, *The Poisoned Loving Cup* (Chicago: National Historical Society, 1928), 18-19
11 Janet Adam Smith, *John Buchan* (London: Rupert Hart-Davis, 1965), 202
12 Ibid. 203
13 Peter Buitenhuis, *The Great War of Words* (Vancouver: University of British Columbia Press, 1987), 54-5
14 Some Americans thought that the Rhodes Scholarships had already succeeded by the time of the Great War in creating an Anglophile fifth column inside the United States. See Charles Grant Miller, *The Poisoned Loving Cup*, 111-4

Chapter 19: Epilogue and Legacy (pp. 287-293)

1 Wilson MacDonald, "Sir George Parkin," typescript

> When a great tree goes down beneath the weight
> Of its own years, in ripeness of completion,
> We keep a noble sorrow, not akin
> To that despair which sounds the grievous passing
> Of lovely, young and incompleted life:
> And when a great man comes at last to earth,
> Urged by his own magnificence of year,
> The hour is not for sorrow or regret;
> And yet it is not free from loneliness—
> The groping ever for departed hands,

The waiting for a word that will not come.

This mighty fugue of life is built on chords—
Some loud, resounding, some quiet as light,
Some that seem discord until our hearts are tuned
To the advancing harmony of Time;
When Parkin went he let a gap in the rhythm
Of the great song. His going was a loss
To chivalry, and the fine-mannered years
Stumbled into his sleep. On friend or foe
He cast no shadow of intolerance,
And took your way of thinking with a warmth,
Or differed with you as a gentleman.

O Youth, your burning wine is in my blood!
May I keep this forever—it is good.
Yet sometimes I have seen, in an old man's face,
That sparkle which is valour in old wine.
Here was one whose flow of soul had gained,
In the cool cellars of near eighty years,
A flavour of great richness. Lay him down,
This fine aristocrat of our young land,
And fold about him that bright cloth of gold
Which all his days have woven for this hour.

2   By Kathleen Scott
3   By E. Whitney Smith
4   The appointment created a family crisis, though, when Vincent asked Maude to be his chatelaine at Rideau Hall. Alice Massey had died on July 27, 1950. When she was dying, Maude went down to Batterwood to be with her sister; Vincent, who did not like being with the sick, kept his distance. On one occasion he came to her room, and Alice told him that she wanted her fur coat to go to Maude. After Alice passed away, Vincent took Maude aside and said he could not afford to give her the coat. He also added that Alice had always spent too much money on Christmas presents, and there would be none this year. Then, when he was offered the

governor-generalship, he asked Maude, whose gracious manners everyone acknowledged, if she would serve as his hostess. Maude refused; she could not afford the clothes required for the position. Vincent said to her, "But I will pay for them," to which Maude replied, "I would never put myself in a position to take anything from you." See William Christian, *George Grant*, 158.
5 http://www.radarpages.co.uk/people/watson-watt/watson-watt2.htm [accessed: 9 December 2005]
6 Parkin's sister Olivia died the same year as he did. Watson Parkin outlived his little brother; he died in 1926 at the age of ninety-six.
7 George Grant, *Lament for a Nation* (Toronto: McClelland and Stewart, 1965), 5–6

Sources

Primary Sources

The most important manuscript sources were the James Bryce and Lord Milner papers in the Bodleian Library at Oxford; the Rhodes House and the Rhodes Trust archives at Rhodes House in Oxford; the Bliss Carman, George T. Denison, G.M. Grant, George P. Grant, W.L. and Maude Grant, D'Alton McCarthy, Vincent and Alice Massey, Lord Minto, Sir George Parkin, Raleigh Parkin, and Harry Wimperis papers at Library and Archives Canada; the Bliss Carman, George M. Grant, and Sir George Parkin papers at the Queen's University Archives; Vincent and Alice Massey papers, and Upper Canada College Archives, University of Toronto

Select Secondary Sources

Adams, John Coldwell. *Sir Charles God Damn: The Life of Sir Charles G.D. Roberts.* Toronto: University of Toronto Press, 1986.

Arnoldi, Frank. *The Endowment of Upper Canada College.* The College Times, 1896, 6–11.

―――. *An Epoch in Canadian History—An Appreciation: Upper Canada College, 1829–1904*. Toronto: Upper Canada College Old Boys' Association, 1904.

Bartholomew, J.G., and John Bartholomew & Co. *British Imperial Federation Map of the World*. [Edinburgh: John Bartholomew & Co.], 1889.

Berger, Carl. *Science, God, and Nature in Victorian Canada*. Toronto: University of Toronto Press, 1983.

Biltcliffe, Pippa. *Walter Crane and the Imperial Federation Map Showing the Extent of the British Empire (1886)*. Imago Mundi: *The International Journal for the History of Cartography* 57 (1) 2005: 63–9.

Birkenhead, Frederick Winston Furneaux Smith. *Rudyard Kipling*. 1st American ed. New York: Random House, 1978.

Bliss Carman: A Reappraisal. Reappraisals, Canadian writers, 16. Ottawa: University of Ottawa Press, 1990.

Brown, R.C. "Goldwin Smith and Anti-Imperialism." In *Imperial Relations in the Age of Laurier*, edited by C. Berger. Toronto: University of Toronto Press, 1969.

Buitenhuis, Peter. *The Great War of Words: British, American and Canadian Propaganda and Fiction, 1914–1933*. Vancouver: University of British Columbia Press, 1987.

Carlyle, Thomas. *The French Revolution: A History*. 3 vols. London: J. Fraser, 1837.

―――. *On Heroes, Hero-worship and the Heroic in History*. London, 1872.

Carlyle, Thomas, and Leonard Henry Courtney. *Sartor Resartus: The Life and Opinions of Herr Teufelsdröckh*. 2nd ed. London, 1841.

Carlyle, Thomas, and Edgar Sanderson. *The Life of Oliver Cromwell*. New York: G.H. Doran, 1924.

―――. *Letters of Bliss Carman*. Kingston, Ont.: McGill-Queen's University Press, 1981.

Chamberlain, Muriel Evelyn. *Lord Aberdeen, a Political Biography*. London; New York: Longman, 1983.

Christian, William. "Canada's Fate: Principal Grant, Sir George Parkin and George Grant." *Journal of Canadian Studies* 34 (4) 1999: 88–104.

Churchill, Winston. *My Early Life: A Roving Commission*. 1st impression ed, Keystone library. London: T. Butterworth, 1934.

Cook, Terry. "John Beverley Robinson and the Conservative Blueprint for the Upper Canada Community." *Ontario History* 64 (2) 1972: 79–94.

———. "The Canadian Conservative Tradition: An Historical Perspective." *Journal of Canadian Studies* 8 (4) 1973: 31–39.

———. "George R. Parkin and the Concept of Britannic Idealism." *Journal of Canadian Studies* 10 (3) 1975: 15–31.

———. "From Backwoods to National Conscience: The Family of Sir G.R. Parkin." *Archivist: Magazine of the National Archives of Canada* 107 (1994): 9–11.

———. "A Reconstruction of the World: George R. Parkin's British Empire Map of 1893." *Cartographica* 21 (1984): 53–65

Craig, Barry L. *Apostle to the Wilderness: Bishop John Medley and the Evolution of the Anglican Church.* Madison N.J.: Fairleigh Dickinson University Press, 2005.

Curry, Ralph L. *Stephen Leacock: Humorist and Humanist.* Shelburne, Ont.: Battered Silicon Dispatch Box, 2005.

Denison, George T. *Struggle for Imperial Unity: Recollections and Experiences.* London: Macmillan, 1909.

Dilke, Charles Wentworth. *Greater Britain: A Record of Travel in English-speaking Countries during 1866 and 1867.* New York: Harper & Brothers, 1869.

Doyle, James. *Stephen Leacock: The Sage of Orillia.* Canadian biography series. Toronto: ECW Press, 1992.

Elton, Godfrey. *The First Fifty Years of the Rhodes Trust and the Rhodes Scholarships, 1903–1953.* Oxford: Blackwell, 1955.

Fisher, R.C. "The Fishers of New Brunswick, 1783–1950." 1998.

Gilmour, David. *The Long Recessional: The Imperial Life of Rudyard Kipling.* London: John Murray, 2002.

Gollin, Alfred M. *Proconsul in Politics: A Study of Lord Milner in Opposition and in Power.* London: A. Blond, 1964.

Graham, John Parkhurst. *Forty Years of Uppingham: Memories and Sketches.* [With plates.] London, 1932.

Grant, George Monro. *Ocean to Ocean: Sandford Fleming's Expedition through Canada in 1872. Being a diary kept during a journey from the Atlantic to the Pacific, with the expedition of the engineering-chief of the*

Sources

Canadian Pacific and Inter-colonial Railways. Toronto: J. Campbell, 1873.

———. *Picturesque Canada: The Country as it Was and Is.* Toronto: Belden Bros., 1882.

———. *Advantages of Imperial Federation.* 1891

Grant, George Parkin. *The Empire, Yes or No?* Toronto: Ryerson Press, 1945.

———. *Lament for a Nation: The Defeat of Canadian Nationalism.* Toronto: McClelland and Stewart, 1965.

Grant, George Parkin, and William Christian. *George Grant: Selected Letters.* Toronto: University of Toronto Press, 1996.

Grant, George Parkin. *Technology and Empire: Perspectives on North America.* Toronto: House of Anansi, 1969.

Grant, William Lawson, and Charles Frederick Hamilton. *Principal Grant.* Toronto: Morang, 1904.

Hall, Walter P. Review of J.E. Tyler, *The Struggle for Imperial Unity (1868–1895). The Journal of Modern History* 11 (1) 1939: 94–6.

Halperin, Vladimir. *Lord Milner and the Empire: The Evolution of British Imperialism.* London: Odhams Press, 1952.

Harrison, Brian, ed. *The History of Oxford University: The Twentieth Century.* Vol. VII. Oxford: Clarendon Press, 1994.

Haultain, T. Arnold. *Goldwin Smith His Life and Opinions.* Toronto: McClelland, 1913. Microform.

Hoyland, Geoffrey. *The Man Who Made a School: Thring of Uppingham.* [With a portrait.] Torch biographies. London, 1946.

James, David. *Lord Roberts.* With a foreword by L.S. Amery. London: Hollis & Carter, 1954.

Jay, Richard. *Joseph Chamberlain: A Political Study*: Oxford University Press, 1981.

Jenkins, Roy. *Sir Charles Dilke: A Victorian Tragedy.* London: Collins, 1958.

———. *Asquith: Portrait of a Man and an Era.* New York: Chilmark Press, 1964.

———. *Gladstone: A Biography.* 1st American ed. New York: Random House, 1997.

———. *The British Liberal Tradition: From Gladstone to Young Churchill, Asquith and Lloyd George—is Blair Their Heir?* Toronto: Published in association with Victoria University by University of Toronto Press, 2001.

———. *Churchill: A Biography*. New York: Farrar, Straus and Giroux, 2001.

Keith, W.J. *Charles G.D. Roberts, Studies in Canadian Literature*. 1. [Toronto]: Copp Clark Pub. Co., 1969.

Kendle, John. *The Colonial and Imperial Conferences, 1887–1911: A Study in Imperial Organization*. London: Published for the Royal Commonwealth Society by Longmans, 1967.

———. *The Round Table Movement and Imperial Union*. Toronto; Buffalo: University of Toronto Press, 1975.

———. *Federal Britain: A History*. London; New York: Routledge, 1997.

Kenny, Anthony, ed. *The History of the Rhodes Trust, 1902–1999*. Oxford: Oxford University Press, 2000.

Knox, Bruce. "The Earl of Carnarvon, Empire, and Imperialism, 1855–90." *Journal of Imperial and Commonwealth History* 26 (2) 1998: 48–66.

LaPierre, Laurier L. *Sir Wilfrid Laurier and the Romance of Canada*. Toronto: Stoddart Publishing Co., 1996.

Marlowe, John. *Cecil Rhodes: The Anatomy of Empire*. London: Elek, 1972.

Martin, Ged. "Empire Federalism and Imperial Parliamentary Union, 1820–1870." *Historical Journal* 16 (1) 1973: 65–92.

Massey, Vincent. *What's Past is Prologue: The Memoirs of the Right Honourable Vincent Massey, C.H*. Toronto: Macmillan of Canada, 1963.

———. *Confederation on the March: Views on Major Canadian Issues during the Sixties*. Toronto: Macmillan of Canada, 1965.

Mensing, Raymond C., Jr. "Cecil Rhodes's Ideas of Race and Empire." *International Social Science Review* 61 (3) 1986: 99–106.

Moore, Steve, and Debi Wells. *Imperialism and the National Question in Canada*. Introduction by Leo Johnson. Toronto: S. Moore, 1975.

Morton, Desmond. *Ministers and Generals: Politics and the Canadian Militia, 1868–1904*. Toronto: University of Toronto Press, 1970.

———. *A Military History of Canada*. Edmonton: Hurtig, 1985.

Murphy, Derrick. 2001. "Joseph Chamberlain: Radical and Imperialist." *Modern History Review* 12 (3) 2001: 27–29.

Nimocks, Walter. *Milner's Young Men: The Kindergarten in Edwardian Imperial Affairs*. Durham, N.C.: Duke University Press, 1968.

Page, Robert J.D. *Imperialism and Canada, 1895–1903*. Canadian history through the press series. Toronto: Holt, Rinehart, and Winston of Canada, 1972.

Parkin, George. "Review: Edward Thring, Theory and Practice of Teaching." *The Nation*, 6 December 1883, 478–9.

———. "The Reorganization of the British Empire." *The Century Magazine*, December 1888, 187–92.

———. "Uppingham: An Ancient School Worked on Modern Ideas." *Century Magazine*, September 1888, 643–57.

———. "The Anglo-Saxon in the Southern Hemisphere: The Workingman in Australia." *Century Magazine*, February 1891, 607–13.

———. "Australian Cities: The Anglo Saxon in the Southern Hemisphere." *Century Magazine*, March 1891, 690–6.

———. "Mr. Goldwin Smith's Book on Canada." *Leeds Mercury*, 31 March, 3 April 1891.

———. "Geographical Unity of the British Empire." *Scottish Georgraphical Magazine*, May 1894, 225–42.

———. 1895. The Principal's Prize Day Address. The College Times, Christmas, 1–11.

———. "A Memoir of Tennyson." *Canadian Magazine*, December 1897, 167–72.

———. Introduction. Book of the Victoria Era Ball Given at Toronto on the Twenty-Eight of December MDCCCXCVII. 1898

———. "Victoria and the Victorian Age." *Canadian Magazine*, March 1901, 395–401.

———. "Imperial Federation." *McGill University Magazine*, April 1902, 180–93.

———. "The Rhodes Scholarships." *Proceedings of the Royal Colonial Institute, 1904–5*, 1–28.

———. "American Rhodes Scholars at Oxford." *North American Review*, June 1909, 900–14.

———. "The Relations of Canada and the United States." *Empire Club of Canada, 1907–08*, 157–68.

———, ed. "Canada since Federation." eleventh ed. Vol. v, *Encyclopedia Britannica*. Cambridge: Cambridge University Press, 1911.

———. "The Rhodes Scholarships." In *Encylclopedia Britannica*. Cambridge: Cambridge University Press, 1911.

———. "Sir John Alexander Macdonald." In *Encyclopedia Britannica*. Cambridge: Cambridge University Press, 1911.

———. "True Imperialism." *United Empire*, December 1911, 837–51.

———. Annual Dinner. *United Empire*, nd, 495–8.

———. "Christian Responsilities of Empire." *The Christian World Pulpit*, 31 May 1916, 301–4.

———. "The Duty of the Empire to the World." In *The Empire and the Future*, edited by A. Newton. London: Macmillan and Co., Ltd., 1916

———. "The Educational Problems and Responsibilities of Empire." *Empire Club of Canada, 1912–13*, Toronto, 1916.

———. "The Integration of the Empire." United Empire, 1916, 669–672.

———. "A Message for Empire Day." *Educational Review*, May 1916, 2501.

———. "Discussion on Sir Walter Raleigh's Paper." *United Empire*, 1917, 32–3.

———. "British and American Democracy as Guardians of Future Peace." Canadian Club of Winnipeg, Addresses of the Year, 1918.

———. "Frontier Work in Western Canda." *East and The West*, 1919, 1–9.

———. "Rhodes Scholarships and American Scholars." *Atlantic Monthly*, September 1919, 365–75.

———. "Sir William Peterson, KCMG." *Nature*, January 1921.

———. "Wireless Telegraphy." *The Times*, 29 December 1902.

———. *Imperial Federation: The Problem of National Unity*. London: Macmillan, 1892.

———. *Round the Empire*. For the use of schools. London: Cassell and Co., 1892

———. *The Great Dominion*. Studies of Canada. London: Macmillan, 1895.

———. *Edward Thring, Headmaster of Uppingham School: Life, Diary and Letters*. 2 vols. London: Macmillan, 1898.

———. *Sir John A. Macdonald*. The Makers of Canada. De luxe ed. Toronto: Morang, 1908.

Sources

———. *The Rhodes Scholarships*. Toronto: Copp, 1912.

Parkin, George Robert, J.G. Bartholomew, and John Bartholomew & Co. *The British Empire Map of the World*. London: Cassell & Co. Ltd., 1893.

Parkin, G.R., and W.E. Duffett. *India Today: An Introduction to Indian Politics*. New York: Longmans, 1946. [Rev. ed. Toronto.]

Percival, Alicia C. *Very Superior Men: Some Early Public School Headmasters and Their Achievements*. London: C. Knight, 1973.

Phillips, Paul T. *The Controversialist: An Intellectual Life of Goldwin Smith*. Praeger, 2002.

Rawnsley, W.F. *Early Days at Uppingham under Edward Thring*. London: Macmillan & Co., 1909,

Roberts, Brian. *Cecil Rhodes: Flawed Colossus*. London: H. Hamilton, 1987.

Roberts, C.G.D. "Bliss Carman." *Dalhousie Review* IX (1930): 409–17.

———. "More Reminiscences of Bliss Carman." *Dalhousie Review* X (1930): 1–9.

Roberts, Charles George Douglas, and Laurel Boone. *The Collected Letters of Charles G.D. Roberts*. Fredericton, N.B.: Goose Lane Editions, 1989.

Saunders, E.M. *The Life and Letters of the Rt. Hon. Sir Charles Tupper*. London: Cassell, 1916.

Schull, Joseph. *Laurier: The First Canadian*. Toronto: Macmillan of Canada, 1965.

———. *Edward Blake*. 2 vols. Toronto: Macmillan, 1975.

Seeley, John Robert. "The expansion of England," two courses of lectures. London, 1883.

Sinclair, Keith. 1955. *Imperial Federation: A Study of New Zealand Policy and Opinion, 1880–1914*. [London]: University of London; Athlone Press, 1955.

Smith, Goldwin. *A Political Destiny of Canada by Goldwin Smith*. With a reply by Sir Francis Hincks. Toronto: Belford, 1877.

———. *Canada and the Canadian Question*. Toronto: Hunter Rose, 1891.

———. "An Imperial Federationist on Canada." *Illustrated London News*, 18 May 1895, 613.

———. "The Rhodes Scholarships." *The Nation*, 1904: 289–90.

Staines, David. *Stephen Leacock: a Reappraisal*. Reappraisals: Canadian writers. Ottawa: University of Ottawa Press, 1986.
Steeves, Leon Parkin. *The Parkins of New Brunswick: The Family of John Parkin (1795–1881)*. Hillsborough? N.B., 1971.
Wallace, Elisabeth. "Goldwin Smith on History." *Journal of Modern History* 26 (3) 1954: 220–32.
Wallace, W. Stewart. *The Memoirs of the Rt. Hon. Sir George Foster, P.C., G.C.M.G.* Toronto: Macmillan, 1933.
Willison, John. *Reminiscences, Political and Personal.* Toronto: McClelland and Stewart, 1919.
———. *Sir George Parkin: A Biography.* London: Macmillan, 1929.
Wiman, Erastus. "The Greater Half of the Continent." *North American Review*, 1889, 54–72.
———. "The Capture of Canada." *North American Review*, August 1890, 212–22.
Wrench, Evelyn. *Alfred Lord Milner: The Man of No Illusions, 1854–1925.* London: Eyre & Spottiswoode, 1958.

Index

Aberdeen, Lady 174, 177, 187
Aberdeen, Lord 177, 180, 186, 278
Adelaide, University of 227
Agassiz, Louis 11
Allen, C.K. 244
All Souls College 74, 209, 241
American Revolution xvi, 49, 61, 83, 206
Amery, L.S. 246, 270, 271
Anson, William 209
Archibald, J.G. 241
Arnold, Thomas 29
Arnold-Foster, Hugh 74, 99, 118, 136, 139, 149, 164, 195
Arnoldi, Frank 166, 178
Ascension Island 119
Ashburn College 235
Asquith, H.H. 36–8, 73, 78
Association of State Universities 217
Association of the Presidents of State Universities 259
Astor, Waldorf and Nancy 259

Athenaeum 138
Australia xiv, 58, 79, 80, 93–9, 104, 112, 116, 119, 131, 184, 185, 194, 197, 212, 226, 227, 237, 238, 244, 246, 257, 258, 266, 267, 271, 350
Aydelotte, Frank 268

Baden-Powell, Robert 189, 247
Bailey, Loring Woart 9–12, 44, 214
Baines, Talbot 132
Baker, Herbert 288
Balfour, Arthur 237
Baliol, John de 2
Balliol College 2, 27, 36, 302
Bartholomew, J.G. 117, 118, 128, 132, 137, 149, 177, 292
Bathurst (New Brunswick) 14, 15, 17, 36
Batterwood 289
Battle of Vimy Ridge 267

Beatty, Mr. 157
Beit, Alfred 207, 208, 249, 255
Bell, Alexander Graham 233
Bell, Moberley 3, 136, 148, 149, 177, 195, 215
Belleau, M. 233
Bermuda 212, 228, 229, 232, 346
Bird, Mr. 90
Blake, Edward 67, 102, 178–81, 278
Boer Republic 189
Boer war 189–93
Borden, Frederick 193
Borden, Robert 109, 173, 199, 200, 246, 258, 259, 267, 273
Boulton, Harriette 57
Bourassa, Henri 190
Bowell, Mackenzie 173
Boyd, Charles 222
Boy Scouts 247
Brasenose College 222
Brassey, Thomas 99, 101, 108, 109, 112, 118, 120, 130, 135, 157
British and Foreign Bible Society 22
British Commonwealth 61, 293
British Empire. *See* imperial federation
British Empire League, 147, 172, 179, 182, 183, 195, 236. *See also* Imperial Federation League
British Information Bureau 270
British Museum 30, 31
British North America Act 61
British Pictorial Services 269
Brock, Mr. 157
Brodie, Douglas 222
Brown, George 128, 131
Bryce, James 133, 135, 138, 150, 209, 271, 282
Buchan, John (Lord Tweedsmuir) 269, 270
Buckle, George 122, 123, 132, 135, 136, 148, 275, 284
Buckmaster, Stanley 254, 255, 261
Buctouche (New Brunswick) 6

Bullers, Redvers 189, 193
Bury, Lord 63
Butler, Benjamin 84
Butler, Geoffrey 270
Butt, Clara 191

Cambridge, Duke of 103
Campobello, Island of 6, 7, 296
Canada (political and trade issues) 53, 54, 56–61, 63, 64, 66, 67, 84, 102–7, 109–14, 116, 124, 126–8, 173, 174, 177–80, 190–200, 249, 258, 259, 267, 273. *See also* French-Canadians; imperial federation: Canada; Rhodes Scholarships: Canada
Canada and the Canadian Question 110, 111
Canada First 54, 57
Canada House 288
Canadian Club 191, 199, 200
Canadian Club of Toronto 191
Canadian Pacific Railway 105, 122, 136, 140, 144, 163
Cape Colony 180, 183, 188, 189, 206
Carleton, Thomas 8
Carlyle, Thomas 95
Carman, Bliss 32, 44, 45, 84, 86, 96, 137–40, 143, 144, 211, 286
Carnarvon, Lord 40
Carnegie, Andrew 112, 206, 218
Carrington, Lord 94
Carter, Downes 79, 93, 96
Cartwright, Richard 109
Century Magazine 69, 70, 97
Chamberlain. Joseph 150, 176, 177, 187, 189, 193, 194, 196, 200, 201, 203, 237
Chandler, E.B. 21
Christchurch 89
Christian Union 22
Churchill, Winston 73, 133, 134, 166, 167, 206, 237

330

Index

Church of England 11, 55, 72, 241
Church Temperance Society 51
Civil War (USA) 7, 58, 61, 116
Clarke, William 59, 60
Clawson, Catherine 50
Cleveland, President 188
Clifton Springs 272
Clinton, Bill xvii
Cockburn, Louise 290
Colbourne, John 154
Collegiate School (Fredericton) 20, 21, 51, 297
Colomb, Captain 73, 103
colonial conferences 61, 177, 201, 246
Colonial Institute 39, 176, 231, 235, 245
Colonial Laws (Validity) Act 61
Companion of the Order of St. Michael and St. George 186
Connaught, Duke of 176
Connell, Charles 50
Cook, Fred 215
Cornell University 56
Corn Laws 125
The Cottage 239, 240, 255, 260, 279, 287, 299
Creelman, A.R. 165
Cross, Ashton 36
Cuba 184, 195, 229
Curtis, Lionel 247, 259
Curzon, Lord 239

Daly, T.C. 137
Darwin, Charles 11, 214
d'Avray, baron. *See* de Brett, Joseph Marshall
Dawson, Geoffrey 259
Dawson, William 65, 279
Deakins, Alfred 246
Delaware 218, 221
Denison, George xiv, 78, 79, 83, 102–4, 106, 109, 110, 117, 118, 123, 124, 128, 131, 134, 146, 153, 172–4, 177, 179, 180, 183, 184, 187, 188, 195, 196, 200, 201, 278, 281, 284, 307
Dewey, Admiral 227
De Beers 207
de Brett, Joseph Marshall 10, 18
Dickson, Casimir 127, 128
Dickson, George 147
Diefenbaker, John 290
Dilke, Charles 39, 99, 115, 145, 206, 323
Dingley Tariff 105
Diocesan Church Society 51, 52
Diocesan School of Rondesbosch 212
Disraeli, Benjamin 35, 40, 58, 63, 64, 71, 281
Doulton, Henry 132
Drummond, George 29, 194, 246
DuBois, W.E.B. 219, 220, 349
Duncan, Robert 132
Dunn, Alexander 161
du Vernet, Ernest 247

East and North of Scotland Liberal Unionist Association 134
Edinburgh, University of 207
Edward VII, King 196, 201, 208
Elizabeth, Queen 289
Emmanuel, King Victor 285
Empire Day 182
Encyclopaedia Britannica 248
Ends of the Earth Club 227
Erskine, Caroline 35, 42, 48, 49, 53, 55, 59, 84, 251, 292
Erskine, Thomas 35
Eton 30–3, 56, 78, 120, 213, 346
Ewing, Juliana Horatia 48
Exeter College 241
The Expansion of England 62

Falklands 119
Fell, Dr. 239
Ferguson, John 15
Fessenden, Celementine 182
Fielding, W.S. 173, 174
Fielding tariff 174
Fischer, Lewis 49
Fisher, Anne 50
Fisher, Annie Connell 49, 50. *See also* Parkin, Annie Connell (née Fisher) (wife)
Fisher, Charles 50, 51
Fisher, Peter 49, 50, 234
Fisher, William 50
Fleming, Sanford 15, 86, 136, 137, 173, 183, 184, 195
Forster, William 54
Foster, George 12, 63, 66, 137, 140, 148, 149, 194, 259
Fredericton 8, 9, 11, 22, 43, 44, 49–51
Fredericton High School 22, 68
Fredericton Juvenile Band 44
Fredericton School Board 22
French, Charity Ann 50
French-Canadians 111, 116, 144–6, 176, 190, 193, 194, 196, 197, 203, 215, 233, 250
Frewen, Morton 73
Froude, J.A. 22, 39, 40, 95, 292

George, Lloyd 271, 277
George V, King 288
Germany 38, 104, 126, 174, 247, 263, 264, 265, 270, 271, 290
Gilder, Richard 70, 76, 83
Gisborn, W. 64
Gladstone, William 11, 35, 54, 63, 71, 78, 82, 85, 125, 126, 127, 131, 176, 281
Glazebrook, Arthur 247, 278
Grant, George Monro xiv, 54, 65, 66, 87, 107, 149, 152, 159, 160, 165, 172, 183, 184, 190, 194, 196, 203, 236, 249, 268, 276, 278, 283, 293, 317, 344, 345
Grant, George Parkin (grandson) 276, 284, 289, 290, 293
Grant, William 159, 160, 169, 172, 249, 255, 256, 265, 268, 269, 275, 289
Gray, Asa 11
Great Dominion 143–6, 292
Grey, Lord 120, 207, 208, 233, 237, 241, 246, 247
Grigg, Edward 259, 277, 279
Groote Schuur 204, 205, 224
Guiana 188

Haggart, Rider 133
Hague, Dyson 159
Haldane, Richard 208
Haley, Joe 118, 132
Hall, G.F.E. 244
Hamilton, Frederick 172
Hamilton, Robert 90
Harrow 133, 213, 346
Harvard 10, 11, 217, 241, 243
Haultain, Arnold 281
Hawksley, Bouchier 207, 208, 220, 222, 241, 250, 251
Hebdomadal Council 213
Henry VI, King 30
Hentschy, Alise 121, 122, 209, 220
Hill, Rowland 182
Hitler, Adolph 264
Home Rule crisis 132, 178
Houstoun, George 130, 132, 195, 284
Howard, Richard 169
Hughes, "Billy" 246
Hughes, James 218
Hughes, Sam 246
Hutton, Edward 189–94, 196, 197, 278

Imperial conferences 61

Index

Imperial Conference on Postal Rates 183
imperial federation (*See also* Parkin, George Robert: imperial federation) 61–4, 82, 85, 104, 116, 129, 130, 172, 236–9, 246, 247, 248, 257
   1891 federal election (Canada) xiv
   Australia 93–7
   Canada 53, 60, 65–7, 102, 103, 236
   Cecil Rhodes 205, 206
   Edward Jenkins 40
   J.A. Froude 39, 40
   New Zealand 89
   objectives xiii
   origins of movement 39–41
   principal proponents xiv
   Tasmania 90–2
Imperial Federation: The Problem of National Unity 112, 117, 120, 123
Imperial Federation (Defence) League 132, 237
Imperial Federation League 72, 78, 79, 99, 101, 103, 126, 127, 129, 172, 203, 237
   Canadian branches 65, 67, 78, 86, 128
   dissolved 131
   New Zealand 89
   Tasmania 90
   See also British Empire League
Imperial War Cabinet 61
India 53, 58, 116, 133, 177, 272, 276, 346
The Influence of Sea Power upon History, 1660–1783 114
Intercolonial Railway 15, 17

Jack, William Brydon 9, 13, 22, 25
Jago, T.E. 288
Jamaica 212, 228–30, 232, 243, 256, 346
James, Henry 234
Jameson, Leander 189, 207, 208, 223, 224, 242
Jameson, Starr 259

Jameson raid 189, 190, 206
Jenkins, Edward 40
Jordan, Louis 159
Jowett, Benjamin 27
Judicial Committee of the Privy Council 16, 61, 180

Kaiser (Germany) 212, 213, 223
Kenny, Anthon 232
Kerr, Phillip (Lord Lothian) 247
Ketchum, Henry 80, 93
King's University, Nova Scotia 147, 148
King, Mackenzie 246, 289
Kingsbury, Dr. 259
Kingsmill, John 155
Kipling, Caroline 205
Kipling, Rudyard 172, 175, 184, 205, 206, 247, 248, 276, 278
Kitchin, G.W. 26, 29
Kitson, Gerald 192–6
Koch, Anna 209, 211
Kruger, Paul 189

Labillière, F.P. de 40
Lament for a Nation 293, 345
Lanctôt 250
Laurier, Wilfrid 1, 86, 102, 106, 109, 144, 173, 176–8, 184, 189–94, 196–200, 203, 246–8, 258, 259, 267, 273
Laval, Université de 215, 233, 250, 259
Leacock, Stephen 152, 160, 161, 237, 238
League of Nations 276, 347
Lee, Arthur 191, 194, 196, 200, 218
Leonard, Mrs. 48, 49
Liddell, Dean 26
Linsday, W.A. 279
Locke, A. LeRoy 241, 242, 243
Loring, A.H. 99, 195
Lucas, Colin xvi

Lyons, H.L. 269

Macdonald, John A. 57, 67, 86, 103, 105, 109, 110, 178, 180, 196, 235, 249, 292, 346
Macdonnell, Jim 265, 275, 290
Mackinder, Halford 247
MacLatchey, James 4
MacLaurin, Normand 226
Macmillan, George 108, 117, 120, 146, 149
Mahan, A.T. 114, 115
Mahomed, James Deen Keriman 27
Malcolm, Ian 166
Maori 47, 88, 89, 98
Marconi, Guglielmo 215, 216
Martin, Chester 241
Mary, Queen 288
Masonic Lodge 205
Massey, Raymond 278
Massey, Vincent 262, 265, 267, 268, 276, 283, 289
Massey Music Hall 191
Mathews, Jehu 40
Mathieu, Monsignor 250
Mavor, James 174
McCarthy, D'Alton 65, 79, 83, 96, 124
McCurdy, J.F. 159
McGill University 65, 119, 160, 165, 193, 199, 208, 209, 216, 233, 241
McKinley Bill 105, 106
McLean, Elizabeth. *See* Parkin, Elizabeth (née McLean) (mother)
Medley, John 1, 9–11, 18, 25, 30, 31, 46–52, 88, 142, 251, 292
Medley, Margaret 48, 142, 143, 163
Medley, Mrs. Spencer 225
Middleton, General 187
Militia Act of 1868 189
Millar, Carman 196
Milner's Kindergarten 223, 247
Milner, Alfred xiv, 28, 38, 41, 73, 117, 129–32, 134, 135, 138–40, 147–50, 156, 163, 173, 180, 181, 183, 187–9, 194, 195, 207, 208, 223, 230, 235, 237, 241–3, 246, 247, 259, 262, 277, 278, 285, 288, 289, 328
Minto, Lord 165, 187, 189–94, 196, 197, 199, 203, 211, 215, 216, 235, 263
Minto, Mary 187
Mitchell, Lewis 8, 208
Mitchell, Nehemiah 8
Monneypenny, W.L. 195
Monroe Doctrine 269
Montgomery-Campbell, George 10
Morgan, Vaughan 163
Morley, John 78
Mormons 221, 256, 259
Morris, William 36
Mount Allison University 214, 215, 228
Mowat, Oliver 147, 148, 173, 183
Mulock, William 102, 173, 182, 183, 194

Natal 183, 212
National Club 153, 171, 177, 178, 180, 183, 278
National Policy 57
National Service League 248
Nettleship, Richard 29
Newcomb, Simon 228
Newfoundland 183, 212, 215, 229, 231, 232, 259
New Brunswick 6, 8, 12, 15
New Brunswick, University of 9–12, 68, 215
New Brunswick Reporter and Fredericton Advertiser 24
New South Wales 93, 94, 118, 212, 244
New Zealand xiv, 46, 47, 58, 60, 64, 88, 89, 97, 98, 116, 119, 131, 185, 212, 225, 226, 232, 237, 246, 258, 266, 347
New Zealand, University of 226
Northcliffe, Lord 254
Northwest Rebellion 187
Notitia of New Brunswick 50

Index

Old Boys' Association 164, 169
Orange Free State 189
Oriel College 207, 213
Osler, William 262
Owen, Admiral 6
Oxford Union 36, 73, 285, 289
Oxford University x, xvi, 1, 2, 11, 25–30, 36–8, 44, 52, 56, 72–4, 159, 160, 206, 207, 209, 210, 212–18, 220, 222, 228, 231, 233–5, 237, 239, 241–5, 249–51, 255, 257, 259, 262, 266, 268, 277, 280, 281, 285, 288, 289, 291

Pacific cable 173, 184, 292
Pacific scandal 178, 249
Padua, University of 284, 285
Papineau, Talbot 233
Park, William (uncle) 3
Parker, Gilbert 95, 96, 97, 238, 270
Parkin, Alice (sister) 4, 168
Parkin, Alice Stuart (daughter) 54, 75, 121, 122, 143, 168, 223, 254, 255, 261, 289, 290
Parkin, Annie Connell (daughter) 75, 142
Parkin, Annie Connell (née Fisher) (wife) x, xvii, 43, 49–51, 54, 55, 69–73, 75, 76, 79, 80, 84, 86, 92, 93, 95, 96, 99, 100, 104, 105, 109, 121, 124, 129, 140, 142, 143, 161–4, 167–9, 200–03, 208, 209, 211, 218, 220, 221, 223–5, 227–31, 234, 235, 239, 240, 245, 251–3, 255–8, 260, 261, 266, 267, 269, 272, 274, 277, 278, 280, 281, 283–5, 288–90
Parkin, Ann (sister) 4
Parkin, Charlotte (sister) 4, 19, 46
Parkin, Christine Marjorie Randolph (daughter) 109
Parkin, Elizabeth (née McLean) (mother) 4, 5
Parkin, Elizabeth (sister) 4, 230, 282
Parkin, Eliza (sister) 4

Parkin, George Raleigh (son) 157, 168, 201, 211, 223, 240, 261, 263, 265, 275, 281, 282, 290
Parkin, George Robert
  alcohol, views on 16, 17, 51, 279
  Anglican church activities 280
  appointed CMG 186
  appointed KCMG 278
  attends Normal School 6
  attends Oxford University 26–9, 36, 37
  attends University of New Brunswick 9–13
  birth of 4
  British Empire map 117, 118, 133, 177, 183
  Canada's role in world 53, 57, 199
  Civil War (USA) 7
  death 285, 287, 288
  Edward Thring's biography 76, 77, 105, 132, 146, 147, 177, 187
  Great Dominion 143, 144, 145, 146, 292, 310
  headmaster of Collegiate School (Frederickton High School)) 20, 21, 45, 46, 52
  headmaster of Gloucester grammar school 14, 15
  headmaster of Upper Canada College 147–9, 152–169, 170, 171, 208, 210, 211
  Imperial Federation League speech 1886 72, 73
  illness 23, 48, 67, 218, 260
  imperial federation 37, 38, 41, 42, 52, 76, 78, 82, 116, 117, 123, 129–34, 171–5, 179, 180, 182–5, 188, 191–200, 238, 239, 245, 246, 248, 257, 266, 272, 273, 276, 292, 293
  marriage 49
  meets Edward Thring 31–4
  philosophy of education 6, 16, 69, 148, 155

335

portrait by F.H. Varley xiii, 278
public speaker 24, 25, 54, 92, 153
race, views on 47, 98, 99, 112, 116, 144, 258
Reka Dom residential school 48
religious influence as child 18
religious life and influences 5, 18, 19, 53, 55, 143, 279, 280
Rhodes Scholarships xvi, 206, 210–23, 226–9, 231–4, 241–5, 250, 252, 259, 260, 262, 267, 268, 291
Round the Empire 118, 119
schooling (as child) 5
school teacher 6
Sir John A. Macdonald 249
studies at Oxford 1
supports Boer war 191–3
USA, view of xvi, 83, 272
visits ancestral home (Yorkshire) 2, 3
Parkin, Grace (daughter) 75, 143, 168, 223, 240, 245, 290
Parkin, James (brother) 4, 20, 21
Parkin, Jane (sister) 4, 19
Parkin, John (brother) 4, 19
Parkin, John (father) 3, 4, 5, 46
Parkin, Maria (née Small) (sister-in-law) 19
Parkin, Marjorie 168, 223, 265, 290
Parkin, Mary (sister) 4
Parkin, Maude Erskine (daughter) 55, 75, 122, 140, 143, 166, 209, 223, 234, 235, 245, 249, 255, 256, 260, 261, 276, 281, 289
Parkin, Muriel Thring (daughter) 71, 75, 142
Parkin, Olivia (sister) 4, 5, 230, 282
Parkin, Robert (uncle) 3
Parkin, Watson (brother) 4, 5, 20, 144, 230, 256, 282
Parkin, William (brother) 4, 19
Parkin, William (grandfather) 3
Parkindale 4, 19
Peacock, Edward 160, 169, 278, 289

Pearson, Mary 163
Peterson, William 119, 208, 216, 233, 282
Philippines 184
Plowden, Pamela 166, 167
The Political Destiny of Canada 56
Pollock, Frederick 237
postal rates 182, 183
Power, Jim xvi, 170
Price, Bonamy 29
Puerto Rico 184

Quebec Act 86
Queen's University xiv, 54, 65, 290
Queensland 226, 244, 256

Raine, Parkin 2
Raleigh, Thomas 38, 73, 85, 117, 132, 135, 139, 149, 157, 163, 276, 277
Rand, T.H. 22, 48
Randolph, A.H. 149
Ransom, Cyril 132
Rawnsley, H.D. 78, 188
Redpath, Peter 118, 122
Reka Dom x, 43, 48, 54, 68, 148, 155, 291
Responsions 217, 243, 244, 291
Rhodes, Cecil xvi, 41, 189, 190, 204–7, 212, 213, 219, 224, 241–3, 252, 272
Rhodesia xvi, 189, 204, 206, 212, 224, 252, 253, 277
Rhodes House xvi, 232, 244, 288
Rhodes Scholarships (*see also* Parkin, George Robert: Rhodes Scholarships) 206, 207, 213, 241, 253, 265, 266, 291
"coloured question" 241, 242, 243, 256
Canada 208, 212, 214, 215, 233
geographical distribution 212
selection criteria 207, 217
USA xvi, 212, 216–21, 232, 241–3, 250,

259, 262, 263, 268
Rhodes Trustees xvi, 208, 210, 211, 219, 220, 222, 237, 241–3, 250, 253, 260, 262, 268, 269, 277, 279, 288, 291, 350
Ridding, George 30, 31
Roberts, Charles G.D. 20, 44–6, 86, 143, 144, 147, 156, 248, 263
Roberts, Dr. 20
Roosevelt, Franklin 6
Roosevelt, Theodore 194, 218, 233
Rose, H.J. 241
Rosebery, Lord xiv, 63, 81, 82, 99, 103, 118, 123, 130, 132, 134, 150, 151, 207, 208, 210, 220, 242
Ross, George 182
Rossetti, Dante Gabriel 36
Round Table movement 247, 258, 259
Round the Empire 118, 119, 123, 136, 281, 292
Royal Colonial Institute 39, 231, 245
Royal Geographical Society 258
Royal Military College 159, 191, 192, 261
Royal Scottish Geographical Society 117
Royal Society of Canada 187
Rugby School 29
Ruskin, John 28, 29, 38, 41, 42, 95, 262, 292
Ryerson, Egerton 154

Saint John 6, 11, 48
Saint John Provincial Training School 6
Saint John River 8, 9, 12, 48, 49
Salisbury, Lord 103, 116, 150
Salisbury (New Brunswick) 4, 19, 20
Schuman, Professor 66
Seeley, George 5
Seeley, J.R. 5, 62, 64, 133
Selwyn, George 46, 47, 52, 88, 98, 292
settler colonies 58, 59
Shaw, Bernard 239
Sherman, John 84

Sifton, Clifford 144, 173
Sketches of New Brunswick 50
Skrine, John 42, 77, 78, 105, 188
Sloman, Arthur 37
Small, John T. 147, 148
Small, Maria. *See* Parkin, Maria (née Small)
Smith, Donald 122, 148
Smith, Goldwin xiv, 56, 57, 59, 60, 64, 84, 89, 110–14, 116, 145, 146, 151, 166, 181, 183, 241, 257, 258, 281
Smith, W.H. 63
Smuts, Jan 270, 271
Society for the Propagation of the Gospel in Foreign Parts 47
Sons of Temperance 16
South Africa xiv, 40, 59, 112, 115, 116, 119, 149, 150, 188–94, 197, 204, 206–8, 212, 223, 232, 235, 246–8, 251, 253, 256–9, 277, 279
South African College School 212
South African Republic 189
South Africa House 288
South Australia 194, 227
Spain 184
Spalding, George 211
Spanish-American war 183, 184, 188, 195
St. Andrews College School Grahamstown 212
St. Joseph's (Memramcook, N.B.) 215
Stanley, Arthur 29
Statute of Westminster 293
Stead, W.T. 73
Stellenbosch School 212
Strathcona, Lord 194, 210, 263
Stupart, R.F. 160
Suez Canal 99, 227
Supreme Court of Canada 61
Sydney, University of 226
Symonds, Richard 41

Taft, Howard 234, 262
Tannegg 121
Tarte, Israel 173, 190, 193
Tasmania 84, 90, 91, 96, 98, 212, 225, 226
Taylor, Henry D'Estère 194, 238
telegraph 215, 216
Temperance Congress 74
Temperance Reform Club Band 44
Tennyson, Alfred 175, 226, 227
Theory and Practice of Teaching 69
Thriftyville 4. *See also* Parkindale
Thring, Edward xv, 31–4, 41, 42, 53, 64, 68–71, 76, 77, 105, 157, 158, 187, 188, 291. *See also* Uppingham School
Thring, Godfrey 78
Thring, Henry 74, 78, 149, 150
Till, Barbara 49
Tilley, S.L. 16, 51, 72, 86
Times (London) 122, 136, 145, 177, 259
Toronto Board of Trade 200
Toynbee, Arnold 28, 41
Tozer, Bishop 47
Trades Unions Council 101
Transvaal 189, 195
Trevelyan, Bruce 78
Trevelyan, George 78
Tupper, Charles xiv, 64, 117, 125–8, 131, 148, 173, 193, 194, 196
Twain, Mark 227

United Empire Loyalists 8, 49, 57, 66, 81
United Empire Trade League 107, 126, 127
United States of America 9, 39, 58, 61, 84, 105, 106, 116, 179, 184, 188, 205, 264, 269–71, 273. *See also* Rhodes Scholarships: USA
Universal Postal Union 182
Upper Canada College xv, xvi, 147–71, 180, 188, 208, 210, 211, 214, 268, 291, 293, 345, 346

Uppingham School xv, 31–4, 42, 68–71, 157, 158, 164. *See also* Thring, Edward
Usher, John 134, 135

Van Horne, William 136, 137, 140, 144, 163, 165, 227, 229
Varley, F.H. xiii, 278
Venables, H.A. 36
Venezuelan crisis 188
Victoria, Queen 125, 174, 175, 196
Victoria College 267
Victorian Order of Nurses 174
Vincent, Howard 107

Wales, Prince and Princess of 209
Walter, A.F. 136
Warre, Edmond 30
Warren, Edward 288
Washington, Booker T. 218, 219
Washington, George 269
Waterstone, Alfred 27
Watson, Elizabeth (paternal grandmother) 3
Way, Samuel 96, 135, 180, 194, 227
Webster, John 132
Wentworth Historical Society 182
Western Australia 212, 227
West Indies 54, 80, 112
Wilde, Oscar 28, 239
Wilkinson, Spencer 133
Willets, Charles 147
Williams, Susannah 50
Willison, John 53, 124, 178, 194, 198–200
Wilmot, Edward 13, 48
Wilmot, L.A. 13
Wilson, Harry 150, 186, 195
Wilson, Woodrow 250, 251, 276
Wilson-Gorman Tariff 105
Wiman, Erastus 105, 106, 112

Index

Wimperis, Harry 245, 248, 265, 275, 280, 290
The Woolsack 204, 205
World War I 263–72, 275, 292
World War II 264
Wylie, Francis 222, 240–4, 262, 263, 268, 279

Yale 217, 262
YMCA 22
Young, Frederick 99, 195
Young Australia movement 93

Credits

My research was made easier by Parkin's son, Raleigh. When he retired, Raleigh set his Oxford-trained mind to collecting the family papers in a thorough and systematic way. As a consequence, Library and Archives Canada has a superb collection of material relating to Parkin's life and his work. Carl Berger's seminal work, *A Sense of Power* (1970), rescued from historical neglect the thought of a group of Canadian thinkers, writers, and political activists such as Colonel George Denison, George Monro Grant, Stephen Leacock, and others who advocated closer ties between member states of the British Empire.

In 1977, Terry Cook took Berger's hint and looked into Parkin's life, work, and thought. He had the good fortune to know Raleigh Parkin and to be able to talk to him about his father, a pleasure I envy him. Cook's Ph.D. thesis from Queen's University in Kingston in 1977 was titled "Apostle of Empire: Sir George Parkin and Imperial Federation." It is a masterpiece of meticulous and comprehensive research. Terry should have published it, but his professional career took him in another direction. It created for me a problem analogous to the one Parkin himself faced. He had undertaken to write a biography of

Credits

Edward Thring, headmaster of Uppingham School. Two of Thring's masters had also produced memoirs before Parkin's book appeared. "I was perhaps too sensitive about saying over again what had been said before," Parkin wrote, "and Skrine has written to reproach me for not using as material everything he has written." Terry Cook was as generous. When he learned I was beginning this project, he encouraged me to make full use of his thesis, and I saw no point in covering again ground that had been so thoroughly and so elegantly covered before. I don't agree with all of Terry's interpretations of Parkin's life and thought, nor he with mine, but in a very deep way, this biography is a collaboration.

I am more than usually grateful to my research assistants: Adam Christian, Barbara Christian, Matthew Christian, Elizabeth Goodyear, Kim Groenendyk, Maureen Smith, Jessica Spence, Melanie Storoschuk. They had faith in my ability to finish this book when I personally had my doubts.

I would also like to thank the following people and institutions: Earhart Foundation; SSHRC; Marian Spence, archivist, Upper Canada College and the archivists at the University of Toronto and Queen's University; John Fraser, master, Massey College, University of Toronto; Maureen Mancuso, provost, University of Guelph; Karen Hand and Susan Senior; Joyce Campbell; University of Guelph Undergraduate Summer Research Programme; Library and the Archives of Canada, especially Rob Fisher; Social Science and Humanities Research Council; Rhodes House Library and Archives, especially Caroline Brown; Biblioteca National de Lisboa; Institute for Advanced Studies, JNU, New Delhi; David Knight; Sir Anthony Kenny; Rev. Graham Eglington; Rev. Barry Craig; Rt. Rev. Harold Nutter; Rudyard Griffiths; Professor Kenneth Minogue; Sir Colin Lucas; Dr. Jim Power; Hon. Michael Chong.

My wife, Barbara, was wonderfully supportive over the very long period I worked on this project. She also did a fine job helping to copy edit the final version. I owe her a great deal, and certainly not just for this. My special thanks are reserved for Patrick Boyer, founder and president of Blue Butterfly Books. The enthusiasm he showed for the book and the patience with which he put up with a temperamental author are remarkable.

George Grant and William Christian, 1980

A graduate of the University of Toronto in political science and economics, William Christian completed his Ph.D. in political philosophy at the London School of Economics in 1970. His first teaching position was at Mount Allison University in Sackville, New Brunswick, not far from where Parkin spent his childhood. While at Mount Allison he met George Grant, author of *Lament for a Nation* and perhaps Canada's most famous political philosopher.

Grant and Christian became friends, and after Grant's death his widow, Sheila, suggested that Christian write her late husband's biography. The book was a national best-seller. During his research, Christian became fascinated by Sir George Parkin, Grant's maternal grandfather, proponent of a movement called imperial federation and founding secretary of the Rhodes Scholarships. Academically, Christian's biography of Parkin continues his study of Canadian political thought, a field in which he is recognized as a pre-eminent expert.

The lively style of this biography reflects Christian's lifelong involvement with journalism, from the student newspaper at the University of Toronto to the *Toronto Star* and the *Globe and Mail*. He writes a regular column for the *Waterloo Region Record* and the *Guelph Mercury*.

He retired from the University of Guelph in 2008.

Interview with the Author

Parkin is forgotten but not by you. You show that Parkin was a welcome guest at the White House and Rideau Hall, a widely respected journalist, a popular speaker who captivated crowds on three continents over four decades, and was arguably the best-known Canadian in the world at the time of his death. How possibly could he be unknown today?

WILLIAM CHRISTIAN: I think it's possibly because he moved about so much. He lived the first forty-two years of his life in New Brunswick as a successful educator. Then he switched his base to England where he was imperial federation's most eloquent spokesman. By 1895, he was extremely well known in the United Kingdom, but money problems forced him to take a job in Toronto. By 1902 he was the most prominent educational figure in Ontario and a powerful political force. Then he was hired to become founding secretary of the Rhodes Scholarships and moved back to England. For the rest of his life, his time was divided between England and his travels to establish the scholarships. Perhaps his roots weren't deep enough in any one place or field of endeavour. But he is still remembered in

New Brunswick. The University of New Brunswick, his alma mater, has a prominent permanent display about him in the university's old building. And a portrait of him by F.H. Varley hangs in the National Gallery of Canada.

 How did you first discover this remarkable Canadian?

CHRISTIAN: His grandson, George Grant, who was one of Canada's greatest political philosophers, was a friend of mine. Parkin was George's grandfather, his mother's father. Grant was a great storyteller and he was fascinated by his grandfather. He told me many stories that had been passed down through the family. Most important for him personally though, and he told me so often that I knew that it was terribly important, was that, when he was growing up, his mother told him over and over that he was supposed to be like his grandfather Parkin, to live by his ideals and to work to make his country a better place. I was fascinated to learn what sort of a man Parkin really was.

As an academic, I also had read about Parkin in Carl Berger's seminal work, *A Sense of Power*. There was enough in Berger's book to tantalize, but nowhere near enough to satisfy.

You can tell another person's life in many ways. Why did you write this book the way you did?

CHRISTIAN: I suppose like any good biographer I am bit nosey and like a bit of a gossip. Here was an incredible success story, the thirteenth child of an immigrant farmer to New Brunswick who ended up with a knighthood and became one of the most famous Canadians in the world. He was an extraordinary political orator, journalist and author, a political visionary. I discovered while researching the book that he was also a radical educationalist who altered the nature of the way children were taught in Ontario. Finally,

Interview with the Author

I was interested in his relationship with his wife, one that seemed so beneficial for him and so debilitating for her. At one point, you know, she walked out on him, took the younger children and went to England. And he was principal of Upper Canada College at the time. Amazing.

People would be far more familiar with Parkin's philosopher grandson George "Lament for a Nation" Grant, whom you mention. Do you see links between their thought?

CHRISTIAN: George Grant was tremendously influenced by Parkin, and I don't think that *Lament for a Nation* can ever be fully understood unless one grasps Parkin's ideals. Grant absorbed his grandfather's vision through his family. His father and his uncles worked toward the same goals Parkin did. Near the end of the Second World War, Grant wrote two short works about Canada's future. Basically, they shared his grandfather's view of the world, which was that Canada should look outward and globally, not inward and restrict itself to the confines of North America. In *Lament for a Nation*, Grant conceded that his grandfather's dream would not come true: Canada was destined to become a prisoner of North America, not a force for good on a worldwide scale.

Our interest in history springs from our fascination about our own times and the future. What is important about Parkin's life that affects people today?

CHRISTIAN: A student from my university recently won a Rhodes Scholarship. She will have an opportunity to study for three years at Oxford and will, for the rest of her life, carry the prestige of being a Rhodes Scholar. You can never second-guess history, but it's unlikely that the Rhodes Scholarship plan would have been a success if it hadn't been for Parkin's intelligence, charm, incredible energy, and his commitment to the principles for which they stood. Upper Canada College, one of Canada's leading secondary schools, would almost certainly have collapsed if Parkin hadn't become principal. I was pleased when I was grading a paper on Sir John A. Macdonald to see a student cite Parkin's biography of Canada's first prime minister. This is also a feel-good story about a man who dedicated his life to making the world a better place and, in the end, was recognized and rewarded for it.

In terms of one of the great causes he devoted his life to, though, isn't Parkin's concept of a "British nation" totally obsolete?

CHRISTIAN: No. By it he meant the cultural unity of the English-speaking peoples and it lives on in concepts such as the Anglosphere, the idea that there is a common bond between countries that have democratic political institutions that were inspired by British traditions, share free market traditions, have common law legal systems, and have common body of literature and philosophy. Although its core includes the countries that Parkin was mostly concerned about, developments in other commonwealth countries such as India, Jamaica, and Bermuda would make them at least cousins.

In this book you present George Parkin as an educational revolutionary. What did he want to change?

CHRISTIAN: He was both democratic and spiritual. Education in his age, you see, was very elitist. Boys from rich families were sent to schools like Eton and Harrow. They were drilled in Latin and Greek and the brightest ones were rewarded with scholarships. It mattered who became prefect and captain of the cricket team. The best ones went on to Oxford or Cambridge where they continued to compete for top grades and prizes. The weaker students were ignored. Parkin believed that the dullest boy in his school had as much right to an

Interview with the Author

education as the brightest. He also wanted a more rounded education. He lessened the emphasis on classics and introduced a range of other subjects. He also wanted his school to create an ethic of service. For Parkin, education was less about training the intellect, more about building character.

As a political philosopher at the University of Guelph and as author of ten prior books, would you like to comment on whether Parkin's role and influence not being known—at least before publication of your new biography about him—is because people don't know their history or because his philosophy is out of date?

CHRISTIAN: I don't think that his philosophy is out of date, though I think that there is one problem in understanding him that is both big and small at the same time. He talks about British and the British Empire and to readers today, that makes him seem out-of-date. But if readers can get past these particularly words, they will realize Parkin's continuing relevance. By "British" Parkin doesn't mean English, you see, he means a set of values: balance, moderation, fair play, order, restraint, impartiality. He makes it clear that anyone can be British, most obviously in his own time French-Canadians, the Maoris of New Zealand, and the Boers of South Africa—if they wanted to.

He talked about the British Empire, but it is clear that he meant some sort of international political unit of global reach that would act as a force for good in the world. He was very critical of the existing British Empire, and never wanted the colonies' interests subordinated to England's. After the Great War, he supported Woodrow Wilson's attempt to create the League of Nations.

If readers can make the slight effort necessary to get past the terms Parkin used and understand his fundamental ideal, the need for a global moral order, they will come to terms with the mission that drove him over his lifetime.

Money plays a big role in Parkin's life, since he always seemed to be living above his means. How can you convey to the contemporary reader the meaning of the £ and the $ from Parkin's time?

CHRISTIAN: That's extremely difficult. Roughly, you could say that one dollar in Parkin's era equalled about forty dollars now, and one British pound equalled about 100 dollars. In many cases, though, that's very misleading. Incomes in Canada weren't taxed until 1917, but there was no public healthcare either: some of what you saved by not paying income tax, you lost by having to pay for medical care. There weren't any benefits or pensions either. By contrast, servants were inexpensive to retain, so once you got to a certain level of income, the quality of life for the middle class dramatically increased. Values were fairly constant during Parkin's life, up to the First World War.

Some of Sir George Parkin's prejudices about other races and attitudes about women don't reflect present-day values of equality. Do you as a biographer explain his views in the context of his times?

CHRISTIAN: I certainly do not leave things out because they are unpalatable today. I believe mature readers are entitled to more than a sanitized story. But I don't spend time in the book trying to explain him away, either, in terms of today's values early in the twenty-first century.

As an historian it is not my place to intrude with my personal views or to critique my subject according to shifting cultural values. If I'd written this book in the 1950s or 1970s, say, standards of those days—as a benchmark to critique Parkin—could seem quaint and anachronistic to many people today. The subject—George Parkin—stands in his own times, not ours. I think readers of biography are sophisticated and grasp that. There are places in the book where I report Parkin using the extremely offensive word "nigger." I would prefer not to use that word ever, but if I don't honestly show the exact words Parkin used, the reader will not be able to understand his attitude, and they won't understand the attitude of people of his time and class.

I certainly don't share his views on French-Canadians, Canada's native peoples, the Chinese, or many other subjects. As a biographer, I think my role is to understand my subject, not to agree with him, and certainly not in this case to defend him.

Don't you risk readers concluding he was bigoted so they won't think much of his other ideas?

CHRISTIAN: This is actually quite interesting, because there's a bit of a puzzle I had to grapple with in writing this book. Parkin's own actions in these matters actually contradicted some of the things he said. For instance, in his letters in this book we see references to Blacks that are bigoted, but then when it comes to his official capacity, he behaves quite differently. He actively worked with the great Black educational leaders such as Booker T. Washington and W.E.B. DuBois to prevent the white universities from developing a system for selecting Rhodes scholars that would exclude the Negro Colleges. When a Black Rhodes Scholar was elected in 1907 and faced fierce opposition from Rhodes scholars from the American South, Parkin worked to ensure that he would be admitted to an Oxford College, and had him to his house.

I think you also have to understand that, in many ways, Parkin's views matured over his lifetime. After all, he was born on a farm in rural New Brunswick and didn't see much of the world outside New Brunswick until he was in his mid-twenties. Although the views he held on racial matters when he died weren't compatible with the diverse, multicultural society we live in today, they were a lot closer to this than the views he had formed in his youth. He learned from his experience.

And, to be fair, he was far more tolerant than most people of his era in religious matters.

ABOUT THIS BOOK

George Parkin was born the thirteenth child of an immigrant New Brunswick farmer and died a knight of the realm and perhaps the most famous Canadian in the world.

Charismatic, eloquent, and dedicated, Parkin devoted his immense energy to two causes. As an orator and journalist, he worked to strengthen the bonds between the English-speaking peoples (a movement known as imperial federation); as principal of Upper Canada College and founding secretary of the Rhodes Scholarships he promoted a vision that education was primarily the formation of character, not the training of the intellect.

Parkin was principal of a high school in Fredericton, New Brunswick, when in 1889 he seized a chance to tour Australia as a spokesman for imperial federation. This was the beginning of his international fame. Sponsored by such prominent Englishmen as the former prime minister Lord Rosebery, Lord Milner, and Lord Grey, he became imperial federation's professional organizer.

After the cause went into decline, Parkin was hired in 1895 as principal of Toronto's prestigious Upper Canada College. Applying revolutionary pedagogical ideas learned from Edward Thring, headmaster of Uppingham School in England, Parkin transformed UCC, and provided a model for educational reform in Ontario and throughout Canada.

When Cecil Rhodes died in 1902, he left an enormous fortune and a sketchy idea of how to turn it into scholarships to knit the English-speaking world more closely together. The Rhodes Trustees chose Parkin to transform Rhodes's vision into reality. By the time he retired, after 18 years of unrelenting toil and an exhausting travel itinerary, Parkin had made them the most prestigious scholarships in the world.

This beautifully written and witty biography is a story of ideas lived through Parkin and those in his wide circle of influence that extended to leaders of many countries. He was one of the first Canadians to see the development of globalization, and produced that famous map to demonstrate his vision, with the British Empire all in red, Canada huge and dominating in the centre. His passionate opposition to free trade and eventual annexation by the United States mark him as an eloquent and perhaps prophetic visionary of Canada's fate under NAFTA.